W9-BET-182

IP
Fundamentals

What Everyone Needs to Know about Addressing & Routing

Thomas A. Maufer

Prentice Hall PTR
Upper Saddle River, NJ 07458
www.phptr.com

ISBN 0-13-975483-0

90000

Library of Congress Cataloging-in-Publication Data

Maufer, Thomas.
    IP fundamentals : what everyone needs to know about addressing &
routing / Thomas A. Maufer .
      p.   cm.
    Includes bibliographical references and index.
    ISBN 0-13-975483-0
    1. TCP/IP (Computer network protocol) I. Title.
TK5105.585.M38 1999
004.6'2--dc21   99-21033
                                       CIP

Editorial/production supervision: *Vincent Janoski*
Acquisitions editor: *Mary Franz*
Marketing manager: *Lisa Konzelmann*
Manufacturing manager: *Alexis R. Heydt*
Editorial assistant: *Noreen Regina*
Cover design director: *Jerry Votta*
Cover designer: *Talar Agasyan*
Illustration renderings: *Vantage Art Studio*

©1999 by Prentice-Hall

Published by Prentice Hall PTR
Prentice-Hall, Inc.
Upper Saddle River, NJ 07458

Prentice Hall books are widely used by corporations and government agencies
for training, marketing, and resale.

The publisher offers discounts on this book when ordered in bulk quantities.
For more information, contact: Corporate Sales Department, Phone: 800-382-3419;
Fax: 201-236-7141; E-mail: corpsales@prenhall.com; or write: Prentice Hall PTR,
Corp. Sales Dept., One Lake Street, Upper Saddle River, NJ 07458.

Figure 7-2 is reprinted by permission from Dr. Robert M. Metcalfe.

Printed in the United States of America
10 9 8 7 6 5 4 3 2 1

ISBN   0-13-975483-0

Prentice-Hall International (UK) Limited, *London*
Prentice-Hall of Australia Pty. Limited, *Sydney*
Prentice-Hall Canada Inc., *Toronto*
Prentice-Hall Hispanoamericana, S.A., *Mexico*
Prentice-Hall of India Private Limited, *New Delhi*
Prentice-Hall of Japan, Inc., *Tokyo*
Prentice-Hall Singapore Pte. Ltd., *Singapore*
Editora Prentice-Hall do Brasil, Ltda., *Rio de Janeiro*

To Deb
(again)

for her enduring love and support
and
for her extreme patience enduring the
creation of my second book

(the last one for a while,
I promise)

CONTENTS

FOREWORD

October 16, 1998. Jon Postel passed away today. No single individual gave more to the Internet, or to the goal of the open standards process. His ideals were the foundation of the Internet Engineering Task Force (IETF) and Internet Architecture Board (IAB). Besides his considerable contributions to the creation of the IETF's processes, he was unmatched in the sheer magnitude of his actual production of IETF standards. No one has authored more Requests for Comments (RFCs), many of which are of core importance to the Internet we know today. In fact, the whole idea for a unified document series, the Requests for Comments, was his. He authored RFCs for Internet Protocol (IP), Internet Control Message Protocol (ICMP), Transmission Control Protocol (TCP), User Datagram Protocol (UDP), Simple Mail Transport Protocol (SMTP), Telnet, File Transfer Protocol (FTP), and more.

Besides the protocols that he actually wrote, his behind-the-scenes work as an IAB member, as the Internet Assigned Numbers Authority (IANA), and as the RFC Editor, along with his active participation in the IETF, exerted a positive, stabilizing influence on many of the standards that do not bear his name. His calm demeanor helped others find compromise where none was apparent. Most people who use the Internet have no idea who Jon was, or how important he was. From what I have heard, he never cared about recognition—only that things worked well.

The Internet Protocol itself was specified by Jon in 1981. Jon coordinated the initial deployment of IP in the ARPANET, having been involved in the ARPANET from the beginning. Later, he was instrumental in the deployment of the Domain Name System (DNS) in the nascent Internet. The DNS was an essential enabler of the Internet's early explosive growth (Yes, even before the World-Wide Web, the Internet was growing exponentially!).

Much of this book is about understanding IP itself, which has transformed our lives. It is the foundation of the Internet. In understanding IP, we come to understand some of Jon's work, but this book only scratches the surface.

I did not know Jon personally, he was an acquaintance from IETF meetings. However, news of his death took the breath out of me. I can imagine how early Americans must have felt when they heard of the death of Ben Franklin or Thomas Jefferson. Jon, among other luminaries such as Vint Cerf, Steve Crocker, Bob Kahn, etc., were the founding fathers of the Internet. The Internet has already revolutionized the world of data communications, and is poised to revolutionize voice communications, but the impact of the Internet extends far beyond the realm of just technology. It seems poised to transcend old-fashioned concepts of borders and governments, as well.

Jon's efforts helped enable the Internet to achieve its fabulous success. How amazing that pure research, which started out as an investigation into a way to do connectionless packet switching, has been able to gain such a foothold in the lives of millions of people. I believe that history will judge the Internet to be the key technological achievement of the twentieth century, even more important than the microprocessor. From this perspective, Jon must be viewed as one of the most influential people of the twentieth century. When people look back on this turbulent century, I hope that they remember how crucial Jon was in making the Internet happen. He will be sorely missed.

Preface

The Internet Protocol has become the dominant networking protocol in use today, and its use continues to grow rapidly, with no end in sight. Thankfully, tools like the World-Wide Web (WWW) have put a friendlier face on the Internet, allowing its users to have a relatively painless experience. From the applications side (top-down), the WWW has made a huge difference, since the pre-WWW Internet was not really what one would call a consumer-oriented service. However, the WWW has done nothing to improve the Internet's plumbing; if anything, it has increased the strain on the infrastructure (due to greatly increased numbers of users, and the very bursty nature of web traffic).

Taking a bottom-up view, it is no easier today to define subnets, configure routers, etc. Even though certain tools now exist to aid in network design, the network managers still may not have the basic knowledge required to make the right design choices for their networks. Given that there is a continuous stream of new networks being attached to the Internet, there is a dramatic increase in the number of people who need to manage these new networks. In order to do a good job, new network managers, and all the network managers that preceded them, need a deeper level of understanding of IP than do users. This book is meant for people who need to understand IP networking-related issues at a deep enough level to ensure that their networks are designed and operated properly. Ideally, the users will have a smooth experience, not realizing how much is really going on beneath the surface.

Part I examines IP addressing. How many hosts should be in some subnet? What is the broadcast address for that subnet? How should the addressing boundaries for a network be defined? Why must each subnetwork's IP prefix be unique (i.e., non-overlapping)? Network managers must be able to design addressing plans and overlay them on their networks' router topologies, configure routing protocols, and understand how the big picture is supposed to work well enough so that they can fix problems when they occur. Also, it is worth noting that a well-designed network will be far more stable than one that is designed haphazardly (or not designed at all). Manipulating IP addresses is a key foundation skill, without which IP routing protocols and forwarding make little sense.

A number of critical, basic skills related to manipulating IP addresses and subnet masks, which are not covered in detail in any one book or RFC, are explained here. I am not satisfied to simply state the rules and move on, however. Thoroughly worked-out examples are provided, and each chapter includes some exercises that should help to cement understanding of the concepts involved. Solutions to each exercise are provided, along with a rationale indicating how the answer was derived. Experienced network managers have learned these lessons through experience and trial-and-error. A goal of this book is to assist new network managers in getting up to speed on the real underlying addressing and routing issues. Mastery of Part I will ensure that no IP addressing-related question will perplex a network manager.

Part II concerns itself with two related issues. First, we need to understand the forwarding decision that each router uses to process a packet. Second, we need to see how IP packets are actually transmitted across the inter-router subnetwork "hops." Over its nearly thirty-year existence,[1] standards have defined how IP works over virtually every subnetwork technology. Luckily, it is not necessary to understand all of them. Only a few have become dominant, and the lessons learned from those generalize fairly well to the others. So, Part II covers how IP packets are carried over the most popular LAN[2] and WAN[3] subnetwork technologies.

Part II begins with a discussion of the IP forwarding decision process. The IP packet header includes a complete destination address, and routers use routing protocols to figure out which outgoing interface is "best," in the sense that it is in the direction of the destination (which will hopefully get the packet closer to its ultimate destination). Every intermediate router uses the same decision process. The differences arise in the subnetwork-specific details of each intermediate subnetwork "hop."

The IP layer is an abstraction, providing the Transport-layer protocols with subnetwork independence. Even though IP makes them all look similar to higher-layer protocols, each subnetwork technology really is quite different from the others.

IP runs over an astounding number of physical media, from ArcNet to X.25. In this book, we examine the most common LAN (Ethernet, token ring, and FDDI) and WAN (PPP and Frame Relay) media. Once these have been understood, IP's operation over other media should be much easier to comprehend by generalizing the mechanisms learned here. Subnetwork technologies that are not mentioned here tend to be niche protocols that are not of general interest.[4]

Not only are addressing-related issues understood by a relatively small percentage of the IP users, but the interactions of addressing and routing are similarly poorly understood. In networks with well-coordinated addressing plans, it is possible to greatly minimize the routing table size at the core of the network. Part III contains an overview of routing technology, showing how the two most popular standards-based routing protocols, RIP and OSPF, operate. This part of the book really drives home the interrelationship between addressing and routing, especially in the chapter on interconnection of routing domains.

A well-designed addressing plan eases network troubleshooting because the addresses used within such a network are more meaningful, or may be related to a subnetwork addressing scheme (e.g., in a frame relay WAN). In such a network design, addresses that are "near" each other will have common prefixes, or leading bits, while "far away" numbers have quite different prefixes, making it easy to look at a number and know what part of the network it refers to. It is critically important that those deploying new networks be aware of addressing and routing issues. People sometimes tend to focus on the network applications and forget about the network itself, which, if well-designed will work smoothly for all applications.

The book concludes with a series of Appendices. Appendix A covers `ping` and `traceroute`, the two most common IP troubleshooting tools. Appendix B covers the Dynamic Host Configuration Protocol (DHCP), which is frequently used today to ease the administration of IP addresses within a network's defined subnetwork prefixes. Appendix C gives a broad overview of the new IEEE 802.1Q and 802.1p standards, which provide for standardized VLANs, multicast filtering at the MAC layer, class-of-service (CoS) prioritization, and other features. These new features seem poised to make a big impact on the way Ethernet-based networks will be deployed in the future. However, since they are still quite new, it did not seem appropriate to include them in the main chapters on Ethernet.

ACKNOWLEDGMENTS

To my wife, Deb, I owe a huge acknowledgment for putting up with a second book right on the heels of the first. I am looking forward to having my spare time back to myself again. I am very grateful to the reviewers, who all offered valuable detailed comments that helped make this book better. Any lingering errors or unclear sections are obviously my responsibility. Once again, I must acknowledge my employer, 3Com. I am especially grateful to Jim Binder, who gave his permission for me to work on this project. Finally, Philippe Byrnes provided valuable moral support, and comic relief when necessary. I look forward to seeing his book(s) published this year.

Many thanks to the team at Prentice Hall PTR, especially Mary Franz, Noreen Regina, and Vince Janoski. Without Mary's constant gentle pressure, this book would not exist. Her patience was considerable, especially considering that this ended up being several months late due to a combination of medical problems and an over-aggressive schedule. Noreen did a great job of making sure that the reviewers' comments made it to me in a timely fashion, and did a great job as "virtual Mary" when necessary. :-) Finally, and very important, Vince Janoski has been doing a great job of managing the whole production process. Once the first draft was done, he took over. Turning 555 pages of double-spaced text into a finished, polished book takes a lot of steps, most of which I am barely aware of. Vince is making it all happen, and based on the results so far, I'm looking forward to seeing the finished product this Spring!

Finally, I feel that I should thank Dr. Kendra Peterson and Dr. John R. Adler of the Stanford University Medical Center.

ENDNOTES

1. IP was first deployed in the Internet in 1981.
2. Ethernet, token ring, and FDDI.
3. PPP and Frame Relay.
4. Note that IP over ATM is not specifically covered here in this book for several reasons. First, when used in PVC mode, ATM is somewhat similar to Frame Relay. Second, IP over ATM is a very broad and complex subject to which whole books have been devoted. Third, IP over ATM LAN Emulation is just the same as IP over Ethernet or token ring, as far as IP is concerned.

Part I

IP: Architecture, Addressing, and Routing

CHAPTER 1

Introduction to the Internet Protocol

WHAT IS IP?

Despite the growing popularity of the Internet Protocol (IP) as a general purpose networking protocol—as evidenced by the explosive growth of the Internet and corporate "intranets"—there is a comparatively low understanding of exactly what IP does and how all its pieces interact. There are many books about the Internet that talk about chat rooms, how to create snazzy web sites, and other applications that are available to users. This book will address the behind-the-scenes infrastructural aspects of the Internet rather than the surface aspects that users see. You will learn the practical aspects of how IP works. Despite the book's focus on nitty-gritty infrastructure, this is not a book about communications theory; it is intended to be more practical and solution-oriented, especially for people who need to get up to speed on how IP works. So, what is IP? It is the fundamental packet format that many computers use to exchange information.

What is a packet? It is a well-defined format, usually consisting of a packet "header" followed by some "data," which could be: 1) portions of files; 2) keystrokes and character echoes within a virtual terminal application; or 3) a portion of an e-mail message. All information that is transmitted over the Internet is broken into *independent* packets. Packet switching was developed in the 1960s to provide a robust communications infrastructure, in the context of military applications. Since the information stream is divided into packets, each may follow its own path through the network, thereby avoiding parts of the network that have been blown up or otherwise incapacitated.

This book is not about web browsers, or writing web pages in XML, or how to find things on the Internet. In this book you will learn how to manipulate IP addresses well enough to design an addressing plan for your network; how IP operates over the most common LAN and WAN media, including diagnosing common connectivity problems; and about the functionality of several common nonproprietary routing protocols, including examples on how to use them in your network. Whenever possible, technical information will be illustrated with concrete examples and illustrative exercises.

In any "packet-switched" protocol, two communicating computers break up their data into "packets" that are transported by the "packet-switching network." There are many packet-switched protocols, but the Internet Protocol alone is the subject of this book. By virtue of its being the building block of the Internet, IP is extremely widespread—and becoming more so every day. Other common packet-switching protocols include the first (international) standards-based packet-switching technology ITU-T's[1] X.25, IBM's Systems Network Architecture (SNA), and Novell's Internetwork Packet Exchange (IPX) protocol. There are others, including AppleTalk Phases I and II, Banyan Vines, ChaosNet, Digital Equipment Corporation's DECnet Phases IV and V, IP version 6, Open Systems Interconnection (OSI), Unix-to-Unix CoPy (UUCP), Xerox's Xerox Network Services (XNS), and others.

The Internet Protocol allows data to flow across computer networks, such as the Internet and the many corporate networks that have elected to deploy IP internally. The "data" carried by IP packets can be traditional computer data, or digitized voice and video traffic which are emerging uses of IP. Once voice and video are digitized, they are just data, but they have specific requirements unlike that of, for example, file transfers. Voice and video are time-sensitive and are less tolerant of delay or delay variability. Curiously, voice and video traffic can tolerate some loss of data without experiencing audible or visible degradation, whereas data traffic must be assured of correct transmission, and so time may be spent retransmitting missing or damaged packets to ensure that the entire transmission arrives intact.

In the early IP world, packet switches were commonly known as "gateways," presumably because they were often served as the gateway between a local campus'

Why Packet Switching?

Why should computers need "packet switching" to communicate? Why not have temporary "phone calls" between computers? The difference comes from the way the phone network is built, and the basic nature of computer communications. Most computer communications are very often brief—on the order of seconds—but intense. The best descriptive word is "bursty." Compare this to voice calls, which may last a long time, but use a predictable amount of "bandwidth" for the entire duration of the call.

The usual phone network is optimized for voice calls, which tend to last a long time relative to the time it takes to set them up. It may take on the order of five seconds to dial and wait for a remote party to pick up the phone. From the phone network's perspective, all the hard work of establishing the resources for the call takes place in those first few seconds, after which the call continues to use the resources that have been allocated to it. Due to the extra effort in establishing a call, versus continuing an already established call, the phone company historically charged a penny or two more for the first minute than the remaining minutes.

Another issue with computers calling each other is knowing when to hang up. In a voice call, both parties mutually end a conversation. On the other hand, computers may wish to keep a channel open for a while (how long?) in case one has data to send to the other in the near future. Maintaining a lot of idle but open connections wastes resources in a dedicated-circuit network, like the voice telephone network. Also, a computer would need to have 10 separate physical phone lines if it wanted to have 10 calls active at the same time, which costs money every month whether or not they are used.

Besides the bursty data versus nonbursty voice issue, the rate at which voice calls are set up is bounded by the limitations of human fingers, since we can't dial quickly enough to overtax the telephone network's control, or "signaling," channels. Computers, on the other hand, may need to send brief bits of data to many peers in a short period of time, necessitating far more call setups per second.

(continued)

Packet switching has two main modes of operation, namely "virtual circuit," also known as "connection-oriented," versus the other mode, known as "datagram," also known as "connectionless." What makes a connection "virtual"? Basically, a number of virtual connections can share a single physical facility, like a single dial-up connection, or a single dedicated serial link to a wide area network (WAN) switch.

While people have difficulty carrying on multiple simultaneous conversations, computers have no such limitations, and can easily maintain simultaneous "conversations" with multiple peer computers. If each connection needed a unique physical facility, such as its own phone line, then having 10 connections to 10 peers would imply that the calling computer would need 10 physical phone lines (or any suitable dedicated physical medium).

However, when intercomputer communications are broken into packets, each packet can share a single wire, even if one packet may be headed for peer#1, while the next three may be headed for peer#7, and so on. All the "virtual" connections share a single physical wire into a packet-switching network. Each packet's header tells the network where the packet should go, which relieves the sending computer from needing separate physical connections to each peer. Logically, the connectivity is the same, since the computer can still send the same data to each peer whether or not there is a separate physical link to each peer. However, packet switching can be much more efficient than the alternative, which is known as "circuit switching."

Remember that there are two fundamental types of packet switching protocols, "virtual circuit" and "datagram." In a virtual circuit scheme, a call setup still happens at the beginning of a virtual call, but all the previously established virtual connections share the same physical access link to the packet-switching network. This eliminates circuit-switching's "problem," wherein multiple connections required multiple physical phone lines. With packet switching, all the virtual connections share the same "phone line" to the packet switch, and each packet has its own destination address that depends on the virtual circuit ID that was assigned during the call setup phase. The virtual circuit ID is a short "label" or "handle," which allows the packet switches to easily forward the packets to their destinations based on a simple table lookup.

Hanging up is less of an issue here, since an established connection consists simply of a table entry in the packet switches between the two computers. However, given

(continued)

that the packet switches do not have infinite memory, it is good to tear down un-needed virtual circuits so there will be room for others. The memory consumed by established virtual circuits is far less expensive than the bandwidth consumed by idle telephone calls. This is in stark contrast to the situation with physical connections, where the scaling limits are pushed out to the edge; in other words, if a computer has 16 modems, and more than 16 other computers want to send it data, then the physical capacity of that system will be exceeded.

The other main form of packet switching, "connectionless," encompasses IP and many other network-layer protocols. In connectionless mode, we preserve the "single access link" aspect of the virtual circuit scheme, in that multiple destinations are reachable via the same connection to the packet switching network. However, in-stead of doing an explicit call setup before any data can be sent, and then using the assigned connection-specific short handle as each packet's destination address, the packets in a connectionless network all carry the full destination address on every packet. Packets are simply sent into the network, relying on each intermediate packet switch (i.e., IP router) to decide how best to forward the packet toward its in-dicated destination.

machines and a wide-area network (e.g., the ARPANET). Today, these devices are most commonly known as "routers."[2]

Figure 1.1 shows an icon for a router which interconnects five "subnetworks." A router receives traffic on any of its interfaces, then must decide how to forward it toward its destination, which often involves the packet leaving the router by a differ-ent interface. The bidirectional arrows indicate the flow of packets to and from the router.

Routers are the fundamental building blocks of any IP-based network, includ-ing the Internet.

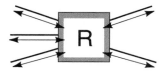

FIGURE 1.1 Representation of a router.

Packet Switching and the ARPANET

Generically, the network elements that move packets around have always been known as "packet switches." Packet switching was invented by Paul Baran and others in the early 1960s. By 1966, plans were beginning for what would become the ARPANET, which was eventually built in 1969.[3] Packet switches in the ARPANET were known as "Information Message Processors," or IMPs. IMPs were Honeywell 516 minicomputers with 12 KB (!) of memory, running ARPANET-specific packet switching software. The IMP software was developed by Bolt Beranek and Newman, Inc. (BBN), currently part of GTE.

In 1970, the ARPANET began using the Network Control Protocol (NCP) packet format, which was used until the ARPANET was converted to employing the Transmission Control Protocol over the Internet Protocol (TCP/IP) suite beginning on 1 January 1983. The ARPANET researchers designed the Internet Protocol, which was the result of many years of experience with packet switching in the real-world testbed that the ARPANET provided.

The ARPANET gradually grew and evolved into the Internet we know today. Throughout the 1970s and 1980s it experienced considerable growth and supported essential research into computer networking. In the late 1980s, the ARPANET had become just one of the many thousands of interconnected IP-based networks of the Internet. After over two decades of faithful service, the ARPANET was deactivated in 1990.

COMMUNICATING OVER LANS AND WANS

When routers talk to other routers, or to endstations (usually over local area networks or LANs), they need a way to send packets to the neighbor. A packet cannot be sent to a neighbor directly using only its IP address; IP addresses are "higher-layer" addresses. What actually happens is that IP packets are "encapsulated," or wrapped up, using a frame format that is specific to the subnetwork type. That frame contains the intended neighbor's destination address, and usually also contains the router's subnetwork-layer source address. Figure 1.2 depicts the relationship between

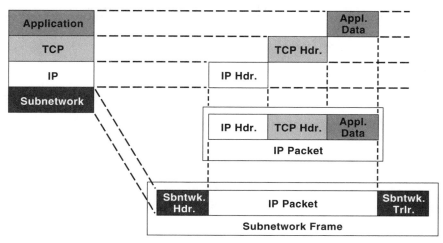

FIGURE 1.2 Layering and encapsulation.

the layers in the IP protocol stack, and the concept of encapsulation. In the diagram the User Datagram Protocol, (UDP) may be exchanged for TCP; they are identical as far as this discussion of layering is concerned.

The LAN and WAN "subnetworks" have their own addressing schemes, which routers must use to communicate with each other. Besides knowing their neighbors' IP addresses, the routers must usually know their neighbor's subnetwork layer addresses. IP uses different techniques, specific to each subnetwork medium, to learn what its neighbors' subnetwork addresses are.

Systems with multiple layers of addresses are commonplace in everyday life. Consider the situation of two people that are in office buildings. One is in the Highgate Tower, suite 2301, and the other is in Trumpet Place, room 3107. Now, in order for them to communicate, they need to know the street address of their correspondent. In real life, each person probably also knows the street address of the other's building, but that's not the point. The point is that we deal every day with systems that have multiple levels of addresses, of different formats.

IP ARCHITECTURE OVERVIEW

IP is a layered protocol, designed to facilitate the exchange of data between two applications on two different computers. The fact that the solution is broken into layers reflects a divide-and-conquer approach to the problem of computer-computer communication. In the IP universe, the application is responsible for formatting data

such that its peer(s) can understand it. Applications employ a Transport layer protocol that provides the capability for multiple applications to be running on one machine. Optionally, a Transport layer protocol may provide reliability services, or ordered delivery services. Transport layer protocols may also provide a checksum over
the Application-layer data, so that correct reception of unaltered data may be verified.

In the IP stack, the Transport layer offers two very common choices, the Transmission Control Protocol (TCP), which is a reliable transport protocol, and the User
Datagram Protocol (UDP), which is a more basic protocol that provides only multiple-
application "demultiplexing."[4] Both transport protocols consider the application's
data to be "opaque." In other words, it has no meaning to the transport protocol.[5]
Below the transport layer is the Internet Protocol (IP) layer. IP carries TCP "segments" or UDP "datagrams," again as opaque data, not knowing anything about
the operation of TCP or UDP, much less the application data they are carrying. IP
"packets" consist of IP's header along with the higher-layer transport data "protocols."

When IP entities need to communicate, they do so by employing any number
of lower-layer "subnetwork" technologies. There are either LAN subnetworks (e.g.,
Ethernet, Token Ring, Arcnet, LocalTalk, etc.) or WAN subnetworks (e.g., static
and dynamic point-to-point links, X.25 "clouds," frame relay clouds, ATM clouds,
Switched Multimegabit Data Service (SMDS) clouds, etc.). Figure 1.3 illustrates all
the various media over which IP can operate. Routers are used to interconnect the
various media; to keep the picture small, the WAN cloud routers do not show LANs
that are present at the remote sites.

Each of these subnetworks has its own internal addressing format and framing
format. Some subnetwork technologies employ both header and trailer fields, and
some encapsulate IP with only a header. Each technology runs at a unique speed, or
set of speeds. In short, each is completely different.

In the early days of IP, a tee shirt was produced that proclaimed "IP over
Everything!"[6] Today, rules do exist that describe how IP can run over virtually any
subnetwork technology that has ever been invented. Lately, running IP over "IP tun-
nels" has become useful for Virtual Private Networks (VPNs) over the Internet; in
this case, IP is using an IP tunnel as if IP itself were yet another subnetwork layer!
Figure 1.4 depicts the layered Internet Protocol "stack," and compares it to the
seven-layer Open Systems Interconnection Reference Model's layering. The IP
model predated the OSI Reference Model (OSI-RM).[7]

Demultiplexing was mentioned above in the context of TCP and UDP, but it
is a concept that recurs at every layer of the IP stack, not just at the Transport layer.
Multiplexing occurs when multiple higher-layer objects share a common lower-layer

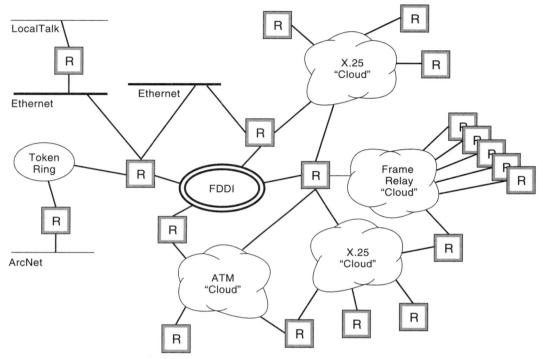

FIGURE 1.3 IP over everything.

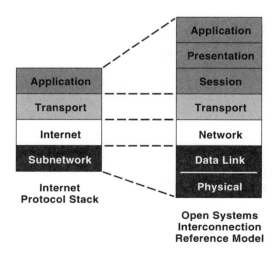

FIGURE 1.4 The layered Internet Protocol stack versus the OSI Reference Model.

facility. Demultiplexing is the process by which lower layers determine which higher-layer entity to deliver some data to. Remember that, ideally, each layer is independent of the others, considering the layer above it to be opaque data. Each layer's header information contains sufficient information so that any decisions regarding the disposition of the opaque payload (the next higher-layer header or data) can be made without needing to peek further inside the packet.

Inbound Packet Processing

In the subnetwork layer, a value in the subnetwork layer header that indicates that IP is the protocol "inside" the frame. At a minimum, there will be a Destination Address and some form of "Protocol Type" in the subnetwork layer header, as indicated in Figure 1.5. The Type field will contain a number X whose value means "the data that begins after the end of this header, and continues until the end of the frame,[8] belongs to protocol X." The DA and SA fields represent the subnetwork-layer destination and source addresses.

Each subnetwork may have its own list of values representing Network-layer protocols. For instance, over one important type of LAN, IP's protocol type value is $0x0800$[9] (one of 65,536 possible values of a two-byte Type field), but in a Frame Relay context, the protocol field is $0xCC$ (one of 256 possible values of a one-byte "Network Layer Protocol Identifier" field).

The subnetwork-layer demultiplexing feature allows multiple protocol stacks to share a common subnetwork medium, or more importantly, for multiple protocol stacks to be active on the same machine at the same time. Think of your PC—you probably have Microsoft® NetBEUI, Novell Internetwork Packet eXchange (IPX), and IP all active. For you Mac users out there,[10] you probably have not only AppleTalk, which is Apple's proprietary protocol stack for printing and file server access, but also an IP stack (either MacTCP or OpenTransport).

Whether a PC, Mac, or Unix workstation is being used, all the active protocol stacks share the same Network Interface Card (NIC) subnetwork address, so when

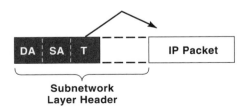

FIGURE 1.5   Subnetwork demultiplexing headers.

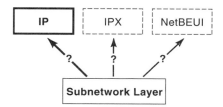

FIGURE 1.6 Passing a packet up the stack.

the NIC receives a frame it is clearly for one of the protocol stacks . . . but which one? The Protocol Type value tells the driver software which protocol stack should get the frame's embedded packet. Figure 1.6 illustrates the decision-making process that the subnetwork-layer protocol software performs.

Once the IP layer has taken delivery of the packet from the subnetwork layer,[11] it must first verify that its locally-assigned address matches the packet's destination address. If this is the case, then the IP layer has its own set of headers that mimic the demultiplexing function of the subnetwork. Figure 1.7 shows the parts of the IP header that are important for demultiplexing.

An important feature that makes the IP layer unique, and valuable, is the fact that it is "subnetwork-independent," so it can run over almost any type of subnetwork. IP insulates the Transport layer above it from all the different underlying characteristics of all the many possible subnetworks that it supports. Just as there can be multiple network-layer protocols that share a common subnetwork layer, multiple-Transport layer protocols can share the Internet Protocol layer, as shown in Figure 1.8.

The IP header's "Protocol" field is the indicator of which higher-layer protocol should receive the data encased within the packet. The most common higher-layer protocols are TCP and UDP (IP Protocol values 6 and 17, respectively). There are also many other protocols that make direct use of IP, including the Internet Control Message Protocol[12] (ICMP, IP Protocol = 1), the Internet Group Management Protocol (IGMP, IP Protocol = 2), the Open Shortest Path First (OSPF, IP Protocol =

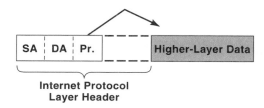

FIGURE 1.7 IP demultiplexing headers.

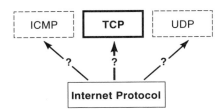

FIGURE 1.8   Passing higher-layer data up the stack.

89) routing protocol, the Protocol-Independent Multicast (PIM, IP Protocol = 103) multicast routing protocol(s), and many others. See the "Assigned Numbers" RFC (RFC-1700, or its successor) for a complete list of the IP Protocol field's possible values. A key thing to remember here is that just because a higher-layer protocol is a client of IP, it is not necessarily a Transport-layer protocol. In such cases, you might say that an application, or an application-like entity, is running directly over IP, with no intervening Transport layer protocol.[13]

In the case where a Transport layer protocol does follow IP, its header it used to help identify which application needs to receive the data. In the case of TCP, which is used for a majority of IP-based applications, there are a lot of fields that facilitate features other than demultiplexing, i.e., sequence numbers so that segments can be delivered in order and so that gaps in the data can be corrected by requesting retransmission, plus flags that are used when opening and closing connections, and other items. Figure 1.9 shows how TCP aids in the delivery of data to the correct application. In this case, we depict both the abstracted packet format and the protocol stacking in the same figure.

In TCP, the Destination "Port" is the indication of which application should receive the data. The DP field is doing double duty as both the "destination address" field and the "protocol type" field. This is perhaps because TCP is the top layer of the protocol stack.

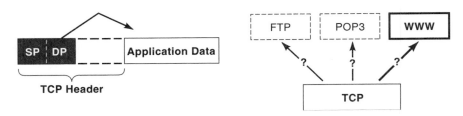

FIGURE 1.9   TCP demultiplexing.

TCP Details

Every TCP "connection" may be represented by a pair of "sockets." A socket is itself a pair of numbers, the IP address and a TCP port. First, a connection is limited to two machines almost by definition, so we need the two machines' IP addresses, i.e., IP_a and IP_b. Secondly, the TCP layer identifies the connection by the source and destination port, so there is $Port_A$ and $Port_B$ as well. So, $Socket_1$ is $(IP_a, Port_A)$, and $Socket_2$ is $(IP_b, Port_B)$. A connection is then represented as either [$Socket_1$, $Socket_2$], or [$(IP_a, Port_A)$, $(IP_b, Port_B)$].

In order to start up a new connection, one needs to know not only the other machine's IP address, but also the port on which the desired application service is "listening" (within that server). Most IP applications make use of "well-known ports" so that the client does not need to look up which port to use. For instance, a client wishing to connect to a WWW server will use destination TCP port 80 by default, but a client wishing to connect to a Post Office Protocol version 3 server will connect to TCP port 110. The client picks a random source port for itself and attempts to open the connection to the desired service's well-known port.

OVERVIEW OF THE IP HEADER

The IP header consists of a lot more than just demultiplexing and addressing functions. In all its glory, Figure 1.10 shows the IP Header. All the IP header's fields are useful, but the highlighted ones are more commonly used. Routers generally pay attention only to the Destination Address as long as the header format is the "simple"

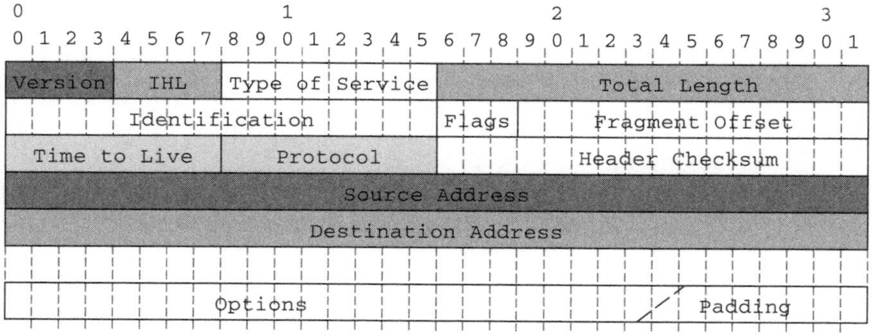

FIGURE 1.10   IP header fields.

one in the figure. The dashed vertical lines delineate bit positions. The header, as drawn, is 32 bits (four bytes) wide.

The most obvious fields are the ones which we are already familiar with, namely the Source and Destination Address fields, and the Protocol field. The other fields are all important, and will be discussed here, in order of relative importance. First, the Total Length field represents the length (in bytes) of the entire IP packet—including the IP header. Since it is a two-byte (16-bit) field, the largest IP packet may be $2^{16} - 1$, or 65,535, bytes long. The Internet Protocol RFC, RFC-791, mandates that all IP endstations be capable of sending and receiving 576-byte packets.

The Internet Protocol header is typically 20 bytes long, though certain "options" have been defined that can be appended to the end of the header. This is represented by the Internet Header Length (IHL) field, which counts the number of four-byte "words" in the IP header. Another way of saying this is that to determine the IHL value, one must take the IP header length and divide it by four. To avoid fractions, the IP header must be padded to a multiple of four bytes. The typical value of the IHL field is five, since five times four is 20. Since the IHL field is four bits long, the maximum value of the field is 15, making the maximum possible IP header 60 bytes long (15 times four bytes).

The Version field is set to four, since this header format is that of IPv4, the version of IP that is in use in today's Internet.[14] The Type of Service (ToS) byte has been getting a lot of attention lately within the industry, as ISPs and customers clamor for a way to provide different "class of service" levels within their networks. Work is under way to define a "Differentiated Services" (DS) model, that redefines the ToS field as the DS field. The first two RFCs defining differentiated services are RFC-2474 and -2475. Work is ongoing to define new "per-hop behaviors" and also to deploy the initial specifications. RFC-2430 is one example of how differentiated services might be deployed, however, other scenarios are likely to emerge as experience with this new technology is accumulated.

The Time to Live (TTL) field is decremented by one each time a packet crosses a router. This practice ensures that the packet will not persist in the Internet forever. The maximum initial TTL is 255, but many endstations will use a lower initial TTL value. Originally, the TTL was literally supposed to be interpreted as up to 255 seconds of time; presumably, the expectation of early-1980s line speeds and software-based routers was that it would take about one second for a router to receive and forward a packet, but the TTL has evolved into nothing more than a hop counter.

The Header Checksum value must be recomputed on a hop-by-hop basis, since each router hop decrements the TTL, thereby changing the header and invalidating the previous hop's calculated checksum. Fragmentation, if performed, also changes the contents of the IP header, thus forcing the checksum to be recomputed.

FRAGMENTATION of IP PACKETS

This section on IP packet fragmentation is somewhat abstract and can safely be skipped on a first reading; however, a discussion of the IP header would not be complete without covering fragmentation.

Three of the IP header fields are used together to support fragmentation. For example, suppose that a packet is sent by an initial endstation with a Total Length of 1500 bytes. Somewhere along the path to the packet's destination, there may be a link that only supports datagrams up to 512 bytes long. We say that the link's maximum transmission unit (MTU) is 512 bytes.

When faced with such a situation, a router can break a packet into fragments such that the pieces will each be small enough to pass through the narrow link. Each fragment has its own complete IP header, much of it the same as the original packet's header, as illustrated in Figure 1.11. This figure assumes the typical Internet Header Length of 20 bytes.

If options were present in the initial header, some of them must be replicated in each fragment, while others may remain in the first fragment. If any options remain in the IP header, the Internet Header Length will be at least 24 bytes, which would make the packets 512 bytes versus 508 bytes. If the Internet Header Length were 28 bytes or larger, the data portion of the packet would be reduced in multiples of eight bytes to keep the Total Length under the 512-byte MTU.

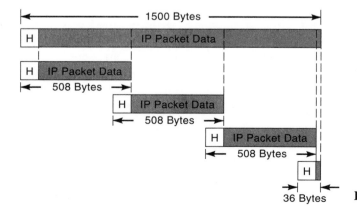

FIGURE 1.11 IP fragmentation.

Each packet fragment is then forwarded independently on its way to the destination, where it is ultimately reassembled. The Identification field is a unique 16-bit value that is used by the transmitting station to help the receiver keep track of related fragments during the reassembly process. It is possible for multiple senders to pick the same one of these 65,536 values, so the receiver must correlate not only the Identification header value, but also the packet's Source Address. Between a given pair of IP addresses, it is unlikely that a sender would pick the same Identification field for two different packets within a small time interval. Senders should increment the Identification field value in each transmitted packet, thereby guaranteeing that the same value will only be used once out of every 65,536 packets sent by any given station.

The Flags field controls the fragmentation process; the most significant of the three bits must be zero, the next one is the "Don't Fragment" bit, and the least significant is the "More Fragments" bit. If the "More Fragments" bit is set (i.e., if the bit is equal to one), then this is not the last fragment. The final fragment will have this bit clear, so the receiving station will know that it is the final fragment of the original packet. The meaning of the "Don't Fragment" bit is clear—the sending station wishes that the packet be carried in one piece, or not at all. If a packet marked with the "Don't Fragment" bit encounters too small a link, the last router before the link will discard the packet and send an error message back to the packet's Source Address.

Once all the packet's fragments have arrived at their Destination Address, the Fragment Offset values in each fragment allow the receiver to put them back together in order. These values also permit the receiver to know when it has received all the fragments, by using the Fragment Offset values for each packet, and the length of each fragment's data field, which is its Total Length minus its Internet Header Length.

Until they all arrive, those fragments that have been received must be buffered, or stored, at the receiver. It is tempting to think that since routers usually fragment packets, that they should re-assemble them as well. This is most definitely not the case! Due to the datagram nature of IP networks, all the fragments may not take the same path through the network. Remember that every IP packet is independently forwarded, based on each router's understanding of the best way to get to the packet's destination when it arrives at that router. A topology or administrative change among the intervening routers could cause some fragments to take a different path than their predecessors. No single "downstream" router is guaranteed to receive all of the fragments,[15] so no single one of them could possibly be expected to re-assemble a fragmented packet. The only sure place where all the fragments ought to reappear is the ultimate destination station.

FRAGMENTATION MINUTIAE

Each fragment must be a multiple of eight bytes long, because there are only 2^{13} Fragment Offset values, but the packet can be up to 2^{16} bytes long. Since $(2^{16})/(2^{13})$ is 2^3, the fragments are forced to be multiples of eight bytes long. Note that the requirement that packet fragments be a multiple of eight bytes long *only applies to the original packet's <u>data</u> field*. A packet fragment's data field length must be a multiple of eight, but its Total Length will never be a multiple of eight, unless there are header options that make the IP header a multiple of eight as well.

Remember that the Total Length of any packet includes the length of the IP header. Since IP fragments are still IP packets in their own right, this is still the case. The Internet Header Length is always a multiple of four bytes long, between 20 and 60, inclusive, i.e., 20, **24**, 28, **32**, 36, **40**, 44, **48**, 52, **56**, or 60. Those IP header lengths that are multiples of eight bytes long are in boldface type. If the original packet had no options, which is the typical case, then all the packet's fragments will have an Internet Header Length of 20, meaning the Total Length of all the fragments will never be a multiple of eight.

Returning to Figure 1.10, one sees that each packet is less than 512 bytes long (the small link's maximum transmission unit). This is because the largest multiple of eight that can fit inside the 512-byte limit is 488, when one takes account of the fact that the header makes the packet another 20 bytes longer, for a Total Length of 508 bytes. The next higher multiple of eight is 496, but 496+20 = 516, which would be too large for the link. The minimum size for a fragment is eight bytes of data, plus 20 bytes of header, or 28 bytes, up to 68 bytes, where the eight bytes of fragment are preceded by a maximum-length 60-byte IP header.

Now, consider the largest IP packet, with a Total Length of 65,535. The data portion of that packet is a variable number of bytes long, depending on the size of the packet's header. In Table 1.1, we see the header lengths versus the resulting data lengths, assuming that each row must add to the maximum Total Length—65,535.

(continued)

TABLE 1.1   VALID DATA SIZES OF A 65,535-BYTE IP PACKET

IHL	65535-IHL
20	65,515
24	65,511
28	65,507
32	65,503
36	65,599
40	65,495
44	65,491
48	65,487
52	65,483
56	65,479
60	65,475

How many minimum-sized fragments would be needed to carry the complete packet in each of these cases? We must simply divide the data packet size by eight. If the answer is a round number, then it represents the number of eight-byte fragments required. If the answer includes a remainder, then another fragment is required to carry the extra data, and the total number of fragments required is indicated in parentheses.

In the case of a 20-byte Internet Header Length, we have a worst-case scenario of 8190 fragments. In such a case, the Fragment Offset field would contain values from 1 (0000000000001) through 8190 (1111111111110). In order to require such extreme fragmentation, a link would need to have a maximum transmission unit of between 28 and 35. IP cannot run over links that have an MTU smaller than 68, so in cases where the header length is 20 bytes, there is room for 48 bytes of data, which just happens to be a multiple of eight. So, the practical upper end on fragmentation is 65,515/48, or 1364 48-byte fragments, with 43 bytes left over, for the 1365th fragment. In the Fragment Offset field, this would be 10101010101, believe it or not.

If all the fragments do not arrive within a reasonable period of time, then those fragments that did make it through must be discarded; losing a fragment is the same as losing the entire packet. The length of each fragment is reflected in its Total Length field. Once the receiver has accumulated all the fragments, it may reconstruct the original packet's Total Length by measuring the length of the concatenated fragments (not including the lengths of their headers).

Important IP "Helper" Protocols

There are other protocols that are part of the IP stack, without which IP would be incomplete. The Internet Control Message Protocol (ICMP, RFC-792) is used for error-reporting and network diagnostic functions. ICMP is actually considered to be part of IP, in the sense that every IP module must support ICMP. The Internet Group Management Protocol (IGMP, RFC-2236) is used to support multicast IP,[16] which is beyond the scope of this book. Most modern IP stacks support IGMP, but IP does not mandate the inclusion of IGMP.

Another absolutely critical protocol that IP could not live without is the Address Resolution Protocol (ARP). ARP is used in a LAN subnetwork to allow IP endstations to learn the subnetwork-layer addresses of their neighbor endstations on that LAN. Several WAN variants of ARP exist, including Inverse ARP and Asynchronous Transfer Mode ARP (ATM-ARP), but not all WAN subnetworks require, or support, address resolution.

WHAT IS ROUTING?

Once packets have been formed with the proper source and destination addresses, they are transmitted into the network; it is then up to the routers to forward them to the indicated destination. A router is a special purpose computer that is designed to "forward" packets. Each of the router's interfaces must be configured with a unique address, each having its own unique prefix[17] (i.e., leading bits). The following chapters will cover the topic of IP addressing completely, but for now just remember that each interface on a router must have a unique IP address. Routers can have anywhere from two to more than 1,000 interfaces, each of which is connected to a LAN or WAN "subnetwork." In the case of a multiaccess subnetwork (there are both LAN and WAN technologies that can be classified as multiaccess), there may be a set of other routers attached to that subnetwork, each of which goes to different places.

Nomenclature

The term "routing" is often used to refer to two completely different, but closely related, concepts. People use "routing" to refer to the process whereby routers exchange special "routing protocol" packets to describe their local topology to one another. "Routing" is also used to describe the process of deciding how to forward a packet, consisting of receiving a packet, looking up its destination in the forwarding table (commonly called the "routing table"), determining the next-hop router, and transmitting to the next-hop router (or perhaps the packet's ultimate destination) on the appropriate outbound interface.

Usually it is clear from the context what a speaker means when they say routing.[18] However, in this book the author will make every effort to say "forwarding" when describing the act of deciding where a packet needs to go and then delivering it on its way, versus "routing" when discussing the act of learning and sharing information about the topology. In short, routing is a process that facilitates packet forwarding.

Figure 1.12 shows a small subset of a topology, including subnetworks that have just one router, and one subnetwork that has three total routers. LAN subnetworks are often drawn as circles or lines, depending on the technology being represented. Symbols for WAN subnetworks are usually either clouds or simply lines.[19] Endstations are almost always attached via the LAN subnetworks.

In order to learn the lay of the land, the routers communicate with each other using routing protocols. It is also possible for an administrator to manually tell their routers that "destination X is reachable via router P," "destination Y is reachable via router Q," and so on. This static method requires no information exchanges among the routers, but only works until the topology changes (e.g., a link or neighbor router fails or otherwise becomes unreachable). In this "static routing" case, a router has no way to detect such failures, and keeps forwarding traffic into oblivion, via a path that is not functional. Another problem with static routing is that it is difficult to configure more than a few routers with all possible destinations. As the network grows, this becomes more and more difficult to do, and thus ever more prone to error.

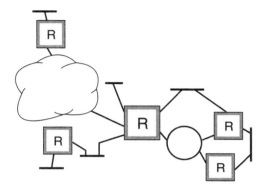

FIGURE 1.12   Router topology.

The alternative, used in the vast majority of situations, is to let the routers use their own knowledge of their individual attachments to build up a routing table dynamically. These messages boil down to a router saying, "here's what I am attached to," or "here's the places you can get to by going through me." Remember that each router must be configured in advance to know what address(es) it has on each of its interfaces. Each router shares this connectivity information with its neighbors, and eventually they all "converge" on a stable understanding of all the reachable destinations, and which neighbor router is the best next-hop to reach each destination.

So, besides data traffic from endstations, which routers must forward as quickly as they can, there are also control messages, mostly routing protocol packets, which routers must listen to (according to their configuration). Most routers support a large suite of routing protocols. There are numerous standards-based routing protocols, and some well-known proprietary ones as well. At this point, it will suffice to say that a given set of routers must all be speaking the same "routing protocol" in order for them to know about the reachability of all destinations within that "routing domain." Routing protocols define a set of messages that let routers advertise and receive information about reachable or unreachable destinations within the routing domain. A routing domain is essentially a collection of routers that speak the same protocol.

Later in the book we will look at ways to effectively use more than one routing protocol at a time. We will also examine ways to use the addressing structure of your network to give your routers strong hints about where certain destinations might be, thereby limiting the need for them to describe each and every little gory detail to each other, yet still maintaining enough reachability information to do the job of forwarding packets.

How is the Internet Built?

The Internet is a large collection of routers, organized as follows. At the highest level, there are a handful of large Internet Service Providers (ISPs), commonly called "Tier-1" providers. Tier-1 providers have networks that may span continents. These providers are attached to each other at convenient places called regional "peering points" or "exchanges," as shown in Figure 1.13 as circles with Xs inside.

Tier-1 providers also typically attach directly to each other at "private peering" points, represented by the dashed lines in the figure. In fact, direct private peering is one of the distinguishing characteristics of a Tier-1 ISP; these ISPs have so much data to exchange that they need private peering points in order to function well. Another characteristic of Tier-1 providers is that they are present at all the major regional peering points. Lower-tier ISPs generally only "peer" with Tier-1 ISPs at the regional exchanges, where many dozens of ISPs of all levels peer with each other and deliver packets.

There are easily more than three Tier-1 ISPs; this figure is meant to illustrate the concept of peering at regional exchange points versus private peering. The end of each of the line in the figure is a router interface.

The large providers also attach to smaller providers, Tier-2, which are usually limited to a continent or a country. Tier-2 providers generally attach to Tier-1 ISPs at the regional peering points. If a Tier-2 ISP is large enough, it may peer with a Tier-1 ISP in more than one geographical location to help balance the traffic between the two, and also to provide a measure of resiliency. Tier-2 ISPs usually attach to multiple Tier-1 providers to provide their customers with richer connectivity.

Generally, Tier-2 peering rules are set up so that they do not inadvertently become a forwarding path between two Tier-1 providers. This is known as becoming a "transit" provider. Tier-1 providers are generally selling "transit services" to Tier-2 and below because the Tier-1 ISPs have high-capacity backbone circuits,

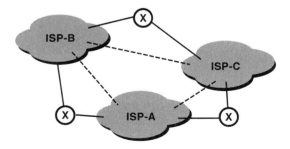

FIGURE 1.13   Tier-1 ISPs.

but the lower-tier providers do not have the capacity to carry data between two Tier-1 ISPs.

Below Tier-2, there are Tier-3 providers that purchase service from the Tier-2 providers, and so on. Each of these providers' networks, from Tier-1 on down, is based on IP routers, devices that understand the format of IP packets and know how to forward them toward their destinations. A large provider's network may have thousands of routers, while a small provider may have a dozen, more or less.

In total, there are hundreds of thousands of routers in the ISP networks, and besides the routers, there are computers that are used by the ISP's "operations" staff to configure, observe, and otherwise manage the network. Each ISP manages its own internal infrastructure, and the peering arrangements that they have with other ISPs represent how they make their money. If ISP A carries traffic for ISP B, then ISP B owes them money for that service. On the other hand, if ISP B carries traffic for ISP A, or its customers, then ISP A owes money to ISP B.

Ultimately, businesses or home-based users attach to some provider, at some level. There is no reason why Tier-1 providers couldn't have customers connecting directly to them, or have businesses attached [semi-]permanently to them. Customers may attach at any level of the hierarchy, wherever they can get a good deal, or otherwise obtain service that meets their specific requirements.

WHY IS THE INTERNET SO USEFUL?

The Internet is a general purpose infrastructure, in the same sense that the highway system is a general purpose infrastructure, as are the Postal service and the telephone network. Each of these are pervasive (in the geographic sense), and they can all carry a variety of payloads to suit their many types of users.

The mere existence of useful general purpose infrastructures actually seems to spur the creation of interesting applications for them. Of course, there had to be some applications or it would not have been built in the first place, but uses of such infrastructures evolve well beyond those envisioned by its creators. A good example is the revolution in commerce that was enabled by the arrival of overnight shipping companies, pioneered by Federal Express. Presumably, the reason it was built was that there was no easy way to get letters and packages delivered overnight. Once the capability existed, new businesses arose that had never been possible before. For example, a high-end florist business now basically cuts flowers to order and ships the floral arrangement overnight. Given the freshness of the flowers, they may last twice as long as those purchased from a local florist. This business would not be possible without a reliable way to ship packages overnight. Because of the success of the pioneers, many other businesses joined the overnight shipping business, creating competition and a healthy marketplace. Many other examples exist of unforeseen applications of new infrastructures.

Examples of General Purpose Infrastructures

Transportation: Roads, Railroads, Airplanes, Shipping, etc.

Motorcycles, tanks, delivery vans, long-haul trucks, and cars all may use the interstate highway system and all its feeder roads. Some roads are wide, with many lanes, and others are narrow; some underpasses limit the size of trucks that can use certain roads. The highway system interconnects with train stations, airports, and shipping ports to facilitate the exchange of people and cargo among the different modes of transportation. Automobiles can be either a user of the transportation system (i.e., when cars are carried on ships or trucks), or a direct application of it (i.e., when people drive their kids to school, or go to a ball game).

Postal Service

The postal service is but one application that makes use of the transportation system. The post carries parcels, postcards, letters, and provides extra services such as certified mail, for which you pay an additional fee. They pick up and deliver mail from all addresses once a day.

Telephone System

Using the telephone network, one can place a call to see how grandma is doing, or set up a job interview, or to order a pizza for delivery. One can also plug in a fax machine and call another fax machine to transfer a document. Other devices such as computers may use modems attached to the telephone network to send data to each other. The trick is that modems, fax machines, etc., have to speak the phone network's "language." Since the phone network was designed to carry human voices, it allows a relatively narrow audio frequency range (about 0 – 4 kHz) to pass through, enough so that voices are recognizable. Thus, any devices making use of the phone network must transmit tones that lie within this frequency range in order to have them pass through successfully.

All of these applications can be performed over local, long-distance, or international circuits, each of which has different rate structures that depend on the length of the call, the geographic distance between the call's endpoints, the time of day, and whether the caller subscribes to a discount calling plan.

The fastest growing use of the telephone network over the last 15 years has been fax and other "data" (i.e., nonvoice) applications, such as two computers calling each other to transmit data on behalf of their users. The Internet is an ever-larger component of this data traffic explosion. Ironically, voice traffic is beginning to be carried over the Internet. Perhaps someday, all (or most) voice traffic will use the Internet.

The Internet as a General Purpose Infrastructure

The Internet has much in common with all of these (and other) general purpose infrastructures. Just as you can send a letter to anyone, drive to almost anywhere, and call almost anyone, the Internet is becoming ubiquitous, asymptotically approaching universal planet-wide connectivity.

The packets which traverse the Internet may be large or small. They may represent any of a large, and growing, list of applications. IP packets cross links whose speed ranges across six orders of magnitude, each potentially congested by the presence of other traffic. Analogies can be made to any of the other "networks" above, but the Internet seems to have more in common with the highways or the postal service than the others. The highway system has some high-capacity roads, some two-lane roads, and some very congested roads (seemingly regardless of their size).[20]

The way IP packets are delivered has much in common with the postal service. There are a lot of dedicated people that work at the postal service, but the quantity of mail they must process dictates that machines must be used to help deliver the mail in a timely fashion. Most of the time, a letter can cross the country in three to five days, but sometimes it takes longer, and sometimes the mail is lost or damaged en route to its destination. Due to unavoidable situations, it is impossible to get all the mail through, despite the best intentions of the post office. So, when you put a letter in the mail, you are not guaranteed how long it will take to get to its destination, nor are you guaranteed that it will even get to its destination. You know that it is very unlikely to be delayed for more than a few days, and you know that it may be destroyed in transit, but that this is also unlikely. The postal service makes their best effort to ensure that your mail will get through. IP networks also offer "best-effort" service.

Each packet that is transmitted into the network has its own "destination address" that tells the network where the packet needs to go. Each packet also has a return address (the packet's "source address"), so that the destination will know which address the packet came from and will be able to send a reply (if necessary). Also, if a packet cannot get through, the network can use the return address to inform the source of the trouble, similar to the way the post office uses the return address on a letter.

IP is also similar to the highway system. Just as a car can drive over a freshly-paved six-lane interstate highway, or a pothole-ridden city street, or across water on a ferry boat, IP packets can be sent over various different types of links, which are known as "subnetworks." IP operates at what is known as the "network layer," so it makes sense that links over which IP operates should be known as "sub-" networks. There are many kinds of subnetworks, the most common of which will be discussed later in the book.

Some IP packets are large and some are small. IP defines a maximum packet size, and some links over which IP operates have minimum packet sizes, or smaller maximum sizes. The fact that some subnetworks have different capacities than others is similar to roads which may have width- or weight-limited bridges, or height-limited underpasses.

INTERNET APPLICATIONS

The feature set of IP will be covered in more detail shortly. For now, it is worthwhile to focus on the subject of applications. There are numerous applications of IP. In the early days of the Internet, the most common applications were remote login and file transfers. Researchers at one university may have needed to access specific computing resources at another university, so they could remotely log in over the Internet rather than traveling there and touching a hard-wired terminal. Once the computers finished with their jobs, the data needed to be transferred back home, so file transfer was another logical application.

Electronic mail was another early application, and it arrived in two forms. First was the point-to-point variety, in which a user sends to only one other user, or a group of users (a "mailing list"). Another form was developed that evolved from a separate network called Usenet. In this case, messages are posted to topical "news-groups" that interested parties subscribe to. One person posts a question or observation and others respond, creating a "thread" of messages. This form of message exchange on Usenet, when it originated, was not based on IP, but the Unix-to-Unix CoPy protocol (uucp). Usenet became a worldwide network in its own right, for a long time much larger than the Internet, but as the Internet became larger and more pervasive, it became possible to use the Internet to transfer Usenet messages. Today, most—but not all—of the old uucp-based Usenet has been replaced by the Network News Transfer Protocol, which operates over the TCP/IP-based Internet.

One of the most important applications of the Internet is its name-lookup system, known as the Domain Name Service (DNS).[21] Virtually every IP-speaking device also supports the DNS application, which allows the devices to convert human-friendly names like "ftp.gnu.ai.mit.edu" into the equivalent IP address 18.159.0.42. This is a critical service, since IP packets must be addressed to IP addresses, but the Internet would be unusable for humans if we all had to remember IP addresses like 18.159.0.42 instead of human-friendly names like ftp.gnu.ai.mit.edu or ftp.ietf.org.

The World Wide Web (WWW) versus the Internet

The Internet is the "packet hauling" infrastructure that has been in place, and growing rapidly, since the early 1980s. The WWW is an application that runs over the Internet. The term "web" is usually used interchangeably with the Internet these days, because so few people know that they are, in fact, different things. Electronic mail, remote terminal access, the domain name system, file transfer, network news, directory services, etc., are all applications of the Internet. They all predated the web, but the web was the "killer app" for the Internet—the application that made everyone want to be "on" the Internet so they could use the WWW applications.

REFERENCES

Kleinrock, Leonard, "Information Flow in Large Communication Nets," MIT, first paper on packet-switching (PS) theory, July 1961.

Licklider, J.C.R., Clark, W. "On-Line Man Computer Communication," MIT, Galactic Network concept encompassing distributed social interactions, August 1962.

Baran, Paul, "On Distributed Communications Networks," RAND, packet-switching networks; no single outage point.

Request for Comment (RFC)

2430 A Provider Architecture for Differentiated Services and Traffic Engineering (PASTE). T. Li, Y. Rekhter. October 1998. (Format: TXT=40148 bytes) (Status: INFORMATIONAL)

2474 Definition of the Differentiated Services Field (DS Field) in the IPv4 and IPv6 Headers. K. Nichols, S. Blake, F. Baker, D. Black. December 1998. (Format: TXT=50576 bytes) (Obsoletes RFC1455, RFC1349) (Updates RFC791, RFC1122, RFC1123, RFC1812) (Status: PROPOSED STANDARD)

2475 An Architecture for Differentiated Service. S. Blake, D. Black, M. Carlson, E. Davies, Z. Wang, W. Weiss. December 1998. (Format: TXT=94786 bytes) (Status: PROPOSED STANDARD)

ENDNOTES

1. The ITU-T is an international standards-setting body, whose acronym stands for International Telecommunications Union, Telecommunication Standardization Sector. The ITU-T was formerly known as the CCITT, or *Comité Consultatif International de Télégraphique et Téléphonique*. The ITU-T is a subset of the ITU, which is an agency of the United Nations.

2. The term gateway lives on as part of the term "default gateway," which is a nearby router to which each IP endstation sends all its nonlocally-destined traffic.

3. The first four sites on the ARPANET were: UCLA, the Stanford Research Institute (SRI), UCSB, and the Univ. of Utah.

4. Transport-layer demultiplexing allows multiple applications to coexist on one machine, by virtue of different transport-layer labels called "ports." Each layer in the protocol stack facilitates demultiplexing, or sharing, that layer's services among multiple higher-layer entities.

5. Each layer in the protocol stack treats the layer above it as opaque; the transport layer is not unique in this characteristic.

6. Anyone familiar with this industry knows that tee shirts are the most influential force at trade shows. Clearly the impact of that tee shirt is still being felt!

7. A suite of "OSI protocols" were developed and implemented that correspond closely to the OSI-RM. Despite the Internet Protocol's insurmountable head start, OSI protocols are in use, predominantly in Europe and in other non-US locations. Despite the OSI suite's lack of commercial success (relative to the Internet Protocol suite), the OSI-RM still provides the context for classification of all layered protocols.

8. Some subnetwork layers have both a header and a trailer. The trailer may provide a data protection function, allowing the receiver to determine if the frame was received error-free or not. In cases where IP operates over such subnetworks, the presence of the trailer is understood, and the packet then includes all data up to, *but not including*, the subnetwork trailer.

9. The 0x (that's a zero and a lower-case 'x') means that the following number is hexadecimal, or base-16. The 0x notation originated in the context of the C programming language, but it has achieved widespread use outside those circles.

10. This book was written on a Macintosh PowerBook 2400c/180 with 80 MB RAM, running Mac OS 8.1.

11. Before handing the packet up to the proper Network-layer protocol, the subnetwork-layer strips off the frame's header (and trailer, if present). The data which is handed up to the Network layer is just the Network-layer packet; no traces of the subnetwork layer remain.

12. Technically, ICMP is a part of the IP software module, but it is still encapsulated in an IP header.

13. After reading that paragraph, you may have the impression that routing protcols run directly over IP. Not quite; the Routing Information Protocol (RIP) is a client of UDP rather than using IP directly.

14. Curiously, version four was the first version of IP.

15. One might be tempted to think that the ultimate destination's router could do this reassembly, but there is no reason why the ultimate destination of the fragments should be served by only one router. In such a case, fragments could be arriving from more than one "direction" (i.e., via more than one router). Again, the only place where the fragments are guaranteed to converge is the original packet's destination address.

16. Interested readers may wish to consult the Bibliography for references on multicast IP.

17. Think of the prefix as a telephone area code. A router interface consumes just one of the many available "phone numbers."

18. Some people pronounce this "rooting," a process performed by "rooters." Others (including the author) pronounce it "rowting," a process performed by "rowters." Either pronunciation is correct.

19. According to a telco "old-timer" friend of mine, a common "mistake" is to draw all point-to-point WAN links as a lightning bolt. The lightning-bolt icon was originally used to represent dial-up links. Permanent "nailed-up" point-to-point "leased line" links will be drawn as straight lines in this book.

20. Have you ever noticed that it doesn't seem to matter how many lanes there are—there is always congestion?

21. Recently, Microsoft has co-opted the acronym DNS to refer to an imaginary Digital Nervous System. Why not just call it the Internet? It is left as an exercise for the reader to consider what the motivation for such an action might be.

CHAPTER 2

Internet Addressing Conventions and Scaling Issues

INTRODUCTION

On the eve of the 21st century, the Internet is a vastly different network than when it was first established in the early 1980's.[1] Today, the Internet has entered the public consciousness as the world's largest public data network, doubling in size more than once a year, at a rate that seems to continually increase. This is reflected in the tremendous popularity of the World Wide Web (WWW), the opportunities that businesses see in reaching customers from virtual storefronts, and the emergence of new types and methods of doing business. It is clear that expanding business and social awareness will continue to increase public demand for access to resources on the Internet.

There is a direct relationship between the value of the Internet and the number of sites connected to the Internet. As the Internet grows, the value of each site's connection to the Internet increases because it provides the organization with access to an ever expanding user/customer population.

INTERNET SCALING PROBLEMS

Over the past and few years, the Internet has experienced two major scaling issues as it has struggled to provide continuous uninterrupted growth:

1. The eventual exhaustion of the IPv4 address space, due to the continued strong demand for addresses.
2. The ability to route traffic between the ever-increasing number of networks that comprise the Internet.

The first problem is concerned with the eventual depletion of the IP address space. The current version of IP, IP version 4 (IPv4), employs a 32-bit address, which means that there are only 2^{32} (4,294,967,296, or just under 4.3 billion) available IPv4 addresses. This might seem like a very large number of addresses, but as new markets open and a significant portion of the world's population become potential consumers of IP addresses, the finite number of IP addresses will eventually be exhausted. It is already impossible to assign a single, unique IP address to everyone on Earth, since there are now more than 6 billion of us sharing this little planet.[2] Some people even personally possess entire network numbers, which are essentially trophies of their early-adopter status of Internet technology. The address shortage problem is aggravated by the fact that portions of the IP address space have not been efficiently allocated. Also, the traditional model of classful addressing does not allow the address space to be used to its maximum potential.

Figure 2.1 illustrates the growth trends in each address class, clearly showing the increasing reliance on "Class C" networks. Also illustrated is the fact that the new address allocation policies caused the rate of depletion of the "Class B" addresses to drop markedly. After 1995, the newer "Classless Inter-Domain Routing" (CIDR) scheme, which will be discussed later in Part I, was basically only handing out blocks of Class C networks, so continuing this graph forward in time would not show much difference; the Class C network allocations would still be growing rapidly, and the Class B would be essentially flat. "Class A" network numbers are essentially not allocated any more, since no single entity can justify needing that many IP addresses.

The Address Lifetime Expectancy (ALE) Working Group of the Internet Engineering Task Force (IETF) expressed concerns that if the then-current address allocation policies were not modified, the Internet would have experienced a near to medium term exhaustion of its unallocated address pool, especially the desirable Class B address space. If the Internet's address supply problem was not solved, new users may have been prevented from connecting to the global Internet!

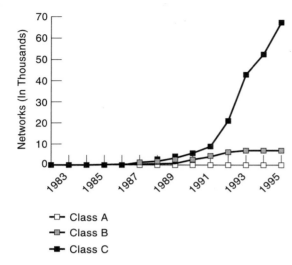

-□- Class A
-■- Class B
-■- Class C

FIGURE 2.1 Assigned and allocated network numbers.

The second problem is caused by the rapid growth in the size of the Internet routing tables. Internet backbone routers are required to maintain complete routing information for every active destination in the entire Internet. Over recent years, routing tables have experienced continuous growth as increasing numbers of organizations connect to the Internet—in December 1990 there were 2,190 routes, in December 1992 there were 8,500 routes, and in December 1995 there were more than 30,000 routes.

As of 1 September 1998, there were approximately 57,500 unique destination routes, or "prefixes" in the Internet routing system. Figure 2.2 is a graph that was derived from data that has been collected by SURFnet in the Netherlands for many years, then by Telstra, a long-established ISP in Australia. The raw data plot was obtained from *<http://www.telstra.net/ops/bgptable.html>*.

Unfortunately, the routing problem cannot be solved by simply installing more router memory, thereby increasing the capacity for holding ever-larger routing tables. Clearly, if a router is not capable of storing a full routing table and its associated data structures, it will not be able to participate in the Internet backbone. Beyond the obvious requirement of simply having enough memory to hold the routing tables, other factors related to the capacity problem include the growing demand for CPU horsepower to process routing table changes,[3] the increasingly dynamic nature of WWW connections and their effect on router forwarding caches,[4] and the sheer volume of information that needs to be managed by people and machines. If the number of en-

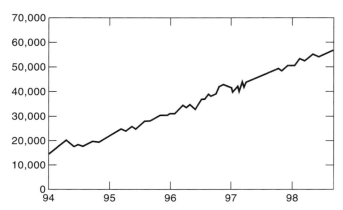

FIGURE 2.2   Growth of internet routing tables.

tries in the global routing table were to increase without bounds, more and more core routers would be unable to maintain a consistent view of reachable Internet destinations, rendering portions of the Internet temporarily unreachable!

One possible long term solution to these problems may be the widespread deployment of IP Next Generation (IPng or IPv6) sometime after the turn of the century. Despite the fact that IPv6 apparently has a complete set of specifications, with well-defined transition strategies, it is unclear whether or not something as large as the Internet can undergo such a fundamental change. Time will tell. However, while the Internet community waits for IPng, IPv4 will need to be patched and modified so that the Internet can continue to provide the universal connectivity its users have come to expect. This patching process may cause a tremendous amount of pain and may alter some of our fundamental concepts about the Internet. At some point, the patches, patches to patches, and so on, that have been applied to IPv4 may make deploying IPv6 more and more attractive, since it has been designed from the ground up based on lessons learned from IPv4.

Classful IP Addressing

When IP was first standardized in September 1981, the specification required that each interface of each system attached to an IP-based internetwork be assigned a unique, 32-bit value, an Internet Protocol address. Systems such as routers, which have interfaces to more than one network, must be assigned a unique IP address for each network interface.

Math

Warning, math ahead. Just kidding! IP addressing and subnet masks are a subject that confuses or intimidates many people. Never fear, understanding IP addressing requires just two simple arithmetic operations: 1) addition, and 2) multiplication by two. Many examples will be provided in this chapter and the remainder of Part I to attempt to illuminate seemingly abstract concepts. Moreover, the rest of the chapters in Part I, including this one, all conclude with a set of exercises so you can test your understanding.

The answers to the exercises are provided, but don't cheat! After some practice with IP addressing, you won't be able to imagine that you once thought it was complicated. The key to comfort with any subject is practice—once you have a basic understanding from this book, you will have many opportunities in the course of your everyday work, which will constantly refresh your knowledge.

The first part of an Internet address identifies the network on which the host resides, while the second part identifies the particular host on the given network. This created the two-level addressing hierarchy which is illustrated in Figure 2.3.

In recent years, the network-number field has been referred to as the "network-prefix," which is a more generic term used because the boundary between the network and host portion is not as rigid as it once was.

All hosts on a given network share the same network-prefix, but must have a unique host-number within that prefix. Similarly, any two hosts on different networks must have different network-prefixes, but may have the same host number. The network number is analogous to a street name, with the host-number akin to a house number. If there are two houses on Basin Street, only one can have 2112 as its house number. However, there is no confusion if there is a 2112 Canal Street in the same neighborhood.[5]

Network-Number	Host-Number

FIGURE 2.3 Two-level internet address structure.

Primary Address Classes

In order to provide the flexibility required to support different size networks, IP's designers decided that the IP address space should be divided into three different address "classes:" Class A, Class B, and Class C. This is often referred to as "classful" addressing because the address space is split into three predefined classes, groupings, or categories. Each class fixes the boundary between the network-prefix and the host-number at a different point within the 32-bit address. The formats of the fundamental address classes are illustrated in Figure 2.4. All the address classes are identified by the pattern of the address' high-order bits.

An address that has its high-order bit set to 0 is a Class A address, which uses only the first byte for the network number, leaving three bytes for the host portion of the address. After the initial 0 bit, seven bits remain for the network number field, allowing Class A networks to have values from 00000000 (zero) through 01111111 (127). By convention, network number fields with the all-0s and all-1s patterns are reserved, so there are a total of 126 Class A network numbers, ranging from 00000001 (one) to 01111110 (126).

The Class A all-0s and all-1s network numbers do have their uses. The all-0s network number is used to represent the "default" route (0.0.0.0), which is a routing table entry that is effectively a wildcard; any destination not matching an explicit route that is in the routing table is forwarded toward the default route. The all-1s pattern is used to represent the loopback network. The address 127.0.0.1 usually refers to "this machine" in a way that does not depend on knowledge of the machine's actual IP address. However, according to RFC-1700 (the Assigned Numbers RFC), all addresses of the form 127.x.y.z are loopback addresses, and must never be seen outside of a machine running IP.

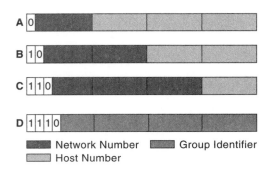

FIGURE 2.4 Summary of principal IP address classes.

Applications of the Loopback Address

The loopback address is quite useful. My machine uses the Dynamic Host Configuration Protocol (DHCP) to obtain its IP address, which may change at some point in the future. I run a Simple Mail Transfer Protocol (SMTP) server on my machine, and my machine's e-mail client software needs a stable configuration so that mail can reliably be sent from the e-mail client software on my machine, to my machine's SMTP server for delivery.

If I were to configure my local e-mail client with a DHCP-supplied address as its SMTP server, I run the risk of not being able to send mail in the future were my address to change, since whoever now has what used to be *my* IP address will not necessarily be running an SMTP server. Moreover, my machine's local server is still alive on the same machine; it just is now reachable by a different IP address, namely the new address that the machine got from DHCP. Unfortunately, while the IP stack can be dynamically configured by DHCP, my e-mail client software's SMTP server configuration is static. To avoid this potential disconnect, my machine's e-mail clients are configured with 127.0.0.1 as their SMTP server, which will always work, regardless of my machine's eventual IP address.

The loopback address greatly simplifies my outgoing e-mail configuration. Incoming mail is fetched by my e-mail client from one of our organization's Post Office Protocol (POP3) servers. The mail had arrived via SMTP from the outside world, ultimately reaching the POP3 server where my e-mail account resides. The POP3 client is configured with the POP server's domain name, so it can look up the server's IP address in the DNS the first time it needs to access my e-mail. The POP server's IP address could change, but hopefully the server administrator will make sure that the old name of the server is changed to point at the new address.

I run an SMTP server on my own machine since it is capable of sending mail directly to the destination of the message, without traversing any intervening mail servers. This is done mostly for reliability and efficiency reasons; if there is a problem

(continued)

delivering my outgoing mail, it will be obvious—the problem will be local to my machine. The efficiency aspect derives from the fact that outbound mail flows from my machine's e-mail client locally to my machine's local server, then directly to the destination's mail exchanger. Any error messages (a.k.a. "bounce" messages) are generated locally on my machine, from the server back to the client. Normally, the postmaster of one of the intervening mail servers would get a copy of my entire e-mail message if it encountered a processing error. This way, I am my own postmaster.

When an address has its high-order bits set to 10, it is a Class B address. Two bytes, less these two bits, form the network number field of a Class B address. Fourteen bits are then available for the network number field after the fixed 10 pattern, for a range of addresses from 10000000.00000000 (128.0) to 10111111. 11111111 (191.255). There are a total of 14 bits of address space, which would allow for 2^{14} (16,384) unique Class B addresses. However, we must remember that the all-0s and all-1s patterns in the 14-bit-wide network number field are reserved and may never be used for actual network numbers. So, the range of Class B addresses is from 128.1 (10000000.00000001) through 191.254 (10111111. 11111110), for a total of 16,382 Class B network numbers.

The final class of unicast IP addresses has its high-order addresses set to 110, which indicates a Class C address. Three bytes, less these three bits, are used to form the network number in this case. Thus, we have 21 bits available for counting network numbers, which may range from 11000000.00000000.00000001 (192.0.1) through 11011111.11111111.11111110 (223.255.254). Note that we have not included the all-0s and all-1s patterns in the 21-bit network number field, since we know they are reserved. A 21-bit network number field would usually be able to represent 2^{21} (2,097,152) unique network numbers, but as usual we needed to reserve those two values, leaving 2,097,150 Class C network numbers.

Class D addresses are used to represent multicast groups. Multicasting is beyond the scope of this book, but it is worth mentioning that a class D address has its high-order bits set to 1110, leaving the remaining 28 bits for use as identifiers for different multicast groups. There are 2^{28} (268,435,456) multicast addresses, ranging from 11100000.00000000.00000000.00000000 (224.0.0.0) through 11101111.11111111.11111111.11111111 (239.255. 255.255).

Classful IP addressing was created so that each address contains a self-encoding "key" that identifies the dividing point between its network-prefix and the host-number. For example, if the first two bits of an IP address are 10, the host portion begins at the third byte. This simplified the routing system during the early years of the Internet. Early routing protocols did not need to carry a "deciphering key" or "mask" with each route to identify the actual length of the network-prefix; the boundary between network and host portion was inferred based on the class of the network number.

Host Portions of IP Address Classes

Each Class A network address has an 8-bit network-prefix with the highest order bit set to 0 and a seven-bit network number, followed by a 24-bit host-number. Today, it is no longer considered 'modern' to refer to a Class A network. Class A networks are now referred to as "/8"s (pronounced "slash eights") since they have an 8-bit network-prefix.

A maximum of 126 (2^7-2) /"8" networks can be defined. The calculation requires that the 2 is subtracted because network 0.0.0.0 is reserved (for use as the default route) and the network 127.0.0.0 (also written 127/8 or 127.0.0.0/8) has been reserved for the "loopback" function. Each /8 supports a maximum of 16,777,214 (2^{24}-2) hosts per network. The host calculation requires that 2 is subtracted because the all-0s ("this network") and all-1s ("broadcast") host-numbers may not be assigned to individual hosts.

Since the entire /8 address block (i.e., all the /8s taken as a whole) contains 2^{31} (2,147,483,648) individual addresses and the IPv4 address space contains a maximum of 2^{32} (4,294,967,296) addresses, the /8 address space is 50 percent of the total IPv4 unicast address space.

Class B Networks (/16 Prefixes)

Each Class B network address has a 16-bit network-prefix with the two highest order bits set to 1-0 and a 14-bit network number, followed by a 16-bit host-number. Class B networks are now referred to as "/16s" since they have a 16-bit network-prefix.

A maximum of 16,384 (2^{14}) /16 networks can be defined with up to 65,534 (2^{16}-2) hosts per network. Since the entire /16 address block contains 2^{30} (1,073,741,824) addresses (since 30 bits remain after the "10" two-bit pattern that identifies all /16s, there are 2^{30} possible bit patterns), it represents 25 percent of the total IPv4 unicast address space.

Class C Networks (/24 Prefixes)

Each Class C network address has a 24-bit network-prefix with the three highest order bits set to 1-1-0 and a 21-bit network number, followed by an 8-bit host-number. Class C networks are now referred to as "/24s" since they have a 24-bit network-prefix.

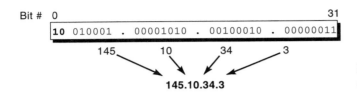

FIGURE 2.5   Dotted-decimal notation.

A maximum of 2,097,152 (2^{21}) /24 networks can be defined with up to 254 (2^8-2) hosts per network. Since the entire /24 address block contains 2^{29} (536,870,912) addresses, it represents 12.5 percent (or one-eighth) of the total IPv4 unicast address space.

In addition to the three most popular classes, there are two additional classes. Class D addresses have their leading four-bits set to 1-1-1-0 and are used to support IP Multicasting. Class E addresses have their leading four-bits set to 1-1-1-1 and are reserved for experimental use.

Dotted-Decimal Notation

To make Internet addresses easier for human users to read and write, IP addresses are often expressed as four decimal numbers, each separated by a dot. This format is called "dotted-decimal notation."

Dotted-decimal notation divides the 32-bit Internet address into four 8-bit (one-byte) fields, and specifies the value of each field independently as a decimal number with the fields separated by dots. Figure 2.5 shows how a typical /16 (Class B) Internet address can be expressed in dotted decimal notation.

Table 2.1 displays the range of dotted-decimal values that can be assigned to each of the three principle address classes. The "xxx" represents the host-number field of the address which is assigned by the local network administrator.

TABLE 2.1   Dotted-decimal ranges for each address class

Address Class	Dotted-Decimal Notation Ranges
A (/8 prefixes)	1.xxx.xxx.xxx through 126.xxx.xxx.xxx
B (/16 prefixes)	128.1.xxx.xxx through 191.254.xxx.xxx
C (/24 prefixes)	192.0.1.xxx through 223.255.254.xxx

UNFORESEEN LIMITATIONS TO CLASSFUL ADDRESSING

The original designers never envisioned that the Internet would grow into what it has become today. Many of the problems that the Internet is facing today can be traced back to the early decisions that were made during its formative years. To be fair, it was impossible to have foreseen the scaling problems that we are now experiencing.

- During the early days of the Internet, the seemingly unlimited address space allowed IP addresses to be allocated to an organization based on its request rather than its actual need. As a result, addresses were freely assigned to those who asked for them without concerns about the eventual depletion of the IP address space.
- The decision to standardize on a 32-bit address space meant that there were "only" 2^{32} (4,294,967,296) IPv4 addresses available. A decision to support a slightly larger address space would have exponentially increased the number of addresses thus delaying the onset of the eventual address shortage problem.
- The classful A, B, and C octet boundaries were easy to understand and implement, but they did not foster the efficient allocation of a finite address space. Problems resulted from the lack of a network class that was designed to support medium-sized organizations. A /24, which supports 254 hosts, is too small, while a /16, which supports up to 65,534 hosts, is too large.

In the past, the Internet registries assigned a single /16 prefix (instead of several consecutive /24 prefix) to sites only having several hundred hosts. Unfortunately, this resulted in a premature depletion of the /16 network address space. The only readily available addresses for medium-size organizations are /24s, which had the initial, deleterious impact of increasing the size of the global Internet's routing table.

Subsequently, Internet address assignment practices have changed to overcome these issues and to support the continued explosive growth of the global Internet.

ADDITIONAL PRACTICE WITH CLASSFUL IP ADDRESSING

PRACTICE EXERCISES

1. Complete the following table which provides practice in converting a number from binary notation to decimal format. Yes, many handheld calculators and PC-based calculators can do this coversion for you. With a little practice you'll be able to do it in your head.

BINARY	128	64	32	16	8	4	2	1	Decimal
11001100	1	1	0	0	1	1	0	0	128+64+8+4 = 204
10101010									
11100011									
10110011									
00110101									

2. Complete the following table which provides practice in converting a number from decimal notation to binary format.

Decimal	128	64	32	16	8	4	2	1	Binary
48	0	0	1	1	0	0	0	0	$48=32+16=00110000_2$
222									
119									
135									
60									

3. Express 145.32.59.24 in binary format and identify the address class:

4. Express 200.42.129.16 in binary format and identify the address class:

5. Express 14.82.19.54 in binary format and identify the address class:

Solutions to Classful IP Addressing Practice Exercises

1. Complete the following table which provides practice in converting a number from binary notation to decimal format.

BINARY	128	64	32	16	8	4	2	1	DECIMAL
11001100	1	1	0	0	1	1	0	0	**204**
10101010	1	0	1	0	1	0	1	0	**170**
11100011	1	1	1	0	0	0	1	1	**227**
10110011	1	0	1	1	0	0	1	1	**179**
00110101	0	0	1	1	0	1	0	1	**53**

2. Complete the following table which provides practice in converting a number from decimal notation to binary format.

DECIMAL	128	64	32	16	8	4	2	1	BINARY
48	0	0	1	1	0	0	0	0	**0011 0000**
222	1	1	0	1	1	1	1	0	**1101 1110**
119	0	1	1	1	0	1	1	1	**0111 0111**
135	1	0	0	0	0	1	1	1	**1000 0111**
60	0	0	1	1	1	1	0	0	**0011 1100**

3. Express 145.32.59.24 in binary format and identify the classful prefix length.

      10010001.00100000.00111011.00011000   /16 or Class B

4. Express 200.42.129.16 in binary format and identify the classful prefix length.

      11001000.00101010.10000001.00010000   /24 or Class C

5. Express 14.82.19.54 in binary format and identify the classful prefix length.

      00001110.01010010.00010011.00110110   /8 or Class A

REFERENCES

REQUEST FOR COMMENT (RFC)

0791 Internet Protocol. J. Postel. Sep-01-1981. (Format: TXT=97779 bytes) (Obsoletes RFC0760) (Status: STANDARD)

0792 Internet Control Message Protocol. J. Postel. Sep-01-1981. (Format: TXT=30404 bytes) Obsoletes RFC0777) (Updated by RFC0950) (Status: STANDARD)

1122 Requirements for internet hosts—communication layers. R.T. Braden. Oct-01-1989. (Format: TXT=295992 bytes) (Status: STANDARD)

1123 Requirements for Internet hosts—application and support. R.T. Braden. Oct-01-1989. (Format: TXT=245503 bytes) (Updates RFC0822) (Updated by RFC2181) (Status: STANDARD)

1517 Applicability Statement for the Implementation of Classless Inter-Domain Routing (CIDR). Internet Engineering Steering Group, R. Hinden. September 1993. (Format: TXT=7357 bytes) (Status: PROPOSED STANDARD)

1518 An Architecture for IP Address Allocaton with CIDR. Y. Rekhter & T. Li. September 1993. (Format: TXT=72609 bytes) (Status: PROPOSED STANDARD)

1519 Classless Inter-Domain Routing (CIDR): An Address Assignment and Aggregation Strategy. V. Fuller, T. Li, J. Yu, & K. Varadhan. September 1993. (format: TXT=59998 bytes) (Obsoletes RFC1338) (Status: PROPOSED STANDARD)

1520 Exchanging Routing Information Across Provider Boundaries in the CIDR Environment. Y. Rekhter & C. Topolcic. September 1993. (Format: TXT=20389 bytes) (Status: INFORMATIONAL)

ENDNOTES

1. The Internet as we know it today began on 1 January 1983 with the adoption of IP as the ARPANET's network-layer protocol (the old protocol was known as the Network Control Protocol, or NCP, which was first used on the ARPANET in 1970). The number of hosts on the *entire Internet* did not exceed 1,000 until sometime in 1984.

2. This does not even account for people like myself, who have multiple addresses. Besides the two machines at work, I have a small subnet at home which contains three machines, plus the address of my router at home.

3. When a route becomes unreachable, it must be withdrawn from all routers' routing tables. Once it comes back up, it must be reinstalled in the routing tables. Routes go away for a variety of reasons, from the spectacular (thunderstorms and earthquakes) to the natural (deteriorating physical cabling, or bad connections), to the intentional (router

upgrades, which necessitate a reboot), to the accidental (power-down the router, un-patch a LAN interface, etc.).

4. In the old days (i.e., before the WWW), connections tended to be long-lived. The primary Internet applications were FTP, Telnet, Usenet, and e-mail. Routers built up caches of forwarding information pertaining to active connections, so they could forward packets more quickly. Router caches are much less useful in today's web-surfing paradigm, since the user may have already surfed over to a different IP destination by the time the cache entry is in place. The router spent valuable CPU time building a cache entry that it did not use for very long.

5. This analogy cannot be carried too far, since the postal address has three or four levels of hierarchy. Houses are subsidiary to streets, which are themselves subsidiary to cities. Cities, then, are part of states, which are part of countries. For those countries which are not subdivided into states, there is only a three-level postal address hierarchy.

CHAPTER 3

Classical Subnetting

WHAT IS SUBNETTING? WHY IS SUBNETTING NEEDED?

In 1985, RFC-950 defined a standard procedure to support the subnetting, or division, of a single Class A, B, or C network number into smaller pieces. Subnetting was introduced to overcome some of the problems that parts of the Internet were beginning to experience with the classful two-level addressing hierarchy. To support network expansion, local administrators had to request additional network numbers from the Internet Network Information Center[1] (NIC). Each new network at their site needs a unique network number.

Each "wire" or "ring" LAN required its own unique network number. Given that there are distance limitations inherent in most LAN technologies, it is not possible to interconnect all machines in a building (or a campus!) with only one LAN segment. The proliferation of LANs ultimately implies the proliferation of network numbers, though there were other proposals besides adding network numbers or subdividing existing network numbers via explicit subnetting. As a result, the Internet's routing tables were beginning to grow "too quickly." As sites needed more network numbers, the Internet's routing tables did not scale proportional to the number of sites, but to the number of network numbers, which began to gradually exceed the number of sites.

When the dust had settled, both of these issues were addressed by squeezing another level of hierarchy into the IP addressing structure. Of course, one cannot get something for nothing—IP addresses are still just 32 bits long; because of that fixed size limit, the extra level of hierarchy must "steal" bits from somewhere, in this case from the host portion of the address. While subnetting is the purest evolution of the IP architecture, there was initial resistance to changing IP, so several other schemes were proposed.

EARLY ALTERNATIVES TO SUBNETTING

Creating an explicit subnetting scheme required modifying the operation of the Internet Protocol. Given the potential difficulty of upgrading what was already a fast-growing Internet (in the early-to-mid 1980s), several alternatives were considered. Clearly explicit subnetting's perceived disadvantage was that it required fundamental (but not radical) changes to IP itself. Explicit subnetting also required that routing protocols have some level of awareness of what subnet mask(s) is (are) in use. Using multiple network numbers was never really a practical alternative, because waste is never a good idea. Still, the problem remained that many campus networks had grown too large for a single LAN "segment" to be able to serve all users on the campus, creating a natural demand for some LAN interconnection solution. (IEEE-standard LAN bridges could have served as LAN interconnection devices within a network number, but were not commonplace until later in the 1980s.)

One proposal for knitting together several subnets was a kind of "ARP-aware bridge," which was sort of a slimmed down IP router. In the mid-1980s, routers were not commonplace as separate hardware devices; early routers were Unix® workstations that ran special software. Later, dedicated hardware devices running special "routing" software appeared, from 3Com, Cisco Systems, Wellfleet, and others. Today we see the emergence of "layer 3 switches" that are hardware based and can perform routing at "wire speed."

Implicit "Subnetting"

This section is provided to show that there were, indeed, other alternatives being pursued besides just getting new network numbers. "Real subnetting" was resisted at first, because it was a change to the fundamental structure of IP. Please note that, while historically interesting, the ideas in this section were eclipsed by explicit subnetting.

The earliest implicit subnetting scheme was documented in RFC-925 "Multi-LAN Address Resolution," in October 1984. By October 1987, when RFC-1027 "Using ARP to Implement Transparent Subnet Gateways" (commonly called "Proxy ARP") was published, a concensus of support for explicit subnetting had developed, as may be seen in this note near the end of RFC-1027 (underlining and italics added by author):

> 4. Availability
>
> The 4.3BSD implementation is currently available by anonymous FTP (login anonymous, password guest) from sally.utexas.edu as pub/subarp, which is a 4.3BSD "diff -c" listing from the 4.3BSD sources that were distributed in September 1986.
>
> <u>This implementation was not included in the 4.3BSD distribution proper because U.C. Berkeley CSRG thought that that would reduce the incentive for vendors to implement subnets per RFC-950.</u> *The authors concur.* Nonetheless, there are circumstances in which the use of transparent subnet ARP gateways is indispensable.

RFC-925 envisioned special boxes that would be multihomed,[2] and that would participate in extending ARP beyond the local LAN. Enough of these special boxes would be required to interconnect all the LANs at a site. Figure 3.1 depicts a set of five LANs with two intervening "boxes." Obviously, one may need up to *n-1* boxes to interconnect *n* LAN segments.

The IP addressing in a transparent gateway topology would be "flat," in that the endstations would be told that the mask was 255.0.0.0 so that they would attempt to ARP for every other address within net 77. This is according to the usual IP forwarding rules, which require that a station ARP for other stations in the same net-

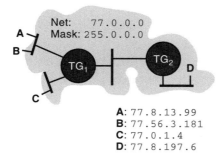

A: 77.8.13.99
B: 77.56.3.181
C: 77.0.1.4
D: 77.8.197.6

FIGURE 3.1 Sample transparent gateway topology.

work number while forwarding nonlocal traffic to a "gateway." This flat addressing structure would also apply in the case of a Class B or Class C network.

This "flatness" allows the organization to use all of their assigned network number prior to needing another. In the case of a Class A network, it is unlikely that there are many organizations which would be able to run out of endstation addresses, given that there are 16,777,214 of them available.[3] Even a Class B network, with 65,534 available addresses, is more than adequate for most organizations' requirements. Class C networks, with only 254 available host addresses, were not perceived as practical until it was possible to bundle them together, as described later in Part I.

Within a given LAN, ARP works as expected. If Station A (77.8.13.99) needs to talk to Station B (77.56.3.181), it will notice that they are both members of net 77, and A will therefore ARP for B. Machine B will hear the ARP request; so will the special box TG_1, which caches the source IP and MAC address from within the ARP packet (provided that this particular IP/MAC was not already in TG_1's cache). Obviously, if TG_1 itself were a target of the ARP request, it would respond, otherwise the real target machine (B), if it is up, will generate an ARP response and begin communicating with machine A.

The gateway caches the information in all ARP broadcast packets, on a per-interface basis. No special effort needs to be made to collect these packets, since they are broadcast and all machines on the LAN must receive them. Since most IP implementations will ARP for their own address when they are initializing, the box will be handed IP/MAC mappings whenever machines boot. The transparent gateway's cache entries gradually age out, just like any ARP cache entry on any "normal" machine.

Suppose that station B sends an ARP request looking for station C. What should the gateway do to make the stations think they share the same LAN? The first thing it notices is that station C is not on the same LAN that the ARP request was transmitted on. Presuming that the gateway has already learned the IP/MAC mapping for station C, it then issues a new broadcast ARP request on station C's LAN, substituting its own MAC address for both the MAC address and the ARP source MAC address in the ARP request packet. The target IP address is, of course, still station C's IP address and the source IP address is still B's IP address. Station C will receive the ARP request and will add the new ARP cache mapping of station B's address to the MAC address that the gateway's NIC has on station C's LAN. Now station C thinks B's MAC address is the gateway's MAC address. If C ever sent a frame to the gateway's MAC address, it would look in its cache and forward the packet to B using B's real MAC address.

At the same time, the gateway can reply to station B's original ARP request as if it were actually station C. The ARP reply will include the gateway's MAC address as the source MAC, but will substitute station C's IP address (the original target IP address) as the ARP reply's source IP address. Now station B thinks that the gateway's MAC address on station B's LAN is station C's MAC address, similar to the way station C views station B. Neither is aware of the presence of the gateway.

Any traffic from B to C is addressed to the gateway's MAC address, and the gateway subsequently forwards it to C by replacing the packet's MAC destination address with C's MAC address. Similarly, data packets from C to B are sent to the gateway, which forwards them to B. The only thing that the gateway must do to the IP packets is to decrement the IP Time to Live (TTL) on the way through. This is a safety feature that will ensure that any loops in the topology do not lead to endless packet forwarding cycles; the packets will eventually die out after they have traversed their 256th gateway.

The packets that arrive at the gateway are forwarded based on the destination IP address. The table of IP/MAC/interface mappings in the gateway allows the gateway to determine the proper outgoing interface and the proper destination MAC address for each packet it needs to forward. The list is used in the forwarding decision, and also in determining when to be a proxy and when to remain silent.

There is one final case that is not covered by the mechanism above. What happens when the gateway knows that the IP destination is not on the same LAN as the source, but the gateway also has not learned the location of the destination? For example, in Figure 3.1, what if station D wanted to send packets to station A?

The mechanism that was suggested had the gateway initiate ARP requests on behalf of the source IP address on all its nonincoming interfaces. These packets are not copies of the original ARP, because the gateway has inserted its MAC address in place of the original source's MAC address on all ARP requests it generates. The gateway must keep a list of all the searches it has in progress.

In this example, TG_2 will issue a new ARP request on its only other LAN interface. This ARP will be received by TG_1, which will see the ARP request (and learn that station D is reachable via one of TG_2's MAC addresses in the process) and realize that it knows the IP/MAC mapping for station A. TG_1 then sends an ARP response to TG_2, which can then close this search and send another ARP response to station D.

The technique of forwarding broadcast packets away from their source (i.e., on all nonincoming interfaces) is known as Reverse Path Broadcasting. A complete discussion of RPB is not appropriate here, but it is covered in detail in my other book "Deploying IP Multicast in the Enterprise." The technique here is not pure RPB, since the TGs are not forwarding exact copies of the ARP broadcasts; however, the rest of the technique is very similar—it was clearly inspired by the RPB forwarding algorithm.

Proxy ARP

Proxy ARP, specified in RFC-1027 "Using ARP to Implement Transparent Subnet Gateways," is a refinement of the previous technique in several ways. First of all, the special boxes are replaced by IP routers that support proxy ARP, which is a per-interface parameter that is either on or off (the default is to have the feature turned off). The objective of proxy ARP is to support subnetting while hiding the presence of subnets from the still unsubnetted portion of the network. This is quite useful if you need to deploy subnets and cannot just sprinkle magic pixie dust over your network to implement your new addressing plan. Proxy ARP can be used during a transition period, allowing subnetting to be deployed gradually. However, proxy ARP can be dangerous, so it must be used carefully.

Operation of Proxy ARP

This discussion uses concepts that are covered later in the book. Don't worry if you don't understand all of this now, just come back to it after you have finished Parts I and II. Proxy ARP is still around today, as opposed to the transparent subnet gateway technique that was discussed in the previous section.

Proxy ARP does not do ARP forwarding as the previous technique did, rather the routers use their knowledge of the network topology to decide whether or not to generate "proxy" ARP Replies on behalf of attached endstations.

How Flat Should An Addressing Plan Be?

Deploying subnetting was a common practice in the late 1980s through the early 1990s. Once "LAN Switching" products emerged (high-speed, hardware-based LAN interconnection devices), the trend reversed and networks tended to flatten out their addressing hierarchies. However, no practical network can ever be entirely flat, and each organization must determine an addressing plan that suits their topology, despite the challenge of understanding subnetting. Hopefully, this book will make this topic more approachable for more people.

Suppose that a network has grown to the point that it needs to be subnetted. Each new subnet may be reachable via a different router. Each of the unsubnetted machines still has only one "default gateway" to which it forwards all its nonlocal traffic. However, because the machines think the network is unsubnetted, their mask indicates to them that they should ARP for all addresses within their network number. They have no way of knowing that certain portions of their address space are reachable via routers. However, if the machines send ARPs when they need to communicate with subnetted hosts, the ARPs will not pass through the router because they are Ethernet broadcast frames. How, then, will the subnetted machines ever be able to talk to an unsubnetted machine?

Let us create a concrete example and try to understand how Proxy ARP might work in a real scenario, as depicted in Figure 3.2. Keep in mind that RFC-1027's Proxy ARP works in environments in which the subnet mask is the same over all the subnets of a network number. At the time it was written, this was a fundamental constraint of the subnetting technology of the day, which relied on classful routing protocols.

The point of Proxy ARP is not to build your network around it—after all, its authors freely admit that it is a hack—but to provide a temporary transition mechanism. In the following example, the network is in the midst of such a transition, with only part of it converted to subnetting; to simplify the example, RFC-1027's "common mask" mandate will be observed.

There are several elements to the diagram that will be important to keep in mind as we explain how machines communicate. First of all, there are two backbones. Only the top backbone is a "real" backbone, in that it only interconnects routers—there are no user machine attachments. The other is the original unsubnetted network that was in place before the deployment of subnets began. This is where the majority of the user machines are still attached to the network. Note that

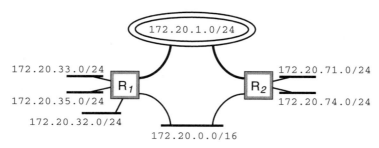

FIGURE 3.2 Operation of proxy ARP.

machines on the original (lower) backbone still think that they are on a completely unsubnetted network, because their subnet masks are /16 (i.e., 255.255.0.0).

The original network's growth ultimately required some degree of traffic segmentation. The subnet routers serve to isolate the new subnets from the old "backbone" while still allowing access to it. They also permit the subnetted hosts to communicate with each other across the new high-speed backbone, thereby offloading their traffic from the original "backbone." The routers are always supposed to use the new backbone to forward traffic to subnets that are reachable via the high-speed backbone. Traffic destined for nonsubnetted portions of the network are sent directly to them, since the routers are still attached to the old unsubnetted LAN "backbone."

Now what happens when 172.20.97.101/16 wishes to communicate with 172.20.71.76/24? (The masks are added only to help you locate the origin subnet in the diagram.) By virtue of its mask, it believes that the network is not subnetted. More precisely, it looks at the destination address (172.20.71.76) and applies its own /16 mask to it, resulting in 172.20.0.0, which is the same result as when the source station applies its /16 mask to itself. This tells the station that the destination shares a common subnetwork with itself. Thus, the station will send an ARP Request, in an attempt to learn the MAC address of 172.20.71.76. Of course, the presence of router R_2 means that ARP broadcasts are not forwarded onto its other interfaces, so the station 172.20.71.76 can never directly hear any ARP broadcasts from 172.20.97.101.

However, R_2 has just received an ARP Request from a machine that is looking for an IP address within a subnet to which R_2 *knows it is directly attached.* R_2 can then, if Proxy ARP is enabled on its "old backbone" interface, send an ARP Reply, telling a lie to the source station. R_2 has the best of intentions, of course, and it is only a little white lie—R_2 knows that as long as it is up it is as good as the "real" destination endstation. Any time R_2 receives an IP packet destined for 172.20.71.76— but with R_2's own MAC address—R_2 looks at its attached interfaces and realizes that it can deliver this packet to the real destination. Upon noticing this, it forwards a frame onto the destination's interface, without changing the IP packet,[4] but this new frame has the real destination's MAC address instead of R_2's MAC DA. The new frame will have the router's MAC address as its SA instead of the original station's source MAC address.

Now let us consider the reverse case, where a "subnetted" endstation wishes to contact one of the as-yet-unsubnetted endstations. If we simply run this example in reverse, we can see that the router need not do anything out of the ordinary in this direction. In this case, we have the source of the IP packets as 172.20.71.76/24. The mask is important! This machine knows that it is subnetted. First, it knows that because the mask is longer than the mask that an unsubnetted class B would have, which is a /16 mask. Also, it knows that the destination is on a *different* subnet by doing the same calculation that the other station did earlier. This station applied its /24 mask to the destination address, which results in a value of 172.20.97.0, which is different than the result when its mask is applied to its own address, which is 172.20.71.0.

Due to the different results, 172.20.71.76 needs to forward packets for 172.20.97.101 to its default gateway, which is R_2. R_2 has an address within the station's subnet, for example, 172.20.71.1. 172.20.71.76 must use ARP to determine the MAC address that corresponds to 172.20.71.1 before it can send any frames to the router. Once the station knows the router's MAC address, it can send the frame, and once R_2 has it, it consults its routing table to decide how to forward the packet.

As luck would have it, the router has one of its interfaces directly attached to the old unsubnetted /16 "backbone;" we may suppose that the router's address on this interface is 172.20.0.2. In order to complete final delivery of the packet, the router must use ARP to discover the MAC address of 172.20.97.101; once it has that station's MAC address, it may send the frame containing the IP packet from 172.20.71.76.

If Proxy ARP is limited to a router's directly attached interfaces, it is a relatively innocuous hack; however, problems can arise if the router implementors try to be a bit more clever.

Dangers of Proxy ARP

It is tempting to envision ways to enhance Proxy ARP to be more helpful. The road to hell is paved with good intentions. Some vendors extended Proxy ARP so that a router might respond not only if it was directly attached to the destination subnet, but also if it had a route to that destination. Consider what might happen if such an implementation were deployed in routers R_1 and R_2 in Figure 3.2. When the ARP Request goes out from 172.10.97.101, both R_1 and R_2 hear it. In a safe Proxy ARP implementation, only R_2 generates a proxy ARP reply, since it is directly connected to the destination subnet.

If the new and improved Proxy ARP were in place, however, either router might respond. If R_1 were to respond, then the station 172.10.97.101 would send packets for 172.20.71.76 to R_1. R_1 would then have to deliver the packets to the destination subnet, which it knows is reachable via R_2. So the packet gets a free trip on the high-speed backbone over to R_2, which performs final delivery to 172.20.71.76. Now, the return path will go from 172.20.71.76, through R_2 (no other router connects this subnet to the outside world), then directly to 172.10.97.101, because R_2 is directly attached to that subnet. This asymmetric traffic pattern is illustrated in Figure 3.3.

If there is a failure of the 172.20.1.0/24 backbone, or if R_1 or R_2 becomes disconnected from it, then R_1 will have no choice but to reroute traffic to 172.20.71.76 *back across the LAN it came from to get to R_2!* Even without this disaster scenario, protocol performance can suffer when the measured delay in each direction is different. If R_1 is especially busy, it may be slow in forwarding traffic to R_2, or it may drop packets. Clearly, if it were not in the loop it would not have the opportunity to adversely affect traffic flow. The performance in this situation can be extremely poor.

Since it is usually out of the question for a customer to modify the router's source code, the only choice was to disable Proxy ARP on all but one router. This way, the "enhanced" Proxy ARP router would proxy for any subnet that it could reach, and all traffic would at least be experiencing a predictable asymmetric path. Proxy ARP is just a tool, and the tool is supposed to help ease the transition to a subnetted environment. It is not meant to be a substitute for a routing protocol, and it does not need to be fancy to serve its purpose. In fact, in the example above, "classic Proxy ARP" would be perfectly safe to enable on both (all of) the routers. Paradoxically, this "enhancement" ended up reducing the usefulness of Proxy ARP.

Beware of "value-added" features; even more so, beware of crutches. The ultimate solution is to finish the conversion of the network to be completely subnetted. One very big danger of features like Proxy ARP, that are designed to aid transitions, is that it is too easy to use them as a crutch, and greatly extend the time over which the transition occurs. In time, you can come to depend on this crutch and forget why you started using it in the first place. This really does happen, honest. This effect may result in delay of adopting IPv6.

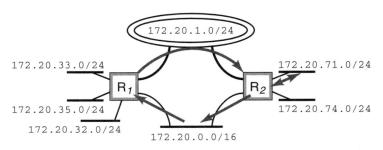

FIGURE 3.3 Asymmetric path due to over-agressive Proxy ARP.

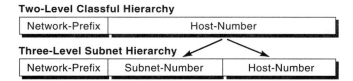

FIGURE 3.4 Subnet address hierarchy.

EXPLICIT SUBNETTING

Figure 3.4 illustrates the third level of addressing hierarchy created by traditional subnetting. In the beginning, there were only two levels in an IP address, with the dividing line at a point determined by the address' "class." The network number was always either 8, 16, or 24 bits long, with the host-number field being 24, 16, or 8 bits long, respectively. Explicit[5] subnetting standardizes the further subdivision of the original classful host-number field into two parts—the new subnet-number field, and finally the remaining bits constitute the host-number, unique to each subnet.

The picture may appear to indicate that the subnet field is half of the host-number field. This is definitely *not* the case! The subnet-number field may be from 1 to $(h - 2)$ bits long,[6] where 'h' is the length of the original host-number field.[7] For instance, if we originally had a Class B network number, then the subnet field could be up to 14 bits in length $(16 - 2)$. Correspondingly, a Class C could have subnet-number lengths up to six bits $(8 - 2)$, and a Class A could have up to 22 bit subnet-numbers $(24 - 2)$. Of course, in each of these extreme cases, only two bits remain for the subnet's host-number field. The ultimate constraint is that $n+s+h = 32$, where n, s, and h are the lengths of the network-number, subnet-number, and host-number fields, respectively.

For now, we will assume the current practice, in which all the subnet bits are contiguous and are located between the network-number and host-number fields. At the end of the chapter there is a sidebar that gives detailed examples of contiguous versus noncontiguous subnet-fields (which are still contained within the host-number field).

HIERARCHICAL INFORMATION HIDING

Subnetting attacked the expanding routing table problem by ensuring that the subnet structure of a network is never visible outside of the organization's private network. By providing a structured way to deploy hierarchical addressing, subnetting made it possible to "hide" the internal structure of networks from the worldwide Internet. This makes sense. After all, no one needs to know if you have 4, 7, or 17 subnets of your network number, or what they are; as long as the outsiders can reach your network number, they can reasonably expect to be able to reach whatever subnets you have defined within your network number. There is no loss of reachability, as far as external observers are concerned. The Internet infrastructure carries packets to your network number's "front door," and your internal infrastructure carries it to the correct "room" within your "house." Some houses may have only a few rooms, while others may have considerably more, in quantities and sizes to properly suit the needs of their occupants. The local administrator may introduce arbitrary levels of complexity into their private network without affecting the size of the Internet's routing tables.

The route from the Internet to any subnet of a given IP address is the same, no matter which subnet the destination host is on. This is because all subnets of a given network number use the same network-prefix but different subnet-numbers.[8] The routers within the private organization need to differentiate between the individual subnets, but as far as the Internet routers are concerned, all of the subnets in the organization are collected into a single routing table entry and are generally reachable via the same router—the one that advertised the network number in the first place!

What does it mean to advertise a route? The advertiser is telling its peer that it is a conduit for traffic destined for the advertised routes. If I tell you that I know how to get to Baltimore, I am also implicitly saying that if you ever need to get to Baltimore, you can reach Baltimore by going through me. Note that the fact that I am advertising that I am a route to Baltimore does not mean that you won't hear a better route to Baltimore from someone else. For instance, I could be saying that I can get to Baltimore, and I am 103 kilometers away from it. You may hear another neighbor tell you that they can get to Baltimore and they are only 87 km away from it. It is up to you to collect all the routing information you receive and make your own local determination of what you think is the best available route.

The routing table in the Internet's core routers is, at its essence, just a list of all the places that make up the Internet at a given instant. A given organization's network number should be reachable by all the Internet's core routers. Do the core routers need to know about subnet six within the network? Not at all. The presence of the single route in the Internet's core routers tells them that any destination matching that network number is reachable within your network. However, once a packet has been delivered to your organization, your internal routers must have more detailed information needed to deliver a packet to, for instance, subnet 6.

For example, we will consider the network number 172.27.0.0.[9] In this example, the organization has decided that they need five subnets, and thus have elected to use a three-bit subnet-number field, as shown in Table 3.1. The available subnets in their scheme are as follows, all of which share a common mask of 255.255.224.0. The binary representation of 224 is 11100000, which is just what is needed to mask off the high-order three bits of the third byte.

Let's imagine that the organization is using subnets 1, 2, 4, 5, and 6, as illustrated in Figure 3.5.

In this case, the organization's routers R_A and R_B will advertise their internal network number, 172.27.0.0, to the Internet routers (not shown, but they would attach to the "exchange LAN" on the left). If router R_A received a packet from the Internet destined for 172.27.182.133 (i.e., subnet 5, host 5765), it would know that it could deliver it there by either R_C or R_D, over either backbone. The choice of next-hop router and backbone path is determined by administrative metrics set within routing protocols, as well as other controls, such as filtering rules within the router.

In this simplified topology, the distance from either R_A or R_B to the subnets on the right, via R_C or R_D, appears to be equal. More complex topologies will usually have paths that are clearly preferred between two given points, but it is always possible that several "equal-cost" paths will exist. If router R_A considers all four possible paths to subnet five equally "good" (by whatever yardstick it is using to measure "goodness"), it may choose to alternatively send packets over one path (e.g., via

TABLE 3.1 THE EIGHT SUBNETS OF 172.27.0.0/16

Subnet Number	Binary Representation of Least-Significant Two Bytes	Available Host Addresses within Each Subnet		
0 172.27.0.0	00000000.00000000	0.1	through	31.254
1 172.27.32.0	00100000.00000000	32.1	through	63.254
2 172.27.64.0	01000000.00000000	64.1	through	95.254
3 172.27.96.0	01100000.00000000	96.1	through	127.254
4 172.27.128.0	10000000.00000000	128.1	through	159.254
5 172.27.160.0	10100000.00000000	160.1	through	191.254
6 172.27.192.0	11000000.00000000	192.1	through	223.254
7 172.27.224.0	11100000.00000000	224.1	through	255.254

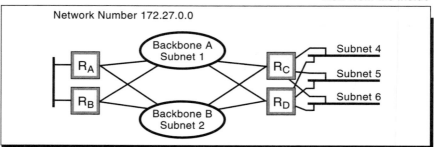

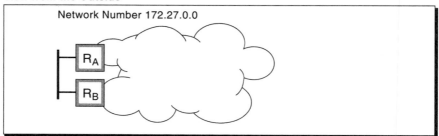

FIGURE 3.5 Example network design.

Backbone A to R_C), then another (e.g., via Backbone B to R_C), then another (e.g., via Backbone A to R_D), and so on.

The deployment of subnetting within the private network provides several benefits:

- The size of the global Internet routing table does not grow because the site administrator does not need to obtain additional address space and the routing advertisements for all of the subnets are combined into a single routing table entry.

- The local administrator has the flexibility to deploy additional subnets without obtaining a new network number.

- Route flapping[10] within the private network does not affect the Internet routing table since Internet routers do not know about the reachability of the individual internal subnets, they just know about the reachability of the

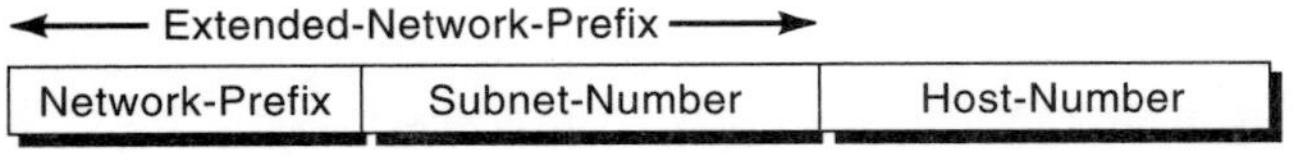

```
◄────── Extended-Network-Prefix ──────►
┌─────────────────┬─────────────────┬─────────────────┐
│ Network-Prefix  │  Subnet-Number  │   Host-Number   │
└─────────────────┴─────────────────┴─────────────────┘
```

FIGURE 3.6 Extended-network-prefix.

whole network number. All the subnets share the same fate: If the Internet loses track of the network number, then they are all unreachable; conversely, if the Internet knows where the network number is, then they are all assumed to be reachable. The Internet does not know or care if subnets even exist within the network number.

EXTENDED-NETWORK-PREFIX

Internet routers use only the network-prefix of the destination address to route traffic to a subnetted environment. Routers within the subnetted environment use the extended network-prefix to route traffic between the individual subnets. The extended network-prefix is the classful network-prefix with the concatenated subnet-number, as illustrated in Figure 3.6.

The extended network-prefix has traditionally been identified by the subnet mask. For example, if you have the /16 address of 130.5.0.0 and you want to use the entire third octet to represent the subnet-number, you need to specify a subnet mask of 255.255.255.0, representing a /24 extended-network prefix. The bits in the subnet mask and the Internet address have a one-to-one correspondence. The bits of the subnet mask are set to 1 if the system examining the address should treat the corresponding bit in the IP address as part of the extended network-prefix. When bits in the mask are set to 0, the corresponding address bits should be treated as the host field, as shown in Figure 3.7.

The standards describing modern routing protocols often refer to just the length of the extended network-prefix, rather than the 32-bit subnet mask value. When subnetting was first defined, there was no requirement that subnet mask bits be contiguous. However, it became clear over time that contiguous bits made sense,

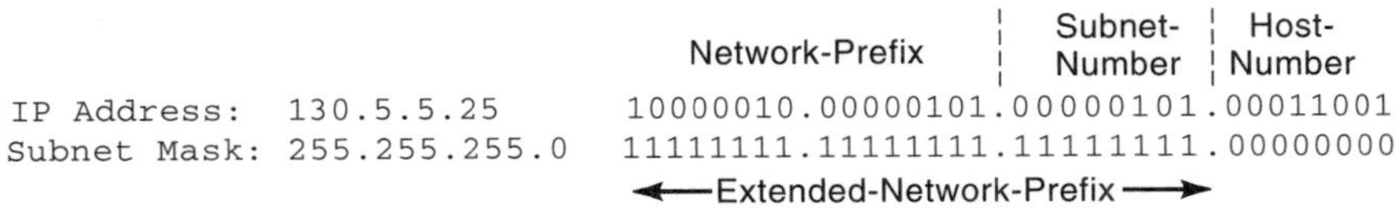

```
                                                        │ Subnet- │ Host-
                                     Network-Prefix      │ Number  │ Number
IP Address:   130.5.5.25      10000010.00000101.00000101.00011001
Subnet Mask: 255.255.255.0    11111111.11111111.11111111.00000000
                             ◄────Extended-Network-Prefix────►
```

FIGURE 3.7 Subnet mask.

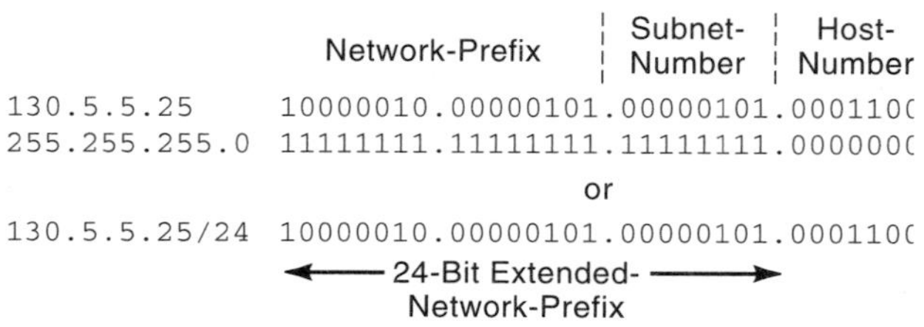

```
                                        | Subnet- |  Host-
                    Network-Prefix       | Number  |  Number
130.5.5.25     10000010.00000101.00000101.0001100
255.255.255.0  11111111.11111111.11111111.0000000
                                or
130.5.5.25/24  10000010.00000101.00000101.0001100
               ◄──── 24-Bit Extended- ────►
                       Network-Prefix
```

FIGURE 3.8 Extended-network-prefix length.

and noncontiguous mask bits did not offer any real value—after all, you still have 32 subnets with 5 subnet bits, whether they are contiguous or not. Contiguous bits are easier to process, more compact, and easier for humans to understand. In the interests of simplifying an already complex subject, noncontiguous subnet masks have been deprecated by the IETF.

The prefix length is simply equal to the total number of contiguous 1-bits in the traditional subnet mask. This means that specifying the network address 130.5.5.25 with a subnet mask of 255.255.255.0 can also be expressed as 130.5.5.25/24. The "/<prefix-length>" notation is more compact and easier to understand than writing out the mask in its traditional dotted-decimal format. This is illustrated in Figure 3.8.

However, it is important to note that many classless routing protocols still carry the subnet mask in its dotted-decimal entirety. There are not yet any Internet standard routing protocols that have a one-byte field in their header that contains the number of bits in the extended-network-prefix. Rather, each routing protocol still carries the complete four-octet subnet mask.

SUBNET ADDRESSING PLAN DESIGN CONSIDERATIONS

The deployment of an addressing plan requires careful thought on the part of the network administrator. There are four key questions that must be answered before any design should be undertaken:

1. How many total subnets does the organization need today?
2. How many total subnets will the organization need in the future?
3. How many hosts are there on the organization's largest subnet today?
4. How many hosts will there be on the organization's largest subnet in the future?

The first step in the planning process is to take the maximum number of subnets required and round up to the nearest power of two. For example, if an organization needs nine subnets, 2^3 (or 8) will not provide enough subnet addressing space, so the network administrator will need to round up to 2^4 (or 16). When performing this assessment, it is critical that the network administrator always allow adequate room for future growth. For example, if 14 subnets are required today, then 16 subnets might not be enough in two years when the 17th subnet needs to be deployed. In this case, it might be wise to allow for more growth and select 2^5 (or 32) as the maximum number of subnets. However, the very act of expanding the number of subnets is also simultaneously reducing the maximum size of each subnet, since the subnet field is stealing bits from the host field.

The second step is to make sure that there are enough host addresses for the organization's largest subnet. If the largest subnet needs to support 50 host addresses today, 2^5 (or 32) will not provide enough host address space so the network administrator will need to round up to 2^6 (or 64).

The final step is to make sure that the organization's address allocation provides enough bits to deploy the required subnet addressing plan. For example, if the organization has a single /16, it could easily deploy 4 bits for the subnet-number and 6 bits for the host number. However, if the organization has several /24s and it needs to deploy nine subnets, it may be required to subnet each of its /24s into four subnets (using 2 bits) and then build the internet work by combining the subnets of three different /24 network numbers. An alternative solution would be to deploy network numbers from the private address space (see RFC-1918) for internal connectivity and use a Network Address Translator (NAT) to provide external Internet access.

SUBNET EXAMPLE #1

Given:

An organization has been assigned the network number 193.1.1.0/24 and it needs to define six subnets. The largest subnet is required to support 25 hosts.

Defining the Subnet Mask / Extended Prefix Length

The first step is to determine the number of bits required to define the six subnets. Since a network address can only be subnetted along binary boundaries, subnets must be created in blocks of powers of two [2 (2^1),

4 (2^2), 8 (2^3), 16 (2^4), etc.]. Thus, it is impossible to define an IP address block such that it contains exactly six subnets. For this example, the network administrator must define a block of 8 (2^3) and have two unused subnets that can be reserved for future growth.

Since 8 = 2^3, 3 bits are required to enumerate the eight subnets in the block. In this example, the organization is subnetting a /24 so it will need 3 more bits, or a /27, as the extended-network-prefix. A 27-bit extended-network-prefix can be expressed in dotted-decimal notation as 255.255.255.224, as depicted in Figure 3.9.

A 27-bit extended-network-prefix leaves 5 bits to define host addresses on each subnet. This means that each subnetwork with a 27-bit prefix represents a contiguous block of 2^5 (32) individual IP addresses. However, since the all-0s and all-1s host addresses cannot be allocated, there are 30 ($2^5 - 2$) assignable host addresses on each subnet. We needed a capacity of 25 hosts, so we have large enough subnets when using a /27 extended-network-prefix.

Defining Each of the Subnet Numbers

The eight subnets will be numbered zero through seven. The 3-bit binary representation of the decimal values zero through seven are: 0 (000), 1 (001), 2 (010), 3 (011), 4 (100), 5 (101), 6 (110), and 7 (111).

In general, to define Subnet #n, the network administrator places the binary representation of "n" into the bits of the subnet-number field. For example, to define Subnet #6, the network administrator simply places the binary representation of 6 (110) into the 3 bits of the subnet-number field.

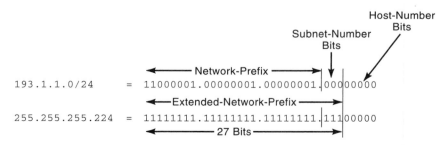

FIGURE 3.9 Example #1: Defining the subnet mask/extended-prefix length.

The eight subnet-numbers for this example are given below. The underlined portion of each address identifies the extended-network-prefix, while the **bold** digits highlight the 3 bits of the subnet-number field:

```
Base Net:   11000001.00000001.00000001.00000000 = 193.1.1.0/24


Subnet #0:  11000001.00000001.00000001.00000000 = 193.1.1.0/27
Subnet #1:  11000001.00000001.00000001.00100000 = 193.1.1.32/27
Subnet #2:  11000001.00000001.00000001.01000000 = 193.1.1.64/27
Subnet #3:  11000001.00000001.00000001.01100000 = 193.1.1.96/27
Subnet #4:  11000001.00000001.00000001.10000000 = 193.1.1.128/27
Subnet #5:  11000001.00000001.00000001.10100000 = 193.1.1.160/27
Subnet #6:  11000001.00000001.00000001.11000000 = 193.1.1.192/27
Subnet #7:  11000001.00000001.00000001.11100000 = 193.1.1.224/27
```

An easy way to check if the subnets are correct is to ensure that they are all multiples of the Subnet #1 address. In this case, all subnets are multiples of 32: 0, 32, 64, 96, etc.

The "All-0s" and "All-1s" Subnets

When subnetting was first defined in RFC-950, it prohibited the use of the all-0s and the all-1s subnet. The reason for this restriction was to eliminate situations that could potentially confuse a classful router. (Note that today a router can be both classless and classful at the same time—it could be running RIP-1 (a classful protocol) and BGP-4 (a classless protocol) simultaneously.)

With respect to the all-0s subnet, a router requires that each routing table update include the <prefix>/<prefix-length> pair to differentiate between a route to the all-0s subnet and a route to the entire network. For example, when using RIP-1, which does not supply a mask or prefix-length with each route, the routing advertisements for subnet 193.1.1.0/27 and for network 193.1.1.0/24 are identical—193.1.1.0. Without somehow knowing the prefix-length or mask, a router cannot tell the difference between a route to a network's all-0s subnet and the route to the entire network! This is illustrated in Figure 3.10.

Regarding the all-1s subnet, a router requires that each routing table entry include the prefix-length so that it can determine if a broadcast (directed or all-subnets) should be sent only to the all-1s subnet or to the entire network. For example, when the routing table does not contain a mask or prefix-length for each route, confusion can

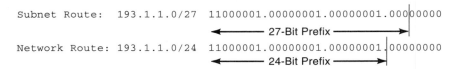

```
Subnet Route:    193.1.1.0/27   11000001.00000001.00000001.000|00000
                                ◄────── 27-Bit Prefix ──────►
Network Route:  193.1.1.0/24   11000001.00000001.00000001.|00000000
                                ◄────── 24-Bit Prefix ──────►
```

FIGURE 3.10 Differentiating between a route to the all-0s subnet and the entire network.

occur because the same broadcast address (193.1.1.255) is used for both for the entire network 193.1.1.0/24 and the all-1s subnet 193.1.1.224/27. This situation is illustrated in Figure 3.11.

With the development of routing protocols that can carry the mask or prefix-length with each route, the address space defined by the all-0s and all-1s subnets is once again usable, despite the cautions in RFC-950. As a result, vendors have begun to accommodate user demand and permit the configuration of the all-0s and all-1s subnets on router interfaces.

To support the deployment of the all-0s and all-1s subnets, the Interior Gateway Protocol (IGP) must either carry extended-network-prefixes or have a mechanism to map each route to its extended-network-prefix, such as statically-defined route/mask information. Both OSPF and I-IS-IS carry extended-network-prefixes, so they support the deployment of the all-0s and all-1s subnets in arbitrarily complex topologies. RIP$_v$1 does not carry extended-network-prefixes, but RIP$_v$2 does. All routers in the organization's network need to be able to correctly interpret, learn, and forward traffic to other subnetworks with all-0s and all-1s in their subnet-number field.

Determining Host Addresses for Each Subnet

According to Internet practices, the host-number field of an IP address cannot contain all 0-bits or all 1-bits. The all-0s host-number identifies the base network (or subnetwork) number, while the all-1s host-number represents the broadcast address for the network (or subnetwork).

```
Broadcast to Subnet:   193.1.1.224/27      11000001.00000001.00000001.111|11111
                                           ◄────── 27-Bit Prefix ──────►
Broadcast to Network:  193.1.1.0/24        11000001.00000001.0000001|.11111111
                                           ◄────── 24-Bit Prefix ──────►
```

FIGURE 3.11 Broadcast to the all-1s subnet versus broadcast to the entire network.

In our current example, there are five bits in the host-number field of each subnet address. This means that each subnet represents a block of 30 host addresses ($2^5 - 2 = 30$, note that the 2 is subtracted because the all-0s and the all-1s host addresses cannot be used by any endstation). Thus, the hosts on each subnet are numbered one through 30.

In general, to define the address assigned to Host #n of a particular subnet, the network administrator places the binary representation of "n" into the subnet's host-number field. For example, to define the address assigned to Host #15 on Subnet #2, the network administrator simply places the binary representation of 15 (01111) into the five bits of Subnet #2's host-number field.

The valid host addresses for Subnet #2 in our example are given below. The underlined portion of each address identifies the extended-network-prefix, while the **bold** digits highlight the 5-bit host-number field:

```
Subnet #2:  11000001.00000001.00000001.01000000  = 193.1.1.64/27

Host #1:    11000001.00000001.00000001.01000001  = 193.1.1.65/27
Host #2:    11000001.00000001.00000001.01000010  = 193.1.1.66/27
Host #3:    11000001.00000001.00000001.01000011  = 193.1.1.67/27
Host #4:    11000001.00000001.00000001.01000100  = 193.1.1.68/27
Host #5:    11000001.00000001.00000001.01000101  = 193.1.1.69/27
              .
              .
              .
Host #15:   11000001.00000001.00000001.01001111  = 193.1.1.79/27
Host #16:   11000001.00000001.00000001.01010000  = 193.1.1.80/27
              .
              .
Host #27:   11000001.00000001.00000001.01011011  = 193.1.1.91/27
Host #28:   11000001.00000001.00000001.01011100  = 193.1.1.92/27
Host #29:   11000001.00000001.00000001.01011101  = 193.1.1.93/27
Host #30:   11000001.00000001.00000001.01011110  = 193.1.1.94/27
```

The valid host addresses for Subnet #6 are given below. The underlined portion of each address identifies the extended-network-prefix, while the **bold** digits identify the host-number field:

```
Subnet #6:  11000001.00000001.00000001.11000000  = 193.1.1.192/27

Host #1:    11000001.00000001.00000001.11000001  = 193.1.1.193/27
Host #2:    11000001.00000001.00000001.11000010  = 193.1.1.194/27
Host #3:    11000001.00000001.00000001.11000011  = 193.1.1.195/27
```

```
Host #4:    11000001.00000001.00000001.11000100 = 193.1.1.196/27
Host #5:    11000001.00000001.00000001.11000101 = 193.1.1.197/27
     .
     .
     .
Host #15:   11000001.00000001.00000001.11001111 = 193.1.1.207/27
Host #16:   11000001.00000001.00000001.11010000 = 193.1.1.208/27
     .
     .
     .
Host #27:   11000001.00000001.00000001.11011011 = 193.1.1.219/27
Host #28:   11000001.00000001.00000001.11011100 = 193.1.1.220/27
Host #29:   11000001.00000001.00000001.11011101 = 193.1.1.221/27
Host #30:   11000001.00000001.00000001.11011110 = 193.1.1.222/27
```

Determining the Broadcast Address for Each Subnet

The broadcast address for Subnet #2 is the all-1s host address, or:

```
11000001.00000001.00000001.01011111 = 193.1.1.95
```

Note that the broadcast address for Subnet #2 is the next-lower address than the base address for Subnet #3 (193.1.1.96). This is always the case; the broadcast address for Subnet #n always has a value that is numerically one less than the base address for Subnet #(n+1).

The broadcast address for Subnet #6 is simply the address value resulting from setting all the bits in the host field to 1 after setting the subnet-number field to six (110):

```
11000001.00000001.00000001.11011111 = 193.1.1.223
```

Again, the broadcast address for Subnet #6 is exactly one less than the base address for Subnet #7 (193.1.1.224).

SUBNET EXAMPLE #2

Given:

An organization has been assigned the network number 140.25.0.0/16 and it needs to create a set of subnets that supports up to 60 hosts on each subnet.

DEFINING THE SUBNET MASK / EXTENDED-NETWORK-PREFIX LENGTH

The first step is to determine the number of bits required to define 60 hosts on each subnet. Since a block of host address can only be assigned along binary boundaries, host addresses blocks can only be created in powers of two. This means that it is impossible to create a block that contains exactly 60 host addresses. To support 60 hosts, the network administrator must define a minimum address block of 62 (2^6–2) host addresses. However, this choice would only provide two unused host addresses on each subnet for future growth. Since this does not appear to be adequate to support additional growth, the network administrator elects to define a block of 126 (2^7–2) host addresses and has 66 addresses on each subnet for future growth. A block of 126 host addresses requires 7 bits in the host-number field.

The next step is to determine the subnet mask/extended-prefix length. Since 7 bits of the 32-bit IP address are required for the host-number field, the extended-network-prefix must be a /25 (because 25 = 32–7). A 25-bit extended-network-prefix can be expressed in dotted-decimal notation as 255.255.255.128. This is illustrated in Figure 3.12.

As shown in Figure 3.12, the 25-bit extended-network-prefix assigns 9 bits to the subnet-number field. Since 2^9 = 512, 9 bits allows room for the definition of up to 512 subnets. Depending on the organization's requirements, the network administrator could have elected to assign more bits to the host-number field and that many fewer bits to the subnet-number field (thereby providing for fewer possible subnets, but more available host addresses within each subnet). Conversely, the administrator may have needed more subnet bits, which necessarily reduces the

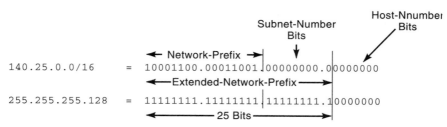

FIGURE 3.12 Example #2: Defining the subnet mask/extended-network-prefix length.

number of bits in the host-number field (i.e., increasing the total number of available subnet bits decreases the available host addresses per subnet, and vice-versa).

Although this example creates a rather large number of subnets, it provides an interesting example because it illustrates what happens to the dotted-decimal representation of a subnet address when the subnet-number bits extend across an octet boundary. (It should be mentioned that the same type of confusion can also occur when the host-number bits extend across an octet boundary.)

Defining Each of the Subnet Numbers

The 512 subnets will be numbered zero through 511. The 9-bit binary representation of the decimal values zero through 511 are: 0 (000000000), 1 (000000001), 2 (000000010), 3 (000000011), . . ., 511 (111111111). To define subnet #3, the network administrator places the binary representation of 3 (000000011) into the 9 bits of the subnet-number field.

Some of the 512 subnet-numbers for this example are given below. The underlined portion of each address identifies the extended-network-prefix, while the **bold** digits identify the 9 bit subnet-number field:

```
Base Net:    10001100.00011001.00000000.00000000 = 140.25.0.0/16

Subnet #0:   10001100.00011001.00000000.00000000 = 140.25.0.0/25
Subnet #1:   10001100.00011001.00000000.10000000 = 140.25.0.128/25
Subnet #2:   10001100.00011001.00000001.00000000 = 140.25.1.0/25
Subnet #3:   10001100.00011001.00000001.10000000 = 140.25.1.128/25
Subnet #4:   10001100.00011001.00000010.00000000 = 140.25.2.0/25
Subnet #5:   10001100.00011001.00000010.10000000 = 140.25.2.128/25
Subnet #6:   10001100.00011001.00000011.00000000 = 140.25.3.0/25
Subnet #7:   10001100.00011001.00000011.10000000 = 140.25.3.128/25
Subnet #8:   10001100.00011001.00000100.00000000 = 140.25.4.0/25
Subnet #9:   10001100.00011001.00000100.10000000 = 140.25.4.128/25
                :
                :
Subnet #510: 10001100.00011001.11111111.00000000 = 140.25.255.0/25
Subnet #511: 10001100.00011001.11111111.10000000 = 140.25.255.128/25
```

Notice how sequential subnet-numbers may not appear to be sequential when expressed in dotted-decimal notation. This can cause a great deal of misunderstanding and confusion since everyone believes that dotted-decimal notation makes it much easier for human users to understand IP addressing. In this example, the dotted-decimal notation obscures rather than clarifies the subnet-numbering scheme!

Only when the extended-network-prefix happens to align with a natural 8-bit boundary does a completely obvious progression appear.

Determining Host Addresses for Each Subnet

In this example there are 7 bits in the host-number field of each subnet address. As discussed earlier, this means that each subnet represents a block of 126 host addresses. The hosts on each subnet will be numbered one through 126.

The valid host addresses for Subnet #3 are given below. The underlined portion of each address identifies the extended-network-prefix, while the **bold** digits identify the 7 bit host-number field:

```
Subnet #3:   10001100.00011001.00000001.10000000 = 140.25.1.128/25

Host #1:     10001100.00011001.00000001.10000001 = 140.25.1.129/25
Host #2:     10001100.00011001.00000001.10000010 = 140.25.1.130/25
Host #3:     10001100.00011001.00000001.10000011 = 140.25.1.131/25
Host #4:     10001100.00011001.00000001.10000100 = 140.25.1.132/25
Host #5:     10001100.00011001.00000001.10000101 = 140.25.1.133/25
Host #6:     10001100.00011001.00000001.10000110 = 140.25.1.134/25
                        .
                        .
Host #62:    10001100.00011001.00000001.10111110 = 140.25.1.190/25
Host #63:    10001100.00011001.00000001.10111111 = 140.25.1.191/25
Host #64:    10001100.00011001.00000001.11000000 = 140.25.1.192/25
Host #65:    10001100.00011001.00000001.11000001 = 140.25.1.193/25
                        .
                        .
Host #123:   10001100.00011001.00000001.11111011 = 140.25.1.251/25
Host #124:   10001100.00011001.00000001.11111100 = 140.25.1.252/25
Host #125:   10001100.00011001.00000001.11111101 = 140.25.1.253/25
Host #126:   10001100.00011001.00000001.11111110 = 140.25.1.254/25
```

Determining the Broadcast Address for Each Subnet

The broadcast address for Subnet #3 is the all-1s host address or:

```
10001100.00011001.00000001.11111111 = 140.25.1.255
```

As is true in general, the broadcast address for Subnet #3 is immediately one less than the base address for Subnet #4 (140.25.2.0).

ADDITIONAL PRACTICE WITH SUBNETWORKS

Subnetting Exercise #1

Assume that you have been assigned the 132.45.0.0/16 network block. You must establish eight subnets.

1. _____ binary digits are required to define eight subnets.

2. Specify the extended network-prefix that allows the creation of eight subnets.

   _____

3. Express the subnets in both binary format and dotted-decimal notation:

   #0 _____

   #1 _____

   #2 _____

   #3 _____

   #4 _____

   #5 _____

   #6 _____

   #7 _____

4. List the range of host addresses that can be assigned to Subnet #3 (132.45.96.0/19). Show your work in binary, and summarize as a range.

   _____

   _____

   _____

   _____

   _____

   _____

   _____

5. What is the broadcast address for Subnet #3 (132.45.96.0/19)?

   _____

SUBNETTING EXERCISE #2

1. Assume that you have been assigned the 200.35.1.0/24 network block. Specify an extended-network-prefix that allows the creation of at least 20 hosts on each subnet.

_____

2. What is the maximum number of hosts that can be assigned to each of these subnets?

_____

3. What is the maximum number of subnets (of this size) that can be defined in this /24?

_____

4. Specify these subnets of 200.35.1.0/24 in binary format and dotted-decimal notation.

_____

_____

_____

_____

_____

_____

5. List the range of host addresses that can be assigned to Subnet #6 (200.35.1.192/27). Show your work in binary, and summarize as a range.

_____

_____

_____

_____

_____

_____

_____

6. What is the broadcast address for subnet 200.35.1.192/27?

_____

Solution for Subnetting Exercise #1

Assume that you have been assigned the 132.45.0.0/16 network block. You must establish eight subnets.

1. <u>Three</u> binary digits are required to define the eight subnets.
2. Specify the extended-network-prefix that allows the creation of eight subnets.

   <u>/19 or 255.255.224.0</u>
3. Express the subnets in binary format and dotted-decimal notation:

```
Subnet #0: 10000100.00101101.00000000.00000000 = 132.45.0.0/19
Subnet #1: 10000100.00101101.00100000.00000000 = 132.45.32.0/19
Subnet #2: 10000100.00101101.01000000.00000000 = 132.45.64.0/19
Subnet #3: 10000100.00101101.01100000.00000000 = 132.45.96.0/19
Subnet #4: 10000100.00101101.10000000.00000000 = 132.45.128.0/19
Subnet #5: 10000100.00101101.10100000.00000000 = 132.45.160.0/19
Subnet #6: 10000100.00101101.11000000.00000000 = 132.45.192.0/19
Subnet #7: 10000100.00101101.11100000.00000000 = 132.45.224.0/19
```

4. List the range of host addresses that can be assigned to Subnet #3 (132.45.96.0/19). Show your work in binary, and summarize as a range.

```
Subnet #3:   10000100.00101101.01100000.00000000 = 132.45.96.0/19

Host #1:     10000100.00101101.01100000.00000001 = 132.45.96.1/19
Host #2:     10000100.00101101.01100000.00000010 = 132.45.96.2/19
Host #3:     10000100.00101101.01100000.00000011 = 132.45.96.3/19
      :
Host #8190:  10000100.00101101.01111111.11111110 = 132.45.127.254/19

Host range for 132.45.96.0/19: 132.45.96.1 - 132.45.127.254
```

5. What is the broadcast address for Subnet #3 (132.45.96.0/19)?

```
10000100.00101101.01111111.11111111 = 132.45.127.255/19
```

Solution for Subnetting Exercise #2

1. Assume that you have been assigned the 200.35.1.0/24 network block. Define an extended-network-prefix that allows the creation of at least 20 hosts on each subnet.

> A minimum of 5 bits are required to define 20 hosts,
> so the extended-network-prefix is a /27 (27 bits remain
> after the 5 host bits are removed from the 32-bit IP address.

2. What is the maximum number of hosts that can be assigned to each subnet?
   The maximum number of hosts on each subnet is $2^5 - 2$, or 30.

3. What is the maximum number of subnets that can be defined?
   The maximum number of subnets is 2^3, or 8.

4. Specify the subnets of 200.35.1.0/24 in binary format and dotted-decimal notation. Show your work in binary, and summarize as a range.

```
Subnet #0:  11001000.00100011.00000001.000 00000 = 200.35.1.0/27
Subnet #1:  11001000.00100011.00000001.001 00000 = 200.35.1.32/27
Subnet #2:  11001000.00100011.00000001.010 00000 = 200.35.1.64/27
Subnet #3:  11001000.00100011.00000001.011 00000 = 200.35.1.96/27
Subnet #4:  11001000.00100011.00000001.100 00000 = 200.35.1.128/27
Subnet #5:  11001000.00100011.00000001.101 00000 = 200.35.1.160/27
Subnet #6:  11001000.00100011.00000001.110 00000 = 200.35.1.192/27
Subnet #7:  11001000.00100011.00000001.111 00000 = 200.35.1.224/27
```

5. List range of host addresses that can be assigned to Subnet #6 (200.35.1.192/27)

```
Subnet #6:  11001000.00100011.00000001.11000000 = 200.35.1.192/27
Host #1:    11001000.00100011.00000001.11000001 = 200.35.1.193/27
Host #2:    11001000.00100011.00000001.11000010 = 200.35.1.194/27
Host #3:    11001000.00100011.00000001.11000011 = 200.35.1.195/27
              :
Host #29:   11001000.00100011.00000001.11011101 = 200.35.1.221/27
Host #30:   11001000.00100011.00000001.11011110 = 200.35.1.222/27

Host range for 200.35.1.192/27: 200.35.1.193 - 200.35.1.222
```

6. What is the broadcast address for subnet 200.35.1.192/27?

```
11001000.00100011.00000001.11011111 = 200.35.1.223
```

Practice Questions

Sidebar 1. Define all the subnet-numbers and their associated broadcast addresses for the following 5-bit subnetting scheme on a Class B network: HHHHHHSS.SSSHHHHH.

Sidebar 2. How many subnets are there?

Sidebar 3. How many host addresses are available per subnet?

LOCATION OF SUBNET BITS

Originally, RFC-950's "Internet Standard Subnetting Procedure" did not explicitly require that the subnet-field's bits be contiguous within the host-number field, or that the subnet-field's bits be located immediately after the network-number field. This quote from RFC-1009 "Requirements for Internet Gateways," the earliest version of the "Router Requirements" RFC, codified this viewpoint:

> The bit positions containing this extended network number are indicated by a 32-bit mask called the "subnet mask" [21]; <u>it is recommended but not required that the <Subnet-number> bits be contiguous and fall between the <Network-number> and the <Host-number> fields.</u>

In principle, computers could handle these arbitrary arrangements, but very few (if any) implementations of IP supported such arbitrary subdivisions of the host-number field. There is no convincing argument that can justify this obfuscation.

If you steal 's' bits from an h-bit-long host-number field, you will have up to 2^s subnets, with $[2^{(h-s)} - 2]$ host addresses per subnet. Clustering all the subnet bits in one place does not in any way restrict the ability to subdivide the network number, and it avoids unnecessarily complication of the mechanics of subnetting—a subject that most people find complex enough already.

For an example of how confusing this can be, let's take a Class B network number of 172.24.0.0 and impose the following structure on the host-number field, where S represents a subnet bit and H represents a bit of the host-number field: SHHSSSHH.HHSHSHHS. The subnet-numbers are derived by setting all the host bits to 0, i.e., S00SSS00.00S0000S. The unusual subnet mask is, in this case, 10011100.00100001, or 156.33, or <u>255.255.156.33</u> in its complete representation that incorporates the fixed network-number portion. Remember, this example only serves to show why noncontiguous subnet numbers are not in use. Feel free to skip this section if you want.

Subnet-number 1 is found by setting the 6 subnet bits to 000001 (0<u>00</u>0<u>00</u>00.00<u>0</u>00000<u>1</u>), the second subnet's bit pattern is 000010

(continued)

(<u>0</u>0<u>0</u>00000.00<u>1</u>00000<u>0</u>), and so on. As usual, all we are doing here is counting in binary: 1, 10, 11, 100, 101, 110, 111, 1000, 1001, etc. The 29th subnet is 011101 (<u>0</u>0<u>0</u>11100.00<u>0</u>0000<u>1</u>).

Here is a summary of the subnet-numbers and their associated broadcast addresses (all the H-bits set to 1), rendered in dotted-decimal notation. Note that only the final two bytes are listed in binary; this saves space, since the first two bytes 172.24 (10101100.00011000) are the same for each subnet.

#	Subnet-Number (Bin & Decimal)		Subnet's Broadcast Address	
0	<u>0</u>0<u>0</u>00000.00<u>0</u>0000<u>0</u>	172.24.0.0	<u>0</u>1<u>1</u>00011.11<u>0</u>1111<u>0</u>	172.24.99.222
1	<u>0</u>0<u>0</u>00000.00<u>0</u>0000<u>1</u>	172.24.0.1	<u>0</u>1<u>1</u>00011.11<u>0</u>1111<u>1</u>	172.24.99.223
2	<u>0</u>0<u>0</u>00000.00<u>1</u>0000<u>0</u>	172.24.0.32	<u>0</u>1<u>1</u>00011.11<u>1</u>1111<u>0</u>	172.24.99.254
3	<u>0</u>0<u>0</u>00000.00<u>1</u>0000<u>1</u>	172.24.0.33	<u>0</u>1<u>1</u>00011.11<u>1</u>1111<u>1</u>	172.24.99.255
4	<u>0</u>0<u>0</u>00100.00<u>0</u>0000<u>0</u>	172.24.4.0	<u>0</u>1<u>1</u>00111.11<u>0</u>1111<u>0</u>	172.24.103.222
5	<u>0</u>0<u>0</u>00100.00<u>0</u>0000<u>1</u>	172.24.4.1	<u>0</u>1<u>1</u>00111.11<u>0</u>1111<u>1</u>	172.24.103.223
6	<u>0</u>0<u>0</u>00100.00<u>1</u>0000<u>0</u>	172.24.4.32	<u>0</u>1<u>1</u>00111.11<u>1</u>1111<u>0</u>	172.24.103.254
7	<u>0</u>0<u>0</u>00100.00<u>1</u>0000<u>1</u>	172.24.4.33	<u>0</u>1<u>1</u>00111.11<u>1</u>1111<u>1</u>	172.24.103.255
8	<u>0</u>0<u>0</u>01000.00<u>0</u>0000<u>0</u>	172.24.8.0	<u>0</u>1<u>1</u>01011.11<u>0</u>1111<u>0</u>	172.24.107.222
9	<u>0</u>0<u>0</u>01000.00<u>0</u>0000<u>1</u>	172.24.8.1	<u>0</u>1<u>1</u>01011.11<u>0</u>1111<u>1</u>	172.24.107.223
10	<u>0</u>0<u>0</u>01000.00<u>1</u>0000<u>0</u>	172.24.8.32	<u>0</u>1<u>1</u>01011.11<u>1</u>1111<u>0</u>	172.24.107.254
11	<u>0</u>0<u>0</u>01000.00<u>1</u>0000<u>1</u>	172.24.8.33	<u>0</u>1<u>1</u>01011.11<u>1</u>1111<u>1</u>	172.24.107.255
12	<u>0</u>0<u>0</u>01100.00<u>0</u>0000<u>0</u>	172.24.12.0	<u>0</u>1<u>1</u>01111.11<u>0</u>1111<u>0</u>	172.24.111.222
13	<u>0</u>0<u>0</u>01100.00<u>0</u>0000<u>1</u>	172.24.12.1	<u>0</u>1<u>1</u>01111.11<u>0</u>1111<u>1</u>	172.24.111.223
14	<u>0</u>0<u>0</u>01100.00<u>1</u>0000<u>0</u>	172.24.12.32	<u>0</u>1<u>1</u>01111.11<u>1</u>1111<u>0</u>	172.24.111.254
15	<u>0</u>0<u>0</u>01100.00<u>1</u>0000<u>1</u>	172.24.12.33	<u>0</u>1<u>1</u>01111.11<u>1</u>1111<u>1</u>	172.24.111.255
16	<u>0</u>0<u>0</u>10000.00<u>0</u>0000<u>0</u>	172.24.16.0	<u>0</u>1<u>1</u>10011.11<u>0</u>1111<u>0</u>	172.24.115.222
17	<u>0</u>0<u>0</u>10000.00<u>0</u>0000<u>1</u>	172.24.16.1	<u>0</u>1<u>1</u>10011.11<u>0</u>1111<u>1</u>	172.24.115.223
18	<u>0</u>0<u>0</u>10000.00<u>1</u>0000<u>0</u>	172.24.16.32	<u>0</u>1<u>1</u>10011.11<u>1</u>1111<u>0</u>	172.24.115.254
19	<u>0</u>0<u>0</u>10000.00<u>1</u>0000<u>1</u>	172.24.16.33	<u>0</u>1<u>1</u>10011.11<u>1</u>1111<u>1</u>	172.24.115.255
20	<u>0</u>0<u>0</u>10100.00<u>0</u>0000<u>0</u>	172.24.20.0	<u>0</u>1<u>1</u>10111.11<u>0</u>1111<u>0</u>	172.24.119.222
21	<u>0</u>0<u>0</u>10100.00<u>0</u>0000<u>1</u>	172.24.20.1	<u>0</u>1<u>1</u>10111.11<u>0</u>1111<u>1</u>	172.24.119.223
22	<u>0</u>0<u>0</u>10100.00<u>1</u>0000<u>0</u>	172.24.20.32	<u>0</u>1<u>1</u>10111.11<u>1</u>1111<u>0</u>	172.24.119.254
23	<u>0</u>0<u>0</u>10100.00<u>1</u>0000<u>1</u>	172.24.20.33	<u>0</u>1<u>1</u>10111.11<u>1</u>1111<u>1</u>	172.24.119.255
24	<u>0</u>0<u>0</u>11000.00<u>0</u>0000<u>0</u>	172.24.24.0	<u>0</u>1<u>1</u>11011.11<u>0</u>1111<u>0</u>	172.24.123.222
25	<u>0</u>0<u>0</u>11000.00<u>0</u>0000<u>1</u>	172.24.24.1	<u>0</u>1<u>1</u>11011.11<u>0</u>1111<u>1</u>	172.24.123.223
26	<u>0</u>0<u>0</u>11000.00<u>1</u>0000<u>0</u>	172.24.24.32	<u>0</u>1<u>1</u>11011.11<u>1</u>1111<u>0</u>	172.24.123.254

(continued)

27	00011000.00100001	172.24.24.33	01111011.11111111	172.24.123.255
28	00011100.00000000	172.24.28.0	01111111.11011110	172.24.127.222
29	00011100.00000001	172.24.28.1	01111111.11011111	172.24.127.223
30	00011100.00100000	172.24.28.32	01111111.11111110	172.24.127.254
31	00011100.00100001	172.24.28.33	01111111.11111111	172.24.127.255
32	10000000.00000000	172.24.128.0	11100011.11011110	172.24.227.222
33	10000000.00000001	172.24.128.1	11100011.11011111	172.24.227.223
34	10000000.00100000	172.24.128.32	11100011.11111110	172.24.227.254
35	10000000.00100001	172.24.128.33	11100011.11111111	172.24.227.255
36	10000100.00000000	172.24.132.0	11100111.11011110	172.24.231.222
37	10000100.00000001	172.24.132.1	11100111.11011111	172.24.231.223
38	10000100.00100000	172.24.132.32	11100111.11111110	172.24.231.254
39	10000100.00100001	172.24.132.33	11100111.11111111	172.24.231.255
40	10001000.00000000	172.24.136.0	11101011.11011110	172.24.235.222
41	10001000.00000001	172.24.136.1	11101011.11011111	172.24.235.223
42	10001000.00100000	172.24.136.32	11101011.11111110	172.24.235.254
43	10001000.00100001	172.24.136.33	11101011.11111111	172.24.235.255
44	10001100.00000000	172.24.140.0	11101111.11011110	172.24.239.222
45	10001100.00000001	172.24.140.1	11101111.11011111	172.24.239.223
46	10001100.00100000	172.24.140.32	11101111.11111110	172.24.239.254
47	10001100.00100001	172.24.140.33	11101111.11111111	172.24.239.255
48	10010000.00000000	172.24.144.0	11110011.11011110	172.24.243.222
49	10010000.00000001	172.24.144.1	11110011.11011111	172.24.243.223
50	10010000.00100000	172.24.144.32	11110011.11111110	172.24.243.254
51	10010000.00100001	172.24.144.33	11110011.11111111	172.24.243.255
52	10010100.00000000	172.24.148.0	11110111.11011110	172.24.247.222
53	10010100.00000001	172.24.1481	11110111.11011111	172.24.247.223
54	10010100.00100000	172.24.148.32	11110111.11111110	172.24.247.254
55	10010100.00100001	172.24.148.33	11110111.11111111	172.24.247.255
56	10011000.00000000	172.24.148.0	11111011.11011110	172.24.251.222
57	10011000.00000001	172.24.1481	11111011.11011111	172.24.251.223
58	10011000.00100000	172.24.148.32	11111011.11111110	172.24.251.254
59	10011000.00100001	172.24.148.33	11111011.11111111	172.24.251.255
60	10011100.00000000	172.24.148.0	11111111.11011110	172.24.255.222
61	10011100.00000001	172.24.1481	11111111.11011111	172.24.255.223
62	10011100.00100000	172.24.148.32	11111111.11111110	172.24.255.254
63	10011100.00100001	172.24.148.33	11111111.11111111	172.24.255.255

(continued)

There are patterns here, but they are not at all obvious, or easily predictable.

In this example, since we have appropriated 6 bits for the subnet field, there must be 10 bits remaining for use as host-numbers, thus providing 2^{10} (1024) unique bit patterns ranging from zero to 1023—in *each* subnet. Host-number 441 (**01 1011 1001**) in subnet 29 works out to the following in this intentionally twisted scheme: 00111110.11010011. In dotted-decimal notation, this becomes 172.24.62.211. The same host number in subnet 30 (011110) would be 00111110.11110010, or 172.24.62.242. Who would guess that 172.24.62.242 and 172.24.62.211 were the same host-number in two adjacent subnets? Even knowing the mask, 255.255.156.33, this is not obvious without "unpacking" the dotted-decimal representations of the addresses and the subnet mask.

To close this sidebar, we will examine the "normal" way to use 6 bits as the subnet-number field: SSSSSSHH.HHHHHHHH. There are clear, obvious patterns in this list, as opposed to the one above, and—as was noted already—there are still the same number of subnets (64), even when the 6 bits are contiguous.

#	Subnet-Number (Bin & Decimal)		Subnet's Broadcast Address	
0	00000000.00000000	172.24.0.0	00000011.11111111	172.24.3.255
1	00000100.00000000	172.24.4.0	00000111.11111111	172.24.7.255
2	00001000.00000000	172.24.8.0	00001011.11111111	172.24.11.255
3	00001100.00000000	172.24.12.0	00001111.11111111	172.24.15.255
4	00010000.00000000	172.24.16.0	00010011.11111111	172.24.19.255
5	00010100.00000000	172.24.20.0	00010111.11111111	172.24.23.255
6	00011000.00000000	172.24.24.0	00011011.11111111	172.24.27.255
7	00011100.00000000	172.24.28.0	00011111.11111111	172.24.31.255
8	00100000.00000000	172.24.32.0	00100011.11111111	172.24.35.255
9	00100100.00000000	172.24.36.0	00100111.11111111	172.24.39.255
10	00101000.00000000	172.24.40.0	00101011.11111111	172.24.43.255
11	00101100.00000000	172.24.44.0	00101111.11111111	172.24.47.255
12	00110000.00000000	172.24.48.0	00110011.11111111	172.24.51.255
13	00110100.00000000	172.24.52.0	00110111.11111111	172.24.55.255
14	00111000.00000000	172.24.56.0	00111011.11111111	172.24.59.255
15	00111100.00000000	172.24.60.0	00111111.11111111	172.24.63.255
16	01000000.00000000	172.24.64.0	01000011.11111111	172.24.67.255
17	01000100.00000000	172.24.68.0	01000111.11111111	172.24.71.255
18	01001000.00000000	172.24.72.0	01001011.11111111	172.24.75.255

(continued)

19	01001100.00000000	172.24.76.0	01001111.11111111	172.24.79.255
20	01010000.00000000	172.24.80.0	01010011.11111111	172.24.83.255
21	01010100.00000000	172.24.84.0	01010111.11111111	172.24.87.255
22	01011000.00000000	172.24.88.0	01011011.11111111	172.24.91.255
23	01011100.00000000	172.24.92.0	01011111.11111111	172.24.95.255
24	01100000.00000000	172.24.96.0	01100011.11111111	172.24.99.255
25	01100100.00000000	172.24.100.0	01100111.11111111	172.24.103.255
26	01101000.00000000	172.24.104.0	01101011.11111111	172.24.107.255
27	01101100.00000000	172.24.108.0	01101111.11111111	172.24.111.255
28	01110000.00000000	172.24.112.0	01110011.11111111	172.24.115.255
29	01110100.00000000	172.24.116.0	01110111.11111111	172.24.119.255
30	01111000.00000000	172.24.120.0	01111011.11111111	172.24.123.255
31	01111100.00000000	172.24.124.0	01111111.11111111	172.24.127.255
32	10000000.00000000	172.24.128.0	10000011.11111111	172.24.131.255
33	10000100.00000000	172.24.132.0	10000111.11111111	172.24.135.255
34	10001000.00000000	172.24.136.0	10001011.11111111	172.24.139.255
35	10001100.00000000	172.24.140.0	10001111.11111111	172.24.143.255
36	10010000.00000000	172.24.144.0	10010011.11111111	172.24.147.255
37	10010100.00000000	172.24.148.0	10010111.11111111	172.24.151.255
38	10011000.00000000	172.24.152.0	10011011.11111111	172.24.155.255
39	10011100.00000000	172.24.156.0	10011111.11111111	172.24.159.255
40	10100000.00000000	172.24.160.0	10100011.11111111	172.24.163.255
41	10100100.00000000	172.24.164.0	10100111.11111111	172.24.167.255
42	10101000.00000000	172.24.168.0	10101011.11111111	172.24.171.255
43	10101100.00000000	172.24.172.0	10101111.11111111	172.24.175.255
44	10110000.00000000	172.24.176.0	10110011.11111111	172.24.179.255
45	10110100.00000000	172.24.180.0	10110111.11111111	172.24.183.255
46	10111000.00000000	172.24.184.0	10111011.11111111	172.24.187.255
47	10111100.00000000	172.24.188.0	10111111.11111111	172.24.191.255
48	11000000.00000000	172.24.192.0	11000011.11111111	172.24.195.255
49	11000100.00000000	172.24.196.0	11000111.11111111	172.24.199.255
50	11001000.00000000	172.24.200.0	11001011.11111111	172.24.203.255
51	11001100.00000000	172.24.204.0	11001111.11111111	172.24.207.255
52	11010000.00000000	172.24.208.0	11010011.11111111	172.24.211.255
53	11010100.00000000	172.24.212.0	11010111.11111111	172.24.215.255
54	11011000.00000000	172.24.216.0	11011011.11111111	172.24.219.255
55	11011100.00000000	172.24.220.0	11011111.11111111	172.24.223.255

(continued)

```
56  11100000.00000000   172.24.224.0   11100011.11111111   172.24.227.255
57  11100100.00000000   172.24.228.0   11100111.11111111   172.24.231.255
58  11101000.00000000   172.24.232.0   11101011.11111111   172.24.235.255
59  11101100.00000000   172.24.236.0   11101111.11111111   172.24.239.255
60  11110000.00000000   172.24.240.0   11110011.11111111   172.24.243.255
61  11110100.00000000   172.24.244.0   11110111.11111111   172.24.247.255
62  11111000.00000000   172.24.248.0   11111011.11111111   172.24.251.255
63  11111100.00000000   172.24.252.0   11111111.11111111   172.24.255.255
```

One of the most obvious patterns above is that all the subnet-numbers are multiples of four. This is because the subnet-number is found by zeroing out the host field, which leaves the lower 2 bits of the third byte always set to zero. The smallest nonzero subnet-number that matches that requirement is 00000100, which is a binary representation of the number four (this is fact one).

Viewed exclusively from within the subnet field, this bit is in the following postion: 000001. Clearly this is the number one. Basic arithmetic tells us that one multiplied by any number results in the same number; 1 * 14 = 14, 1 * 2 = 2, etc. So all the values in the subnet field, from 000000 to 111111, are multiples of "one;" (this is fact two).

Fact one was that, in the context of the 8-bit byte, the first subnet, which has the "one" pattern, (000001) is really the number four (000000100) when viewed in the context of the entire byte. Taken together, these two facts imply that all the subnet-numbers must be multiples of four.

Sidebar 4 a. What patterns can you see in the list of subnets?
          b. Did you expect any of them?
          c. Why?

SOLUTIONS TO SIDEBAR QUESTIONS

Sidebar 1. Define all the subnet-numbers and their associated broadcast addresses for the following 5-bit subnetting scheme on a Class B network: HHHH-HH_SS.SS_SHHHHH.

```
#   Subnet-Number (Bin & Decimal)        Subnet's Broadcast Address

0   00000000.00000000    172.24.0.0     11111100.00011111    172.24.252.31
1   00000000.00100000    172.24.0.32    11111100.00111111    172.24.252.63
```

2	00000000.01000000	172.24.0.64	11111100.01011111	172.24.252.95
3	00000000.01100000	172.24.0.96	11111100.01111111	172.24.252.127
4	00000000.10000000	172.24.0.128	11111100.10011111	172.24.252.159
5	00000000.10100000	172.24.0.160	11111100.10111111	172.24.252.191
6	00000000.11000000	172.24.0.192	11111100.11011111	172.24.252.223
7	00000000.11100000	172.24.0.224	11111100.11111111	172.24.252.255
8	00000001.00000000	172.24.1.0	11111101.00011111	172.24.253.31
9	00000001.00100000	172.24.1.32	11111101.00111111	172.24.253.63
10	00000001.01000000	172.24.1.64	11111101.01011111	172.24.253.95
11	00000001.01100000	172.24.1.96	11111101.01111111	172.24.253.127
12	00000001.10000000	172.24.1.128	11111101.10011111	172.24.253.159
13	00000001.10100000	172.24.1.160	11111101.10111111	172.24.253.191
14	00000001.11000000	172.24.1.192	11111101.11011111	172.24.253.223
15	00000001.11100000	172.24.1.224	11111101.11111111	172.24.253.255
16	00000010.00000000	172.24.2.0	11111110.00011111	172.24.254.31
17	00000010.00100000	172.24.2.32	11111110.00111111	172.24.254.63
18	00000010.01000000	172.24.2.64	11111110.01011111	172.24.254.95
19	00000010.01100000	172.24.2.96	11111110.01111111	172.24.254.127
20	00000010.10000000	172.24.2.128	11111110.10011111	172.24.254.159
21	00000010.10100000	172.24.2.160	11111110.10111111	172.24.254.191
22	00000010.11000000	172.24.2.192	11111110.11011111	172.24.254.223
23	00000010.11100000	172.24.2.224	11111110.11111111	172.24.254.255
24	00000011.00000000	172.24.3.0	11111111.00011111	172.24.255.31
25	00000011.00100000	172.24.3.32	11111111.00111111	172.24.255.63
26	00000011.01000000	172.24.3.64	11111111.01011111	172.24.255.95
27	00000011.01100000	172.24.3.96	11111111.01111111	172.24.255.127
28	00000011.10000000	172.24.3.128	11111111.10011111	172.24.255.159
29	00000011.10100000	172.24.3.160	11111111.10111111	172.24.255.191
30	00000011.11000000	172.24.3.192	11111111.11011111	172.24.255.223
31	00000011.11100000	172.24.3.224	11111111.11111111	172.24.255.255

Sidebar 2. How many subnets are there?

Answer: 32

Sidebar 3. How many host addresses are available per subnet?

Answer: $2^{(16-5)} - 2 = 2^{11} - 2 = 2,048 - 2 = \underline{2,046}$

Sidebar 4a. What patterns can you see in the list of subnets?

Some Answers:

    a. Broadcast addresses increment by 32 in the last octet.

    b. In the broadcast addresses, the same cycle of eight values in the final byte are repeated four times.

      c. The subnet number's fourth octet is a multiple of 32.

      d. In the subnet numbers, the same cycle of eight values in the final byte are repeated four times.

Sidebar 4b. Did you expect any of them?

    Answer: The dependence on the number 32 is due to the fact that 5 bits are part of the host field, and $2^5 = 32$.

                  The reason the addresses are clumped in four related groups of eight is that the third byte ends with the first 2 bits ($2^2 = 4$) of the subnet number, and the last byte begins with the last 3 bits ($2^3 = 8$) of the subnet number.

Sidebar 4c. Why?

                  The separation of the subnet bits across an octet boundary clearly leads to four groups of eight, and the remaining 5 bits of host address lead to the prominence of 32. What other patterns, if any, did you see?

                  Can you derive any general rules for how many hosts per subnet, given the number of original host bits (h) and the number of subnet bits (s)? The answer is $[2^{(h-s)} - 2]$.

ENDNOTES

1. Today, Internet customers get addresses from their Internet Service Provider. The ISP gets addresses from either its "upstream" provider, or the regional "Internet Registries," such as RIPE in Europe, or APNIC in the Asia/Pacific-rim region.

2. A multihomed machine has multiple interfaces, each attached to a different LAN. Single-homed machines are the norm, with only one interface, connected to only one LAN.

3. Of course, there are very few Class A addresses available, so few organizations are put in this enviable situation.

4. R_2 should decrement the packet's TTL, to protect against routing loops.

5. Implicit subnetting was also proposed, and will be discussed later in this chapter.

6. Technically, the minimum number of subnet bits is two (2), if we are considering only classical subnetting. Later in Part I, we will see how to make a 1-bit-wide subnet-number field. Rather than contradict myself, I'll be consistent and say, in both places, that subnet-number fields may be as short as one bit long.

7. The value of 'h' may equal either 24, 16, or 8, in the cases of Class A, B, or C network numbers, respectively.

8. Generally, there is only one place from which an organization's network number is advertised to the Internet. It is possible that a subnet of the organization's network may be independently advertised to the Internet to optimize packet delivery from the Internet to that subnet. Think of this as a side door to a house, perhaps a service entrance. The main entrance handles most of the ingress traffic, but certain kinds of deliveries are made to the side door.

9. This is actually a "private" address, per RFC-1918. In real life, this number may be an actual network number that is so-called "globally routable."

10. A route is said to have "flapped" when a router sees it go down and then come up again.

CHAPTER 4

Generalized Subnetting

INTRODUCTION TO VARIABLE LENGTH SUBNET MASKS (VLSM) AND SUPERNETTING

In order to make more efficient use of any slice of address space, it is often useful to create subnets that are "just the right size" instead of trying to create a "one-size-fits-all" subnet mask. There are routing implications of variable-length subnetting, in that routers must be explicitly informed—usually when a route is advertised—what the route's associated mask is. Older routing protocols such as RIP version 1 and Cisco's Interior Gateway Routing Protocol (IGRP) can only handle classful routes or fixed-length subnets of a route if they have an interface in that prefix.

The term "classful route" means a classfully interpreted route; in other words, if a route to a network number starting with 1–126 is received, it is a class A and thus must be using a mask length of 8 bits (255.0.0.0). (Remember that when the decimal number 255 is expressed in binary, it reads 11111111, which is eight 1-bits). If a route is received whose initial byte falls in the range of 128–191, it must be a class B, having a mask length of 16 bits (255.255.0.0); finally, a route in the range of 192–223 implies a class C network number, with an expected mask length of 24 bits (255.255.255.0).[1]

Classful interpretation of routes implies and requires a degree of guesswork. The mask is not explicitly advertised or known, but is implicitly inferred by examining the first byte of the address. Guessing is not optimal—it would be far better to *know* the correct mask for each route than to guess it. The opposite of classful is classless. Classless routing does advertise a mask along with each route. Therefore, each route's mask is explicitly known and need not be guessed.

If there is a desire to use subnets of differing sizes, or variable-sized subnets within a network number, implemented via variable-length subnet masks, there is an absolute requirement that all routers have a precise understanding of the proper mask that is associated with each route. Thus, there is an implication for the operation of the network: *VLSM addressing cannot be used unless classless routing protocol(s) are also used.* Note that static routing may be considered an instance of classless routing, since a mask may be specified when adding each static route.

VLSM

In 1987, RFC-1009 (later made obsolete by RFC-1812 in 1995) specified how a subdivided network could use more than one subnet mask. When an IP network is subdivided into unequal pieces, each having its own unique subnet mask, it is considered to be a network with "variable-length subnet masks" since the extended-network-prefixes have different lengths. VLSM is useful when the constituent parts of a network number are of different sizes. VLSM allows the size of the subnets to reflect the number of required host addresses in each subdivision.

RIPv1: Fixed-Length (Classful) Subnet Masking

When using RIPv1 (RFC-1058), all subnet masks must be uniform within an entire network-prefix. RIPv1 imposes this restriction because it does not carry subnet mask information as part of its routing table update messages. In the absence of this information, RIPv1 is forced to make some very simple assumptions about what mask values should be applied to the routes it learns.

Processing Received Route Updates

How does a RIPv1 based router know what mask to apply to a new route that it learns from a neighbor? If the router has a subnet of the same network number assigned to one of its other local interfaces, it assumes that the learned subnetwork was defined using the same mask as the locally configured interface. However, if the

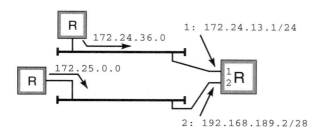

FIGURE 4.1   RIPv1 router operating classfully.

router does not have a subnet of the learned network number assigned to a local interface, the router applies the route's natural classful mask.

As diagrammed in Figure 4.1, interfaces 1 and 2 of a router have been assigned the IP addresses 172.24.13.1/24 and 192.168.189.2/28, respectively. If this router hears a routing update referencing the value "172.24.36.0," it applies a /24 mask since its interface 1 is a) also part of the same classfully-interpreted network number (172.24.0.0) and, b) its only interface in that network is configured with the /24 subnet mask.

Now, continue to assume that interface 1 of a router has been assigned the IP address 172.24.13.1/24 and that interface 2 has been assigned the IP address 192.168.189.2/24. Also, assume that the router has learned about network 172.24.36.0 from a neighbor, in this case the one on the upper left. Since interface 1 is configured with another subnet of the 172.24.0.0 network (namely subnet 13), the router assumes that the advertised route 172.24.36.0 also has a /24 subnet mask.

How will the router interpret an advertisement of the value "172.25.0.0" from the lower neighbor? The router has no other information to base a mask-length decision on (i.e., it has no interface in that network), so it is forced to assign a "natural" /16 mask to this route. This decision is independent of the interface on which the "172.25.0.0" route advertisement was heard. Any advertisement of any network number that is neither 192.168.189.0 nor 172.24.0.0 must be interpreted classfully, because there is no other infomation that the router can use to decide what the "correct" mask is.

Transmitting Route Updates

How does a RIPv1-based router decide whether it should fill in the subnet-number bits in an outgoing routing update? Stated another way, if the router knows about a certain set of active subnets of a network number, how does it decide which routes to transmit on which of its interfaces? Which interfaces should transmit all the detailed routes? Let us assume that the router knows of five other subnets of 172.24.0.0, namely: 172.24.3.0/24, 172.24.8.0/24, 172.24.10.0/24, 172.24.11.0/24, and 172.24.98.0/24.

Some neighboring routers don't need to know about all of those subnets, and it would be wasteful to send five routes when sending a single route for 172.24.0.0 would be sufficient. The requirement is that if the neighbor is inside the same network prefix (in this case 172.24.0.0), it should get the detailed routing update, but an exterior neighbor should not. A router executing RIPv1 will only transmit an update with a nonzero subnet field value via an interface if that interface is attached to a subnet of the same network number.

So, should a router advertise 172.24.98.0 or 172.24.0.0 on an interface? In this example, the subnet bits would not be filled in for routing updates referencing 172.24.0.0's subnets within routing updates to be transmitted onto interface 2, since that is part of a different network number. No matter how many subnets are active within 172.24.0.0, only one update needs to be sent onto interface 2, just 172.24.0.0.

Similarly, if the router had learned of a route to 192.168.189.80 on interface 2 (which must also be a /28 route since interface 2's mask is /28), it may advertise 192.168.189.80 back onto interface 2. However, the router would only transmit a routing update referencing 192.168.189.0 onto interface 1, since interface 1 lies within a different network number. It does this even though it knows of at least one subnet within 192.168.189.0, because it knows that the routers inside of 172.24.0.0 only need to be told that they can reach that entire class C via this router. Even if the router were to advertise 192.168.189.80 onto interface 1, any routers there would not pay attention to the bits beyond the classful /24 boundary, and would treat such an advertisement as a route to 192.168.189.0. However, there exists the possibility that multiple subnets could be advertised, even though only one route (to the whole network number) would suffice.

These methods allow RIPv1 to support subnetting, with the restriction that there be only a single subnet mask used within each network number. However, there are several advantages to be gained if more than one subnet mask can be assigned within a given IP network number:

• Variable-sized subnet masks permit more efficient use of an organization's assigned IP address space.

• RIPv1 can be eliminated as a routing protocol within the organization. Despite the fact that RIPv1 can support the most basic form of subnetting, it is not a very sophisticated routing protocol. Modern routing protocols, in addition to being classless, are also capable of handling more complex topologies, with loops. RIP is well suited to tree topologies, and does not necessarily work well in the presence of loops.

- Multiple subnet masks permit route aggregation which can significantly reduce the amount of routing information at the "backbone" level within an organization's routing domain.

Efficient Use of the Organization's Assigned IP Address Space

VLSM supports more efficient use of an organization's assigned IP address space. One of the major problems with the earlier limitation of supporting only a single subnet mask across a given network-prefix is that once the mask has been selected, it locks the organization into a fixed-number of fixed-sized subnets. For example, assume that a network administrator decided to configure the 172.21.0.0/16 network with a /22 extended-network-prefix, as drawn in Figure 4.2.

A /16 network with a /22 extended-network-prefix permits 64 subnets (2^6), each of which supports a maximum of 1,022 hosts ($2^{10} - 2$). This is fine if the organization wants to deploy a number of large subnets, but what about the occasional small subnet containing only 20 or 30 hosts? Since a classfully-subnetted network can have only a single mask, the network administrator must place the 20 or 30 hosts into their own unique /22 subnet. This assignment would waste approximately 1,000 host addresses for each such small subnet deployed! Restricting a network number to a single mask did not encourage—or allow!—the flexible and efficient use of an organization's address space.

One solution to this problem was to allow a subnetted network to be assigned more than one subnet mask. Assume that in the previous example the network administrator is also allowed to configure the 172.21.0.0/16 network with a /26 extended-network-prefix. Figure 4.3 illustrates how a /16 network address with a /26 extended-network-prefix permits 1024 subnets (2^{10}), each of which supports a maxi-

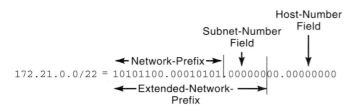

FIGURE 4.2 172.21.0.0/16 with a /22 extended-network-prefix.

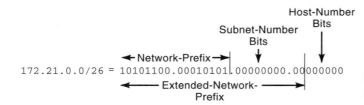

FIGURE 4.3   172.21.0.0/16 with a /26 extended-network-prefix.

mum of 62 hosts ($2^6 - 2$). The /26 prefix would be better for smaller subnets with less than 60 hosts, while the /22 prefix is well suited for larger subnets containing up to 1000 hosts.

The best solution is for network managers to be able to use smaller subnets (longer masks) where there are fewer endstations, and larger subnets (shorter masks) where there are more endstations.

ROUTE AGGREGATION

Probably the most useful application of VLSM is that it also allows the recursive division of an organization's address space in such a way that it can be reassembled and aggregated to reduce the amount of routing information at each level of the logical routing hierarchy.

Conceptually, a network is first divided into subnets, some of the subnets are further divided into sub-subnets, and some of the sub-subnets are divided into sub-sub-subnets, and so on. This allows the detailed structure of routing information for one subnet group to be hidden from routers in another subnet group.

In Figure 4.4, the 10.0.0.0/8 network is first configured with a /16 extended-network-prefix. This allows 256 (2^8) first-level subnets. Then, the 10.1.0.0/16 subnet is configured with a /17 extended-network-prefix, thereby dividing it into two (2^1) second-level subnets. The first half of that block (10.1.0.0/17) is subnetted with a /24 mask, yielding 128 third-level subnets. The second half (10.1.128.0/17) is broken into eight (2^3) /20 third-level subnets. Another of the initial first-level subnets, the 10.254.0.0/16 subnet, has been configured with a /18 extended-network-prefix, yielding four (2^2) second-level subnets. Figure 4.5 illustrates a possible logical router topology that reflects this hierarchical addressing structure.

Figure 4.5 illustrates one possible mapping of the addressing plan of Figure 4.4 into a router topology, but this figure focuses on only the 10.1.0.0/16 portion of the addressing plan. Observe that just because a level of subnetting supports some number of subnets does not mean that all of them must be used. The size of the subnets

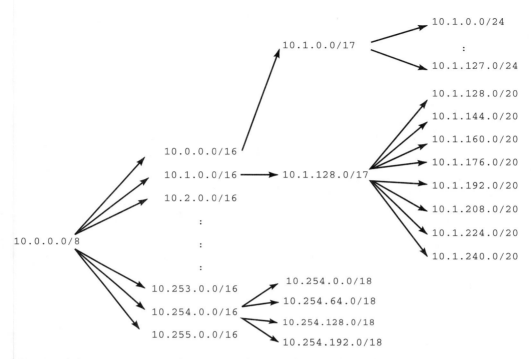

FIGURE 4.4   VLSM permits the recursive division of a network-prefix.

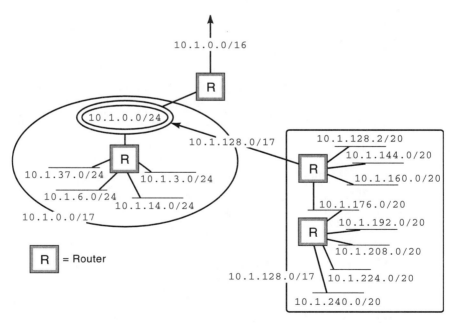

FIGURE 4.5   10.1.0.0/16 logical topology.

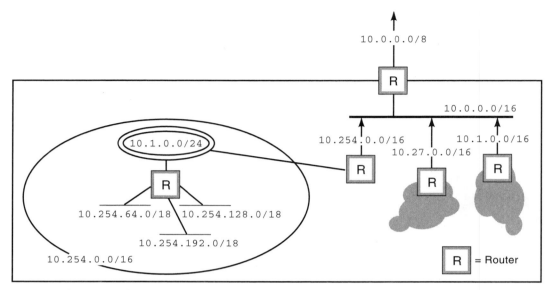

FIGURE 4.6   10.254.0.0/16 logical topology.

at a given level is driven by how many endstations (or lower-level subnets) they need to contain. Just because a level has up to 128 subnets does not mean that they all must be used. However, a network manager should try to pack them in tightly enough so that there is not too much waste, yet also reserve room for growth.

Figure 4.6 illustrates one possible mapping of the 10.254.0.0/16 slice into a logical router topology. As may be seen in Figure 4.6, there is ultimately at least one "border router" that advertises a route to the entire 10.0.0.0/8 network into the worldwide Internet. (Of course, in real life, network 10 is not available for use as a network number, since it has been reserved for private use by RFC-1918. All of the examples in this chapter use private Class A, B, or C addresses to avoid accidentally referring to some actual organization's network number. For the record, the RFC-1918 private address blocks are 10.0.0.0/8, 172.16.0.0/12, and 192.168.0.0/16.)

Observe that the recursive address assignment process does not require that the same extended-network-prefix length be used at each level of the recursion. This recursive subdivision of an organization's address space can be carried out as deep as a network administrator needs to take it, within the boundaries of their assigned address space.

VLSM DESIGN CONSIDERATIONS

When developing a VLSM design, the network designer must recursively ask the same set of questions as for a traditional subnet design. The same set of design decisions must be made at each level of the hierarchy:

1. How many total subnets does this level need today?
   a) How many total subnets will this level need in the future?
2. How many hosts are there on this level's largest subnet today?
   a) How many hosts will there be on this level's largest subnet be in the future?

At each level, the design team must make sure that they have enough extra bits to support the required number of subentities in the next and further levels of recursion. Keeping one bit of "safety margin" is desirable if a sufficient number of subnet and host bits are available.

Assume that a network is spread out over a number of sites. For example, if an organization has three campuses today it probably needs 3 bits of subnetting ($2^3 = 8$) to allow the addition of more campuses in the future. Now, within each campus, there is likely to be a secondary level of subnetting to identify each building. Finally, within each building, a third level of subnetting might identify each of the individual workgroups, or perhaps there might be subnet per floor (or per set of floors).

Following this hierarchical model, the number of subnets needed at the top level is determined by the number of campuses, the mid-level is based on the number of buildings at each site, and the lowest level is determined by the "maximum number of subnets/maximum number of users per subnet" in each building. What this last constraint means is that there must be enough bits left over so that the lowest-level subnets are plentiful enough, and that the number of host-number field bits is sufficient to accomodate both the largest number of buildings on a campus, as well as the largest subnet among all the buildings. Remember that all the subnets in the lowest level need not be the same size, but there must be enough remaining bits for all the combined subnets to be addressed with a common prefix.

EXAMPLE OF HIERARCHICAL ADDRESSING

The deployment of a hierarchical subnetting scheme requires careful planning. It is essential that the network designers recursively work their way down through their addressing plan until they get to the bottom level. At the bottom level, they must make sure that the leaf subnets are large enough to support the required number of hosts. When the addressing plan is deployed, the addresses from each site will be aggregatable, into a single address block to keep the backbone routing tables from becoming too large.

Requirements for the Deployment of VLSM

The successful deployment of VLSM has three prerequisites:

1. The routing protocols must carry extended-network-prefix information with each route advertisement. Modern routing protocols, such as OSPF, RIPv2,[2] I-IS-IS, and Cisco's E-IGRP, all enable the deployment of VLSM by providing the extended-network-prefix length or mask value along with each route advertisement. These routing protocols are "classless." If the routing protocols did not carry prefix information, a router would have to either assume that the locally configured prefix length should be applied, or perform a look-up in a statically configured prefix table that contains all of the required masking information. The first alternative cannot guarantee that the correct prefix is applied, and static tables do not scale since they are difficult to maintain and prone to human error.

    The bottom line is that if your topology requires VLSM, and you want to use your assigned address space efficiently, you *must* select OSPF, RIPv2, or I-IS-IS as the Interior Gateway Protocol (IGP) rather than RIPv1!

2. All routers must implement a consistent forwarding algorithm based on the "longest match." The deployment of VLSM means that the set of networks associated with extended-network-prefixes will exhibit a "subset" relationship. A route with a longer extended-network-prefix describes a smaller set of IP destination addresses than a route with a shorter extended-network-prefix. As a result, a route with a longer extended-network-prefix is said to be "more specific," while a route with a shorter extended-network-prefix is said to be "less specific." When forwarding a packet to a destination, routers must always use the best available route. The best route is the one with the longest matching extended-network-prefix (i.e., the most specific route).

    For example, if a packet's destination IP address is 10.1.2.5 and there are three network prefixes in the routing table (10.1.2.0/24, 10.1.0.0/16, and 10.0.0.0/8), the router would select the route to 10.1.2.0/24. The

10.1.2.0/24 route is selected because its prefix has the greatest number of bits matching the packet's Destination Address, as shown in Figure 4.7.

3. For route aggregation to occur, addresses must be assigned so that they have topological significance. Since OSPF, RIPv2, and I-IS-IS all convey the extended-network-prefix information with each route, the VLSM subnets can be scattered throughout an organization's topology. However, to support hierarchical routing and reduce the size of an organization's routing tables, addresses should be assigned so that they are topologically significant.

In plain English, this means that subnet clusters should share the same set of most-significant bits. This results in a cluster of subnets that is visible externally as just one route with a shorter mask (just the most-significant bits). If subnet addresses were scattered with no regard to the nearby subnet numbers, then there would be little or no chance of aggregating the addresses of nearby subnets, since they will be unrelated to each other (unmatched leading bits). These two contrasting situations are displayed in Figure 4.8.

Hierarchical routing requires that addresses be assigned to reflect the actual network topology. This reduces the amount of routing information by taking the set of addresses assigned to a particular region of the topology and aggregating them into a single routing advertisement for the entire set. The backbone need not know that there are subnets inside a region, only that all addresses within the aggregate are reachable via the same router(s).

Hierarchical routing may be done recursively at various points within the topology. If addresses do not have topological significance, aggregation cannot be performed and all the routers will need to know store routes to *every* subnet in their routing tables. The size of the routing tables will be maximal for a given topology. Remember this point when we discuss Classless Interdomain Routing (CIDR) aggregation in Chapter 5.

```
  Destination  10.1.2.5     =  00001010.00000001.00000010.00000101
    Route #1   10.1.0.0/24  =  00001010.00000001.00000000.00000000
>   Route #2   10.1.2.0/24  =  00001010.00000001.00000010.00000000
    Route #3   10.1.0.0/16  =  00001010.00000001.00000000.00000000
```

FIGURE 4.7 The best route has the longest matching prefix (most specific).

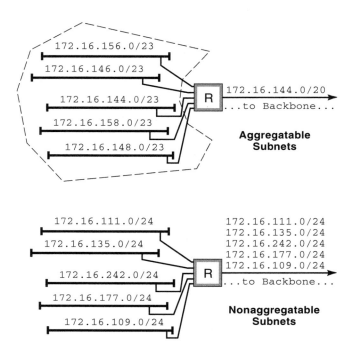

FIGURE 4.8   Aggregatable versus nonaggregatable subnet addresses.

VLSM EXAMPLE

GIVEN:

An organization has decided to use the private network prefix 192.168.0.0/16, and it plans to deploy VLSM. Figure 4.9 illustrates the organization's VLSM design.

The first step of the subnetting process divides the base network address into 16 equal-sized address blocks. Then Subnet #1_4 is divided it into 32 equal-sized address blocks and Subnet #14_4 is divided into 16 equal-sized address blocks. Finally, Subnet #14_4-14_4 is divided into 8 equal-sized address blocks.

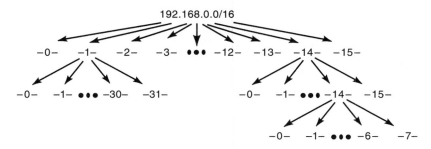

FIGURE 4.9 Address allocation for VLSM example.

Create 16 Subnets of 192.168.0.0/16

The first step in the subnetting process divides the base network address into 16 equal-size address blocks, which are highlighted in Figure 4.10.

Since $16 = 2^4$, 4 bits are required to uniquely identify each of the 16 subnets. This means that to define 16 subnets of 192.168.0.0/16, the organization needs 4 additional bits beyond the initial /16 prefix, or a /20 extended network prefix. Each of these subnets represents a contiguous block of 2^{12} (or 4,096) network addresses.

The 16 subnets of the 192.168.0.0/16 address block are given below. The subnets are numbered 0 through 15. The underlined portion of each address identifies the extended-network-prefix, while the **bold** digits identify the 4 bits representing the subnet-number field:

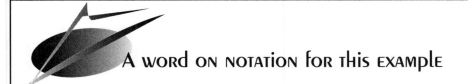

A word on notation for this example

When traversing a hierarchical addressing plan, it helps to know not only the value of the subnet field at a given level, but also how many bits are available at that level. So subnet #14_4 represents subnet 14 out of a 4-bit field. Furthermore, subnet #14_4-14_4 is subnet 14 out of a 4-bit field, under subnet 14 out of another 4-bit field.

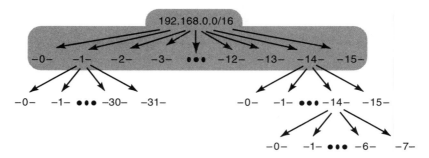

FIGURE 4.10 Define 16 subnets for 192.168.0.0/16.

```
Base Prefix:   11000000.10101000.00000000.00000000 = 192.168.0.0/16

Subnet #0:     11000000.10101000.00000000.00000000 = 192.168.0.0/20
Subnet #1:     11000000.10101000.00010000.00000000 = 192.168.16.0/20
Subnet #2:     11000000.10101000.00100000.00000000 = 192.168.32.0/20
Subnet #3:     11000000.10101000.00110000.00000000 = 192.168.48.0/20
Subnet #4:     11000000.10101000.01000000.00000000 = 192.168.64.0/20
               :
               :
Subnet #13:    11000000.10101000.11010000.00000000 = 192.168.208.0/20
Subnet #14:    11000000.10101000.11100000.00000000 = 192.168.224.0/20
Subnet #15:    11000000.10101000.11110000.00000000 = 192.168.240.0/20
```

DETERMINE THE HOST ADDRESSES FOR SUBNET #3_4 (192.168.48.0/20)

Let's examine the host addresses that are represented by Subnet #3_4 (192.168.48.0/20), which is the shaded subnet in Figure 4.11.

Since the host-number field of Subnet #3_4 contains 12 bits (12 bits remain if a 32-bit IP address includes a 20-bit extended-network-prefix). A 12-bit host-number field contains 4,094 valid host addresses ($2^{12} - 2$). The hosts are numbered 1 through 4,094 (0 and 4095 are the all-0s and all-1s host addresses, respectively, and are not available for assignment).

The valid host addresses for Subnet #3_4 are given below. The underlined portion of each address identifies the extended-network-prefix, while the **bold** digits identify the 12-bit host-number field:

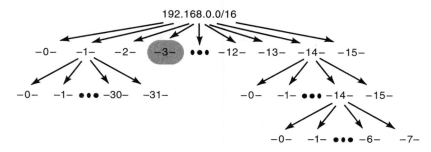

FIGURE 4.11 Define the host addresses for Subnet #3$_4$ (192.168.48.0/20).

```
Subnet #3:  11000000.10101000.00110000.00000000 = 192.168.48.0/20

Host #1:    11000000.10101000.00110000.00000001 = 192.168.48.1
Host #2:    11000000.10101000.00110000.00000010 = 192.168.48.2
Host #3:    11000000.10101000.00110000.00000011 = 192.168.48.3
            :
            :
Host #4093:11000000.10101000.00111111.11111101 = 192.168.63.253
Host #4094:11000000.10101000.00111111.11111110 = 192.168.63.254
```

The broadcast address for Subnet #3$_4$ is found by setting the host-number field to the all-1s value, like so:

```
Broadcast:  11000000.10101000.00111111.11111111 = 192.168.63.255
```

Once again, note that the broadcast address for Subnet #3$_4$ is exactly one less than the base address for Subnet #4$_4$ (192.168.64.0).

Determine 16 Sub-Subnets for Subnet #14$_4$ (192.168.224.0/20)

After the base network address has been divided into 16 subnets, subnet #14$_4$ is further subdivided into 16 equal-sized address blocks, as indicated in Figure 4.12.

Since 16 = 2^4, 4 more bits are required to identify each of these 16 subnets. This means that the extended-network-prefix length for these subnets is 16 + 4 + 4, or /24.

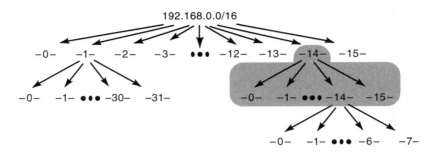

FIGURE 4.12   Define 16 sub-subnets for subnet #14$_4$ (192.168.224.0/20).

The 16 subnets of the 192.168.224.0/20 address block are given below, numbered 0 through 15. The underlined portion of each sub-subnet address identifies the extended-network-prefix, while the **bold** digits identify the 4 bits representing the sub-subnet-number field:

```
Subnet #14:      11000000.10101000.1110 0000.00000000 = 192.168.224.0/20

Subnet #14-0:    11000000.10101000.1110 0000.00000000 = 192.168.224.0/24
Subnet #14-1:    11000000.10101000.1110 0001.00000000 = 192.168.225.0/24
Subnet #14-2:    11000000.10101000.1110 0010.00000000 = 192.168.226.0/24
Subnet #14-3:    11000000.10101000.1110 0011.00000000 = 192.168.227.0/24
Subnet #14-4:    11000000.10101000.1110 0100.00000000 = 192.168.228.0/24
          :
          :
Subnet #14-14:   11000000.10101000.1110 1110.00000000 = 192.168.238.0/24
Subnet #14-15:   11000000.10101000.1110 1111.00000000 = 192.168.239.0/24
```

DETERMINE HOST ADDRESSES FOR SUBNET #14$_4$-3$_4$ (192.168.227.0/24)

Let us now examine the host addresses that can be assigned to subnet #14$_4$-3$_4$ (192.168.227.0/24), which is shaded Figure 4.13. (Note that we could also represent subnet #14$_4$-3$_4$ as subnet #227$_8$.)

Each of the subnets of Subnet #14$_4$-3$_4$ has 8 bits in the host-number field. This means that each subnet represents a block of 254 valid host addresses ($2^8 - 2$). The hosts are numbered 1 through 254.

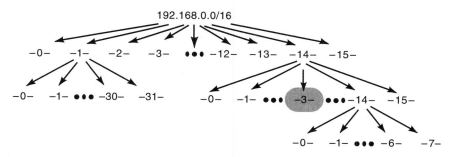

FIGURE 4.13 Define the host addresses for subnet #14_4-3_4 (192.168.227.0/24).

The host addresses for Subnet #14_4-3_4 are listed below. The underlined portion of each address identifies the extended-network-prefix, while the **bold** digits identify the 8-bit host-number field:

```
Subnet #14-3: 11000000.10101000.11100011.00000000 = 192.168.227.0/24

Host #1      11000000.10101000.11100011.00000001 = 192.168.227.1
Host #2      11000000.10101000.11100011.00000010 = 192.168.227.2
Host #3      11000000.10101000.11100011.00000011 = 192.168.227.3
Host #4      11000000.10101000.11100011.00000100 = 192.168.227.4
Host #5      11000000.10101000.11100011.00000101 = 192.168.227.5
                :
                :
Host #253    11000000.10101000.11100011.11111101 = 192.168.227.253
Host #254    11000000.10101000.11100011.11111110 = 192.168.227.254
```

The broadcast address for Subnet #14_4-3_4 is determined by setting all the bits in the host-number field to 1, which is:

```
Broadcast: 11000000.10101000.11100011.11111111 = 192.168.227.255
```

The broadcast address for Subnet #14_4-3_4 is exactly one less than the base address for Subnet #14_4-4_4 (192.168.228.0).

Determine Eight Sub²-Subnets for Subnet #14₄-14₄ (192.168.238.0/24)

After Subnet #14₄ was divided into 16 subnets, subnet #14₄-14₄ was further subdivided into eight equal-sized address blocks, as highlighted in Figure 4.14.

Since $8 = 2^3$, 3 more bits are required to identify each of these eight subnets. This means that the extended-network-prefix length for this level of subnetting will be /27.

The eight subnets of the 192.168.238.0/24 address block are given below, numbered 0 through 7. The underlined portion of each sub²-subnet address identifies the extended-network-prefix, while the **bold** digits identify the 3 bits representing the sub²-subnet-number field:

```
Subnet #14-14:     11000000.10101000.11101110.00000000 = 192.168.238.0/24

Subnet#14-14-0:    11000000.10101000.11101110.00000000 = 192.168.238.0/27
Subnet#14-14-1:    11000000.10101000.11101110.00100000 = 192.168.238.32/27
Subnet#14-14-2:    11000000.10101000.11101110.01000000 = 192.168.238.64/27
Subnet#14-14-3:    11000000.10101000.11101110.01100000 = 192.168.238.96/27
Subnet#14-14-4:    11000000.10101000.11101110.10000000 = 192.168.238.128/27
Subnet#14-14-5:    11000000.10101000.11101110.10100000 = 192.168.238.160/27
Subnet#14-14-6:    11000000.10101000.11101110.11000000 = 192.168.238.192/27
Subnet#14-14-7:    11000000.10101000.11101110.11100000 = 192.168.238.224/27
```

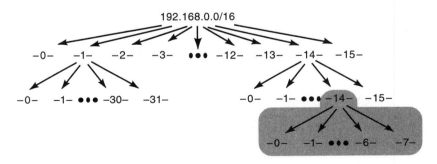

FIGURE 4.14 Define the sub²-subnets for subnet #14₄-14₄ (192.168.238.0/24).

Determine Host Addresses for Subnet #14_4-14_4-2_3 (192.168.238.64/27)

Let's examine the host addresses that can be assigned to Subnet #14_4-14_4-2_3 (192.168.238.64/27), which is shaded in Figure 4.15.

Each of the subnets of Subnet #14_4-14_4-2_3 has 5 bits in the host-number field. This means that each subnet contains 30 valid host addresses ($2^5 - 2$). The valid host addresses for Subnet #14_4-14_4-2_3 are given below. The underlined portion of each address identifies the extended-network-prefix, while the **bold** digits identify the 5-bit host-number field:

```
Subnet#14-14-2:  11000000.10101000.11101110.01000000 = 192.168.238.64/27

    Host #1      11000000.10101000.11101110.01000001 = 192.168.238.65
    Host #2      11000000.10101000.11101110.01000010 = 192.168.238.66
    Host #3      11000000.10101000.11101110.01000011 = 192.168.238.67
    Host #4      11000000.10101000.11101110.01000100 = 192.168.238.68
    Host #5      11000000.10101000.11101110.01000101 = 192.168.238.69
      :
      :
    Host #29     11000000.10101000.11101110.01011101 = 192.168.238.93
    Host #30     11000000.10101000.11101110.01011110 = 192.168.238.94
```

The broadcast address for Subnet #14-14-2 is the all-1s host address, namely:

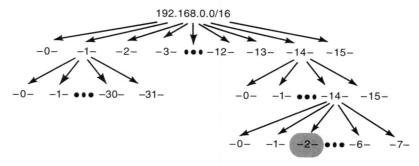

FIGURE 4.15   Define the host addresses for subnet #14_4-14_4-2_3 (192.168.238.64/27).

```
Broadcast 11000000.10101000.11011100.01011111 = 192.168.238.95
```

As usual, the broadcast address for Subnet #14_4-14_4-2_3 is exactly one less than the base address for Subnet #14_4-14_4-3_3 (192.168.238.96).

VLSM EXERCISE

Given:

An organization has been decided to use the network prefix 192.168.0.0/16 and it plans to deploy VLSM, as illustrated in Figure 4.16.

To arrive at this design, the first step of the subnetting process divided the base network address into eight equal-sized address blocks. Then Subnet #1_3 was divided into 32 equal-sized address blocks, while Subnet #6_3 was divided into 16 equal-sized address blocks. Finally, Subnet #6_3-14_4 was further subdivided into eight equal-sized address blocks.

1. Divide 192.168.0.0/16 into eight subnets:

   #0_3 _____

   #1_3 _____

   #2_3 _____

   #3_3 _____

   #4_3 _____

   #5_3 _____

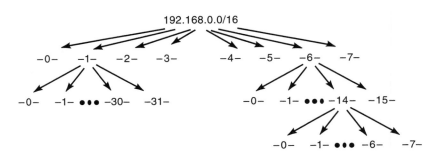

FIGURE 4.16   Address template for VLSM example.

$\#6_3$ _____

$\#7_3$ _____

2. List the host addresses that can be assigned to Subnet $\#3_3$ (192.168.96.0/19), assuming that it is not subnetted further:

_____

_____

_____

_____

_____

_____

_____

3. Calculate the broadcast address for Subnet $\#3_3$ (192.168.96.0):

_____

4. Subdivide Subnet $\#6_3$ (192.168.192.0/19) into 16 sub-subnetworks:

$\#6_3\text{-}0_4$ _____

$\#6_3\text{-}1_4$ _____

$\#6_3\text{-}2_4$ _____

$\#6_3\text{-}3_4$ _____

$\#6_3\text{-}4_4$ _____

$\#6_3\text{-}5_4$ _____

A WORD ON NOTATION

Any given subnet represents, strictly speaking, *exactly* a two-level hierarchy, {Extended-Network-Prefix} + {Host}. However, we are free to create any substructure that suits a network topology, e.g., {Network-Prefix + Subnet + sub-Subnet} + {Host}, as long as there are enough bits for all the desired layers of subnetting. Each subnet must have sufficient bits in its host-number field so that there are adequate quantities of host addresses, for today and allowing for future growth.

$\#6_3\text{-}6_4$ _____

$\#6_3\text{-}7_4$ _____

$\#6_3\text{-}8_4$ _____

$\#6_3\text{-}9_4$ _____

$\#6_3\text{-}10_4$ _____

$\#6_3\text{-}11_4$ _____

$\#6_3\text{-}12_4$ _____

$\#6_3\text{-}13_4$ _____

$\#6_3\text{-}14_4$ _____

$\#6_3\text{-}15_4$ _____

5. List the host addresses that can be assigned to Subnet $\#6_3\text{-}3_4$ (192.168.198.0/23):

_____

_____

_____

_____

_____

_____

6. Calculate the broadcast address for Subnet $\#6_3\text{-}3_4$ (192.168.198.0/23):

_____

7. Divide Subnet $\#6_3\text{-}14_4$ (192.168.220.0/23) into eight subnets:

_____

$\#6_3\text{-}14_4\text{-}1_3$ _____

$\#6_3\text{-}14_4\text{-}2_3$ _____

$\#6_3\text{-}14_4\text{-}3_3$ _____

$\#6_3\text{-}14_4\text{-}4_3$ _____

$\#6_3\text{-}14_4\text{-}5_3$ _____

$\#6_3\text{-}14_4\text{-}6_3$ _____

$\#6_3\text{-}14_4\text{-}7_3$ _____

8. List the host addresses that can be assigned to Subnet $\#6_3\text{-}14_4\text{-}2_3$ (192.168.220.128/26):

_____

_____

_____

_____

_____

_____

9. Calculate   the   broadcast   address   for   Subnet $\#6_3$-14_4-2_3
(192.168.220.128/26):

_____

Solution for VLSM Exercise

1. Divide 192.168.0.0/16 into eight subnets:

```
Base Prefix:   11000000.10101000.00000000.00000000 = 192.168.0.0/16

Subnet #0₃:    11000000.10101000.00000000.00000000 = 192.168.0.0/19
Subnet #1₃:    11000000.10101000.00100000.00000000 = 192.168.32.0/19
Subnet #2₃:    11000000.10101000.01000000.00000000 = 192.168.64.0/19
Subnet #3₃:    11000000.10101000.01100000.00000000 = 192.168.96.0/19
Subnet #4₃:    11000000.10101000.10000000.00000000 = 192.168.128.0/19
Subnet #5₃:    11000000.10101000.10100000.00000000 = 192.168.160.0/19
Subnet #6₃:    11000000.10101000.11000000.00000000 = 192.168.192.0/19
Subnet #7₃:    11000000.10101000.11100000.00000000 = 192.168.224.0/19
```

2. List the host addresses that can be assigned to Subnet $\#3_3$ (192.168.96.0/19), assuming that it is not subnetted further:

```
Subnet #3:     11000000.10101000.01100000.00000000 = 192.168.96.0/19

Host #1:       11000000.10101000.01100000.00000001 = 192.168.96.1
Host #2:       11000000.10101000.01100000.00000010 = 192.168.96.2
Host #3:       11000000.10101000.01100000.00000011 = 192.168.96.3
                   :
                   :
Host #8189:    11000000.10101000.01111111.11111101 = 192.168.127.253
Host #8190:    11000000.10101000.01111111.11111110 = 192.168.127.254
```

3. Calculate the broadcast address for Subnet $\#3_3$ (192.168.96.0):

```
Broadcast:  11000000.10101000.01111111.11111111 = 192.168.127.255
```

4. Subdivide Subnet $\#6_3$ (192.168.192.0/19) into 16 sub-subnetworks:

```
Subnet #6:     11000000.10101000.11000000.00000000 = 192.168.192.0/19

Subnet #6-0:   11000000.10101000.11000000.00000000 = 192.168.192.0/23
Subnet #6-1:   11000000.10101000.11000010.00000000 = 192.168.194.0/23
Subnet #6-2:   11000000.10101000.11000100.00000000 = 192.168.196.0/23
```

```
Subnet #6-3:   11000000.10101000.1100011 0.00000000 = 192.168.198.0/23
Subnet #6-4:   11000000.10101000.1100100 0.00000000 = 192.168.200.0/23
               :
               :
Subnet #6-14:  11000000.10101000.1101110 0.00000000 = 192.168.220.0/23
Subnet #6-15:  11000000.10101000.1101111 0.00000000 = 192.168.222.0/23
```

5. List the host addresses that can be assigned to Subnet $#6_3$-3_4 (192.168.198.0/23):

```
Subnet #6-3:  11000000.10101000.11000110.00000000 = 192.168.198.0/23

Host #1       11000000.10101000.11000110.00000001 = 192.168.198.1
Host #2       11000000.10101000.11000110.00000010 = 192.168.198.2
Host #3       11000000.10101000.11000110.00000011 = 192.168.198.3
Host #4       11000000.10101000.11000110.00000100 = 192.168.198.4
Host #5       11000000.10101000.11000110.00000101 = 192.168.198.5
              :
Host 254      11000000.10101000.11000110.11111110 = 192.168.198.254
Host 255      11000000.10101000.11000110.11111111 = 192.168.198.255
Host 256      11000000.10101000.11000111.00000000 = 192.168.199.0
              :
Host #509     11000000.10101000.11000111.11111101 = 192.168.199.253
Host #510     11000000.10101000.11000111.11111110 = 192.168.199.254
```

6. Calculate the broadcast address for Subnet $#6_3$-3_4 (192.168.198.0/23):

```
Broadcast:  11000000.10101000.11000111.11111111 = 192.168.199.255
```

7. Divide Subnet $#6_3$-14_4 (192.168.220.0/23) into eight subnets:

```
Subnet #6-14:    11000000.10101000.11011100.00000000 = 192.168.220.0/23

Subnet#6-14-0:   11000000.10101000.11011100.00000000 = 192.168.220.0/26
Subnet#6-14-1:   11000000.10101000.11011100.01000000 = 192.168.220.64/26
Subnet#6-14-2:   11000000.10101000.11011100.10000000 = 192.168.220.128/26
Subnet#6-14-3:   11000000.10101000.11011100.11000000 = 192.168.220.192/26
Subnet#6-14-4:   11000000.10101000.11011101.00000000 = 192.168.221.0/26
Subnet#6-14-5:   11000000.10101000.11011101.01000000 = 192.168.221.64/26
Subnet#6-14-6:   11000000.10101000.11011101.10000000 = 192.168.221.128/26
Subnet#6-14-7:   11000000.10101000.11011101.11000000 = 192.168.221.192/26
```

8. List the host addresses that can be assigned to Subnet $#6_3$-14_4-2_3 (192.168.220.128/26):

```
Subnet#6-14-2:   11000000.10101000.11011100.10000000 =
                 192.168.220.128/26

Host #1          11000000.10101000.11011100.10000001 = 192.168.220.129
Host #2          11000000.10101000.11011100.10000010 = 192.168.220.130
```

```
Host #3      11000000.10101000.11011100.10000011 = 192.168.220.131
Host #4      11000000.10101000.11011100.10000100 = 192.168.220.132
Host #5      11000000.10101000.11011100.10000101 = 192.168.220.133
                :
                :
Host #61     11000000.10101000.11011100.10111101 = 192.168.220.189
Host #62     11000000.10101000.11011100.10111110 = 192.168.220.190
```

9. Calculate the broadcast address for Subnet #6_3-14_4-2_3 (192.168.220.128/26):

```
Broadcast 11000000.10101000.11011100.10111111 = 192.168.220.191
```

MANIPULATION OF SUBNETS AND SUPERNETS

Before we continue into the next chapter we need to have a solid understanding of how to manipulate subnets and supernets. And what is a supernet, anyway? Hopefully, at the end of this section, that will be clearer. Please do not be scared off by the math here. It is only simple arithmetic, and as long as you can do simple addition, and multiply or divide by two, you should be able to grasp the concepts. With practice, you will be able to do most of this math in your head, thereby amazing your friends at parties.

In our examples relating to subnets we have already seen how masks must be "longer" in order to represent subnets, which are smaller than a parent network prefix, in terms of how many IP addresses are in the subnet versus the unsubnetted network number. For example, if the prefix 172.16.0.0/16 is subnetted, it may have a subnet that is 172.16.192.0/18. Since 18 is bigger than 16, we say that the subnet has a longer prefix. This works within any prefix; any further lengthening of the prefix will allow a smaller subnet to be identified (both will share the same leading bits, but the one with the longer mask represents fewer host addresses).

As an example, 172.16.192.0/18 may have a subnet that is 172.16.208.0/21, which shares the same first 18 bits, as seen in Figure 4.17. Both subnets share the same initial 16-bit prefix. This fact makes both of them subnets of the /16. The fact that 172.16.208.0/22 shares the same initial 18 bits with 172.16.192.0/18 makes 172.16.208.0/22 a subnet of 172.16.192.0/18.

Note that as a subnet is created within a network or another subnet, the leading bits of the previous level's address remain the same. The subnet mask's additional length covers additional bits that are now effectively part of the prefix. The mask bits only serve to indicate which parts of the address are part of the prefix. The significant address bits are found by a logical AND operation, which is like bitwise multiplica-

172.16.0.0/16
```
10101100.00010000.00000000.00000000 (Prefix)
11111111.11111111.00000000.00000000 (Mask)
```

172.16.192.0/18
```
10101100.00010000.11000000.00000000 (Prefix)
11111111.11111111.11000000.00000000 (Mask)
```

172.16.208.0/22
```
10101100.00010000.11010000.00000000 (Prefix)
11111111.11111111.11111100.00000000 (Mask)
```

FIGURE 4.17 Effect of lengthening a mask.

tion by the zeros and ones in the subnet mask. Figure 4.18 is the "truth table" for AND; note that table is also a multiplication table for the numbers 0 and 1.

Examining Figure 4.17, one sees that the prefix address bits are derived by multiplying, or "AND-ing," each mask bit with its corresponding IP address bit. In bit positions where the mask is zero, the result of the multiplication (i.e., logical AND) operation is zero, which eliminates the nonprefix bits (i.e., the host-number field).

Before we go further, it is worthwhile to provide a conversion chart between mask-length notation and traditional dotted-decimal subnet-mask notation (Figure 4.19). Once this chapter is complete, you should find the new mask-length notation so convenient that you will wonder how you ever managed before.

We will examine the patterns above (the patterns are the key to quickly doing subnet operations in one's head), but first a word about the /31 mask. The reason this is not usable is that there are only two allowed bit patterns in the host field, which is only one bit long if the prefix is 31 bits long. This single bit may take on the value of zero or one. Given that the all-0s and all-1s host-number patterns are reserved, and that the *only* patterns here are zero and one, there is simply no space for actual host addresses.

For comparison, we will examine a /30 mask and see how it allows room for two addresses. Suppose we have the prefix 192.168.47.196/30, which is illustrated in Figure 4.20. As is clear when we write out the binary representation of the subnet's host addresses, there are just two available addresses when we have a /30 mask.

	0	1
0	0	0
1	0	1

FIGURE 4.18 Truth table for logical AND.

```
 /0   0.0.0.0          used only with the default route (0.0.0.0)
 /1   128.0.0.0          128 Class As, or the entire Class A address space
 /2   192.0.0.0           64 Class As, or the entire Class B address space
 /3   224.0.0.0           32 Class As, or the entire Class C address space
 /4   240.0.0.0           16 Class As, or the entire Class D address space
 /5   248.0.0.0            8 Class As
 /6   252.0.0.0            4 Class As
 /7   254.0.0.0            2 Class As
 /8   255.0.0.0        Class A          (or 256 Class Bs, or 65,536 Class Cs)
 /9   255.128.0.0        1/2 Class A, or 128 Class Bs, or 32,768 Class Cs)
/10   255.192.0.0        1/4 Class A, or  64 Class Bs, or 16,384 Class Cs)
/11   255.224.0.0        1/8 Class A, or  32 Class Bs, or  8,192 Class Cs)
/12   255.240.0.0       1/16 Class A, or  16 Class Bs, or  4,096 Class Cs)
/13   255.248.0.0       1/32 Class A, or   8 Class Bs, or  2,048 Class Cs)
/14   255.252.0.0       1/64 Class A, or   4 Class Bs, or  1,024 Class Cs)
/15   255.254.0.0      1/128 Class A, or   2 Class Bs, or    512 Class Cs)
/16   255.255.0.0      Class B                       (or    256 Class Cs)
/17   255.255.128.0                     1/2 Class B, or    128 Class Cs)
/18   255.255.192.0                     1/4 Class B, or     64 Class Cs)
/19   255.255.224.0                     1/8 Class B, or     32 Class Cs)
/20   255.255.240.0                    1/16 Class B, or     16 Class Cs)
/21   255.255.248.0                    1/32 Class B, or      8 Class Cs)
/22   255.255.252.0                    1/64 Class B, or      4 Class Cs)
/23   255.255.254.0                   1/128 Class B, or      2 Class Cs)
/24   255.255.255.0    Class C
/25   255.255.255.128                                    1/2 Class C
/26   255.255.255.192                                    1/4 Class C
/27   255.255.255.224                                    1/8 Class C
/28   255.255.255.240                                   1/16 Class C
/29   255.255.255.248                                   1/32 Class C
/30   255.255.255.252                                   1/64 Class C
/31   255.255.255.254 . . . . > unusable < . . . . . . . 1/128 Class C
/32   255.255.255.255 Exactly one host address
```

FIGURE 4.19 Subnet mask representations.

The rule that the all-0s and all-1s patterns are reserved in every subnet's host-number field implies that the number of available hosts is always $(2^h - 2)$, where h is the number of host bits available.

Since there are 32 bits in an IP address, there must be 32-h addresses in the prefix, so p = 32 − h, or h = 32 − p. So, if we know the prefix length, we immediately have a formula for the number of hosts within a given prefix length: $[2^{(32-p)} - 2]$.

```
192.168.47.196/30

11000000.10101000.00101111.11000100    in binary
11111111.11111111.11111111.11111100    /30 mask

11000000.10101000.00101111.11000100    00 pattern (r)
11000000.10101000.00101111.11000101    01 pattern
11000000.10101000.00101111.11000110    10 pattern
11000000.10101000.00101111.11000111    11 pattern (r)


(r) indicates a reserved pattern:

    00 (all-zeros) is the subnet number, and
    11 (all-ones) is the subnet's broadcast address
```

FIGURE 4.20 Example /30 prefix.

For example, a /14 prefix has $[2^{(32-14)} - 2] = [2^{(18)} - 2] = [262,144 - 2] = 262,142$ host addresses. Figure 4.21 shows the number of hosts available for each possible prefix size (according to the $[2^{(32-p)} - 2]$ formula).

The reason that the /0 prefix capacity is "not applicable" is that the only use of /0 is as part of 0.0.0.0/0 (the default route), and 0.0.0.0 represents no address in particular. Actually, the default route represents all the routes that are *not* in a router's forwarding table. A corporate network's routers need not know about all routes in the Internet; it is much more efficient to just tell the internal routers how to get to the Internet. Then the internal routers can deliver externally-destined packets to the boundary between the corporate network and the Internet. The Internet's core routers will take it from there. Those routers do know about all currently reachable destinations in the Internet.

The reason that /32 is also not applicable is that this mask-length is used to indicate exactly one host address; because of this fact, a /32 route is also known as a "host route." The other prefix lengths (other than 0 and 31) all refer to usable address prefixes, which implicitly contain at least two hosts. It is clear that as the mask lengths increase, the indicated prefix sizes contain fewer and fewer host addresses.

Breaking Up is Easy to Do

Now that we have developed a formula for the number of hosts per prefix (given the prefix length), we need to also have one other formula that relates subnets to each

p	32-p (=h)		$2^h - 2$
/0	32	n/a	4,294,967,294
/1	31		2,147,483,646
/2	30		1,073,741,822
/3	29		536,870,910
/4	28		268,435,454
/5	27		134,217,726
/6	26		67,108,862
/7	25		33,554,430
/8	24		16,777,214
/9	23		8,388,606
/10	22		4,194,302
/11	21		2,097,150
/12	20		1,048,574
/13	19		524,286
/14	18		262,142
/15	17		131,071
/16	16		65,534
/17	15		32,766
/18	14		16382
/19	13		8190
/20	12		4094
/21	11		2046
/22	10		1022
/23	9		510
/24	8		254
/25	7		126
/26	6		62
/27	5		30
/28	4		14
/29	3		6
/30	2		2
/31	1		0
/32	0	n/a	-1

FIGURE 4.21 Capacity of each prefix length.

other. For instance, if you have a /16, how many /19 subnets are inside of it? Or if you have a /18, how many /25s are inside that /18? This formula is even simpler than the other, as long as you are in a purely classless environment. If the two prefix sizes are j and k, then the formula is simply $2^{|j-k|}$, where $|j-k|$ means the absolute value of the difference between the two numbers. (We don't care about the order of subtraction (negative numbers would give strange results), only the separation. If j=13 and k=15, then j-k = −2, but $|j-k|$ = 2.)

The restriction that neither the extended-network-prefix nor the host-number fields may take on either an all-0s or all-1s value still stands, but the all-0s and all-1s prefixes are usable as long as a classless routing protocol is in use. Recall that the all-0s and all-1s host-numbers have special meaning within a subnet, so they are never usable; there is no such reserved use for the all-0s and all-1s *prefixes*.[3]

> If there is a chance that a device may need to be used in the future which is not classless, then you may want to avoid the all-0s and all-1s prefixes. In fact, it is always a good idea to be conservative in your network designs, in which case you may decide not to use these two subnets—just in case.

There are times when using them is unavoidable, such as when you need to divide a /24 into two /25s (or a /16 into two /17s or a /8 into two /9s, though those are not likely to be nearly as common). If one has a /24 and needs to break it in half, then a /25 mask is required; however, since there is only one bit in the subnet-number field, it can only have the values zero and one. If you have elected to not use the all-0s and all-1s subnets, then you must claim *two* bits for the subnet-number field: 00, 01, 10, and 11. After omitting the 00 and 11 values, you are left with 01 and 10. However, each of these values basically represents one-quarter of the /24, thus omitting 00 and 11 renders *half* of the /24 unusable; also the capacities of the /26 subnets are about half of the /25s (62 versus 126 host numbers; see Figure 4.21), which may be too small for the addressing needs of the invovled organization.

In the preceding paragraph we have seen two applications of the subnet-counting formula. If one lenghthens the prefix by one bit, then $|j-k|$ = 1, and 2^1 = 2, so there are twice as many subnets for each 1-bit extension of the prefix. This fact is further borne out by noting that when $|j-k|$ = 2, we see that because 2^2 = 4 there are four times as many subnets for each 2-bit lengthening of the prefix (a /24 may be broken into four /26s). There is a corresponding decrease in the number of host-numbers per subnet. Based on the first formula, there are $2^{(32-26)}$ − 2 = 62 host-numbers in a /26, versus $2^{(32-24)}$ − 2 = 254 available host addresses in a /24 prefix.

It is very important to note that the relationship between two subnets /n and /n+s is always the same—the longer-prefix subnets outnumber the shorter-prefix subnet by a factor of 2^s. So a /17 may be broken into four /19s, a /10 may be broken into eight /13s, a /25 may be broken into two /26s, etc. The size of each subnet, in terms of available host-numbers, will depend on the first formula. The shorter the prefix length, the more host-numbers will be present in that prefix. The number of hosts is approximately double for each single bit shorter the prefix is made.

The reason each subnet's capacity is only *approximately* double (instead of exactly double) is that the all-0s and all-1s host-numbers are unusable at each level. So, a /19 has 8190 host-numbers, while a /18 has 16382; but 2 * 8190 = 16380, which is two less than 16382, so indeed there are fewer than half as many host addresses in a /19 compared to a /18. The differences become more extreme over wider subnet size ranges. Any /23 prefix has $2^9 - 2 = 510$ host-numbers, and any /12 has $2^{20} - 2 = 1,048,574$. Based on the prefix lengths, one would expect a factor of 2048 difference in their capacities (because $2^{|23-12|} = 2^{11} = 2048$), but 2048 * 510 is 1044480, which has 4094 fewer host-numbers than 1,048,574.

Can you explain why the difference is 4094 in this case? Hint: It has something to do with 4096 − 2. Can we work out a formula that gives the "error" (wasted host addresses) whenever a /n is broken into $2^{(n-m)}$ /m's (where m > n)? We can start with this formula:

$$[2^{(32-n)} - 2] - [2^{(m-n)} * (2^{(32-m)} - 2)]$$

The term in the first set of [] is the number of host-numbers in a /n, according to the first formula. The term in the second set of [] is the product of the number of /m's in a /n (a single /n may be broken into 2^{m-n} /m prefixes) times the number of host-numbers in a /m (another application of the first formula, similar to the first term in []). Subtracting them yields the desired result.

Algebraically, these may be easily reduced to an equivalent—and much simpler—formula: $[2^{(m-n+1)} - 2]$. It is not hard to work out this reduction given the full formula above. The reduction is left as an exercise for the reader.

Getting Together is Hard(er) to Do

Up until now, the discussion has been focused on taking a fixed prefix and dividing it into a number of smaller subnets, with longer prefix lengths. We will now look at

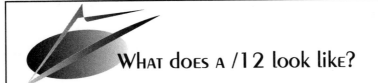

What does a /12 look like?

A /12 is about one-sixteenth of the size of an entire /8, in terms of how many host-numbers lie within a /12 compared to how many host-numbers lie within a /8. There are exactly sixteen /12 prefixes within a /8. For example, using network 10 as a prototypical example, the subnets would be the following:

0	10.0.0.0/12
1	10.16.0.0/12
2	10.32.0.0/12
3	10.48.0.0/12
:	:
:	:
14	10.224.0.0/12
15	10.240.0.0/12

Switching gears from a reductionist to a constructionist mode, we see that relative to a /16, a /12 represents sixteen /16s.

Since a /12 is a shorter prefix than a /16, there must be multiple /16s within a /12. Taking the 172.16.0.0/12 prefix as an example, we have the following sixteen /16 components of the /12:

0	172.16.0.0/16
1	172.17.0.0/16
2	172.18.0.0/16
3	172.19.0.0/16
:	:
:	:
14	172.30.0.0/16
15	172.31.0.0/16

(continued)

A /12 prefix could also represent 2^{12} (or 4,096) /24s, as follows, using 200.0.0.0/12 as a base prefix, or sixteen /16s, using the same base prefix:

0	200.0.0.0/24	0	200.0.0.0/16
1	200.0.1.0/24		
2	200.0.2.0/24		
:	:		
254	200.0.254.0/24		
255	200.0.255.0/24		
256	200.1.0.0/24	1	200.1.0.0/16
:	:		
1022	200.3.254/24		
1023	200.3.255.0/24		
1024	200.4.0.0/24	4	200.4.0.0/16
:	:		
2046	200.7.254.0/24		
2047	200.7.255.0/24		
2048	200.8.0.0/24	8	200.8.0.0/16
:	:		
2070	200.11.254.0/24		
3071	200.11.255.0/24		
3072	200.12.0.0/24	12	200.12.0.0/16
:	:		
3838	200.14.254.0/24		
3839	200.14.255.0/24		
3840	200.15.0.0/24	15	200.15.0.0/16
:	:		
4094	200.15.254.0/24		
4095	200.15.255.0/24		

Verifying that the numbers above are correct requires noticing that there are always 256 /24s in a /16 (because $2^{(24-16)} = 2^8 = 256$). So, if the second byte of the address is 5 and the third is 76, then this is the [(5 * 256) + 76] = 1356th item in the list. Verify that the formula is correct by evaluating it at the end of the range: [(15 * 256) + 255] = 4095. The list from 0 to 4095 has the expected 4096 entries (in any list of

(continued)

numbers from 0 to n, there are n+1 elements...consider {0, 1, 2, 3}—four elements!). Another way to verify that 200.0.0.0/12 contains sixteen /16s (just as a /8 contained sixteen /12s!), is to notice that $2^{(16-12)} = 2^4 = 16$.

Now, the fact is that there is no intrinsic reason why 200.0.0.0/12 should be broken up along (classfully inspired) /24 boundaries. As a single block, 200.0.0.0/12 begins with 200.0.0.0 and ends with 200.15.255.255, containing $2^{20} - 2 = 1,048,574$ host-numbers. If the /12 is broken into 2^{12} (= 4,096) /24s, there are at most 4,096 * 254 = 1,040,384 host-numbers available in the collection of 4096 subnets.

the other side of the coin: For example, how can we combine thirty-two /24s to make a shorter prefix /19 aggregate? And when are thirty-two /24s not a /19?

Today, many Internet users are granted "blocks" of /24s when they need more than one /24 but less than one /16. It is very rare today to get a /16 from an Internet Registry or Provider, though it may happen with sufficient justification of an organization's requirements. Let us imagine that a fictitious company, maufer.com, has been allocated four class Cs, 192.168.66.0/24 through 192.168.69.0/24. Can we convert these four /24s into one /22?

By examining the masks involved, it looks like we should be able to do that (certainly, in the other direction, a /22 is always equal to four /24s). However, a /22 boundary must be a multiple of four, and 66 is not a multiple of four, so we cannot represent these four /24s as a /22. To see another reason why, we can look at the binary expansion of these addresses, in Figure 4.22, for clues.

```
192.168.66.0/24—192.168.69.0/24

66:   11000000.10101000.01000010.00000000
67:   11000000.10101000.01000011.00000000

                  192.168.66.0/23

68:   11000000.10101000.01000100.00000000
69:   11000000.10101000.01000101.00000000

                  192.168.68.0/23
```

FIGURE 4.22   Binary expansion of four /24s.

192.168.67.0/24—192.168.70.0/24

```
67:   11000000.10101000.01000011.00000000
```

                           192.168.66.0/24

```
68:   11000000.10101000.01000100.00000000
69:   11000000.10101000.01000101.00000000
```

                           192.168.68.0/23

```
70:   11000000.10101000.01000110.00000000
```

                           192.168.70.0/24

FIGURE 4.23   Expansion of another four /24s.

In order for any four /24 prefixes to collapse into a /22, all four would have to share the same common first 22 bits in their prefix. Clearly, that is not the case here. However, these four /24s can be collapsed into two /23s. Had the block began with 192.168.67.0, even this level of aggregation would not be possible, as may be seen in Figure 4.23.

In conclusion, Figure 4.24 shows a set of four /24s that does indeed reduce to one /22. Note that all the /24s have their first 22 bits exactly alike, which allows them to be aggregated. Another way to say this is that the initial /24 of a block of four /24s falls on a /22 boundary.

In general, if a block of 2^n /u "long" prefixes is to be aggregated into one /v "shorter" prefix (where u-v = n), then the block must begin on a /v boundary. In other words, the extended-network-prefix of the "long" /u prefix must be a multiple

192.168.68.0/24—192.168.70.0/24

```
68/24: 11000000.10101000.01000100.00000000
69/24: 11000000.10101000.01000101.00000000
70/24: 11000000.10101000.01000110.00000000
71/24: 11000000.10101000.01000111.00000000
```

                           192.168.68.0/22

```
68/22: 11000000.10101000.01000100.00000000
```

FIGURE 4.24   Four /24s aggregated into one /22.

of 2^n. One way to tell if a number is divisible by 2^n is to write it out in binary. If it ends in at least n zeros, then it is divisible by 2^n.

It might help to pop back from the binary world into the decimal world to see the parallel of this factoid. If a decimal number ends in four zeros, it is divisible by 10^4. For example, 430,000 is divisible by 10,000 . . . the result is 43. And if there are more than four zeros, the number is still divisible by 10^4, but it is also divisible by larger factors. So, 17,000,000 is divisible by 10^4 (10,000), with the result being 1700. It is also divisble by 10^5 (100,000), resulting in 170, and 10^6 (1,000,000), which results in 17.

As an exact parallel to the decimal world, in the binary world, a one followed by n zeros is equal to 2^n. So 10 is 2^1 (2 in decimal), and 1000 is 2^3 (8 in decimal). As you would expect, just plain '1' is 2^0 (since it is a 1 followed by zero zeros).

So, again, the test for aggregatability (to coin a word), is that the extended-network-prefix of the first "long" prefix is divisible by 2^n. To determine this, we write out the extended-network-prefix without the dots from dotted decimal notation. For now, we only care about the values of the bits. For example, if we have the following 16 "long" prefixes (/16s), can we aggregate them into a /12 (since $16 = 2^4$)?

```
     0)    172.16.0.0/16
           :
15 (2⁴ - 1)    172.31.0.0/16
```

To test this, we will write out the extended-network-prefix of 172.16.0.0/16 (which is 172.16) as a binary number: 10101100000<u>10000</u>. Since the binary representation of the extended-network-prefix ends in four zeros, as indicated by the underlined portion, it must be divisible by 2^4, and thus aggregatable as 172.16.0.0/12 (since $12 = 16 - 4$). The extended-network-prefix is also divisible by 2^3, 2^2, and 2^1, which means that other possible aggregates that may start with this extended-network-prefix are 172.16.0.0/13, 172.16.0.0/14, and 172.16.0.0/15. Each of those represents 8 (2^3), 4 (2^2), or 2 (2^1) /16s, respectively.

For another example, let us consider the following list of 64 /24s:

```
     0)    192.168.64.0/24
           :
63 (2⁶ - 1)    192.168.127.0/24
```

Can we represent this block of 64 addresses as a single /18? Why do we know that if the aggregate exists, it must be a /18? Because there are 2^6 items in the list, and 24 - 6 = 18. We need to write out 192.168.64 (the /24 extended-network-prefix) as a binary number, which is: 11000000101010001000000. It is clear that the extended-network-prefix does indeed end in six zeros, so it is divisible by 2^6, therefore the 64 items in the list must be aggregatable as 192.168.64.0/18.

Finally, let's pick an example where there are more than 256 (2^8) items to aggregate. Consider the following list of 1024 /28 prefixes that we'd like to test for "aggregatability" into a /18:

```
    0)   172.16.0.0/28
    :
1023 (2^10 - 1)  172.16.63.240/28
```

Before solving the example, what is an easy way to find the highest number in that range, without writing out all the 1024 items in the list? I certainly didn't write them all out. Well, first we just simply assume that the list is aggregatable. If it is, it must take the form:

10101100.00010000.00xxxxxx.xxxx0000.

The /28 boundary is marked by the final x, and the desired /18 boundary is marked by the end of the underline. The first item in the list is determined by setting all the x bits to zero, and the highest item in the list by setting all the x bits to one, which is:

10101100.00010000.00111111.11110000.

In dotted-decimal notation, this is 172.16.63.240/28.

Back to the example, we need to write out the extended-network-prefix and see if it is divisible by 1024 (2^{10}). We just saw above that the initial /28 extended-network-prefix is 10101100.00010000.00000000.   0000, which is 10101100000010000000000000000000 without the dots. The underlined portion indicates that there are, in fact, 16 zeros at the end, so this number is definitely divisible by 2^{10} (it is also divisible by numbers as large as 2^{16}!) Because the extended-network-prefix is, in fact, divisible by 2^{10}, we can aggregate this block of 1024 /28s as a single /18, namely 172.16.0.0/18.

Now that we understand how to manipulate IP prefixes, it is time to delve into the topic of Internet address assignment, known as Classless Interdomain Routing, or CIDR. CIDR is an extension of the the intranet's VLSM concept to the scale of the Internet.

ENDNOTES

1. Addresses in the range 224–239 are class D multicast addresses, but they are never used in the context of a unicast routing protocol. If there is a mask associated with a multicast group address, it is usually /32 (255.255.255.255), since the entire group address represents a whole group as a single entity. Class E addresses are available for experimentation, ranging from 240.0.0.0 to 255.255.255.255.

2. RIPv2, defined in RFC-2453, improves the RIP protocol by allowing it to carry extended-network-prefix information. Therefore, RIPv2 is classless and supports the deployment of VLSM.

CHAPTER 5

Scalable Internet Address Management

CIDR:INTERNET :: VLSM:INTRANET

First, a definition is in order. CIDR stands for Classless Interdomain Routing. CIDR is a strategy that incorporates supernetting (discussed later on) to summarize large blocks of address space into a small number of route advertisements. CIDR helps keep the growth of the Internet's routing tables under control, while in the process hiding details of an Internet Service Provider's (ISP) internal structure from the Internet at large. This information hiding has favorable scaling properties in addition to the reduction of routing information. Just as in the subnetting case, any changes in the internal reachability within a corporate network is invisible outside of the intranet. This keeps the Internet from seeing the organization's internal "route-flaps." CIDR offers the same benefit to ISP networks, in that an ISP's internal structure is invisible to the outside world, so its internal route-flaps are not propagated onto the Internet.

In VLSM, a subnet structure that the organization defines is invisible outside its borders (just as any classful fixed-size subnet structure would be). The organization only advertises a small set of routes to the Internet, to summarize its assigned IP address blocks. Similarly, an ISP may subdivide its allocated address block into various pieces, each of the appropriate size for a given customer. Outside of the ISP's border, only a small number of routes representing the ISP's allocated address space aggregates is visible. This VLSM/CIDR parallelism is depicted in Figure 5.1.

Only the scale is different, the concept is the same. The ISP circle may represent a /12 (as big as 16 /16s, or 4096 /24s), while the corporate network is usually not larger than a few /16s, but typically is around a /22 (four /24s) or less. The ISP address space "pie" is divided into slices appropriate to its customers, similar to the way that a corporate network number is sliced into subnets of appropriate size. Just as with VLSM, deployment of CIDR has three prerequisites:

- The routing protocols must carry network prefix information with each route advertisement.
- All routers must implement a consistent forwarding algorithm based on the "longest match."
- For route aggregation to occur, addresses must be assigned so that they are topologically significant.

CIDR and VLSM are essentially the same thing, since they both allow a portion of the IP address space to be recursively divided into successively smaller pieces. Or, looked at the other way, they allow contiguous small pieces of address space to

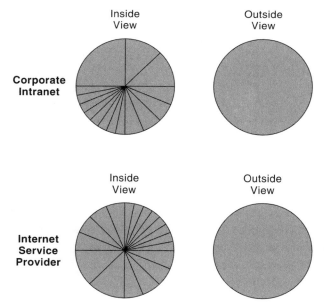

FIGURE 5.1 VLSM/CIDR similarities.

be aggregated into an advertisement with a shorter mask that represents the entire group of small subnets. The difference is that with VLSM, the recursion is performed on address space that has previously been assigned to an organization, and the VLSM structure is invisible to the global Internet.

CIDR operates at the next level up, extending the VLSM concepts to the Internet's routing system. CIDR permits the recursive allocation of an address block by an Internet Registry to a high-level ISP, which can allocate a subset to a mid-level ISP, that can allocate a subset of that subset to an even lower-level ISP, and ultimately a smaller subset is allocated to a private organization's network. The private organization may then, of course, use VLSM to subnet whatever address space their ISP has allocated to them.

CIDR Enables the Efficient Allocation of the IPv4 Address Space

CIDR eliminates the traditional concept of Class A, Class B, and Class C network addresses and replaces them with the generalized concept of a "network-prefix." Routers use the network-prefix, rather than the first 3 bits of the IP address, to determine the dividing point between the network number and the host number. As a result, CIDR supports the deployment of *arbitrarily sized* networks rather than the standard 8-bit, 16-bit, or 24-bit network numbers associated with classful addressing. The only constraint is that the address blocks must always be a power of two; in other words, it is impossible to have an address block of 57 addresses, or 1083. 57 and 0183 are obviously not powers of two, since they are odd numbers, but even blocks of size 866 or 42 are not legal; although they are even, they are also not powers of two, e.g., 2, 4, 8, 16, 32, 64, . . . , 1024, 2048, 4096, . . . , 65,536, . . .

In the CIDR model, each piece of routing information is advertised with a bit mask (or prefix length). The prefix length is a way of specifying the number of left-most contiguous bits in the network-portion of each routing table entry. For example, a network with 20 bits of network-number and 12 bits of host-number would be advertised with a 20-bit prefix length (a /20). The clever thing is that the IP address advertised with the /20 prefix could be a former Class A, Class B, or Class C. Routers that support CIDR do *not* make assumptions based on the first 3 bits of the address, they rely on the prefix length information provided with the route.

In a classless environment, prefixes are viewed as bitwise contiguous blocks of the IP address space. For example, all prefixes with a /20 prefix represent the same amount of address space (2^{12}, or 4096 host addresses). Furthermore, a /20 prefix can be carved out of a traditional Class A, Class B, or Class C network number.

```
Traditional A    10.223.208.0/20    00001010.11011111.11010000.00000000
Traditional B    172.16.144.0/20    10101100.00010000.10010000.00000000
Traditional C    192.168.64.0/20    11000000.10101000.01000000.00000000
```

FIGURE 5.2 Various /20 address blocks.

Figure 5.2 shows how three different /20 blocks all represent 4096 host addresses—10.223.208.0/20, 172.16.144.0/20, and 192.168.64.0/20. As is obvious by inspection, the number of addresses in the host field is the same regardless of the value of the first byte that once defined the classful mask. Instinctively, we often look at a /20 subnet of a Class A or Class B as somehow being "normal," whereas a block of 16 Class Cs is not, even though they all represent the exact same number of host addresses. The real difference between a /20 and 16 consecutive Class Cs is that the /20 is a single entity when interpreted classlessly, but is 16 entities when interpreted classfully.

Table 5.1 provides information about the most commonly deployed CIDR address blocks. This table was inspired by material at the end of Chapter 4. Referring to the table, you can see that a /15 allocation can also be specified using the traditional dotted-decimal mask notation of 255.254.0.0. Also, a /15 allocation represents 2^{17}, or 131,070, IP host addresses, because the host portion of a /15 is 17 bits long (17 = 32 - 15). A /15 can be classfully represented as two Class B networks or 512 Class C networks.

How does all of this lead to the efficient allocation of the IPv4 address space? In a classful environment, an ISP was limited to allocating either /8, /16, or /24 address blocks, regardless of the requirements of the customer. Customers needing more than 254 addresses may have been assigned a class B, which is far more space than required.

In a CIDR environment, the ISP can carve out an appropriately sized block of its allocated address space such that each customer's requirements are specifically met, which minimally consumes the ISP's limited IP address space. By extension, if ISPs can more efficiently allocate addresses, then the Internet will globally have more efficient address space utilization. Similarly, VLSM allows a customer to use its allocated addresses as efficiently as possible. An organization's use of VLSM prevents it from wasting its space, which would create premature demand for more address space from its ISP.

Evolution of Classless Interdomain Routing (CIDR)

By 1992, the exponential growth of the Internet was beginning to raise serious concerns among members of the Internet operations community about the ability of

TABLE 5.1 Classless Address Block Sizes

CIDR prefix-length	Dotted-Decimal Mask Notation	# Individual Addresses	# of Classful Network Numbers
/13	255.248.0.0	524,286	8 Bs or 2,048 Cs
/14	255.252.0.0	262,142	4 Bs or 1,024 Cs
/15	255.254.0.0	131,070	2 Bs or 512 Cs
/16	255.255.0.0	65,534	1 B or 256 Cs
/17	255.255.128.0	32,766	128 Cs
/18	255.255.192.0	16,382	64 Cs
/19	255.255.224.0	8,190	32 Cs
/20	255.255.240.0	4,094	16 Cs
/21	255.255.248.0	2,046	8 Cs
/22	255.255.252.0	1,022	4 Cs
/23	255.255.254.0	510	2 Cs
/24	255.255.255.0	254	1 C
/25	255.255.255.128	126	1/2 C
/26	255.255.255.192	62	1/4 C
/27	255.255.255.224	30	1/8 C

the Internet's routing system to scale and support future growth. These problems manifested themselves as:

1. The apparently imminent exhaustion of the Class B network address space.
2. The rapid growth of the global Internet's routing tables.
3. The eventual exhaustion of the 32-bit IPv4 address space.

Projected Internet growth rates made it seem that the first two problems were likely to become critical by 1994 or 1995. The response to these immediate challenges was the development of the concept of supernetting, also known as CIDR. The third problem, which is more long-term in nature, is seen by some to be solved by the IP Next Generation (IPng or IPv6) protocol. Ultimately, the expectation is that IPv6 may replace IPv4 as the Internet's network layer protocol. The key to a successful migration from IPv4 to IPv6 will be a rich set of transition options, which have been developed by the IETF.

CIDR was documented in September 1993 as RFC-1517, -1518, -1519, and -1520. CIDR supports two important features that benefit the global Internet routing system: 1) CIDR eliminates the traditional concept of Class A, Class B, and Class C network addresses. This enables the efficient allocation of the IPv4 address space which will allow the continued growth of the Internet at least until IPv6 is deployed. 2) CIDR supports route aggregation where a single routing table entry can represent the address space of perhaps thousands of traditional classful routes. Route aggregation limits the amount of necessary routing information in the Internet's backbone routers, reduces route flapping (frequent changes in route availability), and eases the local administrative burden of updating externally visible routing information.

CIDR was rapidly deployed in 1994 and 1995. It is estimated that, without CIDR, the Internet routing tables would now have in excess of 80,000 routes (instead of the today's approximately 60,000 routes). Such a large number of routes would exceed the capacity of some routers, not just because they may not have the memory capacity to store such large amounts of data, but even more critically that they would have to deal with far more "route flapping" than in a CIDR environment. The load on a backbone router's CPU increases very rapidly as a function of the size of the routing tables, due to the increased exposure to route flapping as the number of potentially reachable routes increases. Any routers that still believe that a route exists, when it is not really there, would be forwarding data into a "black hole" rather than toward its destination.

The core routers in the Internet must all have an up-to-date list of all the reachable routes in the Internet. This list is called their routing table. These routes are just numbers to the backbone routers, but way out at the edge, they represent the real Ethernet, Token Ring, FDDI, etc. subnetworks. When there is a thunderstorm in Hong Kong, an electrical disturbance may disable a local ISP's backbone that previously provided access to, for example, 187 different route prefixes. The fact that those prefixes are no longer reachable must be propagated throughout the *entire* Internet backbone. When the power comes back on, the reemergence of those destinations must also be propagated.

Considering not only the effects of mother nature on a worldwide scale, from the spectacular to the mundane—severe storms, squirrels chewing on power and telecommunications wiring, intrusion of moisture into power and telecom wiring, just plain bad wiring,—but also human "operator errors" that could result in routers being rebooted—cables being jostled loose, connectors being improperly secured (leading to intermittent electrical connectivity), heavy construction machinery accidentally digging up part of a fiber backbone—we see that routes being up and stable are the exception, not the rule. The resulting load on core router's CPUs is nontrivial, and may be extreme in some cases.

Managing route flapping is one of the real challenges that has been addressed in the last several years. CIDR "hides" flapping that would otherwise have been visible outside a provider's borders, because the provider is only offering one route. Either all the active pieces of their allocation are active, or all are inactive.[1] There is never an externally visible state where most are active, but 93 are down. Even though CIDR has proved to be an extremely useful tool for controlling the growth of routing tables, there are still large numbers of routes that were assigned before 1993, which cannot be aggregated.[2] These nonaggregatable routes are still a large source of route flaps, which is why there are techniques such as "route flap damping" (RFC-2439) to help the Internet's core routers handle the very dynamic Internet routing environment.

Controlling the Growth of Internet's Routing Tables

Another important benefit of CIDR is that it plays an important role in controlling the growth of the Internet's routing table. The reduction of routing information requires that the Internet be divided into addressing domains. Within a domain, detailed information is available about all of the domain's constituent networks. Outside of an addressing domain, only the common network prefix is advertised. This allows a single routing table entry to specify a route to many individual network addresses.

Figure 5.3 illustrates how the allocation described in the previous CIDR example helps reduce the size of the Internet routing tables. Assume that a portion of the ISP's address block (200.25.16.0/20) has been allocated as described in the previous example. Organization A aggregates eight /24s into a single advertisement (200.25.16.0/21), Organization B aggregates four /24s into a single advertisement (200.25.24.0/22), Organization C aggregates two /24s into a single advertisement (200.25.28.0/23), and finally Organization D aggregates two /24s into a single advertisement (200.25.30.0/23). Finally, the ISP is able to inject all 256 /24s of its allocation (including the 16 /24s in this example) into the Internet with a single advertisement—200.25.0.0/16!

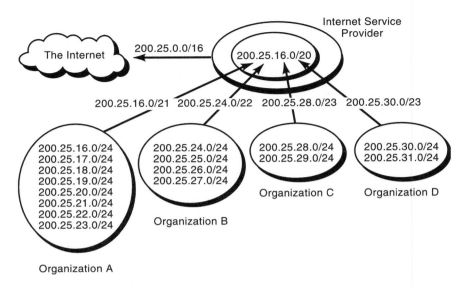

FIGURE 5.3   CIDR reduces the size of Internet routing tables.

It should be emphasized that route aggregation via BGP-4 is not automatic. The network engineers must configure certain specific routers to perform the required aggregation. The successful deployment of CIDR will allow the number of individual networks on the Internet to expand while minimizing the number of routes in the Internet routing tables.

Routing in a Classless Environment

Figure 5.4 illustrates the routing advertisements for Organization A discussed in the previous CIDR Example.

Since all of Organization A's prefixes are part of ISP #1's address block, the routes to Organization A are implicitly aggregated via ISP #1's aggregated announcement to the Internet. In other words, the eight networks assigned to Organization A are hidden behind a single routing advertisement. Using the longest match forwarding algorithm, Internet routers will route traffic to host 200.25.17.25 to ISP #1, which will in turn route the traffic to Organization A, based on the *internal* subaggregate, namely 200.25.16.0/21.

Now, for whatever reasons, assume that Organization A decides to change its network provider to ISP #2. This is illustrated in Figure 5.5.

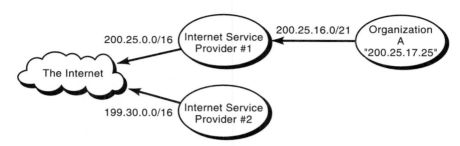

FIGURE 5.4   Routing advertisements for organization A.

The "best" thing for the size of the Internet's routing tables would be to have Organization A obtain a block of ISP #2's address space, and then renumber its network. This would allow the eight networks assigned to Organization A to be hidden behind the aggregate routing advertisement of ISP #2. Unfortunately, renumbering is a labor-intensive task which could be very difficult, if not impossible, for Organization A.

The "best" thing for Organization A is to retain ownership of its address space and have ISP #2 advertise an "exception" (more specific) route into the Internet. The exception route allows all traffic for 200.25.0.0/16 to be sent to ISP #1, with the exception of the traffic to 200.25.16.0/21. This is accomplished by having ISP #2 advertise, in addition to its own 199.30.0.0/16 block, a route for 200.25.16.0/21 (see Figure 5.6). Using the "longest match" forwarding algorithm, Internet routers will route traffic addressed to host 200.25.17.25 to ISP #2, which will in turn route the traffic to Organization A. Clearly, the introduction of a large number of exception routes can reduce the effectiveness of the CIDR deployment and eventually cause Internet routing tables to begin exploding again!

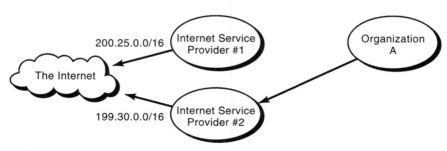

FIGURE 5.5   Organization A changes network providers to ISP #2.

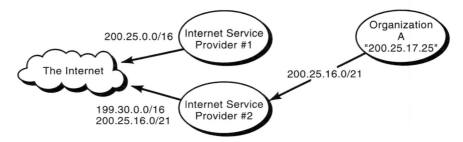

FIGURE 5.6   ISP #2 injects a more specific route into the Internet.

CIDR Allocation Example #1

Suppose that an ISP has been assigned the address block 206.0.64.0/18. This block represents 16,384 (2^{14}) IP addresses, because 14 bits are left of the 32 total IP address bits after removing 18 bits—the /18 prefix. (Note: A single /18 can be classfully interpreted as 64 class Cs.) The ISP's /18 prefix is depicted in Figure 5.7.

Now, suppose that a hypothetical customer organization requires 800 host addresses. Clearly, the customer would not find a single /24 acceptable; in this situation, it is also the case that the ISP would rather not allocate an entire Class B to the customer, thereby wasting around 65,000 addresses. Also, allocating four individual Class Cs is less than optimal because this introduces four new routes into the global Internet routing tables, even though only one new customer has joined the Internet.

The ISP would like to assign the client a /22 prefix, for instance 206.0.68.0/22, which is a block of 1024 (2^{10}) IP addresses (four contiguous /24s). This allocation represents at most one new route in the Internet's routing tables; if the block is simply part of the provider's block, then the allocation of this block to the customer does not add any new routing information to the Internet's routing tables. Figure 5.8 shows the client's allocated CIDR block, which is a subset of the ISP's CIDR block. Note that the first 18 bits of the client's allocation are the same as the ISP's larger block.

Had this allocation been interpreted classfully, as shown in Figure 5.9, it would have been the four class Cs formed by inserting all the possible two-bit patterns (specifically `00`, `01`, `10`, and `11`) into the remaining two bits of the third byte.

```
               206  .  0   .  64   .   0
ISP's Block:   11001110.00000000.01000000.00000000      206.0.64.0/18
```

FIGURE 5.7   Example of an ISP prefix.

```
                        206  .   0  .  64   .    0
ISP's Block:    11001110.00000000.01000000.00000000      206.0.64.0/18

Client Block:   11001110.00000000.01000100.00000000      206.0.68.0/22
```

FIGURE 5.8 Client's /22 block allocated from ISP's /18.

```
                        206  .   0  .  64   .    0
ISP's Block:    11001110.00000000.01000000.00000000      206.0.64.0/18

Client Block:   11001110.00000000.01000100.00000000      206.0.68.0/22


Class C #0:     11001110.00000000.01000100.00000000      206.0.68.0/24
Class C #1:     11001110.00000000.01000101.00000000      206.0.69.0/24
Class C #2:     11001110.00000000.01000110.00000000      206.0.70.0/24
Class C #3:     11001110.00000000.01000111.00000000      206.0.71.0/24
```

FIGURE 5.9 Classful interpretation of client's /22 CIDR block.

CIDR Allocation Example #2

For this example, assume that an ISP owns the address block 200.25.0.0/16. This block represents 65,536 (2^{16}) IP host addresses (or 256 /24s). In size, it is also equivalent to one class B, even though the most significant byte is not in the range of 128 − 191. From the 200.25.0.0/16 block, the ISP wants to allocate the 200.25.16.0/20 address block. This smaller block represents 4096 (2^{12}) IP addresses (classfully equivalent to 16 /24s).

```
Address Block  11001000.00011001.00010000.00000000 200.25.16.0/20
```

In a classful environment, the ISP is forced to use the /20 as 16 individual /24s, indicated by filling out all the possible bit patterns between the /20 and /24 bit positions (indicated in **bold** below).

```
Network #0     11001000.00011001.00010000.00000000 200.25.16.0/24
Network #1     11001000.00011001.00010001.00000000 200.25.17.0/24
Network #2     11001000.00011001.00010010.00000000 200.25.18.0/24
Network #3     11001000.00011001.00010011.00000000 200.25.19.0/24
```

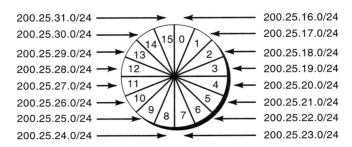

FIGURE 5.10   Slicing the pie—a classful environment.

```
Network #4      11001000.00011001.00010100.00000000 200.25.20.0/24
        :
        :
Network #13     11001000.00011001.00011101.00000000 200.25.29.0/24
Network #14     11001000.00011001.00011110.00000000 200.25.30.0/24
Network #15     11001000.00011001.00011111.00000000 200.25.31.0/24
```

Continuing to take the classful view, the ISP's /20 address block can be represented as a pie that can *only* be cut into 16 pieces of equal size, as illustrated in Figure 5.10. This is because in a classful environment, all routes are either /24s, /16s, or /8s.

However, in a classless environment, the ISP is free to cut up the pie any way it wants. It could slice up the original pie into two pieces (each 1/2 of the address space) and assign one portion to Organization A, then cut the other half into two pieces (each 1/4 of the original address space) and assign one half to Organization B, and finally slice the remaining quarter into two pieces (each 1/8 of the original address space) and assign it to Organizations C and D. Each of the individual organizations is then free to allocate their assigned address space within their intranets as they see fit. The relative size of each organization's allocated address space is illustrated in Figure 5.11.

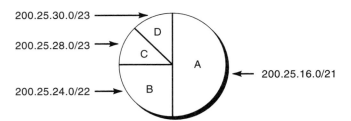

FIGURE 5.11   Slicing the pie—a classless environment.

The following steps were used to derive the values in Figure 5.11

Step 1: Divide the address block 200.25.16.0/20 into two equal size slices by lengthening the mask by 1 bit. Each block represents one-half of the address space, or 2048 (2^{11}) IP addresses.

```
ISP's Block    11001000.00011001.00010000.00000000    200.25.16.0/20

Org A:         11001000.00011001.00010000.00000000    200.25.16.0/21
Reserved:      11001000.00011001.00011000.00000000    200.25.24.0/21
```

Step 2: Divide the "reserved" block from Step 1 (200.25.24.0/21) into two equal-sized slices, by further extending the mask by 1 bit. Each of the new block's represents one-quarter of the original address space, or 1024 (2^{10}) IP host addresses.

```
Reserved    11001000.00011001.00011000.00000000    200.25.24.0/21

Org B:      11001000.00011001.00011000.00000000    200.25.24.0/22
Reserved    11001000.00011001.00011100.00000000    200.25.28.0/22
```

Step 3: Divide the reserved address block from Step 2 (200.25.28.0/22) again into two equal-size blocks, by once again lengthening the subnet mask by 1 bit. The two new blocks represent one-eighth of the original address space, or 512 (2^9) IP addresses.

```
Reserved    11001000.00011001.00011100.00000000    200.25.28.0/22

Org C:      11001000.00011001.00011100.00000000    200.25.28.0/23
Org D:      11001000.00011001.00011110.00000000    200.25.30.0/23
```

What follows is a summary of all the pieces (the original /20 prefix is underlined, with the bold numbers indicating the mask length of each organization's prefix):

```
Org A:      11001000.00011001.00010000.00000000    200.25.16.0/21
Org B:      11001000.00011001.00011000.00000000    200.25.24.0/22
Org C:      11001000.00011001.00011100.00000000    200.25.28.0/23
Org D:      11001000.00011001.00011110.00000000    200.25.30.0/23
```

CIDR PRACTICE EXERCISES

1. List the individual [classful] network numbers encompassed by the CIDR block 200.56.168.0/21.

   _____

   _____

   _____

   _____

   _____

   _____

2. List the classful network numbers contained within the CIDR block 195.24.0.0/13.

   _____

   _____

   _____

   _____

   _____

   _____

   _____

   _____

   _____

3. Aggregate the following set of four /24 network addresses to the highest degree possible.

   212.56.132.0/24

   212.56.133.0/24

   212.56.134.0/24

   212.56.135.0/24

4. Aggregate the following set of four /24 network addresses to the highest degree possible.

   212.56.146.0/24

   212.56.147.0/24

212.56.148.0/24

212.56.149.0/24

5. Aggregate the following set of 64 /24 network addresses to the highest degree possible.

202.1.96.0/24

202.1.97.0/24

202.1.98.0/24

:

202.1.126.0/24

202.1.127.0/24

202.1.128.0/24

202.1.129.0/24

:

202.1.158.0/24

202.1.159.0/24

6. Express the entire Class A address space as a single CIDR advertisement.

_____

7. Express the entire Class B address space as a single CIDR advertisement.

_____

8. Express the entire Class C address space as a single CIDR advertisement.

_____

Solutions for CIDR Practice Exercises

1. List the individual [classful] network numbers encompassed by the CIDR block 200.56.168.0/21.

   a. First, express the CIDR block in binary format:

   `200.56.168.0/21   11001000.00111000.10101000.00000000`

   b. The /21 mask is 3 bits shorter than the /24 mask for a class C. This means that the CIDR block identifies a block of eight consecutive /24 network numbers, because $2^3 = 8$.

   c. The range of classful /24 network numbers defined by the CIDR block 200.56.168.0/21 includes all possible patterns starting with the fixed

/21 prefix (underlined) and each possible combination of three remaining bits in the third byte (**bold**):

```
Net #0:    11001000.00111000.10101000.00000000    200.56.168.0
Net #1:    11001000.00111000.10101001.00000000    200.56.169.0
Net #2:    11001000.00111000.10101010.00000000    200.56.170.0
Net #3:    11001000.00111000.10101011.00000000    200.56.171.0
Net #4:    11001000.00111000.10101100.00000000    200.56.172.0
Net #5:    11001000.00111000.10101101.00000000    200.56.173.0
Net #6:    11001000.00111000.10101110.00000000    200.56.174.0
Net #7:    11001000.00111000.10101111.00000000    200.56.175.0
```

2. List the classful network numbers contained within the CIDR block 195.24.0.0/13.

   a. First, express the CIDR block in binary format:

```
195.24.0.0/13         11000011.00011000.00000000.00000000
```

   b. The /13 mask is 11 bits shorter than the /24 mask for a class C. We do not consider the /13 as a collection of eight class Bs (even though that is the size of the block), because the network number starts with 195, indicating that all classful members of the address block are class Cs. This means that the CIDR block identifies a block of 2048 (or 2^{11}) consecutive class Cs.

   c. The range of class C network numbers defined by the CIDR block 195.24.0.0/13 include:

```
Net #0:     11000011.00011000.00000000.xxxxxxxx    195.24.0.0
Net #1:     11000011.00011000.00000001.xxxxxxxx    195.24.1.0
Net #2:     11000011.00011000.00000010.xxxxxxxx    195.24.2.0
                            :
                            :
Net #2045:  11000011.00011111.11111101.xxxxxxxx    195.31.253.0
Net #2046:  11000011.00011111.11111110.xxxxxxxx    195.31.254.0
Net #2047:  11000011.00011111.11111111.xxxxxxxx    195.31.255.0
```

3. Aggregate the following set of four /24 network addresses to the highest degree possible.

```
212.56.132.0/24
212.56.133.0/24
212.56.134.0/24
212.56.135.0/24
```

   a. List each address in binary format and determine the common prefix (if any!) for all of the addresses:

```
212.56.132.0/24     11010100.00111000.10000100.00000000
212.56.133.0/24     11010100.00111000.10000101.00000000
```

```
212.56.134.0/24      11010100.00111000.10000110.00000000
212.56.135.0/24      11010100.00111000.10000111.00000000

Common Prefix:       11010100.00111000.10000100.00000000
```

b. The CIDR aggregation is:

```
212.56.132.0/22
```

4. Aggregate the following set of four /24 network addresses to the highest degree possible.

```
212.56.146.0/24
212.56.147.0/24
212.56.148.0/24
212.56.149.0/24
```

a. List each address in binary format and determine the common prefix for all of the addresses:

```
212.56.146.0/24      11010100.00111000.10010010.00000000
212.56.147.0/24      11010100.00111000.10010011.00000000

212.56.148.0/24      11010100.00111000.10010100.00000000
212.56.149.0/24      11010100.00111000.10010101.00000000
```

b. Note that this set of four /24s cannot be summarized as a single /22! The best we can do is to summarize these four /24s as two /23s:

```
212.56.146.0/23      11010100.00111000.10010010.00000000
212.56.148.0/23      11010100.00111000.10010100.00000000
```

c. Thus, the CIDR aggregation is:

```
212.56.146.0/23
212.56.148.0/23
```

Note that if two /23s are to be aggregated into a /22, then both /23s must fall within a single /22 block. A /22 block must begin with an address whose third address byte is divisible by four (because $4 = 2^{24 - 22}$). Since each of the two /23s is a member of a different /22 block, they cannot be aggregated into a single /22 (even though they are consecutive, and even though they represent the same number of IP addresses as a /22!). They could be aggregated into 222.56.144/21, but this aggregation would include four additional /24s that were not part of the original problem statement. Hence, the smallest possible aggregate is two /23s.

5. Aggregate the following set of 64 /24 network addresses to the highest degree possible.

```
202.1.96.0/24
202.1.97.0/24
```

```
202.1.98.0/24
     :
202.1.126.0/24
202.1.127.0/24
202.1.128.0/24
202.1.129.0/24
     :
202.1.158.0/24
202.1.159.0/24
```

a. List each address in binary format and determine the common prefix for all of the addresses:

```
202.1.96.0/24    11001010.00000001.01100000.00000000
202.1.97.0/24    11001010.00000001.01100001.00000000
202.1.98.0/24    11001010.00000001.01100010.00000000
     :
202.1.126.0/24   11001010.00000001.01111110.00000000
202.1.127.0/24   11001010.00000001.01111111.00000000
     :
202.1.128.0/24   11001010.00000001.10000000.00000000
202.1.129.0/24   11001010.00000001.10000001.00000000
     :
202.1.158.0/24   11001010.00000001.10011110.00000000
202.1.159.0/24   11001010.00000001.10011111.00000000
```

b. Note that this set of 64 /24s cannot be summarized as a single /18!

```
202.1.96.0/19     11001010.00000001.01100000.00000000
202.1.128.0/19    11001010.00000001.10000000.00000000
```

c. Thus, the CIDR aggregation is:

```
202.1.96.0/19
202.1.128.0/19
```

Similar to question 4, if two /19s are to be aggregated into a /18, the /19s must fall within a single /18 block (which means in this case that the third byte of the start of the range would need to be a multiple of 64, since $2^{(24-18)} = 64$). Since each of these two /19s is a member of a different /18 block, they cannot be aggregated into a single /18. They could be aggregated into 202.1.0.0/16, but this aggregation would include 192 network numbers that were not part of the original allocation. Again, the smallest possible aggregate is two /19s.

6. Express the entire Class A address space as a single CIDR advertisement.

Since the <u>leading bit</u> of all Class A addresses is a "0," the entire Class A address space can be expressed as 0.0.0.0/1. "/1" means that only the first, or leftmost, bit is significant. Since 0.0.0.0 has no bits other than zero bits, the first bit must be "0," which by definition makes any matching network a Class A network.

7. Express the entire Class B address space as a single CIDR advertisement.

   Since the <u>leading two bits</u> of all Class B addresses are "10," the entire Class B address space can be expressed as 128.0.0.0/2.

8. Express the entire Class C address space as a single CIDR advertisement.

   Since the <u>leading three bits</u> of all Class C addresses are "110," the entire Class C address space can be expressed as 192.0.0.0/3.

ENDSTATION IMPLICATIONS FOR CIDR DEPLOYMENT

It is important to note that there may be some endstation implications when you deploy CIDR-based addressing. Since many endstations are still classful, their user interface will not permit them to be configured with a mask that is shorter than the "natural" mask for the classfully interpreted address. For example, potential problems could exist if someone wanted to deploy 200.25.16.0/22 to support up to 1022 endstations ($2^{10} - 2$).

The IP software on some endstations might not allow what it sees as a traditional Class C address within this range (200.25.**16**.1 – 200.25.**19**.254) to be configured with a 20-bit mask, instead insisting on the classful 24-bit mask. If the endstation software supports CIDR, it will permit shorter than natural masks to be configured on its interfaces.

Mixing CIDR-aware and non-CIDR-aware endstations will result in some "interesting" asymmetries, which will be described in the following example and illustrated in Figure 5.12.

First, consider traffic from the CIDR-aware endstation on the left (200.25.17.190) to the non-CIDR-aware endstation on the right (200.25.18.76). The CIDR-aware endstation will believe, based on its configured mask, that the local router (200.25.16.1) and the destination (200.25.18.76) endstation all share the same subnet prefix. Because the CIDR-capable endstation believes they all share a common subnet prefix, it will use ARP to discover the MAC addresses corresponding to each of these remote IP addresses.

The router, also being classless, shares the belief that all three of these devices lie within the same subnet-prefix. It will be able to successfully respond to ARPs sent by the CIDR-aware endstation. However, the non-CIDR-aware endstation would inter-

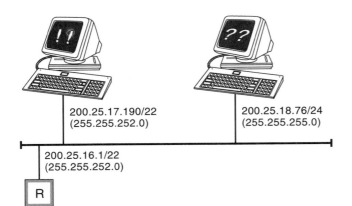

200.25.17.190/22
(255.255.252.0)

200.25.18.76/24
(255.255.255.0)

200.25.16.1/22
(255.255.252.0)

R

FIGURE 5.12   Implications of
non-CIDR-aware endstations.

pret both of the other addresses as being on foreign subnet prefixes, since it sees itself as
being in a class C subnet (200.25.18.0/24). Unfortunately for it, there is no default
gateway in its [classful] prefix, so it can't reach the CIDR-aware endstation! It will be
able to reach any endstation within (what it sees as) its class C, whether or not the endstations that happen to lay within 200.25.18.x are classless.

Workarounds to Support Classful Endstations?

Please consider returning to this discussion after you have read Part II, which contains detailed information on IP's forwarding decision procedure.

We need to examine traffic in each direction. From the non-CIDR-aware endstation outward, addresses outside of 200.25.18.x will be treated as nonlocal, and
will therefore expect to forward such traffic to a default gateway. So far in this example, the classless (CIDR) subnet had only one default gateway, which was not addressed as part of the 200.25.18.x prefix.

Rather than segmenting the four /24s with additional routers, it maybe possible to add secondary addresses to the existing router's interface. Note that some
routers may not support configuring one interface with multiple, overlapping IP
subnet prefixes. There must be a router interface in every "subnet" where non-
CIDR-aware endstations reside. In this case, the router could assume the secondary
address 200.25.18.1, with an associated mask of 255.255.255.0 (a.k.a. /24), as
shown in Figure 5.13. This address and mask gives the router a logical presence in
the endstation's "subnet."

The non-CIDR-aware endstation now has a default gateway in its subnet.
Traffic to other endstations on the classless subnet—or other "real" subnets reach-

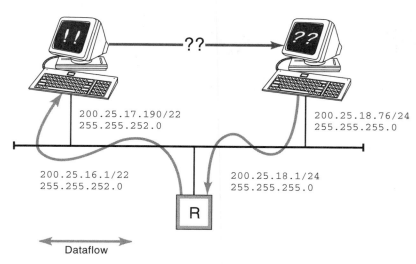

200.25.17.190/22
255.255.252.0

200.25.18.76/24
255.255.255.0

200.25.16.1/22
255.255.252.0

200.25.18.1/24
255.255.255.0

R

Dataflow

FIGURE 5.13   Workarounds?

able via the router—must go out via this router. However, the return traffic *might* not have to pass through the router. The CIDR-aware endstation will view the non-CIDR-aware one as being in its own subnet, thus it will not use the router to return traffic to the classful station.

Given that it will not want to speak indirectly to the classful endstation via the router, the non-CIDR-aware endstation in Figure 5.13 will send an ARP Request for the non-CIDR-aware endstation, and the CIDR-aware endstation will then have a chance to add the CIDR-aware endstation's IP-to-MAC address mapping to its ARP cache.

A careful ARP implementation may notice that the IP address is nonlocal and thus it should not add the CIDR-aware "neighbor's" address to its ARP cache, perhaps believing that the ARP packet was received in error. Even if the ARP process accepted the information, it should not be usable. The IP forwarding decision will calculate that the destination is nonlocal, and so it should not ever even consult the ARP cache—it should send packets to its default gateway in this case. So, even if the address mapping were present (within the non-CIDR-aware endstation) it could not be used!

Only a very sloppy implementation would be able to make use of this information. The bottom line is that the CIDR-aware endstation may not get an ARP response from the non-CIDR-aware endstation, and will not be able to reach it. The CIDR-aware endstation would not send the traffic back via its default gateway; after all, it sees the destination as being local!

A possible conclusion is that while one may add secondary addresses to the router to allow it to serve the non-CIDR-aware endstations, it is not possible to "fix" the CIDR-aware endstations so they can talk to the non-CIDR-aware ones—at least not if we want to rely upon the operation of ARP and other such automatic protocols. So, all we have is one-directional traffic at this point, which amounts to no communication.

However, if one were to statically configure an ARP cache entry on the CIDR-aware machine, telling it the MAC address of the non-CIDR-aware machine, then traffic could flow from CIDR-aware to non-CIDR-aware—directly. The return traffic (from non-CIDR-aware to CIDR-aware) would continue to be forced through the router, however. This is really only a theoretical "solution," since it is not practical to statically manipulate this information on more than 2 or 3 machines.

Another partial "solution" would be for the router to give a proxy response when it sees ARP requests from CIDR-aware endstations wanting to communicate with non-CIDR-aware endstations. The router will know that the broadcast ARP Request will not yield a useful response, since the router is present in the both overlapping subnets. The proxy response will fool the CIDR-aware endstation into thinking that the router's MAC address is the non-CIDR-aware endstation's MAC address, thereby forcing traffic from CIDR-aware to non-CIDR-aware to go through the router.[3] This would enable connectivity between the two worlds, which is far better than there being no connectivity between the CIDR-aware and non-CIDR-aware endstations.

The author is not aware of any router implementations supporting this "solution." The best solution is to collect non-CIDR-aware endstations into subnets that make sense to their classful IP stacks. Of course, only segregate old-fashioned machines after upgrading those endstations that can be upgraded so that they can freely use "shorter than natural" masks.

NEW SOLUTIONS FOR SCALING THE INTERNET ADDRESS SPACE

As we approach the 21st century, the problems of IPv4 address shortages and expanding Internet routing tables are still with us. The good news is that CIDR has been working. The bad news is that recent growth trends indicate that the number of Internet routes is still increasing. The Internet must find a way to keep the routing table growth linear. The IETF is continuing its efforts to develop solutions that will overcome these problems, enabling the continued growth and scalability of the Internet.

Appeal to Return Unused IP Network Prefixes

RFC-1917 requested that the Internet community return unused address blocks to the Internet Assigned Numbers Authority (IANA) for redistribution. This includes unused network numbers, addresses for networks that will never be connected to the global Internet for security reasons, and sites that are using a small percentage of their address space. RFC-1917 also petitions ISPs to return unused network-prefixes that are outside of their assigned CIDR prefixes.

Address Allocation for Private Internets

RFC-1918 suggests that organizations make use of the private Internet address space for use within their enterprise network, with translation performed into a much smaller "routable" pool of addresses at the edge of their network. The IANA has reserved the following three address blocks for use within private internets:

```
10.0.0.0    - 10.255.255.255   (10.0.0.0/8 prefix)
172.16.0.0  - 172.31.255.255   (172.16.0.0/12 prefix, or 16 /16s)
192.168.0.0 - 192.168.255.255  (192.168.0.0/16 prefix, or 256 /24s)
```

These private addresses are not routable on the Internet. No ISP should accept any route within any of these prefixes from any of its customers. Organizations electing to use addresses from these reserved blocks can do so without contacting the IANA or an Internet registry. Since these addresses are never injected into the global Internet routing system, the address space can be used simultaneously by many different organizations.

The disadvantage to this addressing scheme is that it requires an organization to use a Network Address Translator (NAT) for its Internet access. However, there is a hidden advantage, in that the use of the private address space and a NAT device make it much easier for customers to change their ISP. Their internal private addressing structure is always the same, independent of their ISP choice. Changing ISPs means a simple change to the configuration of the NAT box—now it will use an address pool delegated from the new ISP.

The benefits of this addressing scheme to the Internet is that it reduces the demand for IP addresses, so large organizations may require only a small block of the globally unique IPv4 address space. It is estimated that only 10 percent or less of an organization's endstations are communicating with *external* devices at any given time. This fact allows the public address pool to be much smaller than the total number of endstations in the organization's network. NAT is very commonly deployed today. Most router vendors support this; firewalls and special-purpose NAT boxes also exist to perform IP address translation.

NAT is not without its undesirable side effects, however. For instance, NAT breaks IP Security (IPsec) because changing the IP address in between the endpoints will invalidate the cryptographic transforms. NAT also interferes with applications that directly manipulate IP addresses, such as FTP. NAT boxes need special code to look for IP addresses in unusual locations and translate them in all the right places. Alternatives to NAT are being sought by the IETF, such that private addressing is usable in contexts that are not supported by NAT.

Address Allocation from the Reserved Class A Address Space

RFC-1797, entitled "Class A Subnet Experiment," explores the allocation of the upper-half of the currently reserved Class A address space, which is class A network numbers from 64 – 126, or 64.0.0.0/2 in CIDR notation (note that 64.0.0.0/2 includes net 127.0.0.0, which is already spoken for as the loopback address).

The entire class A space is *half* of the total IP addresses. The Class B space is one-quarter of the total IP addresses. Half of the Class A space is, then, *the same size as the **entire** Class B space!* As the demand for IP addresses continues to grow, it appears that it will be necessary to allocate CIDR blocks from the 64.0.0.0/2 address space wihtin the next several years.

Implications of Address Allocation Policies

RFC-2008, entitled "Implications of Various Address Allocation Policies for Internet Routing," discusses the fundamental issues that were considered as the Internet developed CIDR-era unicast address allocation and management policies. The RFC compares the benefits and limitations of an "address ownership" policy with an "address lending" policy. Since its publication in October of 1996, it has been designated a "Best Current Practice" RFC.

"Address ownership" means that when an address block is assigned to an organization, it remains allocated to that organization for as long as the organization wants to keep it. This means that the address block is "portable" and that the organization would be able to use it to gain access to the Internet no matter which ISP the organization uses to connect to the Internet. On the other hand, "address lending" means that an organization obtains its address block on a "loan" basis. If the loan ends, the organization can no longer use the borrowed address block, and it must obtain new addresses and renumber its endstations into the new address block.

As we have seen, efficient hierarchical routing happens when allocated addresses reflect the network topology in order to permit route aggregation along address block boundaries. The RFC argued that there were (and are) two fundamental problems that disrupt the hierarchical addressing and routing model advocated by CIDR:

- The continued existence of pre-CIDR routes that cannot be aggregated.
- Organizations that switch ISPs and continue to use addresses from their previous ISP's address block. The new ISP cannot aggregate the old address block as part of its aggregation, so it must inject a more specific exception route into the Internet on behalf of this organization. As the number of exception routes increases, they tend to erode the benefits of CIDR, thereby diminishing the scalability of the Internet's routing system.

The RFC concluded by recommending that large providers, which can express their destinations with a single prefix, be assigned address blocks following the "address ownership" model. However, all allocations from these providers to a downstream client should follow the "address lending" model. This means that if an organization changes its provider, the loan is canceled and the client will be required to renumber.

If a customer moves from one ISP that is subsidiary to ZZnet ISP, Inc., to another ISP that also gets addresses (and service) from ZZnet ISP, Inc., then the exception route never leaves ZZnet ISP, Inc., thus saving the rest of the Internet from needing to learn that route. Of course, ZZnet ISP, Inc., does have to carry that extra route internally. However, if the customer moves to a new ISP that is a client of TelcoISP Corp., then TelcoISP Corp. would need to advertise the exception route to the whole Internet.

RFC-2008 generated a tremendous amount of discussion within the Internet community about the concept of address ownership and what it means in the context of global routing. The authors presented a strong argument that the Internet has to make a choice between either address ownership for all or a routable Internet—we can't have both!

Smaller organizations had concerns about the difficulty of renumbering and their lack of self-determination if their provider or their provider's upstream provider changes its provider. Finally, ISPs had concerns because the term "large provider" has not been defined.

The "largeness problem" was solved by delegating large portable blocks to regional or continental Internet Address Registries. Those registries then delegate to ISPs within the region or continent, and the registry's policies decide which ISPs get portable versus nonportable addresses. Customer blocks are almost always nonportable these days. All the pre-RFC-2008 network number assignments also predated CIDR, so they are not aggregatable, and most certainly must be portable. There are certain address users that are inter-regional, or inter-continental. Finally, for such organizations, it is possible for the IANA to assign the addresses directly, rather than delegating them to a registry first. The IANA is effectively the highest-level registry.

REFERENCES

REQUEST FOR COMMENT (RFC)

1517 Applicability Statement for the implementation of Classless Inter-Doman Routing (CIDR). Internet Engineering Steering Group, R. Hinden. September 1993. (Format: TXT=7357 bytes) (Status: PROPOSED STANDARD)

1518 An Architecture for IP Address Allocation with CIDR. Y. Rekhter & T. Li. September 1993. (Format: TXT=72609 bytes) (Status: PROPOSED STANDARD)

1519 Classless Inter-Domain Routing (CIDR): an Address Assignment and Aggregation Strategy. V. Fuller, T. Li, J. Yu, & Varadhan. September 1993. (Format: TXT=59998 bytes) (Obsoletes RFC1338) (Status: PROPOSED STANDARD)

1520 Exchanging Routing Information Across Provider Boundaries in the CIDR Environment. Y. Rekhter & C. Topolcic. September 1993. (Format: TXT=20389 bytes) (Status: INFORMATIONAL)

1631 The IP Network Address Translator (NAT). K. Egevang & P. Francis. May 1994. (Format: TXT=22714 bytes) (Status: INFORMATIONAL)

1917 An Appeal to the Internet Community to Return Unused IP Networks (Prefixes) to the IANA. P. Nesser II. February 1996. (Format: TXT=23623 bytes) (Also BCP0004) (Status: BEST CURRENT PRACTICE)

1918 Address Allocation for Private Internets. Y. Rekhter, B. Moskowitz, D. Karrenberg, G. J. de Groot & E. Lear. February 1996. (Format: TXT=22270 bytes) (Obsoletes RFC1627, RFC1597) (Also BCP0005) (Status: BEST CURRENT PRACTICE)

2439 BGP Route Flap Damping. C. Villamizar, R. Chandra, R. Govindan. November 1998. (Format: TXT=86376 bytes) (Status: PROPOSED STANDARD)

ENDNOTES

1. The routes are still flapping, but this information is localized to the inside of the ISP's network, hidden from the world by CIDR aggregation. In an ideal Internet, an ISP would only have to process flaps pertaining to its own customers' routes (and to other *entire* ISPs, of course). The backbone flapping rate would then scale with the number of ISPs, not routes.

2. In fact, over 20,000 of the Internet's routes are part of "The Swamp," the 192.x.y.0 class C address space.

3. You might wonder how the router could know which endstations were classful? Well, they would be the ones that send packets through the router, trying to reach another endstation in the broader classless subnet.

PART II

LAN AND WAN SUBNETWORKS UNDER IP

The IP protocol stack is comprised of four layers, namely Subnetwork, IP, Transport, and Application, as described in Part I. Each layer provides service(s) to the layer above it, and depends on the service(s) offered by the layer below it. The next several chapters will focus on the subnetwork layer of the IP model. Both LAN and WAN subnetwork technologies will be described.

What services does IP need from the subnetwork layer? IP is an unreliable data-gram service, so the link layer need not offer reliable delivery or any performance guarantees. What IP needs is simply a service that will transport its packets from one IP–speaking device to the next. However, as the 1990s draw to a close, more and more QoS[1]– and CoS[2]–aware subnetwork technologies are being developed, such as ATM LAN Emulation (specifically LANE version 2.0), and IEEE 802.1p/Q-enhanced switched LANs, specifically 10/100/1000 Mbps Ethernet. Additionally, the IP "Type of Service" byte has been redefined to implement so-called "Differenti-ated Services," which may allow different classes of service within an IP-based net-work, other than the default which is "best effort." At the same time, applications of IP are being developed that will leverage these new capabilities, perhaps providing enhanced "multimedia" services over "converged" networks.[3]

Traditional IP-enabled applications are for "data" transfers, in varying amounts, with generally few time-related performance constraints, except for interac-tive applications such as Telnet, the Internet's virtual terminal protocol. Broadly, ap-plications can be classified as in Figure II.1.

In the Internet of the late 20th century, data-oriented applications are clearly dominant, as they have been since the Internet's inception. Rather than leave the im-pression that data protocols have no timing requirements, note that Telnet and other protocols, with whose applications users interact directly, are delay-sensitive for that reason alone. If these protocols perform sluggishly, the users will be unproductive, and perhaps unhappy, too.

Emerging applications are creating requirements for IP-based networks to support enhanced classes of service. A small list of such emerging IP-based applications include: voice-over IP (VoIP), video- and audio-streaming, and video- and audio-conferencing.

The Internet enhancements required to support these new applications often boil down to some statistical assurance that most packets will arrive within a certain

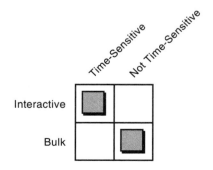

FIGURE II.1   Broad classes of In-ternet applications.

maximum amount of time (i.e., packets will have bounded delay). Time-sensitive applications such as interactive voice may also require that a certain bandwidth be reserved, or that the variation of packet delay (also known as jitter) be kept within certain levels.

The topic of multimedia networking has already filled many books, and for now it will suffice to observe that such applications appear to be the Internet's "Next Big Thing." Certainly, VoIP is real enough that Internet Telephony Service Providers (ITSPs) are sprouting up, such as L3, Qwest, and others. Even established telephony providers such as Bell Atlantic and AT&T are making significant investments in VoIP technology. These companies are willing to make billion-dollar-scale investments in the technology.

If the Internet can be successfully enhanced to support voice, which is one of the most demanding of all "multimedia" applications, the floodgates may open on a whole new class of both data and nondata applications that can leverage these new capabilities.

SUBNETWORK FUNCTIONS

Encapsulation and Framing

At a minimum, WAN and LAN link layer protocols provide for the encapsulation and transmission of higher-layer protocol packets, including IP packets. The link-layer encapsulation enables the higher-layer protocol's packet to travel through the subnetwork medium and be distinguished from other packets, which may be IP packets or packets of some other protocol stack. Generically, many of the subnetwork technologies (both LAN and WAN) have frames that follow the format illustrated in Figure II.2.

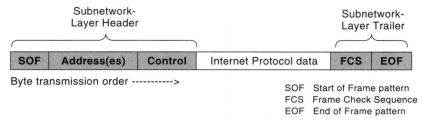

FIGURE II.2 Generic subnetwork frame format.

Framing, or the process of prepending a data-link header (and, optionally, appending a trailer) to the higher-layer protocol packet, provides for the synchronous transmission of large sequences of bits. Each frame starts with a pattern that allows for the destination station to synchronize its clock with the transmitter.[4]

The frame's synchronization pattern, which is transmitted immediately prior to the actual start of the frame, allows the receiver's hardware to synchronize itself to the transmitter's exact frequency. Once the receiver has been synchronized to the transmitter's frequency, it can then maintain synchronization throughout the duration of the frame. Synchronous subnetwork protocols, such as we have been discussing, require that timing be maintained over an entire frame (up to many thousands of bits). Clock recovery begins at the framing sequence and then the bits are transmitted such that the bit stream is self-clocking, once synchronization has been established.

Character-based asynchronous[5] protocols transmit a character at a time, each with its own start and stop bit(s). The start and stop bits permit synchronization to be maintained for the temporal duration of the character—usually, but not necessarily, 8 bits.

Why is synchronization important? If a LAN is supposed to run at 10 Mbps, there is no guarantee that every station will have precisely identical clock frequencies. This is due to manufacturing differences, power supply voltage differences, temperature variations, and other environmental variables such as the temperature, the age of the clock chip, and possibly even the ambient humidity. Considering these real-world factors, it would be a bad idea for each station to use its own local clock to receive data bits from another sender, since the transmitted bit timing would almost certainly not match up with the receiving station's bit frequency, ensuring data corruption.

Subnetwork-Layer Addressing

The addressing information that is carried in the subnetwork-layer header identifies the subnetwork-layer destination address (DA) as well as the subnetwork-layer source address (SA).[6] IEEE LANs commonly use 48-bit (i.e., six-byte) addresses, though you may see 16-bit addresses occasionally.[7] IEEE LAN addresses may be globally assigned and uniquely "burned-in" to the hardware (by the manufacturer), or be manually assigned.

Besides the source and destination addresses, it is often important to have some mechanism for indicating how long the frame is. Length indications can be explicit or implicit. One feature that is almost never implicit is marking a frame to indicate what higher-layer protocol it is carrying. In a LAN context, these data-link layer protocol IDs are often referred to as "EtherTypes," because Ethernet was the first commercially successful LAN technology. (IP's EtherType is 0x0800.) In the ATM world, it is possible to create multiple virtual circuits between two points and then agree that VC#x is only for AppleTalk, while VC#y is only for IP. When sending over these links, a few bytes may be saved because there is no need for explicit higher-layer-protocol marking, as the mere fact that the packet was sent on VC#y indicated that it was an IP packet. ATM is the only subnetwork technology that has defined "null encapsulation," though conceivably frame relay or X.25 could do similar things.

Interestingly, the original Ethernet standard did not have a length field. When the transmitting station was done transmitting, it drops its carrier which is supposed to indicate to the receiver that the frame is complete. It is also possible to encode the length in the header, which gives the receiver an idea of how long this frame is going to be. Many subnetwork technologies' frames do include an explicit length indication in their header, but implicit means are also used, as in the case of Ethernet. In either case, once the frame has been completely received, its Frame Check Sequence (FCS) is compared with the calculated FCS to verify that the frame was unaltered in transit. Each data link layer has a specific minimum and maximum frame length,[8] which must be adhered to by the LAN or WAN devices.

Specifications exist that define how IP should operate over most existing subnetwork technologies. In order for a station to be able to send a link-layer frame, it must know the link-layer address of the (next-hop toward the) destination. The process of discovering a neighbor's link-layer address is known as Address Resolution in the IP model.

Address Resolution

IP's "Address Resolution Protocol" (ARP) operates over LANs and allows IP endstations to learn the MAC-layer addresses of neighbors. ARP is a "helper" protocol to IP, not actually an IP-based protocol itself.[9] Figure II.3 depicts ARP's status as a peer protocol to IP, also using the transmission services of the subnetwork layer to do its job. ARP is most often seen in LAN environments.

ARP uses a subnetwork frame that contains the IP address of the desired target station, and includes the source's MAC and IP addresses. The frame is sent to the broadcast destination address since the IP stack doesn't know the correct MAC-layer address to send this packet to—that's what it is trying to learn![10] If a station with a

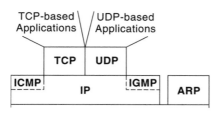

FIGURE II.3 ARP relative to the IP protocol stack.

matching IP address exists, then that station will respond to the ARP request directly, and the requesting station will know how to reach this destination. Figure II.4 shows the procedure two endstations must follow in using ARP before they can communicate.

ARP operates over any "broadcast-capable" subnetwork layer, such as Ethernet, Token Ring, FDDI, and other LANs, even including the LAN-like SMDS, which does not have a true broadcast service in the same sense that a LAN does. Broadcast-capable subnetworks are inherently "multiple access." A degenerate form of broadcast exists on point-to-point subnetworks, in that broadcasting is equivalent to sending a frame to the other side. Thus, point-to-point networks have an implicit broadcast mechanism.

However, there are WAN subnetwork technologies that do support multiple access (i.e., at least two nodes on the medium) despite not having broadcast mechanisms. The generic name for such technologies is a mouthful: "Non-Broadcast Mul-

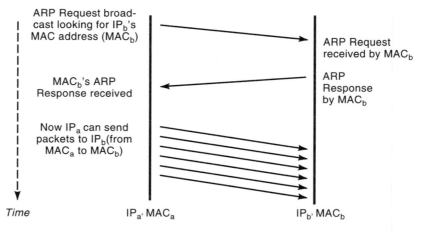

FIGURE II.4 ARP procedure.

tiple Access," or NBMA for short. Examples of NBMA technologies are X.25, Frame Relay, and Asynchronous Transfer Mode (ATM) (not LAN Emulation).

WAN encapsulations look very similar to the LAN encapsulations described earlier. The main difference is that WANs frequently carry only a destination address in their headers, while LAN frames carry both source and destination addresses. WAN subnetwork layers span from the point-to-point protocol (PPP), which always has at most two participants, and thus a very limited need for link addressing, to more complex packet- and cell-switched "cloud" NBMA technologies such as Frame Relay, X.25, ATM, and SMDS.

Despite the nonbroadcast nature of most WAN subnetworks, certain ARP variants do exist, supporting address resolution over some—but not all!—WAN subnetwork technologies. Over WANs, which generally lack broadcast capabilities, address resolution must employ very different mechanisms than the simpler LAN case. Each WAN technology's unique features determine what form an ARP-like protocol may take, or if such a protocol is even definable. Contrary to LANs, there is no generic NBMA address resolution protocol.

Inverse ARP (InARP) has been designed to work with Frame Relay networks. InARP leverages information derived from Frame Relay's associated Layer Management Interface (LMI) protocol, which periodically reports the status of each defined virtual circuit. ATM-ARP has been designed to work with RFC-1577-style "IP over ATM" networks. RFC-2225 defines an ATM-ARP server to which all address resolution queries are addressed; the ATM-ARP server maintains a centralized database of IP-to-ATM address mappings. When systems initialize their IP-over-ATM stacks, they register with the ATM-ARP server, which enables the ATM-ARP server to provide accurate address mapping information to the other stations within that logical IP subnetwork (LIS).

The Next Hop Resolution[11] Protocol (NHRP) has also been designed to support address resolution over ATM for next generation applications including the Multi-Protocol Over ATM standards (MPOA) from the ATM Forum. NHRP is most certainly *not* a routing protocol; it is a generic address resolution protocol for NBMA networks (it could even be used with X.25). NHRP is designed to communicate with "Next-Hop Servers," which are NHRP-capable routers, to determine the best exit point from the NBMA cloud en route to a given destination. It is a matter of policy whether "shortcut calls" across the NBMA-layer may be established, allowing packets to bypass some number of router hops, proceeding directly to the best egress router for some destination.

For NBMA subnetworks that have no defined ARP variant, static configuration of each relevant (neighbor IP address, neighbor subnetwork-layer address) mapping is required. In some carefully controlled private X.25 environments, where the X.121[12] addressing plan and the IP addressing plan are managed by the same organization, it is possible to create a configuration in which an algorithmic mapping between IP and X.121 addresses is possible. See RFC-1236 for an example from the U.S. military's Defense Data Network (DDN).

Even when ARP variants do exist, static mappings have the attractive property of being extremely stable over time. The WAN "addresses" associated with neighbors usually have very long lifetimes, so a dynamic address resolution protocol mainly serves to ease activation of new neighbor sites. Once up, however, adding a static entry for the new site captures its likely long-term presence and stability. Whether or not a site is reachable at some future time becomes a routing protocol issue. If a neighbor router becomes unreachable, then its formerly adjacent WAN neighbors will not have a route to destinations that previously were reachable via the dead router .

Without a forwarding table entry, then, any neighbor router will simply generate an error message if it ever gets a packet heading to one of those now-unreachable destinations. The router will never forward the packet over the WAN, even if it has a static entry for the now-dead remote router's subnetwork address, because no destination forwarding table entries will be using that IP address as their next hop.

Conversely, whenever a router *does* need to send a packet to the Boise, Idaho, branch office, the subnetwork-layer address will almost certainly be the same whether the router in Boise is up or down. Dynamically discovering the IP-to-subnetwork address mapping every time a site is activated is a waste of effort for the routers. The network administrator knows in advance that the answer will always be the same, and setting a static mapping in the router(s) reflects this quasi-permanence of the WAN address mappings, thus enabling the routers to send data to each other provided that the link-layer path between them is up. Stale mappings are harmless because there will be no forwarding table entries that might use that mapping.

IP FORWARDING PROCEDURE

Regardless of the type of subnetwork involved, the forwarding decision is very similar. Of course, there are always subnet-specific details, but before diving into the details, it will be useful to take a high-level view and look at the forest. The trees will be examined closely enough in the remainder of Part II.

Endstation Forwarding Decision

The first step of the journey of an IP packet begins inside an endstation. The endstation needs to determine the best way to send out a packet, and then deliver it to the next hop. A special case is when the endstation is on the same subnetwork as the destination; in this case, the IP packet can be sent "directly" to the destination. This case involves only ARP or an Address Mapping Table lookup, since all that needs to be known is the subnetwork-layer address of the destination.

If an endstation can tell that the ultimate destination of the packet is not on one of its local subnetworks, then it must send the packet to a router. The endstation's IP stack configuration includes the IP address of a "default gateway," which is the IP address of a router within (one of) the endstation's assigned prefix/mask(s). The endstation will send all non-locally-destined traffic to the default gateway for further delivery. The endstation hopes that the default gateway will know how to reach the packet's destination. Note that the default gateway *must* share the same IP subnetwork prefix with the endstation, or else they could not exchange packets. Sending to a router on an endstation's LAN is just like sending to any other local destination,[13] with the exception that the router is not the ultimate destination.

IP uses a hop-by-hop forwarding paradigm, which in and of itself does not distinguish IP from other protocols. Since IP is connectionless, the packet's destination address (DA) is always the address of the ultimate destination. In connection-oriented networking technologies, it is common to use a label-switching paradigm in which the destination's label is only significant on a hop-by-hop basis. IP also uses link-layer addresses hop-by-hop, but the key difference is that there is no preestablished series of link-layer addresses that tell you how to get from point A to point B, as there is once a virtual connection is set up.

Figure II.5 illustrates a simple topology with four routers, two of which are on the path from A to B. A word on the notation: Each of the router's interfaces have at least one IP address. These router IP addresses are denoted by $R_X(i, a.b.c.d)$, indicating that interface i of router X has the indicated IP address. The MAC address of that same interface is $R_X(MAC_i)$.

The following steps show how a packet proceeds from A to B.

Step 1: A needs to send a packet to B. First, A (172.16.96.214) notices that B's address (172.16.96.165) is not within A's local prefix, 172.16.96.192/27, which implies that the packet must be sent to A's default gateway, R_B. The first time that A needs to send a packet to R_B, A must send an ARP Request looking for $R_B(MAC_3)$.

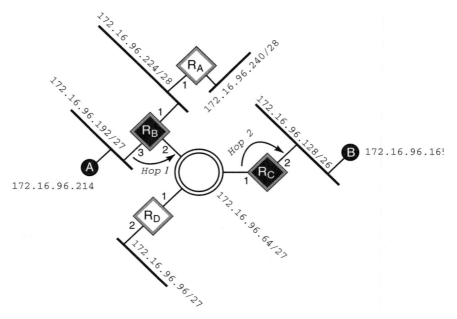

FIGURE II.5   Hop-by-hop IP forwarding.

A's IP stack is preconfigured with its default gateway set to 3, 172.16.96.193, which is how A knows the IP address for which it must broadcast an ARP Request. A stores $R_B(MAC_3)$ in its ARP cache for later use, in case any other packets need to be sent to nonlocal destinations.

A then transmits the IP packet, with its IP destination address field set to B's IP address (172.16.96.165), and its source IP address field set to A's own address (172.16.96.214). The packet is encapsulated within a MAC-layer frame that is addressed to a destination of $R_B(MAC_3)$. The MAC-layer source address will be set to MAC_A. The initial frame and packet are illustrated in Figure II.6.

Step 2: Now let's assume that the frame made it across the first LAN subnetwork, and that the router R_B has received the frame. It examines the frame and looks at the IP DA field, comparing the value in that field with its forwarding table,[14] which might be something like what is displayed in Figure II.7. Note that the parenthetical labels in the next-hop gateway column were added by the author as an aid in understanding the example. A real forwarding table would only have the next-hop routers' IP addresses.

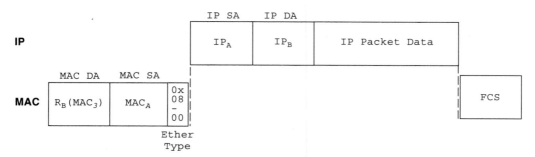

FIGURE II.6 The packet's initial encapsulation.

The destination prefix that has the most leading bits in common with the packet's DA (172.16.96.165) is the third entry, carrying a destination prefix of 172.16.96.128/26. Expressed in binary, that prefix and the destination address are:

Prefix (172.16.96.128/26)   10101100.00010000.01100000.10000000, and
IP_B (172.16.96.165)   **10101100.00010000.01100000.10**100101.

For reference, the other prefixes are:

Prefix (172.16.96.64/27)   10101100.00010000.01100000.01000000,
Prefix (172.16.96.96/27)   10101100.00010000.01100000.01100000,
Prefix (172.16.96.192/27) 10101100.00010000.01100000.11000000,
Prefix (172.16.96.224/28) 10101100.00010000.01100000.11100000, and
Prefix (172.16.96.240/28) 10101100.00010000.01100000.11110000.

The best-matching forwarding table entry's /26 mask boundary is marked by the extent of the underlining, which ends at the 26th bit. The destination address'

Known Prefixes	Next-Hop Gateway	Metric	Status
172.16.96.64/27	172.16.96.67	0 (connected)	Up
172.16.96.96/27	172.16.96.66 (R_D)	11	--
172.16.96.128/26	172.16.96.65 (R_C)	11	--
172.16.96.192/27	172.16.96.193	0 (connected)	Up
172.16.96.224/28	172.16.96.225	9 (connected)	Up
172.16.96.240/28	172.16.96.226 (R_A)	20	--

FIGURE II.7 Router R_B's forwarding table.

best-matching prefix is $172.16.96.128/26$.[15] Thus, according to R_B's forwarding table, the packet needs to be forwarded to R_C. By the same exact calculation that A did when it decided that IP_B was a nonlocal address, R_B also sees that IP_B is nonlocal, and additionally, it sees that R_C claims to know how to reach this packet's destination prefix.

Just as A needed to use ARP to find $R_B(MAC_3)$, R_B needs to use ARP to find $R_C(MAC_1)$. Once R_B knows R_C's MAC address on their common subnetwork, R_B can forward the packet to R_C. The appearance of the new frame is illustrated in Figure II.8. The MAC header structure is a bit different over FDDI, which will be covered later in Part II. The important part for this discussion is observing that the MAC-layer source and destination addresses change at each hop, as well as noting that the IP packet's addressing is unchanged at each hop.

Observe that the IP portion of the packet is unchanged, except that the Time-To-Live field will have been decremented by one, forcing the recomputation of the IP Header Checksum at each intervening router. At the MAC layer, the SA and DA fields reflect the fact that R_B is the now the source and R_C is now the destination on this example's in intermediate hop. Finally, due to the changes in the MAC and IP headers, the FCS will end up being a different value from the first frame as well.

Step 3: Once R_C receives the packet, it also needs to examine the packet's destination address and decide how to forward it. In this case, the packet's destination

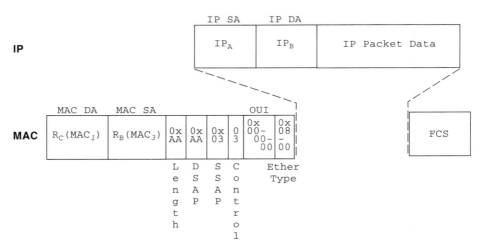

FIGURE II.8   The packet's intermediate encapsulation.

(172.16.96.165) happens to match one of R_C's attached subnetworks. Recalling the binary representations of the prefixes above, we see that the 172.16.96.128/26 prefix is, indeed, the longest match.

```
Prefix (172.16.96.128/26)   10101100.00010000.01100000.10000000, and
IPB (172.16.96.165)  10101100.00010000.01100000.10100101.
```

This is the very same calculation that R_B did, with the difference that R_C is actually directly connected to the destination's subnetwork, rather than the case with R_B, in which R_C was simply the next hop on the way to the final destination. Figure II.9 shows R_C's forwarding table; note the differences from R_B's forwarding table. Note that there is one fewer destination prefix than in R_B's forwarding table, apparently because R_B has aggregated 172.16.96.224/28 and 172.16.96.240/28 into a single prefix, namely 172.16.96.224/27.

Now that R_C has realized that it needs to deliver the packet to a directly connected subnetwork, it requires information derived from ARP as we have seen in every step thus far. Once the router knows MAC_B, it can send a frame directly to the destination, IP_B. The final encapsulation will appear as illustrated in Figure II.10. This packet is definitely the final hop packet because the subnetwork-layer destination address (MAC_B) and the IP destination address (IP_B) are associated with the same machine.

This example had the first-hop and last-hop subnetworks using the same technology, but obviously that is not a requirement. An IP packet may originate on any subnetwork type, e.g., a Token Ring LAN, and after crossing some intermediate Ethernet, FDDI, ATM, or Frame Relay subnetworks, may ultimately land on an SMDS subnetwork—or any other type of LAN or WAN destination subnetwork.

The important thing to carry away from this example is that each step in the forwarding process is the same as all the others. Whether it is the endstation deciding whether a destination is local or not, or a router along the path making the same decision, the forwarding decision is the same algorithm. What is interesting is how

Known Prefixes	Next-Hop Gateway	Metric	Status
172.16.96.64/27	172.16.96.65	0 (connected)	Up
172.16.96.96/27	172.16.96.66 (RD)	11	--
172.16.96.128/26	172.16.96.129	0 (connected)	--
172.16.96.192/27	172.16.96.67 (RB)	11	Up
172.16.96.224/27	172.16.96.67 (RB)	11	Up

FIGURE II.9 Router R_C's forwarding table.

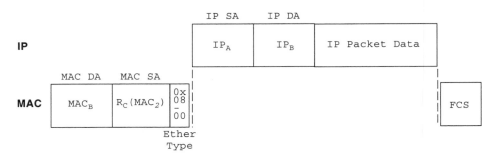

FIGURE II.10   The last hop: Delivery to the packet's destination.

the intermediate routers build their forwarding tables. This is the realm of routing protocols, two of which (RIP and OSPF) will be covered in Part III.

There are more routing protocols, however, they share many similarities with RIP and OSPF. The fact that RIP and OSPF are commonplace makes them good prototypical examples. The job that routing protocols do is to exchange information among themselves so that they will know what destination prefixes are reachable.[16] Also, the routing information is often tagged with "metrics." These metrics allow the routers to decide which path toward a destination is "best," in the event that multiple paths appear to exist.

For the moment, we don't need to understand the operation of routing protocols. With this foundation—understanding the IP forwarding procedure—we will now begin a detailed examination of subnetwork technologies, beginning with Ethernet.

REFERENCES

Kercheval, Berry, *"DHCP: A Guide to Dynamic TCP/IP Configuration,"* Prentice Hall, Upper Saddle River, NJ. 1999. ISBN 0-13-099721-0.

Request for Comment (RFC)

RFC-1236 IP to X.121 address mapping for DDN. Jr. Morales, L.F., P.R. Hasse. June-01-1991.
InARP, NHRP, ATM-ARP, Classical IP over ATM (1483, 1577, 1755, etc.)
Classical IP and ARP over ATM. M. Laubach, J. Halpern, April 1998. (Format: TXT=-65779 bytes) (Obsoletes RFC1626, RFC1577) (Status: PROPOSED STANDARD)

ENDNOTES

1. Quality of Service. A term used to indicate fine-grained parameters related to the connection, or "flow," such as end-to-end bandwidth, delay, variation of delay (i.e., jitter), etc.

2. Class of Service. A term used to indicate coarse-grained QoS-like parameters related to perhaps a handful of different priorities or service levels by which traffic flows may be classified.

3. The author regrets invoking the terms "multimedia" and "converged," because they have become overused and are now practically meaningless. However, they may convey the type of applications, and the evolutionary direction of networking, so in that sense they help paint the proper picture.

4. Typically, WAN subnetworks operate alongside a reference clock that is provided by the subnetwork. In this event, the only service that the framing provides is to delimit one frame from the next; clock synchronization "just happens."

5. Despite its name, Asynchronous Transfer Mode (ATM) is not such a protocol; it is asynchronous in the sense that its cells have no fixed timing relationship(s).

6. WAN subnetworks may only have a destination address in the frame, especially switched WAN services such as ATM, frame relay, and X.25. Point-to-point links have implicit addressing, in that the other side is unique, so sending to "the other side" is logically the same as sending to "every other station." So, in the point-to-point case, unicast and broadcast are effectively the same thing.

7. The IEEE has officially deprecated 16-bit LAN addresses, but certain subnetworks such as FDDI and token ring do support them, and it is possible that certain installations are still using them.

8. This maximum frame length is more commonly known as the medium's Maximum Transmission Unit (MTU).

9. ARP frames have no IP header; they are layered immediately above the MAC-layer LAN header.

10. Broadcast is less than optimal, but some method must be used to bootstrap the address discovery process. An IP-specific "ARP multicast" address could have been used, so that only IP endstations would hear the ARP traffic. Contrast this with the broadcast method, in which even non-IP endstations must receive the broadcast frame.

11. The R in NHRP is often decoded as "Routing," which is incorrect. That R actually stands for "Resolution." See RFC-2332 or its successor for all the gory details (including the correct name, available on page 1).

12. CCITT X.121 is the standard that specifies the format of X.25 addresses.

13. Local destinations are on the same subnetwork medium as the endstation, and share the same IP prefix.

14. The forwarding table is built by the routers using routing protocols. The job of routing protocols is to exchange information among themselves so that they will know what destination prefixes are reachable.

15. Because we consider a matching prefix to be "best" when its mask is longest, this type of forwarding style is known as "longest-match forwarding." Another form of forwarding is "exact match," which is used by Novell's IPX, as well as other protocols that have fixed-size network numbers (as opposed to IP's variable-sized extended-network-prefixes)

16. I have always found it to be somewhat magical that the routers use the network itself to find out about the network. Hoisted up by its own petard, indeed!

CHAPTER 6

LAN INTERCONNECTION

INTRODUCTION

All LAN types need to be interconnected; it is not practical for one LAN to span the whole world, or even an entire company (unless it is very small). LAN interconnection devices typically operate at either OSI Layer 1 (the Physical layer), Layer 2 (the Data Link layer), or Layer 3 (the Network layer).

As shown in Figure 6.1, frames arriving on a LAN interconnection device's interface have three processing choices: 1) simply flow straight through the device [literally bit-by-bit, in the case of pure layer-1 repeaters], 2) be received by the device, which verifies the layer-2 frame check sequence to ensure error-free reception[1] then forwards the packet based on its layer-2 destination address, or 3) be received by the device, pass layer-2 input error checks (e.g., FCS), and then be forwarded based on the layer-3 destination address, after having proper outgoing layer-2 header and trailer attached.[2] Each layer depends on the one immediately below it.

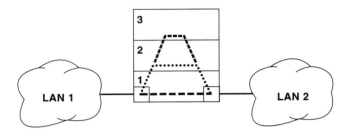

FIGURE 6.1   Generic LAN interconnection device.

INTERCONNECTION AT OSI LAYER 1

Layer 1 Ethernet interconnection devices are called "repeaters" or "hubs."[3] Layer 1 devices simply pass bits along, with little or no knowledge of the Data Link layer frame structure. A repeater is depicted in Figure 6.2. A hub may attach to multiple endstations, or to other hubs (within limits set by the Ethernet standard). Repeaters allow the physical extent of a LAN to be expanded beyond the distance constraints of a single wire, and they allow different Ethernet media to be mixed within the same extended LAN.

Multiport transceivers, used with thick Ethernet, are a kind of hub, in that they allow multiple stations to share one "vampire tap." There are also many special-purpose repeaters, allowing dissimilar Ethernet physical layers to be interconnected. So-called "micro-transceivers" are a kind of repeater, allowing an AUI port to supply power to a small device that may have 10BASE-T, 10BASE-FL, or 10BASE2 thin Ethernet output.[4] These devices allow the thick Ethernet AUI port to be a kind of universal Ethernet port. Today, most devices ship with either an AUI port or a native 10BASE-T port, since twisted pair is now, by far, the most prevalent physical layer over which Ethernet is run.

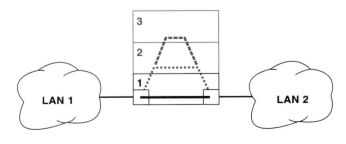

FIGURE 6.2   Logical internal diagram of a repeater.

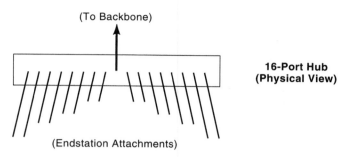

FIGURE 6.3 Physical view of a 16-port hub.

Ethernet repeaters are like a "wire in a box," in that they are usually diagrammed just as an Ethernet cable. In all important ways, hubs behave just as if all the attached stations were sharing an internal 10 Mbps cable. Figure 6.3 shows a physical diagram of a repeater/hub.

This example hub has 16 ports, with one "backbone" port. Most hubs have some sort of backbone slot, allowing the hub to attach to another type of Ethernet. An AUI port could be used to attach to a thick Ethernet "backbone," or hubs could be chained from one medium to another. Returning to the hub in Figure 6.3, it is sometimes drawn as a wire with tick marks representing endstation attachments. It is most often drawn simply as a wire, as one might draw a thicknet. Figure 6.4 shows these two different logical views of a hub.[5]

Backbone attachment can be accomplished in 10BASE-T environments by using a dual-mode port (labeled MDI/MDIX) with a "straight-through" patch cable, or any regular MDI port with a crossover cable. MDI stands for "medium-dependent interface," referring to the Ethernet physical layer reference model, as shown in Figure 6.5.[6]

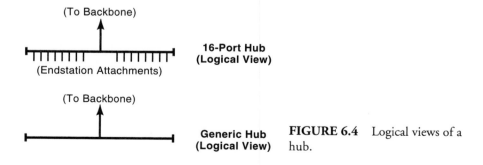

FIGURE 6.4 Logical views of a hub.

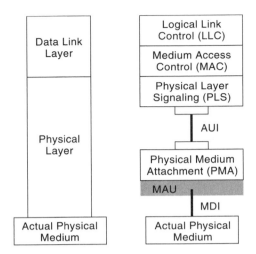

AUI   Attachment Unit Interface
MAU   Medium Attachment Unit
MDI   Medium-Dependent Interface

FIGURE 6.5   10 Mbps 802.3 reference model.

10BASE-T Wiring

In the context of 10BASE-T, a hub's ports are typically MDIX ports, allowing the MDI ports of the endstation to be directly patched in with a "straight-through" patch cable. Fundamentally, an endstation's "transmit" pins need to be connected to a hub's "receive" pins; likewise, the hub's "transmit" pins need to be connected to

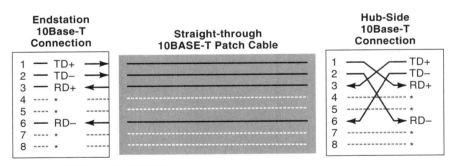

*   Pins 4, 5, 7, and 8 are
Unused in 10BASE-T

FIGURE 6.6   10BASE-T pinout and hub attachment.

the endstation's "receive" pins. One of the hub's functions is to perform this electrical crossover function—the crossover happens inside the hub. Figure 6.6 illustrates the 10BASE-T patch cable connector wiring diagram, as well as a schematic of the way the patch cable facilitates the endstation's attachment to the hub.

When a hub has a port labeled MDI/MDIX, this port may be switched so it acts like a endstation, which facilitates the chaining of one hub to another using a straight-through patch cable. Another way to interconnect two hubs (when one of the two does not have a switchable MDI/MDIX port) is to use a 10BASE-T crossover cable. Figure 6.7 shows how a "crossover cable" swaps transmit and receive inside the cable, so two endstations or two hubs may be interconnected. In a way, a crossover cable is like a two-port hub.

LAYER 1: REPEATERS

Repeaters are the least sophisticated devices that may be used to interconnect two or more Ethernets. A repeater does nothing more than copy bits from one port to all the other ports. Repeaters are strictly Physical Layer devices, with little intelligence. One limitation of repeaters is that they propagate errored frames because they have no concept of what they are doing beyond the bit level.

Repeaters exist to extend the size of an Ethernet. A 10BASE5 Ethernet may only have 100 nodes, and a 10BASE2 segment is limited to 30 nodes. Interconnecting more nodes than that requires some kind of LAN extension device. Remember that 10BASE5 is limited to 500 meters per segment, and 10BASE2 segments cannot exceed 185 meters. Given a need to cover a larger distance, a repeater was the sim-

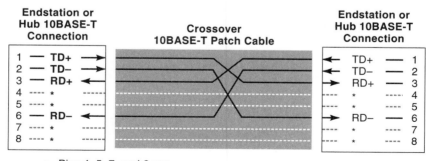

* Pins 4, 5, 7, and 8 are
Unused in 10BASE-T

FIGURE 6.7 Crossover cable functionality.

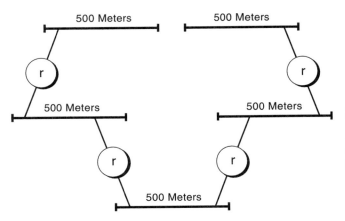

FIGURE 6.8   No more than four repeaters per Ethernet.

plest device that could do the job. One cannot add repeaters indefinitely. The "four-repeater rule" holds regardless of which physical manifestations of Ethernet are being interconnected. It is easy to forget this rule and interconnect some set of Ethernets with more than four repeaters, which can lead to error conditions such as late collisions.[7] The four-repeater rule is illustrated in Figure 6.8.

Multiport repeaters were commonplace in many networks at one time. Often these were modular "multi-media" devices, in the sense that they could interconnect thick and thin Ethernet media. Multiport repeaters evolved into hubs, especially once 10BASE-T was standardized. Later, so-called "enterprise" hubs, often supporting multiple logical repeaters within one chassis, and perhaps enhanced network management capabilities, arrived on the scene. Some of these devices also included bridging or routing features, or server cards. Hubs became a strategic product that centralized essential network functionality in the wiring closet.

INTERCONNECTION AT OSI LAYER 2

Layer 2 interconnection devices, for all LAN types, are known as "bridges." Since only four repeater hops can be in a collision domain and still have it be compliant with Ethernet's topology rules, "bridges"[8] serve to interconnect Ethernets and help to further extend the distance over which they could operate. Plus, remember that a single Ethernet cable (or an extended LAN), logically a bus, is a shared medium—only one station may transmit at a time. This is another part of the motivation for bridges, which isolate conversations so that local traffic (traffic that does not need to cross the bridge) cannot collide with conversations taking place on other "collision domains" to which the bridge is attached. This traffic isolation is indicated in Figure 6.9, in which traffic between stations A and B can happen at the exact same instant as traffic between stations C and D.[9]

Ethernet bridges are designed to be "transparent." They are supposed to be invisible in the sense that endstations operating over a bridged LAN cannot tell it from a "repeater-ed" LAN, or a piece of coaxial cable for that matter. After repeaters, bridges are the next most sophisticated Ethernet interconnection devices. Bridges operate at the Data Link layer. Transparent bridges are one major type of bridge; they receive at least the destination address of each frame, forwarding the frames based on a table they have learned by simply observing which (source) addresses are seen on each port.

One of the advantages of transparent bridges is that they are easy to deploy. (Be warned, however: The IEEE recommends that a given topology be no more than seven bridges in diameter.) Another benefit of bridges is that their presence is transparent to all higher-layer protocols. Bridges only forward packets based on the destination address in the Data Link layer frame.[10] Figure 6.10 indicates where bridges fit within the OSI Reference Model, and logically illustrates the layer processing that happens within a bridge.

In the mid-to-late 1990s, marketing lingo dispensed with the older label, so "bridges" first evolved into "switches," then into "layer-2 switches" (to distinguish

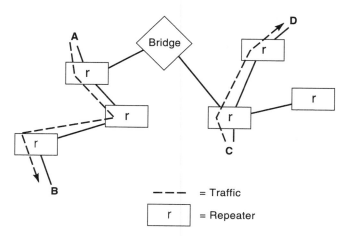

FIGURE 6.9 Bridges enable simultaneous data transfer.

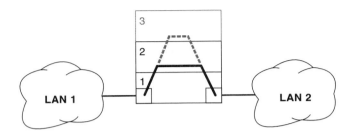

FIGURE 6.10 Logical internal diagram of a bridge.

them from "layer-3 switches," which is the new term for products that are otherwise known as "routers"). Despite their "new" name, they are still bridges. The principal difference between bridges and switches is speed. As far as their layer-2 functionality goes, they are identical.

Bridges were originally software-based devices that had relatively few ports (e.g., eight or less). Even though each frame was forwarded by software, it was still possible to achieve wire-speed or near-wire-speed performance with reasonably fast microprocessors—and efficient forwarding code! Switches are mostly hardware-based, especially the components related to receiving, forwarding, and transmitting frames. These are well-defined and relatively straightforward tasks, suitable for implementation in hardware.

Various companies have put the necessary MAC-layer and bridging functionality on a single chip (usually an Application-Specific Integrated Circuit, or ASIC), allowing much higher port density and enabling aggregate forwarding capacity to increase as the number of ports increases, without increasing the cost of the devices. Switches used to be more expensive, per port, than hubs, but competition and market maturity have made switches so much cheaper that hubs are fading away. Switches offer far more performance for the price, even if they cost slightly more per port than a hub.

Bridge Types

Transparent Bridging (Ethernet)

Ethernet bridges are known as "transparent bridges" because they are "plug and play" devices. If you insert a transparent bridge in the middle of a repeater-interconnected Ethernet, it just learns where stations are by watching them talk. If a source address is seen on a given port, then any traffic destined for that station should be forwarded out that port. The "bridge forwarding table" is simply a list of MAC addresses alongside the ports on which they were learned.

If a frame is seen that has an as-yet unknown destination, the bridge must flood that frame across all ports (except the one the frame arrived on)[11] so that it can reach the destination station, if it exists. When a transparent bridge first starts up, it spends time in a "learning" mode so it learns which of its ports lead to which of the stations it has seen traffic from.

Source-Route Bridging (Token Ring)

Token Ring bridges are called "source-route bridges" and do not operate by learning where MAC addresses are.[12] Transparent bridges are semi-intelligent so that the endstations can operate the same in either bridged or nonbridged environments. On the other hand, source route bridges are less intelligent, forcing the endstations to do more work to operate in a bridged environment. The bridges serve to define "ring numbers" for each unique ring, which are used by the bridges to determine how to follow the frame's source "routing" header.

The forwarding tables in the source-routing bridges are entries of the form (ring number, interface number), thus the forwarding state in the bridges depends on their number of interfaces, not the number of endstations in the bridged LAN.

Source-route bridging puts extra demands on the endstations, while the bridges need only know how to forward the "explorer frames"[13] to all rings without creating duplicates, and how to follow the source route tag[14] in the frame header. Since all the bridged frames will have a source route tag, the bridges need not do any real work to figure out how to forward frames—the frames' headers contain instructions on how to forward them, in the form of a list of ring numbers.

Every time a token ring station wants to contact another staton, it sends out a special "all-routes explorer frame," which is flooded by the bridges until the station is reached (if it exists). The destination station then responds with another broadcast frame, which the station that originally transmitted the explorer frame will presumably hear.[15] Now that the original station has a "source route," or a list of bridges a frame must cross in order to reach the destination station, it can create the proper Routing Information Field in the Token Ring header. Each endstation keeps a local cache of information (destination MAC address, source-route tag), so that it need not transmit a broadcast explorer frame every time it wishes to communicate with that MAC address.

"Learning Bridges" and the Spanning Tree Protocol

Transparent bridges learn where stations are by remembering which port each active source address was heard on. When a frame needs to be forwarded to some destination, the bridge looks up that destination in its "bridge forwarding table" and sends the frame out the port on which that MAC address was learned. Destinations that have not yet been learned are flooded along a "spanning tree" that is constructed among the set of bridges so that there are no loops in the topology. A spanning tree is literally a tree that spans (connects) each bridge in the topology. Trees have the property that they are free of loops in the topology.

A topology with a loop would create broadcast storms, and would even replicate unicast frames endlessly. A spanning tree is constructed because it is a tree that spans all the links in the topology. The tree ensures that only one copy of a packet will be seen on any LAN in the entire topology. The Spanning Tree Protocol is the very simple protocol that ensures that the topology is loop free and that creates the spanning tree. Each bridge periodically transmits a Bridge Protocol Data Unit (BPDU), which serves to inform all other bridges (if they exist) of its presence.

The Spanning Tree Protocol was invented by Dr. Radia Perlman, then of Digital Equipment Corporation (DEC).[16] It was later standardized by the IEEE as part of the 802.1D bridging specification. The two versions are not quite identical, and you will sometimes see bridges that can be configured to speak either the DEC or IEEE dialect of the protocol. Figure 6.11 shows an example of a spanning tree. Note that certain bridge ports are "blocked," (indicated by dashed lines) so that duplicate frames are not created by the loops that would otherwise have been present.

As indicated in the topology, one of the bridges has been elected as the "root" bridge. All frames that are either broadcast, multicast, or being sent to unknown des-

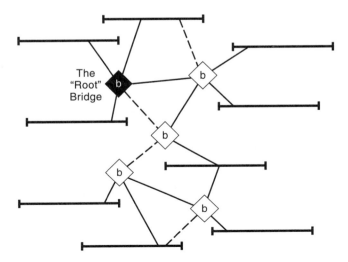

FIGURE 6.11   A spanning tree.

tinations are flooded toward the root bridge.[17] This ensures that the frames are conveyed to all the LANs in the bridged topology.

Normally, the Bridge PDUs have a default bridge priority of 32,768 (out of a range from 0–65,535). If no configuration tuning has been done, the bridge with numerically lowest MAC address will be elected as the root bridge. This might be fine if you have a small bridged network (bandwidth is plentiful and it doesn't really matter to you where the root bridge is). However, in the event of a bridged WAN, it may be very important that the root bridge be on the main campus, near most of the users. If your main office were in New York, with small branch offices scattered throughout the U.S., you wouldn't want all your broadcast packets to be forwarded through Council Bluffs, Iowa. To prevent this from happening, it is possible to configure a bridge with a lower bridge priority value, which makes it win and become the root bridge.[18] Conversely, bridges that you do not ever wish to become the root may be configured with a very high bridge priority, even as high as 65,535.

Some bridges begin forwarding frames as soon as they have received the first six bytes (the destination address), which means that the frames incur little delay in passing through the bridge. Of course, errored frames will get through, so this "cut-through" technique is not perfect. Other bridges wait until they have received entire packets and verify the Frame Check Sequence before forwarding it. The delay incurred varies with packet size, since it takes much longer to receive a 1500-byte frame than a 64-byte frame.

Bridge designers always had this choice of forwarding while receiving versus receiving before forwarding. These different forwarding approaches were mostly academic while bridges were still relatively slow, software-based devices. However, as bridging performance approached "wire speed," these differing delay characteristics became a key marketing differentiator for first-generation Layer-2 switches.

Collision Domains and Broadcast Domains

Today's Ethernet environments are increasingly dominated by Ethernet "switching," so collisions are less and less likely since the switch (still a transparent bridge) limits the "collision domain" to those stations reachable via a given switch port. Ultimately, this trend indicates that there may be just one endstation attached to a port, with its own private collision domain that it shares with the switch port. Note that this is the degenerate case for the binary exponential backoff algorithm, and thus is vulnerable to the *capture effect*.[19] However, a switch port may also connect to a set of hubs and/or switches, which could potentially reach hundreds of endstations.

The collision domain is the set of Ethernet segments that can directly "hear" each other's frames. Remember that any collision must happen within the frame's first slot-time (512 bits, i.e., 64 bytes), so the time it takes for a signal to propagate across a LAN and return to the starting point must be less than the time it takes to transmit 512 bits. Any set of Ethernets connected with repeaters is a single collision domain, since the repeaters simply copy the bits from one port to every other port. MAC-layer bridges terminate the collision domains, but preserve the broadcast MAX-layer or multicast domain, which is the set of stations that will receive a broadcast frame sent by any of them. Collision domains and their relationship to broadcast domains is illustrated in Figure 6.12.

When there are no bridges, the collision domain and broadcast domain both encompass the same set of end-nodes. Once bridges are added, each collision domain is a proper subset of the broadcast MAC-layer or multicast domain, which is the superset of all the end-nodes. Each bridge port defines the edge of a collision domain.

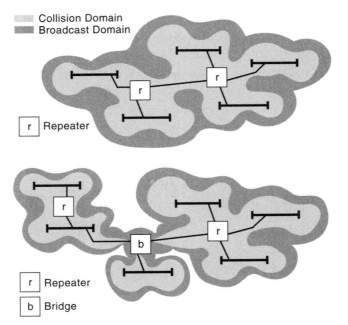

FIGURE 6.12 Collision domain versus broadcast domain.

Evolution of Bridging: Switching

Throughout the late 1980s and early 1990s bridges had few ports, on the order of four to twelve. Bridges also were not "wire speed" devices, meaning that if they had eight ports, they could not necessarily support 40 Mbps of unicast traffic. Why not 80 Mbps? Clearly, since 10 Mbps Ethernet is a half-duplex technology, the most traffic that can ever be on a link is 10 Mbps. Any traffic that the bridge receives has obviously arrived on some port, and it needs to exit via a different port. If one considers the eight ports as being four "in" ports and four "out" ports, then there is clearly only enough capacity in the *links* to support 10 Mbps throughput per in/out *pair*. Granted, each port will have a mix of in and out traffic, but the maximum is still 10 Mbps total *per pair of ports*. Generically, a switch with N half-duplex 10 Mbps ports needs to have a maximum internal forwarding capacity of N/2 Mbps. This discussion is illustrated in Figure 6.13.

In 1992 or so hardware implementations of "a bridge on a chip" enabled the emergence of the first Ethernet "switches." Ethernet switches were nothing more than bridges that were capable of near wire-speed or wire-speed performance. Generally, they also had more ports than the bridges which had preceded them. The inevitable

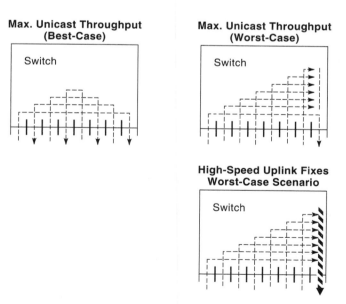

FIGURE 6.13 Rationale for high-speed uplinks.

march of technology has given us switches today that are fully wire-speed devices, and performance has ceased to be a differentiator for switches. Today, all switches are expected to be wire-speed and vendors differentiate their switches by incorporatng extra value-added features, such as VLANs or class-of-service queueing.

A 10 Mbps Ethernet switch will usually support Fast Ethernet (100 Mbps, half- or full-duplex) uplinks, or Asynchronous Transfer Mode OC-3 uplinks (155.52 Mbps, full duplex) supporting LAN Emulation. ATM LAN Emulation, or "LANE" for short, is a standard from the ATM Forum that standardizes Ethernet and Token Ring bridging over ATM backbones. Switches with Fiber Distributed Data Interface (FDDI) uplinks are also very common, and Gigabit Ethernet uplinks (1000 Mbps) began emerging in 1998.

Rather than give the impression that Ethernet switches are the only type, note that DEC's GigaSwitch™ was an early FDDI switch, and is still used at many Internet Exchange points. Many other vendors sell FDDI switches today, and Token Ring switches are also available. Of course, as implied by LANE, ATM switches are also on the market.

Practical Overview of Switch Design

The earliest LAN switches to appear on the market were not necessarily wire-speed devices. At the time, only one form of Ethernet existed: 10 Mbps, which is half-duplex by design. As discussed above, a switch can only handle (N/2)*10 Mbps, where N is the number of ports. For example, the switch on the left in Figure 6.13 can clearly only accomodate four simultaneous 10 Mbps data flows.

If multiple ports have data needing to exit via the same output port, then the switch must buffer the data. The worst-case scenario for a single-speed switch is that all N-1 of the ports will have data needing to exit via only one of the ports. In this case, the switch offers no more speed than a hub, and probably less.[20] Bear in mind that these best- and worst-case scenarios have only considered unicast traffic flows. If any port receives a broadcast or multicast, that frame must be flooded out the other N-1 ports (except ones which the Spanning Tree Protocol has placed in the "blocked" state).

Now that Fast Ethernet exists, a switch may have 12 to 36 (or more) 10 Mbps Ethernet ports, with one to three (or more) Fast Ethernet "uplink" ports. These faster ports may be attached to "in-demand" devices such as links to core switches, or routers, or popular servers. This neatly addresses the unicast worst-case scenario, provided the popular device has been attached to a high-speed port. However, traffic management is still an issue that must be carefully considered, as it is still possible for more than 10 Mbps of traffic to be waiting for a 10 Mbps port at any given time.

INTERCONNECTION AT OSI LAYER 3

Routers can also be viewed as LAN interconnection devices, but they isolate each LAN domain into a separate "subnet" or "network number," depending on which protocol stack you are "routing." Routers forward packets based on the destination address at the Network layer (layer 3). A router's logical structure is shown in Figure 6.14.

Like any LAN endstation, a router receives a frame if it is either a) a unicast frame addressed to one of the router's interfaces, b) a frame addressed to the LAN broadcast address, or c) a frame addressed to a multicast address. Broadcast packets for protocols that the router is not participating in may be dropped. Multicast packets for groups with no internal forwarding state may be dropped.[21] Unicast frames addressed to one of its interfaces must be interpreted, and possibly forwarded, provided the packet corresponds to a protocol that is currently being routed.

If a frame is addressed to one of the router's interfaces, and the packet inside is also addressed to one of the router's layer-3 interface addresses, then the packet is meant for the router itself. Packets that the router must forward are addressed to the router at layer 2, *but not at layer 3*; their ultimate (network-layer) destination is elsewhere. Packets addressed to the router itself will have one of the router's interface MAC addresses in the Data Link layer Destination Address field, and one of the router's Network layer addresses in the packet's Destination Address field.

A router acts as a protocol endstation on each of its interfaces, as well as supporting forwarding between interfaces, but not all packets that a router receives need to be forwarded. For instance, if a telnet session is connected to the router, packets are sent to and fro between the router and the device at the other end of the connection. Again, these packets are actually addressed to one of the router's interface addresses, at both layer 2 and layer 3. Other packets that may be directly addressed to the router are Internet Control Message Protocol (ICMP) packets and Simple Network Management Protocol packets (SNMP), as well as packets associated with

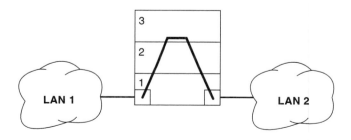

FIGURE 6.14 Logical internal diagram of a router.

routing protocols, such as routing updates, etc. Lately, many routers are also manageable via Hyper-Text Transport Protocol (HTTP) in so-called "Web-based management."

The size of a network layer address depends on the protocol stack. AppleTalk Phase II has a three-byte address consisting of a two-byte network number and a one-byte node address. DECnet Phase IV addresses are only two bytes, consisting of a 10-bit node address and a 6-bit network number. Novell's IPX is a close derivative of Xerox's XNS "Internet Datagram Protocol," which both use four-byte network numbers concatenated with six-byte MAC addresses, which are used as the node addresses.[22] IPv4 addresses are four bytes long, with no fixed boundary between the "network number" and node address. IPv6 addresses are 16 bytes, allowing for multilevel hierarchical addressing structures. The prize for the largest addresses goes to OSI's Connectionless Network Protocol (CLNP), which uses hierarchical addresses that are up to 20 bytes long. Both IPv6 and CLNP addresses support using a node's literal MAC address as a token within the host portion of the network-layer address, because the MAC address is a convenient six-byte number that is virtually guaranteed to be unique.[23]

Routers forward packets based on their destination address at the Network layer of the OSI Reference Model. Bridges are independent of higher-layer protocols, while routers are intimately protocol-dependent. Routers define boundaries for protocols, allowing them to scale beyond operation over a single LAN. To one degree or another, each Network layer protocol depends on the judicious placement of routers for its scalability. Some protocols, such as DECnet Phase IV and AppleTalk have very small address spaces that are incapable of supporting operation on a global scale. Generally speaking, a protocol's addresses need to be big enough to support at least two layers of hierarchical structure.

Remember that bridges forward frames based on their Data Link layer destination address, also known as MAC address in the case of most LANs.[24] Routers, for "routable" protocols (including IP), terminate both broadcast domains and collision domains. Broadcast domains have a one-to-one correspondence with distinct IP prefixes (a.k.a. "subnets"), or distinct network numbers in other protocols. Despite the fact that routers terminate broadcast domains, they may be configurable to selectively forward certain types of broadcast traffic, e.g., UDP/IP broadcasts of DHCP, NetBIOS, etc. In such cases, the routers are configured to pick up only certain broadcast packets and send their data—within a new unicast IP header—to a particular server.

Besides the very special cases of broadcast traffic above, the only traffic that crosses a router is unicast or network-layer multicast traffic. Unicast traffic leaving a broadcast domain is addressed to a router's MAC address, with the destination IP address indicating the ultimate target. Multicast traffic, in the case of multicast IP, is not addressed to the router's MAC layer address, but simply sent to the MAC-layer equivalent of the IP multicast destination address. IP multicast packets are not addressed to the router at either the Network or Data Link layer! The router's job is to take such packets off the wire (by noticing that they have a MAC-address prefix used by IP multicast), decide if they should be forwarded, and if so, where. How the packet is forwarded depends partly on the multicast routing protocol(s) in use, and partly on the multicast forwarding state that has already been built up within the router. (Note that OSI's CLNP also supports multicast at the network layer.)

Typically, routers are multiprotocol devices, usually also capable of supporting concurrent bridging of protocols which it is not configured to "route." If a router is bridging and routing at the same time, how can it tell if it needs to bridge a packet (i.e., forward it based on its destination MAC address alone), or route it (i.e., forward it based on its destination network-layer address)? There are two possibilities. The one that was commonplace in the late 1980s and early 1990s was based on the EtherType. If a bridge/router received a packet for an EtherType that it was configured to route, it would "route" that packet, forwarding it according to the packet's Network-layer destination address and that protocol's "routing table." If the frame's EtherType did not match a protocol that the bridge/router was configured to route, then it was bridged, or forwarded, based solely on its destination MAC address.

Another, perhaps more efficient, way to tell "bridgeable" packets from "routeable" ones is to use the packet's destination MAC address alone. If the frame is addressed to one of the bridge/router's own interface MAC addresses, then it must correspond to a routed protocol. If the frame is received and not addressed to the bridge/router itself, then it must need to be bridged. (Another possibility would be that the packet was misdelivered, or a broadcast or multicast packet. Before bridging a packet, it must be examined to ensure that it should be bridged.)

REFERENCES

Perlman, R., *Interconnections,* Addison-Wesley, Reading, MA. 1992.

ENDNOTES

1. Bridges need not receive an entire frame before making their forwarding decision (in a mode known as "store-and-forward" operation). Alternatively once the first six bytes have been received (i.e., the MAC-layer destination address), the frame may be streamed directly to the appropriate output interface. That mode of operation is known as "cut-through."

2. Note that in the case of a bridge, the frame's FCS, as received, is unaltered inside the bridge. In a router, the inbound FCS is stripped, and a new FCS is created on the output LAN interface. Why is the FCS different? The LAN headers are different—in particular, the MAC SA is now the router's output interface address, and the MAC DA is that of the next-hop gateway (or of the ultimate destination). Other elements of the LAN frame should be the same. The layer-3 packet is usually unaltered by the router, except for decrementing the packet's Time-to-Live (TTL), and updating the header checksum (if it is present).

3. Token Ring layer-1 interconnection devices are Multistation Access Units (MAUs), which are essentially token ring hubs. The closest product in FDDI technology is the concentrator. Both Token Ring MAUs and FDDI concentrators participate in the layer-2 protocol, performing ring maintenance functions.

4. If attachment to thick Ethernet is desired, simply use an AUI cable to a transceiver.

5. Of course, the number of ports is irrelevant, as long as Ethernet's topology rules are observed.

6. In 10BASE5 environments, the MDI is the vampire tap. In 10BASE2, it is a thinnet coaxial "T" connector.

7. All collisions should happen within the first 64 bytes (i.e., 512 bits) of the frame. At 10 Mbps, it takes 51.2 microseconds to transmit 512 bits, which is Ethernet's "slot time." The binary exponential backoff algorithm's chosen random numbers represent how many slot times that a station must wait before attempting a retransmission.

8. Layer-2 interconnction devices are generically known as bridges. These devices make forwarding decisions based solely on information present in the Data Link layer header, generally just the MAC DA.

9. Of course, the repeaters are actually flooding the traffic out all their interfaces, one bit at a time. The figure focuses on the path between the communicating nodes, but remember that all nodes on the left side, including the bridge, receive each and every bit of every frame between A and B. Likewise, all stations on the right side receeive every frame that C transmits to D.

10. IEEE LAN standards formerly allowed both a 16-bit and 48-bit address format. 16-bit addressing has been officially deprecated by the IEEE, but it is still supported by certain equipment, notably FDDI.

11. Broadcast and multicasts are handled the same way, in that they are forwarded out of all ports—*except the port on which the frame arrived.*

12. Despite the name including the word "routing," source-route bridges operate at the Data Link layer. Source-routing is a bridging technique, in which the source must discover the route to the destination MAC address.

13. Explorer frames are a special kind of broadcast packet that bridges use to "thread the needle" from the source to the requested destination. Source-route bridges ensure that

the explorer frame is forwarded onto every ring in the bridged topology. If the destination MAC address exists, that station simply responds by reversing the explorer frame's accumulated source route. Once the original station has the source route, then it can send packets directly to that destination.

14. The actual name for the source-route tag is the "Routing Information Field" (RIF). See Chapter 9 for a more in-depth discussion of Token Ring (IEEE 802.5) LANs.

15. Yes, it would have been a lot more efficient if the "found station" would have responded via unicast to the searching station. However, the use of broadcast does allow the other stations on the LAN to promiscuously build up their source-routing information caches. In this manner, future broadcasts are limited to stations who have restarted or aged-out old information.

16. Dr. Perlman's book, *Interconnections*, contains a very detailed, yet readable, description of all types of bridging and the Spanning Tree Protocol. I heartily recommend this book if you are interested in learning more about bridging. (*Interconnections* also covers Network layer issues, including the theory of routing protocols.)

17. Once the root bridge forwards the frame away from itself, the other bridges note the frame arriving from the *direction* of the root bridge, so they flood the frame on all their non-blocking parts. The universal forwarding rule that all the bridges follow is to flood out all non-blocking parts—except the one on which the frame arrived.

18. In the event that there is more than one bridge at the lowest priority level, the one with the numerically lowest MAC address becomes the root.

19. See Chapter 7 for a discussion of the binary exponential backoff algorithm and the capture effect.

20. At least with a hub, each station could participate in the collective CSMA/CD algorithm and the collisions would ensure fair access to the popular device. In this case, the switch must implement some fairness algorithm within itself, and provide enough memory to buffer packets during the inevitable times of congestion.

21. Such packets are also dropped if multicast routing is not enabled.

22. Using the endstation's MAC address as part of the network-layer address eliminates the need for an ARP-like protocol alongside the IPX protocol stack. The router that attaches to the destination network number can easily form a MAC-layer frame to the destination, by simply extracting the destination MAC address from the host portion of the network-layer destination address field (the least-significant six bytes).

23. Manufacturers, despite their best efforts, may accidentally ship duplicate MAC addresses. As long as two such devices are not connected to the same Layer-3 network number, there is no chance for confusion.

24. The term "MAC layer" is often used interchangeably with the term "Data Link layer," though the MAC layer is, strictly speaking, a sublayer of the Data Link layer.

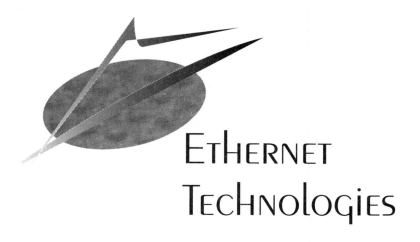

CHAPTER 7

Ethernet Technologies

D ue to its market dominance, Ethernet will be the first subnetwork technology to be discussed. Because there are many details surrounding Ethernet, it will be described in two chapters. The first chapter will be on Ethernet basics, including what media it runs over, how its medium access control protocol works, and physical layer-specific issues. The second will be on Ethernet LAN interconnection specifics, finishing off with a description of how IP works over Ethernet.

Subsequent chapters on other LANs will highlight differences from Ethernet. All LANs have some common features from IP's perspective, however, they may be very different at the subnetwork layer, both in how the LAN protocols work, as well as how the different LANs are interconnected.

INTRODUCTION

Local Area Networks (LANs) were invented in the mid-1970s to late-1980s. It is possible that the future will provide more examples of LAN technologies, but the industry seems to have settled on a small number of choices.[1] The immediate future development of LANs seems centered on enhancing what exists today; for example, making existing LAN technologies faster,[2] or adding support for enhanced reliablility or extra priority levels, rather than inventing something completely new.

LAN technologies operate at the Data Link layer (layer 2 of the OSI Reference Model), and Ethernet is just one of a variety of different LAN types. Figure 7.1 illustrates the OSI and IP Reference Models and places Ethernet and its other LAN cousins in the context of the rest of the protocol stack.

While Figure 7.1 only depicts LAN subnetwork technologies, IP also works over WAN subnetworks, which will be discussed later in Part II. As far as IP is concerned, LANs are all similar—they are all broadcast-capable, multiple access technologies.[3] We'll use Ethernet as the prototypical example in discussing how IP works over LANs, then in later chapters we will highlight the accommodations that IP must make to operate over the other LAN types.

By almost any measure, Ethernet has been the most successful LAN technology. Ethernet is not a singular Medium Access Control (MAC) layer protocol, but a family of closely related protocols that share a common set of frame formats. Ethernet was invented in 1973 (see paper in *ACM Communications* by Metcalfe, *et. al.*), conceived as a passive coaxial cable medium (a physical and logical bus topology) with a contention-based medium access protocol. Contention-based means that only

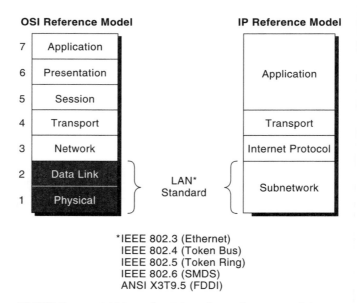

FIGURE 7.1   LANs in the OSI and IP reference models.

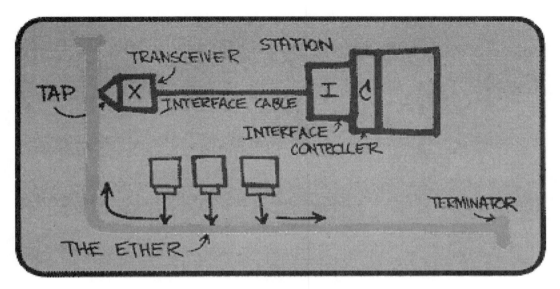

FIGURE 7.2   An early Ethernet diagram by Dr. Metcalfe (June, 1976).

one station may transmit at a time, so a protocol is needed to fairly share access to the wire among all its stations. Carrier Sense Multiple Access with Collision Detection (CSMA/CD) is the protocol that enables the medium to be shared fairly among all the stations. Other LAN technologies use different techniques to control access to their media; CSMA/CD is only pertinent to Ethernet.

Figure 7.2 is a copy of an early diagram of Ethernet, drawn by Dr. Metcalfe as part of a presentation to the National Computer Conference.

MEDIUM ACCESS CONTROL: CSMA/CD

The gist of CSMA/CD is that each station continually monitors the wire to keep track of whether or not any other station is transmitting. If another station is already transmitting when this station has a frame it wants to transmit, it must defer transmission until the other station is finished. That is the "carrier sense" portion of the technique. For diagnostic purposes, Ethernet devices may keep a counter of such "deferrals" or times when a frame was queued for transmission but the wire was already in use. Large numbers of deferrals may indicate that the Ethernet is becoming too busy, in which case network managers can respond by breaking up the LAN into smaller pieces using bridges.

When the medium is not being used, any station may attempt to transmit. Each station must not only monitor the wire to ensure it is free before a frame is transmitted, but also to see that its transmission is not garbled by a "collision" with a frame from another station. Once a collision has been detected, a station *should* cease transmitting immediately. In a shared medium in which only one machine can talk at a time, collisions are an expected and unavoidable event that must be dealt with fairly.

Binary Exponential Backoff Retransmission Algorithm

When a station encounters its first collision, it randomly selects a number from the set {0, 1}. The other station also picks a random value, which depends on how many times it has already collided with any other station. A collision must be observable by a transmitting endstation during the transmission of a frame. When determining its backoff interval, these randomly chosen values represent how many "slot times"[4] a station must wait before attempting a retransmission. Once the random delay timer expires, a station is not guaranteed to be able to transmit because yet another station may be using the wire at that time. Even if the coast is clear, any transmission it begins could experience a collision with any other station before the frame has been successfully transmitted.

In an Ethernet with only two stations, we can get a feeling for how the binary exponential backoff algorithm works. After the first collision, both stations select a value from the set {0, 1}. A tie results in a new collision (because each station will pause for the same time interval before retransmitting the packet). In this event, the stations then each pick a random value from the set {0, 1, 2, 3}, which has twice as many elements as the first set. At this point—on an Ethernet with only two stations—a tie is less likely. Keep in mind that on an Ethernet with more than two stations, a further collision is still possible given that there are perhaps dozens or even hundreds of machines that could be trying to transmit at any given time.

Each new collision that a station experiences doubles the size of the set from which random values are chosen. Successive rounds would use the following sets that keep doubling in size, ultimately reaching the set {0, . . . ,1023} after 10 successive collisions. Table 7.1 summarizes the randomization sets for the first ten rounds of the backoff algorithm.

The binary exponential backoff procedure continues selecting random numbers from the set {0, 1, . . . , 1023} in the 11th through the 16th rounds. In the un-

TABLE 7.1   The First Ten Rounds of the Binary Exponential Backoff Algorithm

Round	Size of Set	Elements of the Set
1 2		{0, 1}
2 4		{0, 1, 2, 3}
3 8		{0, 1, 2, 3, . . . , 7}
4 16		{0, 1, 2, 3, 4, . . . , 15}
5 32		{0, 1, 2, 3, 4, 5, . . . , 31}
6 64		{0, 1, 2, 3, 4, 5, 6, . . . , 63}
7 128		{0, 1, 2, 3, 4, 5, 6, 7, . . . , 127}
8 256		{0, 1, 2, 3, 4, 5, 6, 7, 8, . . . , 255}
9 512		{0, 1, 2, 3, 4, 5, 6, 7, 8, 9, . . . , 511}
10 1024		{0, 1, 2, 3, 4, 5, 6, 7, 8, 9, 10, . . . , 1023}

likely event that 16 consecutive transmission attempts result in 16 consecutive collisions, the Ethernet controller must report an error to the higher-layer protocol which was trying to send the packet. This is an example of an "excess collisions" error condition.

There is a benefit to "winning" a collision battle. Every time a station successfully transmits a frame, it gets to reset its backoff choice set to {0, 1}. In our degenerate example with only two nodes, this means that the station that wins the first collision—call it "A"—is very likely to win the next collision, a situation known as the "capture effect." Why? If another collision happens, station A will still be choosing either 0 or 1, while station B will (at best) be choosing from {0, 1, 2, 3}. In this case, A can lose if it chooses 1 while B chooses 0. The rest of the eight combinations result in A winning, or A tied with B (which simply results, in a new collision—which causes each station to choose from the next larger set). If station B loses the first new collision (5 out of 8 possibilities have B losing), it will then have to choose from {0, 1, . . . , 7}, while station A will still be choosing from {0, 1}.

Once station A wins, it is likely to win the next 16 collisions, with its worst exposure to loss coming after the second collision, when station B at least has a one in eight chance of winning. Any tie (A=0 versus B=0, or A=1 versus B=1) results in worsening odds for station B (3/16 chance of winning, 1/8 chance of a tie, to A's 9/16 chance of winning); station A will move up to {0, 1, 2, 3}, with station B choosing from{0, 1, . . . , 7}. Station B only gets to reset to {0, 1} after it has been through 16 collision events, or in the increasingly unlikely event that it wins a round by choosing a number such that B < A.

Because an Ethernet is a shared medium, potentially supporting hundreds of endstations, it is not difficult to imagine scenarios in which a long series of collisions could occur. Much has been made of the fact that *theoretically* it may take an *infinite* amount of time for a station to gain access to the medium. In reality this is rare; shared Ethernets with many hundreds of nodes have been built successfully.

Ethernet sans Collisions

The shared Ethernet medium we have been discussing thus far depends on collisions for its proper operation. The CSMA/CD protocol assumes a half-duplex bus topology in which only one endstation may be transmitting at any time.

The term "half-duplex," meaning that only one station may transmit at a time, is borrowed from the serial communications world. For most of its existence, Ethernet was purely half-duplex. Given that, at the time, there was no other kind of Ethernet, the term "half-duplex" was not heavily used. It did not come into common usage until after 10BASE-T was defined. The relationship between the hub and the endstation is much like that between two devices sharing a half-duplex serial link. In Ethernet, either the endstation is transmitting or the hub is transmitting; they cannot each transmit simultaneously. While 10BASE-T is also half-duplex, 100 Mbps Ethernet has an option allowing it to run in "Full Duplex" mode.

When Fast Ethernet was defined, an autonegotiation procedure was specified that permitted nodes on either end of a copper (not fiber) link to negotiate not only the speed at which they would communicate, but also the duplex setting—but only if they had already agreed to 100 Mbps operation. It is not possible to autonegotiate full duplex operation over 10 Mbps Ethernet. Some vendors do support full-duplex 10 Mbps operation, but the participating devices must be manually configured to operate in that mode.

In full-duplex mode, either end may transmit, even while the other end is transmitting. Since it is not possible to have a collision event, much of the CSMA/CD protocol is unneeded. One important side effect of full-duplex is that the temporal diameter of an Ethernet may be larger than if it was operating in half-duplex mode. In half-duplex mode, the size of an Ethernet is limited by the fact that a collision must be detected within the first 512 bits (64 bytes) of a frame.

Full-duplex operation is well-suited to deployment between switches, or between a server and a switch, since it eliminates the chance for collisions. Since collisions need not be detected, the size of an Ethernet may be larger; there are still upper limits to the size, but as Ethernet is pushed to higher and higher speeds, full-duplex operation is increasingly important, allowing practical-sized Ethernets to be constructed.

ETHERNET FRAME FORMATS

The history of Ethernet could fill a chapter or two by itself. Actually, there are many entire books on the subject of LANs, and several excellent titles only about Ethernet, which are mentioned in the bibliography. Briefly, the original protocol envisioned by Metcalfe was "standardized" by a consortium of companies, namely Digital Equipment, Intel, and Xerox.[5] Due to the names of the companies, this flavor of very early Ethernet was known as "DIX" Ethernet. An updated Ethernet specification came to be known as Ethernet version 2, and it followed the original frame formats as specified by the DIX consortium.

In the early 1980s, the IEEE stepped in to create a formal standardization framework to encompass all existing and yet-to-be-invented LAN technologies. This effort within the IEEE was known as "Project 802." Within Project 802, the committtee responsible for standardizing Ethernet was named "802.3." Figure 7.3 depicts the structure of Project 802 in the 1990s.

The standard that eventually emerged from 802.3 was similar to, but not the same as, the Ethernet version 2 specification that was the extant *de facto* standard. The most obvious difference was in the frame format. Figure 7.4 indicates the differences between the older Ethernet version 2 frame format and the format that was settled upon by the 802.3 committee. Jargon simplification: References to pre-802.3 Ethernet, e.g., Ethernet version 2, or just plain Ethernet, will just be called "Ethernet" from now on, while 802.3 Ethernet will simply be called 802.3.

The Preamble is not really part of a frame, but indicates that a frame is about to begin. The Preamble always consists of the following 8-byte pattern:

```
AA AA AA AA AA AA AA AB
```

This is just 60 bits of alternating `1010 1010 1010 1010 . . .`, until the last four bits which are `1011`. Strictly speaking, the Preamble is just the first seven

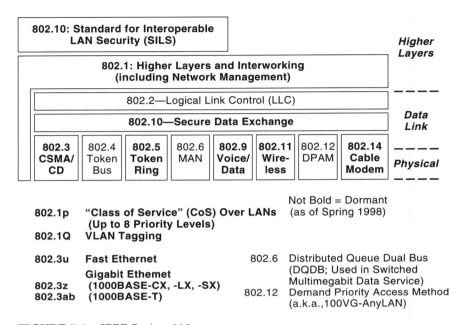

FIGURE 7.3   IEEE Project 802.

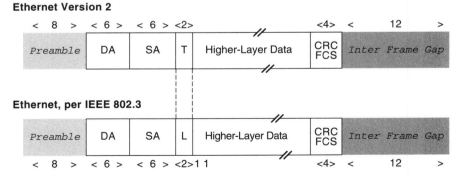

FIGURE 7.4   Evolution of Ethernet's frame structure.

bytes of alternating 1s and 0s, enabling all the other LAN stations to scynchronize with the transmitter's precise clock frequency. The final 'AB' byte is the "Start of Frame Delimiter," indicating that the next byte is the first byte of the actual frame. Once the packet is complete, stations must observe a 96-bit Interpacket Gap (IPG). Due to the fact that Ethernet transmits 10 million bits per second, each bit is transmitted in one-tenth of a microsecond (0.1 μs); by extension, the IPG lasts 96 times 0.1 μs, or 9.6 μs. The gap helps improve the fairness of the collision-detection algorithm, since all stations that have frames to transmit must wait an equal amount of time after the current frame ends before they may attempt to transmit their frames.

The primary difference between 802.3's frame format and the pre-standard Ethernet was that Ethernet's 2-byte "Type" field following the Destination and Source Addresses was instead used as a "Length" field in 802.3.

Without a length field, how did Ethernet version 2 controllers know when their frames were over? At the MAC layer, a receiver can detect that the medium has returned to a quiet state; once this happens the received frame's FCS is checked. If the frame is good, it is stored for further processing. The higher-layer protocol should be well-behaved and verify that the length is correct. A related question concerns receiving frames: If you're receiving an Ethernet packet, how can you tell if you have an Ethernet frame or an 802.3 frame? This is important, since 802.3 and "classic" Ethernet devices may share the same physical medium.

The numerical value of the Type/Length field holds the key: Luckily, the DIX consortium had assigned very few "EtherTypes" prior to the establishment of Project 802. As it turns out, few EtherTypes with numerical values less than 0x0600 had been assigned,[6] which is 1536 in decimal. Since the maximum size of an Ethernet frame is 1518 bytes, we simply interpret values in this two-byte field as shown in Figure 7.5.

If a frame is received with a type/length value of 0x05DC (decimal 1500) or less, then these two bytes are the frame's length, and the rest of the header is inter-

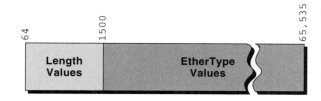

FIGURE 7.5 Type versus length.

preted as in IEEE 802.3; conversely, values in excess of 0x05DC are EtherTypes, and indicate that the frame header is now over, with the next byte corresponding to the indicated higher-layer protocol.

Note that an Ethernet frame may not be less than 64 bytes long. Packets must be long enough so that they will have time to reach the farthest parts of the Ethernet before the station stops transmitting, otherwise another station might collide with this frame—without the original sending station realizing that there had been a collision! Smaller packets must be padded so they are 64 bytes long.

Transmission Order

The IEEE draws an Ethernet frame as depicted in Figure 7.6. The bytes (rows) are transmitted from top to bottom, and each bit in each row is transmitted from left to right.

Ethernet uses what the IEEE calls "canonical" transmission order, in which the least significant bit is transmitted first. The English-speaking world tends to read from

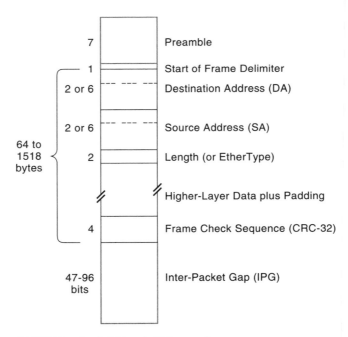

FIGURE 7.6   IEEE-style Ethernet frame.

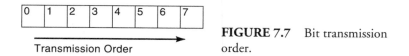

FIGURE 7.7 Bit transmission order.

left to right, so the natural order of transmission is from the left to the right. Figure 7.7 depicts the bit transmission order for Ethernet, which indicates that the leftmost bit is transmitted first, then continues on to the right. However, in Figure 7.6 the bytes are written "backward," with the most-significant bit on the *right*.

Confusion comes from two sources: A) Binary numbers are usually written with the most-significant digits on the left, just as decimal numbers are. The decimal number 4421 means 4000 plus 400 plus 20 plus 1, not 4 plus 40 plus 200 plus 1000. B) In Ethernet, the first bit onto the wire must be the least significant bit. If you write the decimal number eleven in binary, you have 0000 1011 (expressed as an 8-bit number). The transmission order of this byte would be 1-1-0-1-0-0-0-0, since the least significant bit must go first.

The IEEE could have written the binary numbers in the usual order,[7] with the most significant bits on the right, and defined the transmission order within each byte as "backwards," or right-to-left. This would have preserved the numerical values of the bytes within the frame. Really, the only requirement was that there be a consistent way of writing frames, and of transmitting frames. In practice, this is only an important distinction if you feel compelled to either a) read the IEEE Project 802 standards, or b) observe the physical medium with a "logic analyzer," a device that can show the electrical representation of the bit pattern on the wire. The transmitting MAC entity takes a value such as "8B" (in binary: 1000 1011) and transmits it as "1-1-0-1-0-0-0-1." The receiving MAC entity, knowing the rules for transmitting bits, takes these 8 bits off the wire and interprets "1-1-0-1-0-0-0-1" as 1000 1011, or 8B. Even a packet analyzer will not allow you to see the bit reversal, since any packets it displays must be received through its MAC chip, which necessarily undoes the reversal and presents the numbers in hex or decimal as one would expect to see them.

ETHERNET MEDIA

Ethernet frames may be sent over many different physical media (e.g., coaxial cable(s), twisted pair wiring, optical fiber). Ethernets may also run at different speeds. There was a very early "experimental Ethernet," built by Xerox,[8] that ran at

2.94 Mbps.[9] DIX Ethernet was a 10 Mbps system, but 802.3 originally ran at either 1 or 10 Mbps. All these Ethernets support both the Ethernet version 2 and IEEE 802.3 frame formats, as discussed above, but they are deployed over different physical media and operate at different speeds. The slowest standardized form of Ethernet is 1BASE5, which operates at 1 Mbps. It will be very difficult to find Ethernets running at less than 10 Mbps these days.

Thick Ethernet: 10BASE5

This original type of Ethernet, which ran over thick, typically yellow, cables, came to be known as "thicknet." Due to practical problems with this physical medium, other physical media were invented in an attempt to improve upon the original thicknet medium. Some practical problems were:

- the thick yellow cable was difficult to work with due to its stiffness and weight
- the cable was difficult to manage, requiring that it run close[10] to each machine in one long, winding, bus
- vampire taps were difficult to make properly
- vampire taps could wiggle loose fairly easily, causing intermittent electrical contact
- improper grounding could lead to unexpected errors, including having the cable becoming a short circuit between different power circuits (potentially dangerous!)

The 802.3 physical layer corresponding to thick Ethernet is formally known as "10BASE5," which means that it runs at 10 Mbps, uses baseband transmission, and may be up to 500 meters in "diameter."

Vampire taps must be at least 2.5 meters apart from each other, and the yellow Ethernet cable was typically marked every 2.5 m to help ensure correct tap placement. In order to simplify deployment in close quarters, multiport transceivers were produced that allowed multiple stations (up to eight) to share a common vampire tap. A 500 meter 10BASE5 Ethernet segment, with vampire taps every 2.5 meters (198 taps, allowing for 2.5 meters at each end between the terminator and the last tap), and an eight-port multiport transceiver attached to each could supposedly support 1584 endstations. However, the 10BASE5 LAN standard sets a limit of 100 endstations per 10BASE5 LAN segment.

The Attachment Unit Interface (AUI) between the transceiver and the Ethernet controller in the workstation/PC could be up to 50 meters in length, which allowed machines in offices to tap into ceiling-mounted thicknet cables, or into multiport transceivers. The AUI "transceiver cable" connects the Ethernet controller with the transceiver, the device that actually puts bits on and takes bits off the wire. The AUI cable is terminated in a 15-pin D-style connector with a universally-hated slide lock mechanism. Not only does the Ethernet controller exchange frames with the transceiver, it also provides the transceiver with power.

Other forms of Ethernet to be discussed next, namely 10BASE2, 10BASE-T, and 10BASE-F, integrate the transceiver onto the Ethernet controller itself. They are still logically separate, but they are physically co-located on the Ethernet controller.

The AUI connector that is part of nearly every 10 Mbps Ethernet device has become a convenient place to attach "microtransceivers," small boxes that attach directly to the AUI port, and draw power from it. These small boxes house a transceiver, so that they may have 10BASE2, 10BASE-T, or 10BASE-F ports, thus providing an inexpensive and easy way for thick Ethernet devices to be integrated into newer Ethernet infrastructures.

10BASE5 Issues

Thick Ethernet can have problems due to the attachment to the wire, or to the wire itself. Some wire-related problems include excess length, improper electrical grounding, and damaged cable. Excess length could result in late collisions, or an excessive number of collisions. Damage to the yellow cable may include such things as a broken outer casing, or an excessively bent cable that perhaps occurred during installation. If the casing is cracked, that could allow accidental contact between the shielding and some external metal, or the wire could act as an antenna, allowing radio-frequency energy to interfere with the internal signals. Environmental variables such as humidity can also cause problems. If moisture invades the wire, it will gradually degrade it. Excessively bending the cable could break the center conductor or the insulating layer, perhaps even forcing the center conductor to touch the shielding, which would cause a short circuit and render the cable useless. Finally, the cable must be properly grounded (i.e., "terminated") at each end. If not, strange electrical reflections may interfere with real traffic on the wire, causing higher numbers of collisions.

Excess length is tested with a device known as a Time-Domain Reflectometer (TDR). A TDR works by sending an electrical pulse into the wire and measuring the time delay until its reflection is seen. The measured time covers a trip from the beginning to the end, and back from the end to the beginning. The length (in units of time), then, is the measured round-trip time divided by two. Knowing the speed of electrical propagation in the medium, one can deduce how long the cable must be by multiplying the measured time-length by the signal propagation speed.

Attachment to the wire is where many problems happen. In the heyday of thicknet, making a good vampire tap was an art form. Even the best installers sometimes made the taps too deep, or not quite deep enough. A tap might work in the position the installer left it in, but then a shift in the position of the cable could separate the tap from the center conductor. Environmental factors can also lead to tap failure. If it is in an area with excessive heat or humidity, it is possible that the copper will oxidize and become a poor electrical conductor.

One final issue had to do, again, with the thickness of the cable. Due to its weight, one person could only carry so much when installing it. In order to create networks that were big enough, splices were required to interconnect multiple pieces of coax.[11] Splices are prone to being severed, and provide a location for electrical problems to arise. Similar to taps, splices that were exposed to excess heat or humidity were apt to degrade the coax's transmission quality at that point.

THIN ETHERNET: 10BASE2

The so-called "thin-net" employed thinner coaxial cable, which was much easier to work with but still had some practical problems, including that it was difficult to ensure that the system had been grounded properly and that it was too easy to add extra cable, which could make the overall length of the bus exceed the specification. The biggest liability was that it still had to snake from one machine to the next, which hindered wire management. In fact, it lacked thicknet's AUI cables, which meant that the cable now literally had to visit each endstation, instead of just getting to within 50 meters of each of them.

Thinnet was easier, and cheaper, to install due to the lighter-weight cable that did not require as many splices.[12] In the 802.3 context, thinnet's formal name is "10BASE2," indicating that it is also 10 Mbps, also employs baseband transmission, but is limited to about 200 meters in diameter (actually 185 meters, which is just under 607 feet). Due to the shorter overall length of a 10BASE2 segment, fewer endstations may attach to it. In fact, the 10BASE2 standard sets an upper bound of 30 endstations per segment. Despite the identified limitations, thinnet was very successful, mostly because it greatly reduced the cost of attaching the endstations.

10BASE2 Issues

Thinnet shares many electical vulnerabilities with thicknet. Thinnet segments also need to be terminated and grounded properly. One difference from thicknet is that the transceivers are integrated onto thinnet's network interface cards (NICs), so the card attaches directly to the wire. If the wire is not properly grounded, then it can actually carry an electric current! If a thinnet interconnects machines that are served by different electrical circuits, which may have slightly different electrical ground levels, then current will flow in an attempt to equalize the voltage differential. Most Ethernet adapters are not designed to receive power from the network, so this situation can result in fried adapters or motherboards—or a "shocking" experience for the user!

Thinnet was easy to deploy compared to thicknet, but it was also much easier to deploy it incorrectly, including failure to terminate it properly. The ends are just as easy to terminate as a thicknet; however, the nodes in the middle present a problem. Usually a station attaches to the wire with a BNC "T" connector. If the user didn't have a T handy, they may have used other connector types, resulting in improper impedance at that point in the wire. These mismatched impedances cause electrical reflections which can interfere with normal data transmissions. A time-domain reflectometer can be used to search for these impedance mismatches. Actually locating them is quite challenging since the TDR only tells you how far away the impedance mismatch is. You need to estimate where, among the coils of thinnet, that point may be.

One of the trickiest problems with thinnet that I have ever seen was due to cable length. The 10BASE2 standard says that the cable is supposed to be less than or equal to 185 meters long. That is just under 607 feet. As a marketing tool, at least one large NIC vendor made their thinnet NICs so that they could support 1000-foot "thinnets." This worked great, as long as all the NICs on that thinnet were from this vendor.

When inserting a new station in the thinnet bus, it is often easier to just insert a cable that is longer than necessary. Obviously, if the cable is too short (less than two meters), it won't work. Also obviously, finding a cable that is "just right" takes effort. Thus, cables that are too long are almost always chosen. Sometimes the cables are just a little too long, but who hasn't needed to insert a machine into a thinnet and grabbed a 10- or 25-foot piece of coax when you really only needed six feet? Such practices can rapidly make a thinnet much longer than is actually required to span the physical separations of the machines it serves.

It turns out that "enhanced" NICs could work with distances well beyond 1000 feet. The vendor can't guarantee it, but you might be able to get away with a thinnet that is 1300 or 1400 feet long. That is just what happened in a case I know all too well. All the existing machines on a thinnet were using nonstandard NICs, and then some new machines were added that had built-in Ethernet ports. Unfortunately, those new NICs "only" supported the standard's requirements of around 600 feet.

What was observed? The new machines didn't work . . . at all. Well, actually, new machines that were near each other could see each other, but not the rest of the network. The preexisting machines had no trouble; in fact, one office had an old and a new machine. The old machine worked just fine, but the new one did not. Thinking that perhaps there was a problem with the coaxial T-connector, the machines were swapped so they exchanged attachment points. The result was the same.

After several days of trying to isolate the problem, and having noticed that proximity seemed to be a factor for machines working or not, a TDR was used to measure the thinnet. It was just a tad long: 1650 feet! After looking in the ceiling and deciding that untangling the large coils of coax would be far too difficult,[13] two bridges were inserted in such a way that the oversized segment was broken into three legal-sized pieces. Ultimately this problem was solved by 10BASE-T, which did away with the shared coaxial medium, effectively hiding the coaxial cable in a box called a 10BASE-T hub.

Ethernet over Twisted Pair: 10BASE-T

Ethernet did not explode commercially until it could run over structured wiring, such as unshielded twisted-pair (UTP) phone wiring. Because the wires all come together in one wiring closet, it is easy to patch machines into hubs at this point. A very important practical advantage is that it is also easy to disconnect a misbehaving endstation from a hub without disturbing the rest of the machines on the LAN.

This 802.3 variant is known as "10BASE-T," with the "T" standing for twisted pair. Each "run" from a hub to an endstation may be up to 100 meters on "good-enough" wiring—"category 3" wiring, which is older but has the advantage of being nearly ubiquitous. Higher speeds such as 100 Mbps may require "category 5" wiring.

10BASE-T uses one pair of wires for transmitting data and another pair for receiving data. The connector used by 10BASE-T has eight pins, and is known as an RJ-45 connector. The six-pin connector used for telephones is known as an RJ-11. Typically, the remaining four wires of an RJ-45 are unused. Rather than install multiple twisted-pair wires to each desktop, some installations take advantage of the unused four wires for telephone lines or other communication capabilities.[14] This division of resources works fine in 10BASE-T environments, but certain faster technologies (such as 100BASE-T4, a way of running Fast Ethernet over category 3) require all four pair for the data connection, leaving no leftover wires to be used by other services. In such cases, new wire must be pulled to desktops.

10BASE-T Issues

10BASE-T is an improvement on virtually all of the media-specific issues of earlier Ethernets. The advantages of 10BASE-T, especially the fact that it could run over most of the world's installed twisted-pair telephone wiring, made it an overnight success. Its 100 meter radius (between a hub and all its attached endstations) ensured that a large percentage of most office buildings would be suitable for 10BASE-T, since very few buildings have floors large enough that 100 meters would not reach all the desktops. 10BASE-T was significantly easier to install, manage, and troubleshoot than earlier forms of Ethernet. For this reason, companies were willing to spend money on hubs and transition away from their prior investments in their installed thicknet or thinnet infrastructures. Despite its improvements, 10BASE-T is not without its own unique set of issues.

A Clean Patch Cord is a Happy Patch Cord. The first time I used 10BASE-T, the only patch cords that were handy had been sitting in a box under a co-worker's desk for a *long* time. They were unbelieveably dusty, but I didn't think that would be a problem; I thought the connector would clean the end of the patch cord when we inserted it into the hub. Given the large number of transmit-direction errors, especially the unbelievable numbers of collisions seen by the local device, but not by other devices, we decided to go out and buy some brand new cabling. The new cabling worked perfectly with the same router interface and hub interface. I learned to check for dirty connectors and sockets if unusual error statistics were seen—especially errors that seem to be localized to one port.

All Patch Cords Are Not Created Equal. One subtlety with 10BASE-T is that there is a "hub-side" and "device-side" of the standard. Normal "straight-through" patch cords are meant to connect a 10BASE-T endstation interface to a hub. There are also "crossover" cables that are used to interconnect two Ethernet devices back-to-back. Figure 7.8 illustrates how a hub plus two straight-through patches can be used to interconnect two endstations, and how a single crossover may substitute for a hub when only two devices need to be interconnected. The crossover may also be used to interconnect two hubs.

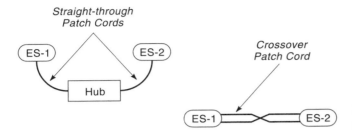

FIGURE 7.8   10BASE-T interconnection choices.

An Ethernet crossover cable is analogous to a null-modem cable. The modem situation is more familiar to most people. If a PC is attached to a modem, the serial cable is wired to connect a DTE (the PC) to a DCE device (the modem). If there is a desire to interconnect two PCs' serial ports without using modems, a "null-modem" cable is used, which swaps the transmit and receive wires so data can flow from transmit to receive in each direction (one wire is used to transmit from DTE to DCE, and a different wire is used to transmit from DCE to DTE . . . or said another way, to allow the DTE to receive bits from the DCE).

Similarly, 10BASE-T has a *pair* of wires that are used to transmit data, and another pair to receive transmissions from the other side. If two devices wish to be interconnected, whether two hubs or two PCs, you need to make sure that the cable swaps transmit and receive so that each side can hear the other. A 10BASE-T crossover cable is directly analogous to a serial null-modem cable.

The somewhat difficult issue here is that crossover and normal cables are very easy to mix up. Many shops try to choose one color for normal cables and another for crossovers, but this is more difficult to maintain than it sounds. The only real way to tell if a cable is "normal" is to hold the two connectors next to each other, upside-down. The left-to-right sequence of colors inside the connector should be the same on both sides. If it is not, then you have a crossover cable. It isn't necessary to know the pinout of a 10BASE-T connector to tell if a patch cable is crossed-over or not.

Length Issues.   What if you have a desktop that is 99 meters from the wiring closet? Attaching a one-meter patch cord from the hub to the patch panel, and another one-meter patch at the desktop will exceed the 100 meter length from the hub to the device. This is a rather extreme example, but it can arise in less obvious ways. If a desktop is 80 meters from the wiring closet, you might think you have plenty of slack. If you can't find a one- or two-meter patch cord, you may have to make do with a 10-meter patch, just to achieve connectivity between the hub and the patch panel. If you also must resort to using a long patch at the desktop, you could be near the edge of reliable operation (late collisions would be a symptom that such an endstation would experience).

It is easy to forget about the distance of the wire between the outlet at the desktop and the patch panel in the wiring closet, since you usually can't see that wire. In general, if you have a properly-designed horizontal cabling plant, and if you make sure you always have plenty of one- and two-meter patch cords on hand, you shouldn't have to worry.

ETHERNET OVER FIBER: 10BASE-F

One of the most important Ethernet media, besides 10BASE-T, is 10BASE-F. The 10BASE-F standards define how to carry Ethernet frames over optical fiber. 10BASE-FL (FL stands for Fiber Link) defines how a device such as a router or bridge might attach to a hub using a pair of fibers. 10BASE-FB (FB stands for Fiber Backbone) specifies the interconnection of hubs with fiber. There is one other 10BASE-F standard, 10BASE-FP. This variant uses a passive optical "repeater" to interconnect devices. The repeater is not an active device; it simply serves as a point where the optical signals may mix together. 10BASE-FP is a niche standard, in the same way that 10BROAD-36 was/is a niche standard—even though it is a standard it is not greatly demanded by the market.

The 10BASE-F specifications evolved from an earlier standard known as FOIRL, which stood for Fiber Optic Inter-Repeater Link. 10BASE-F is very important for interconnecting Ethernet devices between floors in buildings, or between buildings, where coaxial cable or twisted pair is not likely to be available. 10BASE-FL is completely backward compatible with FOIRL, with the added feature that end-devices such as bridges or routers may use 10BASE-FL, while FOIRL was limited to inter-repeater applications.

Inside buildings, the 100 meter limit of 10BASE-T (between the hub port and the NIC) means that fiber must be used between floors, since the distances would be too great for copper runs. Interbuilding distances are clearly the realm of fiber, which can easily exceed the 100 meter limit of 10BASE-T. Fiber also has the advantage similar to 10BASE-T of being a structured system, allowing buildings to be patched together in star or ring topologies.

10BASE-F Issues

FOIRL/10BASE-FL was used to interconnect hubs across distances greater than 100 meters. In fact, links between repeaters may be up to 2 km using either 10BASE-FL or 10BASE-FB. FOIRL was limited to 1 km, and has largely been superseded by

10BASE-FL. A common use of Ethernet-over-fiber standards is to connect routers or other devices to a hub at a remote location. Usually, a router or switch is located in the basement of a building, with vertical fiber to each floor, at which point a repeater serves to interconnect users over the horizontal copper wiring. Many organizations adopted such "collapsed backbone" architectures in the early 1990s.

An indirect benefit of using fiber to interconnect devices is that it provides electrical isolation. If lightning strikes a building, some of the millions of volts of electrical energy could be carried by interbuilding copper, resulting in damage far beyond the original strike. Fiber doesn't carry electricity, so electical damage cannot spread far beyond the original strike site.

Ethernet frames are carried over two fibers. At each 10BASE-FL endpoint, one fiber is used to transmit, and the other to receive. Most 10BASE-FL devices indicate that the link is 'up' when they receive optical power from the other side. If you only connect device A's transmit to device B's receive, this will make device B think the link is up.[15] Device B may believe it is successfully transmitting frames out its transmit connector, but with no fiber to pick them up, these light pulses won't be carried anywhere.

For 10BASE-F, and to a lesser extent 10BASE-T, you need to see positive link status on both ends as a basis for a working connection. Damaged or dirty optical patch cables could allow enough light through to trigger the 'link up' condition, but be of poor quality as far as actual frame transmission goes.

ETHERNET OVER CATV: 10BROAD36

Other variants of Ethernet exist, such as 10BROAD36, which specifies how Ethernet may run over broadband infrastructures, such as CATV cable plants. 10BROAD36 is quite different from the baseband (digital transmission) forms of Ethernet, since it has separate analog transmission, receive, and collision channels, which are carved out of two adjacent 6 MHz cable TV channels. Despite having been standardized, this form of Ethernet never really established itself in the marketplace. This may have been due to the emergence of Ethernet-over-fiber standards that could flexibly support interbuilding connectivity. It could also have been due to the fact that it required a rather high quality cable TV infrastructure, and people with strong RF engineering skills to keep it running well.

10BROAD36 Issues

10BROAD36 worked very well as a campus LAN backbone in the eary days of Ethernet. Applitek, Digital, and 3Com, among a few others, made equipment that complied with this standard. However, because the system was based on analog transmission equipment, it required significant RF engineering expertise to keep the system tuned—literally! The amplifiers, over time, gradually shifted away from the frequencies that they had been set for. The system must be carefully monitored for weird Ethernet errors (excess bad frames, indicated by FCS mismatches, and other problems). Approximately every six months, a 10BROAD36 system needs to be taken out of service for a tune-up. All the amplifiers need to be retuned to the exact center frequencies of the two channels used for transmit and receive.

One strange effect to watch out for is when you attach a device that thinks it is talking to a regular thicknet 10BASE5 network, via an AUI-to-10BROAD36 transceiver. Due to the separate channels being used for transmit, receive, and collision, the Ethernet controller will see many more framing errors, giants, and runts than a "normal" thicknet. This is because the transmit and receive channels are independent, so a collision is indicated to the controller, but data is still being received, instead of being jammed as in baseband Ethernet technologies.

Ethernet Beyond 10 Mbps

A discussion of Ethernet would not be complete without describing how Ethernet has evolved—and continues to evolve—from its 10 Mbps roots. On 14 June 1995, the IEEE 802.3 committee completed work on the 802.3u specifications for what was and is known as "Fast Ethernet." Fast Ethernet, also known as 100BASE-T, runs at 100 Mbps, and operates over two main physical media: unshielded twised pair copper and multimode fiber.

Copper-based Fast Ethernet has a choice of several physical layers: 100BASE-T2, 100BASE-T4, and 100BASE-TX. A critical requirement of the new standard was that it should, as 10BASE-T did, support operation of machines at up to 100 meters from the wiring closet. If this criterion were not met, then it would not be possible to transparently upgrade to Fast Ethernet by simply upgrading the endpoints; major capital expenditures would be required to install new wiring closets (and physical wiring) to support a Fast Ethernet upgrade. For Fast Ethernet to be successful, the 100 meter hub-to-station distance was a necessary requirement.

FIGURE 7.9 100BASE-T media summary.

The most common variant of 100BASE-T in new installations uses two pairs of wire within the 4-pair RJ-45 connector, over category 5 wiring. This type is known as 100BASE-TX. For compatibility with older cable plants, 100BASE-T4 was defined, which allowed 100 Mbps operation over category 3 (or better) wiring.[16] The tradeoff was that 100BASE-T4 required the use of all four pairs of the RJ-45 connector.[17] Later, 100BASE-T2 allowed operation over only two pairs of category 3 wiring, but by the time this was standardized, 100BASE-TX over category 5 wiring had acquired significant market share as the key enabler of high-speed desktop networking.

Table 7.2 summarizes the characteristics of all Fast Ethernet physical media. The following shorthand was used so the table could fit in a small space: Under the "Pairs" column, c/d/e represent category 3/4/5 of copper wiring, and mm/sm represents multimode or single mode fiber (only a single pair of fiber is ever needed to interconnect two Fast Ethernet devices). FDX and HDX stand for Full Duplex and Half Duplex, respectively. The 100BASE-FX standard does not officially specify single-mode media, but several vendors are shipping such products. 100BASE-FX uses a pair of multimode fibers, often terminated in "SC" connectors at each end. Other connectors, such as "ST," are also in use.

An autonegotiation scheme was defined so that a pair of Ethernet devices may choose 100 Mbps operation if they both support it, or 10 Mbps if one of them does not support 100 Mbps. The default mode of operation between Fast Ethernet nodes is half duplex, just like 10 Mbps Ethernet. The IEEE 802.3x and 802.3y standards specify how to operate in Full Duplex mode, in which either end may transmit at any time.[18] Whether a link is full or half duplex is also autonegotiable at link activation time, but only after both ends have already agreed to operate at 100 Mbps.

TABLE 7.2 COMPARISON OF 100BASE-T MEDIA

Medium	Pairs	Length	RJ-45 Pinouts
100BASE-TX	2 (e)	100 m	1:3, 2:6 (FDX capable)
100BASE-T4	4 (c/d/e)	100 m	1:3, 2:6, 4:7, 5:8 (HDX only)
100BASE-T2	2 (c/d/e)	100 m	same pairs as -TX (FDX-capable)
100BASE-FX	1 mm	412 m (HDX)	n/a
	1 mm	2000 m (FDX)	n/a
	1 sm	20000 m (FDX)	n/a

Autonegotiation is not possible between 10BASE-F* and 100BASE-FX devices. Their optical components are fundamentally incompatible. Efforts were made to enable autonegotiation over fiber, but in the end the choice was made to require that 100BASE-FX use a different wavelength of light. Thus, 10BASE-F* and 100BASE-FX devices will not even see each other if they are interconnected.

Fast Ethernet has become very popular. One reason must be that it feels like 10 Mbps Ethernet, with which many people had already become familiar. However, there are significant differences, notably in the physical layer. The backoff algorithm is preserved, but 10 Mbps Ethernet has no option for Full Duplex operation (newer devices can be manually configured do this, but it can't be autonegotiated), nor does 100 Mbps Ethernet work over coaxial cable—it is strictly designed for twisted pair copper wiring and optical fiber.

The one family resemblance that is preserved between the two different speeds is the Ethernet/802.3 frame formats. The common frame formats allow the construction of bridges that may transparently interconnect 10 and 100 Mbps Ethernet segments.

Ethernet beyond 100 Mbps

In 1998, the IEEE 802.3z group completed work on an even faster type of Ethernet, which runs at 1000 Mbps (1 gigabit per second, abbreviated 1 Gbps). This newest form of Ethernet is called Gigabit Ethernet, often abbreviated "GE." Gigabit Ethernet preserves the Ethernet/802.3 frame format, so devices may be built to transparently integrate LAN segments running at 100 and 1000 Mbps, just as devices integrate 10 and 100 Mbps operation today. This hierarchy of speeds conceivably will allow tiered deployments of Ethernet, with 10 and 100 Mbps to the endstations, and with 100 and 1000 Mbps in the "LAN core." (See Chapter 6 for a discussion of LAN interconnection.)

The work on GE has been split among two projects within the IEEE 802.3 committee. As mentioned above, the initial project was known as 802.3z, which has produced the 1000BASE-X family of standards. This project has defined three physical layers: 1000BASE-CX (short-haul copper), 1000BASE-LX (long-wavelength optics), and 1000BASE-SX (short-wavelength optics), all of which will be discussed shortly.

Another project was spun off, due to the more complex nature of its work. The 802.3ab project was tasked with creating a physical layer that would allow GE to work over four pairs of category 5 unshielded twisted pair copper, at the amazing distance of 100 meters. Not surprisingly, this work has been dubbed 1000BASE-T, imitating the names of the wildly successful 10BASE-T and 100BASE-T standards. The 1000BASE-T standard will be a natural upgrade for 10BASE-T or 100BASE-TX when products become available (1999).

There are two fiber-optic variants of GE: 1000BASE-LX and 1000BASE-SX, both of which use laser transmitters. 1000BASE-SX operates *only* over multimode fiber, over relatively short distances. 1000BASE-SX uses short-wavelength (770 – 860 nm) laser transmitters, running over multimode fiber. 1000BASE-LX version uses long-wavelength laser transmitters (1270 – 1355 nm), and spans the greatest distances when used over the less-commonly deployed single-mode fiber.[19] 1000BASE-LX can also run over multimode fiber, but over shorter distances. The common name for short-wavelength lasers is "850 nm," and the common name for long-wavelength lasers is "1300 nm." Both of those wavelengths identify the point of minimum optical attenuation within the range of wavelengths specified above.

Of the four physical layers that exist, 1000BASE-SX is likely to be the most popular in early GE devices due to its innate ability to leverage the large installed base of multimode fiber. Ultimately, 1000BASE-T will exceed 1000BASE-SX in terms of ports shipped, especially as 100/1000 and 10/100/1000 NICs arrive on the market.

1000BASE-X supports both 50/125 nm and 62.5/125 nm multimode fiber, as well as 10 nm single-mode fiber. These different fibers are illustrated in Figure 7.10.

Table 7.3 shows the maximum distance (assuming full duplex operation) that is supported by 1000BASE-LX and 1000BASE-SX. The distances depend on the type of fiber, as well as which wavelength is used.

Given all these choices, which are likely to be the most popular? It depends on the application, and also on the prevalence of installed fiber at a site. Multimode fiber is far more widely installed today than single mode. Of the two possible multimode fiber types, 62.5/125 nm is more popular in the U.S., though there is some 50/125 nm. 50/125 nm fiber is more common in Europe and elsewhere in the world. At present, long-wavelength lasers are more expensive than short-wavelength.

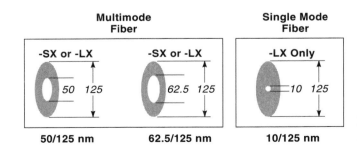

FIGURE 7.10 1000BASE-X fiber media.

TABLE 7.3 Gigabit Ethernet over Fiber

Fiber Dimensions	1000BASE-SX (770 – 860 nm)	1000BASE-LX (1270 – 1355 nm)
multimode........50/125 nm	525 m	550 m
multimode.....62.5/125 nm	260 m	550 m
single mode......10/125 nm	n/a	3000 m

Also note that when using these more expensive lasers with 50/125 nm fiber there is less than a 5 percent increase in distance. It is unlikely that anyone would plan to use 1000BASE-LX over 50/125 fiber when 1000BASE-SX is cheaper and goes nearly as far.

The 1000BASE-X family of standards includes one copper-based variant, 1000BASE-CX (the "C" stands for Copper). 1000BASE-CX operates over two pairs of 150 Ω shielded twisted pair cable,[20] terminating in two possible electrical connectors. This physical layer was designed for server-to-switch interconnection in relatively small rooms, which is why the distance is limited to 25 meters. Table 7.4 compares 1000BASE-CX to the forthcoming 1000BASE-T, which is intended to be used for desktop interconnection at 1000 Mbps.

1000BASE-T is being developed with a goal of 1000 Mbps operation over a 100 meter category 5 unshielded twised pair infrastructure. 1000BASE-T is related to the 100BASE-T2 standard, which allowed 100 Mbps operation over two pairs of category 3 (or better) wiring. 1000BASE-T will use all four pairs of the RJ-45 connector and squeeze five times the bandwidth out of each pair, compared to 100BASE-T2. The key is that for 1000 Mbps operation to be practical, it must be full duplex, which is just one of the many challenges involved in operating at such a high speed over twisted pair wiring, even category 5 wiring.

TABLE 7.4 Comparison of Nonfiber-optic Gigabit Ethernet Media

Medium	Length	Medium Type
1000BASE-CX	25 m	150 Ω (STP)
1000BASE-T	target: 100 m	100 Ω (UTP)

Possible Deployment Scenarios for Gigabit Ethernet.   In most campus backbone scenarios, 1000BASE-SX will be adequate for intrabuilding uses, such as interconnecting 10/100 "edge switches" on each floor, which provide connectivity to desktops, with backbone switches in the basement, reached via Gigabit Ethernet "uplinks." Another use for 1000BASE-SX might be interconnecting backbone switches in different buildings, provided the devices need not be more than 260 meters (just over 853 feet) from each other. Interbuilding applications may warrant 1000BASE-LX since it can cover more than twice the distance than 1000BASE-SX can (550 meters is about 1804 feet, which is just over a third of a mile). For applications requiring truly long distances, 1000BASE-LX over single mode is really the only choice.

For patching high-end servers into the LAN infrastructure, either 1000BASE-CX, 1000BASE-SX, or 1000BASE-T could be used. Due to the low cost of short-wavelength lasers,[21] and the abundance of multimode fiber patch cords, it is likely that 1000BASE-SX will be used by early adopters in wiring closets and server rooms rather than 1000BASE-CX, which would require a patch cable that is not common today. Once the 1000BASE-T standard exists, it is likely that server NICs will begin to support 1000BASE-T if it is cheaper than 1000BASE-SX. It is possible that 1000BASE-CX will find a niche, though it may not be used for its original purpose of attaching servers to the Gigabit Ethernet infrastructure over very short distances.

Can Ethernet Go Even Faster?

Will there be a 10 Gbps Ethernet? 100 Gbps?

10 Gbps (i.e., 10,000 Mbps) operation is quite challenging for current state-of-the-art electro-optical technology. As time goes by, it is almost inevitable that 10 Gbps Ethernet will become technologically feasible. Until then, it appears that the industry is looking to "trunking" as an interim solution. Trunking is an emerging technology that logically bundles multiple LAN connections (e.g., multiple 1 Gbps links) together. The bundle then appears as if it were a single, faster link. For example, four GE links may be trunked together to form an approximately 4 Gbps link.

Proprietary trunking techniques such as Cisco's Fast EtherChannel™ exist today,[22] and the IEEE is beginning to standardize link trunking as a way of providing speeds greater than 1 Gbps. It is unlikely that speeds in excess of 1 Gbps will be a market requirement until sometime in 1999 or 2000, and trunking will likely be an adequate solution in that time frame. Note that any trunking standard would also work for bundled 100 Mbps links as well, though the existence of Gigabit Ethernet in the marketplace may limit the demand for Fast Ethernet link trunking.

TROUBLESHOOTING ETHERNET

Ethernet may seem simple, but appearances can be deceiving. As with any technology, it is possible for things to go wrong, and Ethernet is no exception. Each of Ethernet's physical layers have different possible failure modes. Some observations about robustness may be obvious, but they apply across the board and are worth mentioning.

1. **Be suspicious of cabling**

   When things are broken, always check the cabling first! I'd estimate that more than half the time, I've traced problems to bad cables (too long, crushed, broken) or bad connectors (dirty or loose) .

   Don't be fooled by link lights. In 10BASE-T environments, it is possible for one end of a link to see the other's link pulse, with the other end seeing none. This is not supposed to be possible, but it does happen in the real world. If you can see link lights, but can't get packets across the link, replace the patch cord with one you know is good. If the link light still works, but now you can also exchange data across it, then the original cable is bad and should be discarded or re-terminated. If reterminating the patch cord with new connectors doesn't help, then discard it (after destroying it).

   10BASE-T is not the only variety of Ethernet for which the link status may be deceiving. 10BASE-F fiber patch cords can be damaged such that only one of the fibers is working, so one fiber of the pair will transmit light, and the other won't. If you see asymmetric link light status, you should replace the fiber patch with a known good patch. If the new one works, then the old one is at least dirty. You might want to try cleaning the ends of the fiber to see if it works any better. If not, then destroy it so it won't cause problems in the future.

   Even 10BASE5 transceivers have been known to go deaf, but not mute, so that you might see frames coming from some MAC address, but frames sent to it will not be heard. Conversely, it is possible for an interface to become mute. It may be able to hear inbound traffic, but outbound traffic never makes it onto the wire. Contrary to the problems with 10BASE-T and 10BASE-F, which are hardware- or firmware-related, these problems may be hardware- or software-related.

   If the device exhibiting either condition is a router, sometimes reinitializing the interface will fix the problem. A warm or cold boot may be required to correct it. If a PC or other endstation on a 10BASE5 network has gone deaf or mute, it may be possible to fix it by disconnecting the AUI cable and reconnecting it. If a 10BASE-T station exhibits deafness or muteness, it may also be corrected by disconnecting and reconnecting the patch cable.

2. Avoid complexity for its own sake

The more complex a device is, the more likely it is to fail in unusual ways. Today's network environments have many requirements and are by nature complex. Try to follow Einstein's maxim: "Make things as simple as possible, but no simpler."

A full-blown Enterprise Hub, with multiple logical LANs, integrated network management, multiple backplanes, multiple LAN types and LAN media, etc., has more opportunities for misbehavior than a simple stand-alone hub, or a piece of wire. Granted, your requirements may force you to use a complex device, but you should still deploy it in ways that minimize complexity. The more complex the configuration, the more difficult it will be to maintain. Troubleshooting and fixing devices with complex configurations are also much more challenging.

Don't just consider how easy a device is to set up and maintain, consider too how easy it is to fix when it's broken. If a device is doing eight different things, can you fix one without disturbing the others? Perhaps more importantly, how well-isolated are the internal components? Will a problem with one adversely affect the others?

Notwithstanding the rather rare partial failures mentioned above, a piece of wire tends to either work or not, while complex devices can exhibit intermittent partial failures, which are maddeningly difficult to pin down. Note that patch cords can exhibit unidirectional behavior, but that is very easy to identify and fix. Intrinsic problems with wire, such as being too long, may cause bizarre partial connectivity. Further discussion of some of these problems can be found above in the 10BASE2 section.

Besides avoiding gratuitously complex equipment, it is also wise to keep LAN topologies as simple as possible. If loops are present in the topology, they could adversely affect performance. Note that loops are often created by users, who may accidentally interconnect two or more independent LAN segments with a hub. The LAN topology should be carefully designed so that such accidents create only localized problems. The Spanning Tree Protocol is one feature in bridges which can help the network eliminate loops and still maintain maximum connectivity.

3. Watch your link statistics

Many devices keep statistics about receive and transmit errors. Routers, hubs, switches, and even endstations may have stats that you can use to help isolate problems. Some especially interesting error statistics on Ethernets are:

a) Transmit-direction statistics

- Late collisions (look for excess cable length, or too many repeater hops)
- Collision rate (should be a small percentage on a healthy Ethernet; if the number of collisions is large relative to the number of frames transmitted (over 5 percent as a rule of thumb), consider breaking up your collision domain by strategically adding some bridges)
- Carrier loss (indicates physical connectivity loss, e.g., between a router and a hub)

b) Receive-direction statistics

- CRC errors
- Framing errors
- Giants
- Runts
- Jabbers

All of these receive statistics may indicate that there is a physical problem. Each Ethernet medium may experience these at times.

REFERENCES

Metcalfe, R. M., and Boggs, D. R., *Ethernet: Distributed Packet Switching for Local Computer Networks*. Association for Computing Machinery, Vol. 19/No. 7, July 1976.

Digital Equipment Corporation, "The Ethernet, A Local Area Network: Data Link Layer and Physical Layer Specification", AA-K759B-TK. Maynard, MA.

Digital Equipment Corporation, Intel Corporation, Xerox Corporation. "The Ethernet - A Local Area Network," Version 1.0. September 1980.

Digital Equipment Corporation, Intel Corporation, and Xerox Corporation, "The Ethernet, A Local Area Network: Data Link Layer and Physical Layer Specifications." November 1982.

International Standard ISO/IEC 8802-3: 1996(E), ANSI/IEEE Std 802.3, 1996 Edition. Information technology—Telecommunications and information exchange between systems—Local and metropolitan area networks—Specific requirements—Part 3: Carrier sense multiple access with collision detection (CSMA/CD) access method and physical layer specifications.

X3T51/80-50. Xerox Corporation, "The Ethernet, A Local Area Network: Data Link Layer and Physical Layer Specification," Stamford, CT. October 1980.

ENDNOTES

1. Namely, Ethernet, Token Ring, FDDI, and ATM LAN Emulation (which is really just another way to implement Ethernet and Token Ring).

2. For example, Ethernet running at 10, then 100, then 1000 Mbps; and Token Ring running at 4, then 16 Mbps.

3. Those two adjectives are the most important defining characteristics of LANs compared to WANs. WANs are typically *non*broadcast, multiple access. Point-to-point WAN technologies are barely broadcast (sending to the other side is the same as sending to everyone!) and barely multiple access (only two devices attach to a point-to-point link).

4. Ethernet is a derivative of the "slotted ALOHA" protocol, developed at the University of Hawaii in the early 1970s to share access to a slice of radio frequency spectrum. Ethernet's slot time is 512 bits (64 bytes) long. Since one bit requires 0.1 microseconds to transmit (one ten-millionth of a second), the slot time is 51.2 microseconds. (Note that minimum-sized Ethernet frames are transmitted in exactly one slot time.) If a collision happens after the first 512 bits of a frame have been transmitted, then a "late collision" error has occurred.

5. In 1979 Metcalfe founded his own company, 3Com Corporation, to commercialize his invention. His vision was that Ethernet would enable <u>com</u>puters to <u>com</u>municate <u>com</u>patibly (the three "com"s in 3Com).

6. In particular, 0x0600 was assigned to the Xerox Network Services (XNS) suite of protocols.

7. Some computer architectures store numbers "backwards" (i.e., most significant bit on the right). The internal representation of numbers is not important . . . only that there is an unambiguous definition for how to interpret bits on the wire. Translations to machine-dependent data representations are the job of each different machine.

8. RFC-895 describes how IP should run over this type of "Experimental Ethernet." RFC-895's techniques are very similar to those documented in RFC-894, which describes how IP runs over "normal" 10 Mbps Ethernet.

9. This variant interconnected 100 workstations across a 1 km cable.

10. "Near" means that all machines requiring connectivity must be within 50 meters of the yellow cable.

11. Due to the extra time (i.e., labor) involved, this also made thick Ethernet rather expensive to install.

12. Thinnet's length being limited to 185 meters, rather than 500, also helped minimize the need for splices.

13. In the future, I believe that copper mining inside old office buildings will be a very profitable enterprise. I am virtually certain that the coiled-up coaxial cable that had been hiden away in the ceilings was never removed, and is still just sitting there.

14. Anecdotally, this practice is more common in Europe than elsewhere.

15. Device A will still think the link is down because nothing is connected to its receive port.

16. The fact that Fast Ethernet can operate over all four pairs of category **3** wiring, implies that it can also run using four pairs of better wiring (e.g., category 4 or 5).

17. This did not guarantee ubiquitous deployment over category 3 cable plants. A typical older installation would run one 4-pair wire bundle to a desktop, using one pair for the phone, and two pair for 10BASE-T. In such installations, deploying 100BaseT4 would require that new copper be pulled to each desktop. Now, if you are already spending the money to rewire your desktops, why wouldn't you install top-of-the line category 5 wiring? (The extra cost of the better quality wire is dwarfed by the cost of labor to install the wire.)

18. In Full Duplex mode, no collisions are possible. Generally, this mode is used between switches and servers, or between switches.

19. Single-mode fiber is more time-consuming to terminate, and therefore more costly to install. Given the extra cost (compared with multimode fiber), and the fact that no campus-scale networking technologies have yet required single-mode fiber, it is not surprising that it has not been widely installed.

20. Token Ring LANs also use 150 Ω cable, but the electrical tolerances for GE are much tighter, having a smaller upper-bound for differential (temporal) skew between the two pairs of cable.

21. There is a very large market for such lasers, as they are components of CD players, CD-ROM drives, DVD-ROM drives, etc.

22. In this case, for aggregating multiple Fast Ethernet "channels" between Cisco's routers and switches, in lieu of Gigabit Ethernet support.

IP over Ethernet

INTRODUCTION

Because Ethernet is a broadcast-oriented medium, it is well suited to the requirements of IP and other higher-layer protocols. All LAN media, because they are broadcast-oriented, are similarly well-suited to supporting IP. Granted, their methods may be radically different from Ethernet, but their essential broadcast-oriented, multiple-access nature unifies them despite the differing details of their operation.

IP, being a connectionless datagram protocol, does not require any special reliability features from the subnetwork layer. Emerging IP applications such as Internet-based telephony and videoconferencing can benefit from subnetworks with reduced latency and jitter. Ethernet is evolving to support these next-generation applications by incorporating class-of-service features into Ethernet switches (i.e., IEEE 802.1Q's 3-bit priority field).

Protocol Demultiplexing

Multiplexing refers to sharing something among a number of "users." In the case of Time Division Multiplexing, a fixed-bandwidth circuit is shared among a number of users by breaking it up into time slots. For instance, a T-1 circuit is divided into 24 8-bit channels plus one extra "framing" bit. These 193 bits are transmitted 8000 times per second, therefore the entire circuit's bandwidth is 1,544,000 bits per second. Each channel is 8 bits, and is sent 8000 times per second, which works out to 64,000 bits per second (per channel). Each channel serves a different user, and each user may feed 8000 bytes per second into its channel. A single T-1 may be broken up into odd-sized pieces among fewer than 24 users (e.g., eight users may share the 24 channels as 1+3+6+2+8+1+2+1), so that more bandwidth may be granted to more demanding users.

There are several kinds of multiplexing on an Ethernet. First, there is the statistical multiplexing implemented by the CSMA/CD protocol, in which numerous machines share the common medium. Here, demultiplexing is achieved by each station having its own unique MAC-layer addresses. Each station examines the bit patterns in the destination address field of every passing frame, receiving only frames that have a destination address matching its own hardware address.[1]

Another form of multiplexing, protocol multiplexing, allows an Ethernet to carry multiple distinct network-layer protocols. Protocol multiplexing is facilitated by Ethernet's EtherType field, or 802.3's DSAP/SSAP fields. After a station receives a packet that is addressed to it (whether unicast, broadcast, or multicast), and verifies the Frame Check Sequence, it must then decide which protocol stack within the machine should receive the packet. It bases this decision on the frame's EtherType or DSAP field. A logical picture of the interrelationships among an Ethernet station's networking modules is shown in Figure 8.1.

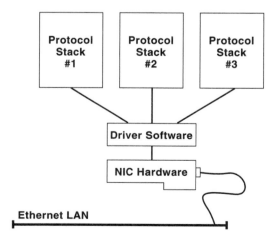

FIGURE 8.1 Multiple protocol stacks bound to one driver.

TABLE 8.1 Some common EtherTypes

• AppleTalk	0x809B
• AppleTalk ARP	0x80F3
• DECnet	0x6003
• IP	0x0800
• IPX	0x8137-8138
• Loopback	0x9000
• XNS	0x0600

The EtherType field enables networking hardware to hand up the packet to the correct protocol stack within the machine. In the case of IP, its EtherType is 0x0800. For example, several EtherTypes are summarized in Table 8.1. The "Assigned Numbers" RFC, currently RFC-1700, lists even more EtherTypes.

Another way that Ethernet supports protocol demultiplexing is with the DSAP and SSAP fields. Though it is not commonly seen in Ethernet environments, IP does have an assigned SAP value, which is 96 (in decimal, 0x60 in hex). IP over 802.3 is specified in RFC-948, while IP over Ethernet is specified in RFC-894.[2]

Neighbor Address Discovery

In order for IP to use Ethernet, or any other LAN, it must have a way to discover the MAC-layer addresses of its IP neighbors. Taking a purely MAC-layer view, two Ethernet stations are sending each other data, and you don't care what higher-layer protocol is inside those Ethernet frames. The IP layer needs to know those remote MAC addresses or else it cannot communicate with its neighbors on this LAN. After all, it only knows about IP addresses. A static table of neighbor IP addresses and their associated MAC addresses would suffice for limited applications, but a dynamic method offers much less administrative overhead and is normally used in LAN environments.[3]

The Address Translation Table, of which Figure 8.2 is one example, is often referred to as an "ARP cache."[4]

```
---------------------IP Address Translation Table---------------------
Address         Port  Type       Media Address     Header Format   Address Source

224.0.0.1       --    Multicast  0x01005E000001    Ethernet        Static
224.0.0.2       --    Multicast  0x01005E000002    Ethernet        Static
10.87.174.64    1     Broadcast  0xFFFFFFFFFFFF    Ethernet        Static
10.87.174.65    1     Local      0x0800021CF3FA    Ethernet        Static
10.87.174.66    1     External   0x00401002E278    Ethernet        ARP
10.87.174.67    1     External   0x0000861826F6    Ethernet        ARP
10.87.174.71    1     Broadcast  0xFFFFFFFFFFFF    Ethernet        Static
```

FIGURE 8.2 Address translation table a.k.a. ARP cache.

ARP Overview

The IP suite has a "helper" protocol called the Address Resolution Protocol or "ARP" for short. ARP runs directly over Ethernet and does not include an IP header. ARP is a protocol that is used by IP endstations to find neighbors with a certain IP address (the one it wants to talk to), and then the owner of that address will respond directly to the requester if it hears the request. ARP is documented in RFC-826.

Let's make an analogy to a fictional street where we can only communicate by couriers, or by shouting.[5] The thing is that when we wake up in the morning, we do not know anyone's addresses. Let's say we need to send information via courier to Georgette, but we do not know Georgette's address. It is not rational to instruct our courier to visit every possible address on our street looking for Georgette, so we do the following: we shout, "Georgette! I need to talk to you! If you're at home and awake, please shout out your address. Here's my name and address so your courier will be able to reach me in the future." Georgette replies directly by courier. Future communication between them is by courier, and does not bother anyone else on the street. Because everyone on the street hears our original request, they need not shout across the street the next time they need to contact us . . . they must simply remember our address, which we shouted in the process of searching for Georgette.

What problems could arise in this system? First of all, it is clear that if there are too many people shouting at once, it will be difficult for each person to hear themselves think. Each person must listen to all the shouts, in case someone is trying to reach *them*. Another issue is that the street has a fixed size, and only so many couriers can occupy it at a time, no matter how many people need to send information. Each courier can only carry so much at a time, so multiple trips may be required before all the information is transmitted between any two parties. This effect, accumulated over all the users, contributes to filling up the street.

ARP Protocol Operation

ARP works much this way. A frame is sent to the broadcast address, so that all stations on this LAN will hear it. This is both good and bad; it might be okay if everyone on the Ethernet were using IP. However, all Ethernet endstations—even ones that are not running IP—must receive broadcast packets, which they will then delete. Another design choice might have used an IP-specific MAC-layer multicast address to which only IP stations would pay attention. This would have limited ARP's impact to the endstations that are running IP. One reason to use the broadcast address is that not all LANs support multicasting at the data link layer, though they all support broadcast. Therefore, if ARP uses broadcast, it can work the same way across any LAN. Figure 8.3 illustrates the frame format of an ARP packet.

The source MAC address ARP frames is the requester's or responder's MAC address. The EtherType for ARP is 0x0806 (distinct from IP's EtherType, which is 0x0800). The first two bytes of the ARP packet indicate the hardware type that the station is transmitting onto. In the case of Ethernet, the hardware type is 1. The next two bytes express the Protocol Type, which indicates the "partner protocol" that this ARP frame is associated with.[6] IP's EtherType, 0x0800, goes here. Then there are two address length fields. First, the hardware address length, then the protocol address length. These allow the remainder of the packet to be interpreted. In the case of Ethernet and IPv4, the hardware address length is 6, and the protocol address length is 4. There is one more byte which indicates whether this is an ARP Request (1) or Response[7] (2).

The next six bytes (according to the hardware address length field) hold the source's MAC address,[8] and then the source's protocol address (i.e., its IP address) occupy the next four bytes (according to the protocol length field). Now that the requester has expressed all the information it knows about itself, it finishes with four bytes containing the target's protocol address. This is the station being sought, whose MAC address is needed before communication can happen across this LAN.

If the target machine is up, and hears our broadcast, it will transmit an ARP Reply directly to us (i.e., from its source MAC address to our MAC address). The difference between an ARP Request and a Reply is that the OpCode is 2 for a Reply, and the source hardware and protocol addresses will be those of the original target station. Now, the original requester will have the target's MAC address, and will be able to send it a frame.

Also, every IP endstation on this LAN will receive every ARP Request, each of which contains a mapping for some IP address to some MAC address. Since CPU cycles already had to be spent to receive the broadcast and notice that it was an ARP

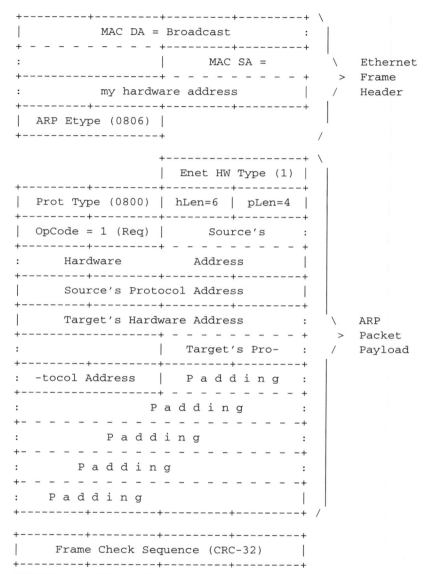

```
+---------+---------+---------+---------+  \
|           MAC DA = Broadcast      :   |
+ - - - - - - - +---------+---------+  |
:                       |      MAC SA =        \   Ethernet
+-----------------+ - - - - - - - +  >  Frame
:         my hardware address       |  /   Header
+---------+---------+---------+---------+  |
|  ARP Etype (0806) |                       |
+-----------------+                       /

                  +-------------------+  \
                  |  Enet HW Type (1) |   |
+---------+---------+---------+---------+  |
|  Prot Type (0800) | hLen=6  | pLen=4 |   |
+---------+---------+---------+---------+  |
|  OpCode = 1 (Req) |     Source's     :   |
+---------+---------+ - - - - - - - +  |
:     Hardware         Address      |   |
+---------+---------+---------+---------+  |
|     Source's Protocol Address     |   |
+---------+---------+---------+---------+  |
|     Target's Hardware Address     :   \   ARP
+-----------------+ - - - - - - - +  >  Packet
:                       |  Target's Pro-   :  /   Payload
+---------+---------+---------+---------+  |
:  -tocol Address   | P a d d i n g  :   |
+-----------------+ - - - - - - - +  |
:             P a d d i n g        :   |
+- - - - - - - - - - - - - - - - -+  |
:           P a d d i n g          :   |
+- - - - - - - - - - - - - - - - -+  |
:         P a d d i n g            :   |
+- - - - - - - - - - - - - - - - -+  |
:  P a d d i n g                    |   |
+---------+---------+---------+---------+  /

+---------+---------+---------+---------+
|     Frame Check Sequence (CRC-32)  |
+---------+---------+---------+---------+
```

FIGURE 8.3   Ethernet frame carrying ARP packet.

packet, every station may as well continue processing the packet and extract the useful information from each ARP Request it must receive. In the future, should any of them need to send a packet to that IP address, all of them will already have its MAC address, therefore none of them will need to send a duplicate request for it. This technique is known as "snooping on ARP Requests."

Once the requester receives an ARP Reply, it will typically remember the association between the remote IP address and its MAC address for some "hold time." RFC-826 suggests no default for the length of this timer, but common choices include times ranging from 15 or 60 minutes up to 24 hours.

IP OVER IEEE 802.3

As was observed in Chapter 7, Ethernet version 2 and the IEEE 802.3 version of Ethernet are not quite the same. The first attempt to define a way for IP to run over 802.3 was for the IETF to acquire a SAP value for IP, which ended up being 0x60 (96 in decimal). Thus, it was possible to layer IP directly over Logical Link Control or LLC (the DSAP and SSAP fields are part of the LLC header, along with the Control field, which IP always sets to 0x03). RFC-948 documented this first attempt to specify how IP might operate over IEEE 802.3, using IEEE 802.2 LLC as an intermediate layer. This first attempt at layering IP over 802.3 is depicted in Figure 8.4.

Curiously, RFC-948 did not tell which SAP value ARP should use, so it was of limited value (of course, since Ethernet version 2 and IEEE 802.3 frames may share the same subnetwork, a station could use ARP over Ethernet version 2 to do its address discovery functions, then once the endstation knew the proper MAC address to send to, it could use IEEE 802.3 encapsulation for the IP packets). This would work, but it has kludge written all over it.

As the 802.2 standard evolved, the IEEE eventually put in a clean way for EtherType values to be used in the context of LLC. They defined a special value of

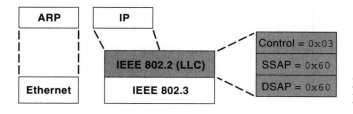

FIGURE 8.4 RFC-948 layering of IP over IEEE 802.3.

the SAP fields, 0xAA, which indicated that another set of headers was present above the normal three bytes of LLC headers. The DSAP = SSAP = 0xAA indicated the presence of the Subnetwork Access Protocol (SNAP) header, consisting of an Organizationally Unique Identifier (OUI) and a Type field. In the case where an EtherType field was desired, the OUI was to be set to 0x00-00-00. If a private organization wished to specify its own set of Types, then it would preface its Type values with its own OUI (to distinguish these Type values from those of other organizations).

Once the SNAP header had been defined as an enhancement to LLC, the IETF wrote a document that specified how IP- and ARP- would work over *any* IEEE 802-based LAN. This document, RFC-1042, made RFC-948 obsolete. The new method was simple: Always use the IEEE 802 SNAP header over 802.2 LLC (shown in Figure 8.5).

When using SNAP, the data link header ends with an EtherType, just as in the case of Ethernet version 2. The only twist in RFC-1042 is that all the IEEE 802 LAN types share a single ARP Hardware_Type value, specifically "6," as opposed to Ethernet, which used a value of "1" for the ARP Hardware Type.

IP Forwarding Decision

Why was the ARP procedure necessary? Presumably because the IP module, on behalf of some higher-layer application, wanted to send a packet to another station on the same subnetwork. In order to be functional, an IP endstation must have at least one active interface with at least one IP address, the interface's associated subnet mask, and an active default gateway.[9]

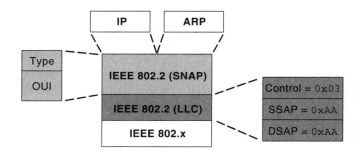

FIGURE 8.5 RFC-1042 layering of IP and ARP over SNAP/LLC/802.x.

The Local/Not-Local Decision

When IP needs to send a packet, the endstation needs to make a "routing" decision. It knows the IP destination address of the packet,[10] now it must decide if it is a local neighbor on one of its subnetworks, or if it is on a remote subnetwork (in which case it must be sent to its default gateway). Most endstations only have one interface running IP, but extra interfaces do not significantly complicate this procedure.

When the IP stack first needs to transmit a packet, or when it is initialized, it will create a table of its attached subnet prefixes (at least one subnet prefix per interface). Here is an example of a machine with one interface. Other interfaces would increase the number of rows in the table beyond just one. Imagine that the endstation's IP address is 10.87.174.67/29 (which indicates a subnet mask of 255.255.255.248 in the old dotted-decimal notation). To extract the subnet prefix, we apply the interface's mask to its IP address by means of a bitwise logical "AND" operation. For every 1-bit in the mask, we preserve that bit position's value in the address. For every 0-bit in the mask, we zero out that bit of the address. Figure 8.6 summarizes the logical "truth table" for the AND operation.

Based on the knowledge gained in Part I, we can see that the local interface's prefix is 10.87.174.64. An IP stack always remembers its local subnet prefix(es), which were determined when it was initialized.

At some later point in time, the IP stack needs to transmit a packet. It needs to decide if it is a local neighbor (local means that it is in the same prefix), or a nonlocal address that must be forwarded to the station's default "gateway."[11] In order to see if the packet is local, it compares the (masked) IP destination address with its table of interface subnet prefixes. If any match, then the destination IP address is a local neighbor and may be transmitted from the appropriate subnet's interface.

IP Forwarding Decision in Action

For example, suppose that the packet's destination address were 10.87.174.68. The machine we are considering only has one interface, so it needs to apply that interface's mask (which was /29) to the destination address. The operation, again, is

AND	0	1
0	0	0
1	0	1

FIGURE 8.6 "Truth Table" for the AND function.

the logical AND function. This is depicted in Figure 8.7. The goal is to see whether or not the destination IP address is within the sender's own prefix.

Once the interface's mask is applied to that address, the result is 10.87.174.64, as shown in Figure 8.7. The shaded area in the AND computation is the portion of the address that is covered by the mask. These bits are preserved, unchanged from their values in the destination address. The resulting destination prefix, in this example, matches the interface's subnet prefix. Now the IP stack can transmit the packet from that interface directly to the destination IP address with no need to employ the services of the default gateway.

If the destination address had been 10.3.8.106, it would have reduced to 10.3.8.104, which does not match the source station's single interface prefix. Figure 8.8 shows the same calculation, indicating a clear mismatch between this IP address' destination prefix (10.3.8.104) and the local interface's prefix (10.87.174.64).

If the destination were local, then the Address Translation Table, or "ARP cache," would be examined. If an entry for 10.87.174.68 were present, then the station simply sends an Ethernet frame to 10.87.174.68's MAC address. If there is not yet an ARP cache entry for this target IP address, then an ARP Request is broadcast on this LAN to see if that machine will send an ARP Reply supplying its MAC address. If it does, then the station will record it in its ARP cache before transmitting the frame.

Destination Address (DA):
```
(decimal)    10    .   87    .   174   .    68
   (hex)    0 A    .   5 7   .   A E   .   4 4
(binary) 0000_1010.0101_0111.1010_1110.0100_0100
```

Interface Mask (/29):
```
(decimal)   255    .   255   .   255   .   248
   (hex)    F F    .   F F   .   F F   .   F 8
(binary) 1111_1111.1111_1111.1111_1111.1111_1000
```

```
          0000_1010.0101_0111.1010_1110.0100_0100  (DA)
   AND    1111_1111.1111_1111.1111_1111.1111_1000  (mask)
          _____
          0000_1010.0101_0111.1010_1110.0100_0000  (prefix)

            0 A    .   5 7   .   A E   .   4 0      (hex)
            10     .   87    .   174   .   64       (decimal)
```

FIGURE 8.7 Determining the destination's IP prefix.

Destination Address (DA):

```
(decimal)    10   .    3    .    8    .    106
    (hex)    0 A  .   0 3   .   0 8   .    6 A
 (binary) 0000_1010.0000_0011.0000_1000.0110_1010
```

Interface Mask (/29):

```
(decimal)   255  .   255   .   255   .   248
    (hex)   F F  .   F F    .   F F   .   F 8
 (binary) 1111_1111.1111_1111.1111_1111.1111_1000
```

```
        0000_1010.0000_0011.0000_1000.0110_1010 (DA)
 AND    1111_1111.1111_1111.1111_1111.1111_1000 (mask)

        0000_1010.0000_0011.0000_1000.0110_1000 (prefix)
        0 A  .   0 3   .   0 8   .   6 8        (hex)
        10   .   3     .   8     .   104        (decimal)
```

FIGURE 8.8 Mismatched destination prefix.

If the destination is not local, then the packet must be forwarded to the default gateway. As noted earlier, the default gateway must have an address in one of our interface's prefixes. If a station has multiple interfaces, it can only have one default gateway (at a time). This should be obvious by inspection of the term "default gateway," which implies uniqueness. In order for a station to be able to use multiple gateways, it would have to participate in the local routing protocols so it would know which routers were the "best" ones to reach certain destinations. Alternatively it could attempt to use some "secondary" default gateway if it appeared that the primary default gateway had become unreachable.

Generally, the default gateway is statically configured as part of the IP stack's configuration.[12] In this example, imagine that the default gateway's address is 10.87.174.65. Now the problem is reduced to the first case—since the router is a [LAN-local] neighbor of the station, the station needs to be able to send a MAC layer frame that is addressed to the default gateway's MAC address. The critical difference in this case is that the IP Destination Address is *not* the address of the default gateway, but the address of the packet's ultimate destination.

Again, the station must check for the default gateway's IP address in its ARP cache (as opposed to the ultimate destination's address), and send an ARP Request if there is no entry for the default gateway in the ARP Cache. The router will decide how to forward the packet toward its ultimate destination. Routing protocols, and the forwarding of IP packets by routers, is the topic of Part III.

IP Forwarding Procedure on "Multihomed" Endstations

Multihoming is a situation in which an endstation is attached to multiple subnets. End-user machines are typically not multihomed, but servers often are. Figure 8.9 depicts an endstation that is multihomed.

Note that multihomed endstations usually do not forward traffic between their interfaces. A multihomed endstation that does perform interinterface forwarding is called a router. The most common uses of multihoming are in servers. One use is to connect the machine to as many different client subnets as possible; another use is just to provide redundant connectivity.

The modifications required for an IP stack to support multihoming are relatively straightforward. There are changes when the IP stack is initialized, and when each packet is forwarded. Both kinds of changes boil down to the fact that there is more than one "local prefix" for this machine, implying that multiple comparisons must be made before transmitting the packet.

Initialization Changes Due to Multihoming.   At initialization time, a single-homed machine computed its local prefix by ANDing its only interface's mask with its address. This value was stored for later use when forwarding packets.

A multihomed machine must do this calculation for each of its interfaces. Rather than storing a single value for future use, it must keep a set of (local-interface prefix, mask) pairs. For example, imagine a machine with three interfaces, as depicted in Figure 8.10.

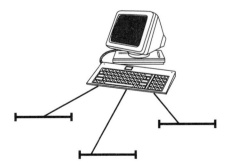

FIGURE 8.9   A multihomed end-station.

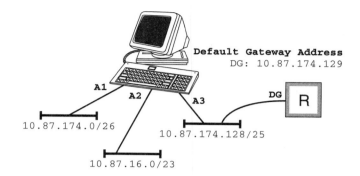

FIGURE 8.10 Example of a multihomed endstation.

Packet-Delivery Changes Due to Multihoming.   As with the single-homing example, the endstation must still determine which outgoing interface to use. If the packet's destination is within interface A1's subnet (10.87.174.0/26, or addresses ranging from 10.87.174.1 – 10.87.174.62), then the packet is sent from interface A1. Similarly, if the packet is within either 10.87.16.0/23 (10.87.16.1 – 10.87.17.254) or 10.87.174.128/25 (10.87.174.129 – 10.87.174.254), it would be sent from either interface A2 or A3, respectively. The station still has only one default gateway, which has an IP address that is within one of the station's attached subnets. Any traffic not destined for one of these three local subnetworks will be forwarded to the default gateway for further processing.

Determining Which Outgoing Interface to Use.   The endstation must use each of its masks against the packet's destination address. For instance, if the station's IP stack needed to send a packet to 10.43.1.2, it would try to determine if that address was within any of its locally attached IP prefixes. To a human, it is obvious that it is not going to be, but let's see how the computer determines this. First, it computes the logical AND of this address with each of its masks, as shown in Figure 8.11.

To summarize the results, we see that none of them match any of the interface prefixes that were computed at initialization time, namely 10.87.174.0/26,

Destination Address (DA):

```
(decimal)     10    .   43    .    1    .    2
   (hex)      0 A   .  2 B    .   0 1   .   0 2
(binary) 0000_1010.0010_1011.0000_0001.0000_0010
```

A1: Interface Mask (/23):

```
(decimal)    255    .    255   .    254   .    0
   (hex)     F F    .    F F   .    F E   .   0 0
(binary) 1111_1111.1111_1111.1111_1110.0000_0000
```

```
        0000_1010.0010_1011.0000_0001.0000_0010  (DA)
AND     1111_1111.1111_1111.1111_1110.0000_0000  (A1 mask)

        0000_1010.0010_1011.0000_0000.0000_0000  (prefix)

           0 A   .   2 B   .   0 0   .   0 0     (hex)
           10    .   43    .   0     .   0       (decimal)
```

A2: Interface Mask (/25):

```
(decimal)    255    .    255   .    255   .    128
   (hex)     F F    .    F F   .    F F   .    8 0
(binary) 1111_1111.1111_1111.1111_1111.1000_0000
```

```
        0000_1010.0010_1011.0000_0001.0000_0010  (DA)
AND     1111_1111.1111_1111.1111_1111.1000_0000  (A2 mask)

        0000_1010.0010_1011.0000_0001.0000_0000  (prefix)

           0 A       2 B       0 1       0 0     (hex)
           10        43        1         0       (decimal)
```

A3: Interface Mask (/26):

```
(decimal)    255    .    255   .    255   .    192
   (hex)     F F    .    F F   .    F F   .    C 0
(binary) 1111_1111.1111_1111.1111_1111.1100_0000
```

```
        0000_1010.0010_1011.0000_0001.0000_0010  (DA)
AND     1111_1111.1111_1111.1111_1111.1100_0000  (A3 mask)

        0000_1010.0010_1011.0000_0001.0000_0000  (prefix)

           0 A       2 B       0 1       0 0     (hex)
           10        43        1         0       (decimal)
```

FIGURE 8.11   Masking the destination address.

10.87.16.0/23 or 10.87.174.128/25. In this case, the IP stack now knows that the destination is nonlocal and must forward it to the default gateway, which is 10.87.174.129 in this example. Forwarding to the default gateway is the same as in the single-homing example, with one final twist: The *source* IP address in the packet must be set to the outgoing interface's IP address. If another of the machine's interface addresses were used, the packets would return to an interface on the multi-homed machine that is different than the transmitting interface. Generally, implementations will automatically set the source address in the IP header to be the address of the interface from which the packet is to be transmitted.

IP Scaling Issues over Large Switched LANs

As we have seen, layer 2 switching is a marketing term for wire-speed transparent bridging. The term switching has a lot of mindshare, but there is little fundamental difference between bridging and switching. The term "bridging" has become old-fashioned, despite still being accurate.

Traditionally, subnetworks rarely had more than several hundred stations (except in the case of large campus-scale bridged networks of the late 1980s and early 1990s[13]). To provide better traffic isolation and increased performance, Ethernet switching (layer 2 bridging) has been deployed, often over a star-wired fiber backbone.

In the early 1990s, large bridged networks were more difficult to build than they are today. The only suitable backbone technology, 10BROAD36, was not something that every large campus could deploy. If you didn't have a high-quality cable TV infrastructure with a couple free channels, you were out of luck. Now that it is possible to run Ethernet over fiber, and with the advent of Fast Ethernet, FDDI, ATM LAN Emulation, and Gigabit Ethernet, it is possible to assemble a fiber backbone and interconnect large quantities of endstations. The switches used today are much much faster than those of yesteryear, and scaling issues may be encountered that never arose in the old days.

Unicast

A significant problem that unicast IP faces as many subnetworks have grown to have more and more stations, is that the "default gateway" becomes a potentially catastrophic single point of failure. To ensure that the routing system has redundant paths to every subnetwork, there will typically be at least two router attachments to every subnetwork. Modern routing protocols have no difficulty performing path selection in such an environment, but endstations don't run routing protocols. Since endstations have a single default gateway *statically defined* in their IP stacks, there is no quick or easy way for them to notice that the default gateway has become un-reachable, then switch to a backup.

All the data that leaves a station for nonlocal destinations is forwarded toward this single router. If the subnets were small (few endstations), then any given outage would affect few users, but the trend today is to make networks as "flat" as possible, thereby creating large subnets with hundreds of users. The larger the subnet, the more reliable the default gateway must be, because an outage would be extremely disruptive.

Some IP stacks, notably that in Windows 95, provide an option for a "backup" default gateway. If the IP stack notices that there are excessive TCP retransmissions toward the primary default gateway, it will shift to the backup. The logic is that if TCP flows stop, the cause may be the first-hop router. Of course, the outage could be anywhere along the path from this endstation to its peer, so switching default gateways may not help at all. This scheme also does nothing for UDP-based applica-tions, since UDP has no transport-layer acknowledgments; any retransmission

Rivalry between HSRP and its Siblings

In 1997, the IETF began the process of standardizing a protocol that would be a nonproprietary solution to this problem. Cisco even offered HSRP as a candidate for such an open standard.[14] The IETF, for various technical and political reasons (mostly political, in the author's opinion), instead chose to design a new protocol, called Virtual Router Redundancy Protocol (VRRP). Cisco has asserted that it will consider implementations of VRRP as infringing on their HSRP patents. (Mean-while, HSRP uses a "Hello" protocol largely borrowed from the Open Shortest Path First (OSPF) routing protocol. IBM claims that certain aspects of the OSPF proto-col infringes on some of its Advanced Peer-to-Peer Networking (APPN) patents.) Of course, this is all rather unseemly[15] corporate posturing, which does not reflect well on any of the participants.

schemes are application-specific. To be effective for UDP-based applications, this endstation-based router-redundancy scheme would have to monitor each application's traffic for telltale signs that traffic is not getting through. Historically, most applications used TCP, with the notable exception of the Simple Network Management Protocol (SNMP), but UDP-based applications are becoming more prevalent such as IP telephony and other multimedia applications begin to be deployed, so a "solution" that only works for TCP-based applications is insufficient.

As subnetworks have grown, the need for an endstation-independent solution was increasingly apparent. Around 1994, Cisco Systems began shipping a new feature, called "Hot Standby Router Protocol," designed to address this problem. The key advantage of HSRP is that it is totally transparent to the endstations. Deploying HSRP is as nondisruptive as any other planned router software upgrade.

HSRP/VRRP solves the "hundreds of endstations statically pointing at a single-point-of-failure" problem by enabling a set of routers to back each other up. These routers share a virtual MAC/IP address pair, along with "Hello" messages that revalidate their mutual aliveness. This virtual IP address is the default gateway's address, which is configured into those hundreds of endstations. One router is elected from the group to be the owner of the virtual IP/MAC pair. Any endstation needing to send nonlocal traffic from this subnet will be sending such traffic to this IP address.

The routers use a "Hello" protocol to maintain their mutual status. Should the current owner of the virtual IP address disappear, then the previously-elected backup immediately takes over.[16] This changeover is designed to be transparent to the endstations whose IP stacks still use the same IP and MAC addresses (unaware that those addresses now belong to a different physical device). During the changeover, there may be some transitory packet loss, but higher-level protocols can recover from brief outages, and sessions should be preserved.

The situation HSRP/VRRP is really trying to avoid is that of hundreds of users being forced to log in to their networked applications again. Without HSRP/VRRP, if the default gateway was down for a long time (defined as more than 30 seconds), users that wanted to continue using the network would need to change their IP stack configuration to use a different default gateway,[17] or rely on proprietary "dead gateway detection." They may even have to reboot their computer after making these changes (Windows 95 users definitely cannot make changes to their IP stack config without rebooting; Windows NT 4.0 does allow changing the IP configuration on the fly, and Macintosh users, if they have installed Apple's Open Transport networking software, also have this "change on the fly" capability).

You might observe that ARP should be a viable substitute for HSRP/VRRP. According to RFC-826, the source-IP/source-MAC addresses in broadcast ARP Re-

IPv6 NOTE:

Dead Gateway Detection is a built-in feature of the Neighbor Discovery protocols (see RFC-2471) known as Neighbor Unreachablility Detection (NUD) in the RFC. Timers allow the responsiveness of the protocol to be tailored depending on each individual network manager's assessed requirements; the IETF is providing sensible defaults that should be widely useful.

The IETF also plans to specify an IPv6 version of VRRP, which may be able to provide even better failover times, at the expense of a small bit of extra network traffic.

quests must override the contents of local ARP caches, updating any stored IP/MAC address mappings. If all IP implemetations complied with this requirement, then HSRP/VRRP could be considerably simpler—in fact, they would not need to exist! No one believes that there are large numbers of noncompliant ARP implemetations in the field; however, HSRP/VRRP solves the problem in an endstation-independent manner, regardless of the compliance of endstation ARP implementations.

Multicast

Sending IP multicast over a LAN is very straightforward. The IP Class D group address is mapped directly into a MAC-layer multicast destination address. When a multicast is transmitted onto a bridged LAN, it is flooded along the spanning tree, just as broadcasts and unknown-destination unicasts are. Broadcast traffic can hopefully be managed and kept to a minimum. Unknown-destination unicasts are probably not a very frequent occurrence.

Both broadcasts and unknown-destination unicasts must be flooded out every nonblocking bridge port in the LAN. They must reach every segment of the LAN in order for the LAN to function correctly. Multicast, however, could account for a large amount of traffic on a switched LAN. All this multicast traffic is real data, flowing on this LAN because some number of users have instructed their stations to join some multicast groups. Despite the fact that only some stations are members of a given group, the group's traffic is flooded to all stations on the LAN under the default IEEE 802.1D bridge forwarding rules, just as if it were broadcast traffic.

As multicast-based applications are deployed, such as multimedia applications, "push" applications, multidestination file transfer, etc., the wasted LAN bandwidth (due to multicast being treated as if it were broadcast) becomes an increasingly critical issue. In addition to the fact that all the links on the spanning tree will be quite busy with traffic that is being dutifully delivered where it is not needed, most endstations will be inundated with traffic that they never signed up for. Multicast traffic is much different from broadcast or unknown-destination unicast traffic because:

- Broadcast is primarily used[18] for administrative protocols (e.g., routing protocols) and other infrequent uses (e.g., ARP), certainly not for bulk data transfer.
- Unknown-destination unicast forwarding is a rather rare event. Most protocols send broadcasts to help discover a target peer's address, which necessitates the target station sending a reply packet, thereby allowing the switches to learn which port leads to it.

A desirable solution for multicast would be to allow layer-2 switches to filter multicasts so they are only sent out ports that lead to group members. This is similar to what happens at the IP layer, where routers only forward multicasts to group members, not to all subnetworks in the multicast domain, regardless of expressed group membership knowledge. To implement such a scheme at the Data Link layer, the switches need a way to identify the location(s) of group members.

Early attempts to solve this problem centered on techniques that are broadly known as "IGMP Snooping."[19] The cornerstone of these techniques is that a switch can tell where group members are if it simply watches IGMP traffic from endstations, noting which group addresses (MAC-layer group addresses!) the IGMP Reports are destined for. There are many subtle nuances that make this harder than it sounds, but it is now technically feasible to implement the full technique in a low-cost layer-2 switch.

Cisco has taken a different approach, called CGMP (Cisco Group Multicast Protocol) in which the router receives the IGMP Reports, and records the IGMP Report frame's source MAC address. The router then sends a special multicast control packet to the switches serving that subnetwork, telling them that this new MAC address is now a member of some group. Similarly, when IGMP Leave Group messages are issued by endstations, the router can send a follow-up message to the switches that serves to remove the MAC address from a group. The switches use their bridge forwarding tables to determine the downstream[20] interfaces that should get a copy of multicasts for this group. The router has told them that MAC address X has joined a group, and it is straightforward for the switches to see which port they have learned that MAC address on, and thus which port should now be receiving traffic for this multicast group.

The IEEE 802.1 committee has standardized a nonproprietary MAC layer solution, comprised of two related standards, called 802.1Q and 802.1p, the latter of which is responsible for controlling MAC-layer multicast (802.1Q deals with VLAN filtering). With respect to multicast data, 802.1p's functionality lies somewhere between IGMP, IGMP Snooping, and CGMP.

Unfortunately, the differing sizes of the IP multicast address space (2^{28} addresses) versus IP's allotted MAC-layer multicast address space (2^{23} addresses) means that each MAC-layer multicast address represents 2^5 (32) IP multicast addresses. The implication of this mismatch is that up to 32 IP multicast addresses could share a MAC-layer multicast address. Conversely, joining or leaving a single MAC-layer multicast address is equivalent to joining or leaving 32 IP-layer multicast addresses. All the MAC-layer multicast control techniques share this "feature."

As in CGMP, the switches receive explicit group membership directives, so they need not attempt to infer what is going on, as IGMP Snooping does. Unlike CGMP, in 802.1p the endstations explicitly tell the switches what groups they want to join, rather than relying on the router to control the switches on their behalf.

As in IGMP, the endstations send messages to inform the network devices directly about their group membership; contrary to IGMP, 802.1p's "Join" and "Leave" messages operate at the MAC layer, whereas IGMP operates at the IP layer. The role of the switches in GMRP is opposite of the routers in IGMP. IGMP sends periodic Query packets to see if there are any members, while 802.1p is always trying to cut off inactive groups by sending "Leave All" messages. Those stations that are still interested are supposed to reissue their Joins. In IGMP, the stations actively participate in both the Joining and Leaving processes. IGMP's Queries (from a multicast router) serve to induce at least one group member, from each active group, to identify itself.

As in IGMP Snooping, the switches learn the group membership information directly from the endstations, but the new protocol is explicit, rather than forcing the switches to infer MAC-layer group membership based on multicast IP's network-layer control packets (i.e., IGMP). See Appendix B for a more detailed description of the IEEE 802.1Q and 802.1p standards.

REFERENCES

0791 Internet Protocol. J. Postel. Sep-01-1981. (Format: TXT=97779 bytes) Obsoletes RFC0760) (Also STD0005) (Status: STANDARD)

0826 Ethernet Address Resolution Protocol: Or converting network protocol addresses to 48.bit Ethernet address for transmission on Ethernet hardware. D.C. Plummer. Nov-01-1982. (Format: TXT=22026 bytes) (Status: STANDARD)

0894 Standard for the transmission of IP datagrams over Ethernet networks. C. Hornig. Apr-01-1984. (Format: TXT=5697 bytes) (Status: STANDARD)

0895 Standard for the transmission of IP datagrams over experimental Ethernet networks. J. Postel. Apr-01-1984. (Format: TXT=4985 bytes) (Status: STANDARD)

0948 Two methods for the transmission of IP datagrams over IEEE 802.3 networks. I. Winston. Jun-01-1985. (Format: TXT=11495 bytes) (Obsoleted by RFC1042, STD0043) (Also STD0043) (Status: UNKNOWN)

1042 Standard for the transmission of IP datagrams over IEEE 802 neworks. J. Postel, J.K. Reynolds. Feb-01-1988. (Format: TXT=34359 bytes) (Obsoletes RFC0948) (Status: STANDARD)

2281 Cisco Hot Standby Router Protocol (HSRP). T. Li, B. Cole, P. Morton, D. Li. March 1998. (Format: TXT=35161 bytes) (Status: INFORMATIONAL)

2338 Virtual Router Redundancy Protocol. S. Knight, D. Weaver, D. Whipple, R. Hinden, D. Mitzel, P. Hunt, P. Higginson, M. Shand, A. Lindem. April 1998. (Format: TXT=59871 bytes) (Status: PROPOSED STANDARD)

2461 Neighbor Discovery for IP Version 6 (IPv6). T. Narten, E. Nordmark, W. Simpson. Debemcer 1998. (Format: TXT=222516 bytes) (Obsoletes RC1970) (Status: DRAFT STANDARD)

ENDNOTES

1. Note that Ethernet stations rely on the "broadcast" nature of the medium as they watch for frames that are addressed to them. Besides frames that are addressed directly to them, Ethernet stations must receive frames sent to the broadcast address (0xFF-FF-FF-FF-FF-FF, or 48 one-bits in a row). Finally, an Ethernet controller will receive any multicast addresses which it has been instructed to filter.

2. An insignificant observation is that, coincidentally, "894" and "948" are permutations of each other.

3. In WAN environments, with generally fewer neighbors connected over nonbroadcast media, static tables are much more commonplace.

4. Address Translation Table is a better term than ARP Cache because ARP is only one way that entries can get into this table. There are other link-layer address discovery protocols besides ARP (i.e., Inverse ARP and ATM-ARP), plus default entries are created that bind each IP address to its physical interface's address. Manually-defined static entries are also possible. "ARP Cache," however, is easy to say and gets the point across; just remember that there is more going on here than just ARP.

5. We'll assume that everyone worth talking to is within earshot, or that we can shout as loudly as we need to.

6. ARP is not limited to use with IP. It could be used with other protocols, but I have only seen this once. I remember it well, because the "ARP-on-behalf-of-a-non-IP-protocol" packet, while theoretically legal, caused an IP-speaking networked printer to crash. That printer's software had been designed with the assumption that the Protocol Type would always be 0x0800. This is an example of a violation of good network software design. The programmers should have been more liberal in what they accepted. If they want to be strict, that strictness should only be enforced on what they send.

7. Note that RFC-826 uses a different name for what I call "ARP Response," namely an ARP Reply. My experience has been that "response" is used more in the field than "reply." Strictly speaking, only Reply is correct, but in my opinion there is little ambiguity in the usage of "response" in this context.

8. Some network hardware may discard the MAC-layer headers before the higher-layer protocol, in this case ARP can see them. To ensure that the information is available, the source's MAC address is stored again in the ARP header. The ARP Response's destination will be the requester's MAC address.

9. The default gateway's address must lie within the endstation's subnetwork. If the endstation is attached to more than one subnetwork, it may only have one default gateway—not one per subnetwork!

10. The destination IP address is either supplied directly by the user (that's actually rare), or the user supplies a domain name such as "ftp.ietf.org," which is then looked up in the Domain Name System (DNS). The result of that query is the IP address(es) that correspond to that domain name.

11. Gateway is an old-fashioned term for "router," or "intermediate system" in OSI parlance. Today, the term gateway is more often used to describe a machine that converts from one protocol stack to another, except in the case of IP's "default gateway." This term has been used for so long that "default router" just doesn't sound correct.

12. It might be learned dynamically by the Dynamic Host Configuration Protocol (DHCP), the Internet Control Message Protocol's (ICMP's) Router Discovery Protocol (RDP), or by "wiretapping" on routing protocol packets (a device that sends a routing protocol update is likely to be a router).

13. Large, bridged Ethernets, even a broadband cable TV cable plant "backbone," supported thousands of users in the days when the most bandwidth-hungry application was

FTP. Once the Web burst onto the scene, it became inconceivable to imagine 6,000+ users sharing a single broadcast domain.

14. HSRP was eventually published by the IETF as RFC-2281 in March of 1998. It is an "Informational" RFC, which means it *does not specify an IETF standard of any kind.* Cisco documented it for the community, and Cisco is free to change the protocol at their discretion. Cisco may also update the specification if they choose to do so, with no requirement that the changes be reflected in a new Informational RFC. Of course, Cisco is bound by their installed base of users to provide backward-compatible extensions.

15. "Unseemly" is the author's opinion. This debate is the networking industry equivalent of professional wrestling.

16. In practice, "immediately" is on the order of 3 – 10 seconds.

17. Most users would not be comfortable with this process, and the network support staff would be temporarily overtaxed at a time when they should be fixing the problem, not helping users with temporary workarounds.

18. Some say misused.

19. 3Com holds a patent on IGMP Snooping, which has been licensed to at least one other large networking company.

20. "Downstream" is reckoned relative to the root of the spanning tree: it is the direction <u>away from</u> the root. In short, it is any non-blocked interface, except the one leading to the root.

CHAPTER 9

Token Ring and FDDI

INTRODUCTION TO TOKEN-PASSING RING TECHNOLOGY

As we have seen, Ethernet is fundamentally based on contention for a shared medium. Token-passing rings are also shared media, but they are very different from Ethernet, in that their medium access does not depend on contention. A "ring" is a closed sequence of point-to-point connections which interconnect the nodes into the shape of a ring. As shown in Figure 9.1, each node's interface to the ring consists of a "ring-in" and "ring-out" portion. Note that the ring-out port of one station is connected to the ring-in port of the next station. This process is repeated until the ring returns to the original station's ring-in port.

For diagrammatic consistency, there is a preferred direction of rotation in the drawings of token rings, namely clockwise. All the data on the ring passes through each node (at a very low level), but stations only pay attention to frames that are addressed to them.

For convenience in wiring, the ring-in and ring-out ports are usually pulled back into a wiring closet device to facilitate easy use of structured wiring.[1] Figure 9.2 depicts a token ring "multistation access unit" (MAU). MAUs typically also have a spare ring-in/ring-out connection so the MAU can be part of a larger ring. The

245

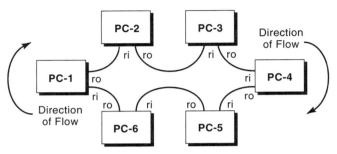

FIGURE 9.1   A simple token-passing ring.

MAU interconnects the ports inside it in much the same way that an Ethernet hub behaves as if there were a coaxial-cable shared medium inside the hub.

The MAU is essentially a ring in a box,[2] with the physical ports for PC attachments containing one pair of wires for the "ring-in" direction and one pair for "ring-out." The cable between the MAU and the endstation is known as a "lobe cable." The MAU's ring-out is patched to the endstation's ring-in, and the endstation's ring-out is patched back to the MAU's ring-in (both pairs occupy different pins within the same lobe cable). The two other wires out of the 8-wire 150 Ω shielded twisted pair bundle (or 100 Ω unshielded twisted pair[3]) are unused.

Token ring was pioneered by IBM in the 1980s as an alternative to Ethernet. In order to support applications with well-defined timing requirements,[4] token ring was specifically designed to facilitate predictable access to the LAN medium. Because the ring is a finite size,[5] each station has a chance to transmit data every so often. The token rotation time depends on the size of the ring and the speed of the ring.

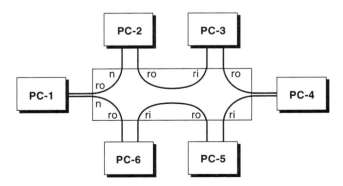

FIGURE 9.2   Multistation access unit (MAU).

Token ring begat the Fiber Distributed Data Interface (FDDI), which has been very successful. In its day, FDDI was the only "high-speed" LAN, so it was the default choice as the LAN or campus backbone, supporting either Ethernet (10 Mbps) or token ring (4 or 16 Mbps[6]). Not only was FDDI's speed an advantage, but it incorporated dual counter-rotating rings for built-in redundancy, which allowed high-availability backbones to be constructed. For a backbone technology, high availability is at least as important as high speed.[7] FDDI was used in high-end servers and Unix workstations, but was far more popular in LAN backbones. Routers with FDDI interfaces appeared in the early 1990s, and shortly thereafter switches emerged that supported one or two dozen 10BASE-T ports, which could be used either for hub connectivity or for direct connections to servers or power users, and one or two FDDI ports for connectivity to the local backbone.

At the time FDDI was conceived (initial work began in 1983), all IEEE 802 LANs were limited in speed from 1 to 20 Mbps. Of course, now that Fast Ethernet and Gigabit Ethernet have equaled or surpassed the 100 Mbps speed, FDDI no longer holds the LAN speed record. However, FDDI is still quite popular due to its reliability features. In addition, there is a lot to be said for a technology that is robust and well understood. Even though FDDI was designed by ANSI,[8] it was designed in the context of the IEEE's layered LAN architecture, effectively becoming another MAC layer under LLC.

TOKEN RING SPECIFICS

Token ring is so named because there is a special frame, called the "token," that constantly circulates around this closed sequence of point-to-point links or "ring." Individual token rings may operate at either 4 or 16 Mbps; FDDI rings only operate at 100 Mbps. In a quiescent state, in which no stations need to transmit data, the token circulates continuously. The token does not have a source or destination MAC address because it is at the lowest part of what one would normally call the MAC layer.

What follows is a brief overview of the token ring MAC-layer protocol. There are few inexpensive references that cover token ring, so if more details are needed than what is presented below, I recommend consulting the IEEE 802.5, 802.2 and 802.1D standards. Another good source of information is product documentation from internetworking devices such as routers and switches. One topic that is not discussed is the whole topic of "station management." There are some relatively complex protocols that are used when a station inserts itself into the ring, and when it is removed. Also, if the ring is broken, there are ring management functions which are also quite involved. These topics could fill a chapter on their own, but they are not very relevant to how IP works over token ring. The information below will cover the frame formats and addressing conventions, which should be just enough to understand how IP and ARP operate over token ring.

Token Ring Functional Description

When a station wishes to transmit, it must wait for the token to arrive. Tokens and data-carrying frames both begin with the same sequence of fields with a single bit in the outer header indicating whether the frame is a token or data. The Starting Delimiter, a special one-byte sequence that can never occur in the data, begins the frame. After the Starting Delimiter, there is an "Access Control" field that includes the token/data bit. (See Figures 9.3 and 9.6 for the format of the token frame and the Access Control field, respectively.) If the frame is a token, it then concludes with an Ending Delimiter. Once an endstation has received the token, it may then transmit some frames before reissuing a token onto the ring. Any frames that the station does transmit begin with a new Start-of-Frame Sequence; in this case, "token" bit is set to indicate that this frame is data, not a token. This process is called "claiming the token."

Now that the station has the token, it may transmit as many frames as it wishes,[9] until the "token holding timer" (THT) expires. The value of the THT is 9.1 ms, which means that a station may transmit up to 4550 bytes at 4 Mbps before it must release the token (4550 bytes * 8 bits/byte = 36,400 bits / 4,000,000 bits/sec = 9.1 ms). If it does not have 4,550 bytes that it needs to transmit, it simply reissues a fresh token to the wire once it has finished transmitting its frame(s). The station must remove its frames from the ring when they come back around, by recognizing its own MAC address as the frame's MAC Source Address.

When an endstation releases a new token as soon as it is done transmitting its frames, it is performing an optimization known as "Early Token Release," or ETR. Before ETR was conceived, endstations did not reissue a new token until after they had taken their frame(s) off the wire. This was a viable technique in the days of 1 Mbps and 4 Mbps rings, but 16 Mbps rings run much more efficiently with ETR than without it.[10] Obviously, at 16 Mbps, one can transmit four times as much data in the same 9.1 milliseconds, so 18,200 bytes of data may be transmitted each time the station possesses the token. All the stations on a given token ring must operate at the same speed. Once the station's frame(s) have circulated around the ring, it will notice its own source address in them and remove them from the ring.

The THT is implemented as a credit function in the endstation. On 16 Mbps rings, all stations start with 18,200 bytes of credit each time they claim the token. For each byte that they transmit, their credit is reduced by one byte, until there is not enough credit left to transmit any remaining frames. For instance, if 363 bytes of credit remain, but the frame the station needs to transmit is 616 bytes long, the station will defer transmitting that frame until the next time it claims the token. Similarly, on a 4 Mbps ring, an endstation starts out with 4550 bytes of credit when it claims the token, which is decremented by one byte for each byte it transmits.

In Ethernet networks, we saw that there was a minimum packet size that was based on how many bits an endstation could transmit during Ethernet's "slot time." Token ring (and FDDI) networks do not have a minimum frame size. Of course, if one is running IP over token ring, a minimum-sized packet would need to at least have a full set of ARP or IP headers, but contrary to the case of Ethernet, no padding[11] is required. Also, contrary to the case of Ethernet, there is no well-defined maximum frame size (i.e., Maximum Transmission Unit, or MTU). The MTU depends on the speed of the ring and the token holding time.

TOKEN RING FRAME FORMATS

Format of the Token

The frame format of the token is much simpler than a full-blown token ring data frame. A token is depicted in Figure 9.3.

The Starting Delimiter field is a pattern that can never occur in a legitimate data frame, and the Ending Delimiter serves to indicate several status conditions. There is an Error bit that indicates if the frame, from the SD up through just before the ED field,[12] has been altered in its trip around the ring. The other Ending Delimiter bit of interest is the I bit, which indicates that this frame is an intermediate frame. Only the last frame of a multiframe transmission has this bit clear.

Format of the IEEE 802.5 MAC Frame

Figure 9.4 depicts the token ring frame structure and indicates where the MAC header (IEEE 802.5) begins. Note that the data frame starts with SD/AC and ends with ED, just as the token does. The Frame Status provides extra information to the

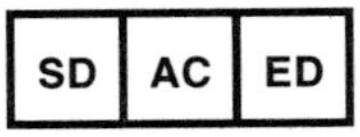

SD	AC	ED

SD = Starting Delimiter (1 byte)
AC = Access Control (1 byte)
ED = Ending Delimiter (1 byte)

FIGURE 9.3 Format of the token.

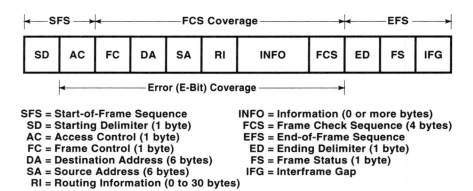

FIGURE 9.4　Token ring frame format.

source station so that it knows if the frame was successfully received (the token needs no such verification).

The token ring frame is more complex than Ethernet's, offering increased functionality (at the cost of increased complexity). Some of this extra functionality results in perceptible benefits to end users, while other functionality serves only to support the operation of this more complex MAC protocol.

The starting delimiter is a series of special "symbols"[12] that are used to indicate that a frame is beginning. Token ring uses "differential Manchester" encoding to represent its bits at the physical layer.[13] Figure 9.5 displays the four possible differen-

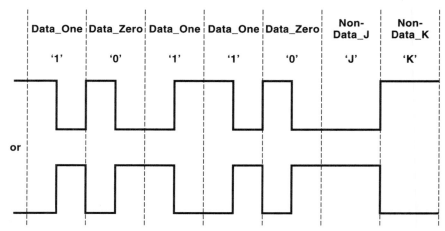

FIGURE 9.5　Differential Manchester symbols.

tial Manchester symbols. Two are used to represent "data_zero" and "data_one" and the other two symbols are called "J" and "K," which are used for special purposes, such as in the SD and ED fields.

Note that both of the data symbols spend one half of the bit time in the high state, and the other half in the low state. The "data_zero" symbol begins with a state transition from the previous bit's ending state, transitioning back to the previous bit's ending state after half the bit time has expired. In contrast, the "data_one" symbol remains in the previous bit's state for the first half of the bit time, then transitions to the opposite state.

The nondata "J" symbol is a whole bit time in the same state as the end of the preceding bit, while the nondata "K" symbol is a whole bit time in the state opposite that of the preceding bit. Both of the data symbols have a state transition halfway through the bit, while both the nondata symbols have no intrabit state transition.

Following the Starting Delimiter is the Access Control (AC) byte, shown in Figure 9.6, which is used to encode the frame's priority level (token ring supports eight priority levels, from 0 – 7; with the default being 3). The AC field also indicates whether this frame is the token (T=0), or whether it is a data packet (T=1). The AC field's M-bit is used in the course of monitoring the ring, used by ring monitors and other ring management entities. Normally, the M-bit is set to zero.

Continuing on into the frame, we find the Frame Control byte. This byte is responsible for identifying a frame as either a MAC frame or an LLC frame, and in the case of an LLC frame, conveying priority information. Next comes the familiar MAC layer Destination and Source Address fields, which may be either two or six bytes long (i.e., 16 or 48 bits long). Historically, many token ring installations used locally administered 16-bit addressing, but 48-bit universally-unique addressing has become more dominant lately.[14]

Locally administered 16-bit addresses were used by LAN administrators in order to make it obvious which nodes were transmitting. Older protocols that operated directly over the MAC layer, such as NetBEUI, use no other form of addressing, so familiar numbers eased troubleshooting ("Oh, that's node 67. I know where that is"). The locally administered 16-bit addresses look like the following: mbbbbbbbbbbbbbbb, where m is set to zero for unicast addresses and one for multi-

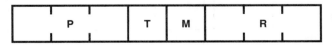

P = Priority Bits
T = Token Bit
M = Monitor Bit
R = Reservation Bits

FIGURE 9.6 Access control byte.

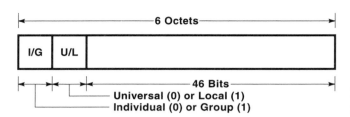

FIGURE 9.7 Token ring destination address format.

cast addresses (m is otherwise known as the Individual/Group bit), and the 15 other bits are manually defined at each station.

Following the frame's addresses is the Routing Information, which facilitates operation in (source-route bridged) multiring environments. The presence of Routing Information in the frame is indicated by stealing a bit from the Source Address Field. The destination address is interpreted just as in Ethernet, as indicated in Figure 9.7.

In Ethernet, the source address is interpreted exactly like the destination address, but in the token ring frame, we see the following structure (Figure 9.8).

The leftmost bit of a source address must always be zero, because a multicast or broadcast address may never be the source address of any frame, only its destination. In token ring, the I/G bit of the source address is not used to indicate the source address' I/G status, since any source address, by definition, must be an individual address, i.e., source addresses cannot be multicast addresses. Instead, 802.5 uses this bit to indicate the presence of "source routing" Information. The source address' I/G bit is renamed RII (the Routing Information Indicator) so its function is clear. If RII = 1, then Source Routing Information is present, and if it is present it must follow the format depicted in Figure 9.9. The structure of this field specified in the 802.1D bridging standard, not within 802.5.

The first two bytes of the Routing Information field contain control information, as depicted in Figure 9.10. The RT field indicates the Routing Type. There are three types, namely "specifically routed" frames (RT = 0xx), "all-routes explorer" frames (RT = 10x), and "spanning tree explorer" frames (RT = 11x). The LTH in-

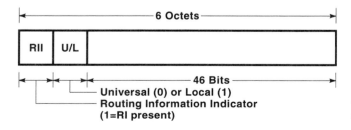

FIGURE 9.8 Token ring source address format.

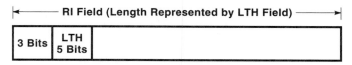

RI = Routing Information (2 to 30 octets when present)
LTH = Length (5 bits)(number of octets)

FIGURE 9.9 Routing information field.

dicates the Length of the Routing Information Field (the RIF must be at least two bytes long, and is at most 30 bytes long, so we need 5 bits to express its length). From Figure 9.10, observe that the length must also always be a multiple of two. The D bit indicates the sense of direction of the routing information; D=0 means the Route Descriptors must be followed in the order specified within the RIF, with D=1 indicating that they be followed in the reverse order. Finally, the "r" bit is reserved, and must be transmitted as zero.

Finally, the LF bits are coded to convey the size of the largest information field that can traverse the source route described by this specified sequence of route de-

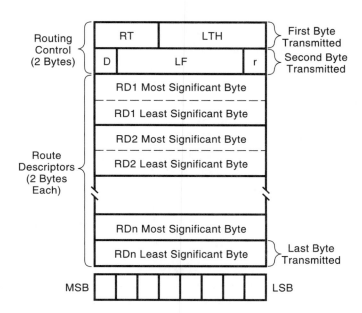

FIGURE 9.10 Internal structure of the routing information field.

MSB	LAN ID (12 Bits)	Bridge No. (4 Bits)	MSB

FIGURE 9.11   Route descriptor field.

scriptors. The LF bits are not significant for Specifically Routed frames; however, they are significant for the all-routes explorer and spanning tree explorer frame types. When a station transmits an explorer frame, it initializes the LF field to indicate the maximum frame size that it can receive. As the explorer frame is propagated throughout the bridged LAN, each bridge may reduce the value in the LF field if the outbound interface cannot handle that large of a frame. This process continues until the destination endstation is reached. If found, the destination may also reduce the value if it wants to receive even smaller frames than its local LAN can support.

After the Routing Control, the Routing Information Field contains up to 14 two-byte Route Descriptors, whose internal structure is depicted in Figure 9.11.

A 12-bit LAN ID is the "ring number," which means that at most 4096 rings may be present in a given source-routed extended LAN. The bridge number must be unique among the LANs to which they attach, and since there are only 4 bits, that means that there may be "only" 15 parallel bridges between any two rings in a source-routed LAN. The practical limit on source-routed domains derives from size of the Routing Information Field. Since it is limited to 14 Route Descriptors, a source-route-bridged extended LAN's "diameter" is no more than 14 bridges.

The end of a frame is indicated explicitly, as was its beginning, by a special delimiter, in this case the Ending Delimiter. Again, the nondata J and K symbols are used to distinguish this byte from any that could ever occur within the data. Figure 9.12 shows the format of the Ending Delimiter.

The Intermediate Frame bit is used when a station is sending multiple frames per token. For each frame transmitted, until the last one, the I-bit is set. The last frame before the token has the I-bit clear, which indicates to downstream stations that the token's arrival is imminent. The E-bit is set when an error is detected within the frame. It is initially set to zero when the frame is transmitted. As you can see in Figure 9.4, the coverage of the FCS and the E-bit are different. Also, since the token has no FCS, the E-bit is the only indication of a broken token.

J	K	1	J	K	1	I	E

J = Data_J Symbol
K = Data_K Symbol
1 = Data_One Symbol
I = Intermediate Frame Bit
E = Error-Detected Bit

FIGURE 9.12   Token ring frame's ending delimiter field.

The FCS is a CRC-32 function as in Ethernet. In 802.5, however, it "covers" the frame from the FC field up through the end of the FCS. In Ethernet, there is no FC field, so Ethernet's FCS coverage begins with the Destination Address field. After the FCS, there is a Frame Status field that is used to inform a transmitting station about whether or not its frame has been received by the intended recipient. The structure of the Frame Status field is shown in Figure 9.13.

The Frame Status field contains control bits which can indicate that the frame has been copied (the C bit), and that the destination address has been recognized (the A bit). The A and C bits are set to zero by the transmitting station, and set to one by the target station. The A bit is duplicated in the FS field and both should be set together, i.e., a station that recognizes its address in the DA of this frame must set both A bits. The same is true for the C bits, which indicate that the frame was successfully copied (i.e., received) by the destination.

It is possible that a station may be able to indicate that it recognized its address in the frame, but it may temporarily not have had the resources to copy the frame into local memory. In this case, the transmitting station may choose to retransmit the frame, hoping that the destination will now have the resources necessary to receive the frame. The four reserved bits are to be transmitted as zeros and should be received as zeros.

The Info field is where the higher-layer protocol packet is, and in token ring LANs the only higher-layer protocol is LLC (802.2 Logical Link Control). In token ring, not surprisingly, there is no (Ether)Type field. LLC uses the one-byte DSAP and SSAP fields to indicate higher-layer protocols. NetBIOS, NetBEUI, IPX, and some other protocols can directly use DSAP or SSAP values over IEEE 802 MAC layers.

Protocols that tend to use EtherTypes may use the Subnetwork Access Protocol (SNAP) header, which is layered on top of LLC. LLC and SNAP are both part of the IEEE 802.2 specification. IP and ARP are encapsulated in SNAP over LLC headers on all IEEE 802 LAN media, the important ones being 802.3, 802.5, and FDDI.

Bit Ordering Issues

In 802.5, bits are transmitted onto the wire in order of the most-significant bit first. FDDI also shares this bit ordering, which is opposite that of

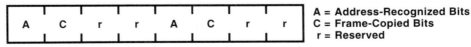

FIGURE 9.13 Token ring header's frame status field.

Ethernet (and Token Bus, too). The effect of this is that bytes are bit-reversed, and this would only be a local issue except that token ring and FDDI can be bridged to Ethernets, and the MAC addresses are interpreted differently in each domain.

This bit order reversal within a byte affects protocols like ARP, since they directly contain MAC addresses that are *not* in the data link header. Bridges must translate the MAC addresses, inside the ARP header when exchanging packets across token ring or FDDI to Ethernet boundaries.

The ordering of the bits in Ethernet is called "canonical" and is bit-wise big-endian. In other words, the most significant bit is on the left. The LSB is transmitted first. This is how one would normally write a binary number (decimal numbers are written this way, too; larger "denominations" are further to the left within written numbers). Token ring binary numbers are also written with the MSB on the left, but they are transmitted MSB-first. Figure 9.14 shows what is meant by canonical order, both abstractly and with a concrete example.

One implication is that ARP, which carries hardware addresses as part of its payload, needed to pick a single, unique bit ordering. In order to be consistent with the bit ordering in other IETF protocols, ARP uses canonical ordering internally. Thus, the source's and target's MAC addresses inside the ARP packet will be bit-reversed from the values used in the SA and DA fields of the 802.5 header.

Here is a quick way to convert between canonical and noncanonical ordering. Hold up both hands in front of you, with your fingers in the indicated bit pattern, as indicated in Figure 9.15. For instance, if the pattern were 1010 0001 (0xA1), you would hold up the first and third fingers of your left hand, and the little finger of your right hand.

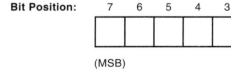

Bit Position:

7	6	5	4	3	2	1	0

(MSB)   (LSB)

0	1	1	1	1	0	1	0
128	64	32	16	8	4	2	1

= 64+32+16+8+2 = 122
                = 0x7A

FIGURE 9.14 Canonical order.

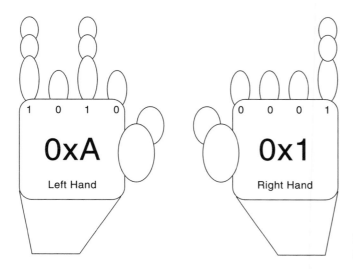

FIGURE 9.15 Finger representation of 1010 0001.

Now, rotate your hands front to back, then cross your right arm over your left arm (or your left arm over your right if you're left-handed). Magically, your right little finger is now on the very left, followed by three "down" fingers (1000, or 8 in [hexa]decimal), and your left hand now reads as 0101 (5 in [hexa]decimal) from left to right. So 0xA1 in canonical becomes 0x85 in noncanonical form, as in Figure 9.16.

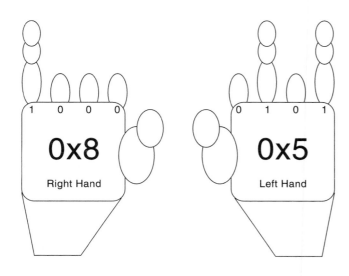

FIGURE 9.16 Finger representation of 1000 0101.

So-Called "Functional" Addressing

Token ring does not support multicast addressing like Ethernet does, rather it has a more-limited "group address" capability known as a "functional" address. (FDDI has Ethernet-like multicast support at the MAC layer and does not support functional addressing.) All LAN types have a special multicast address, consisting of the I/G bit plus all the other 47 bits being set. This 48 bit all-1s address is the broadcast address. Generically, a multicast address is any address that starts with the I/G bit set (equal to "1"), and whose other bits are not all-1s. Also, remember that only destination addresses may have the multicast bit set; this is true for every LAN.

Token ring LANs, however, do not support Ethernet-like multicast addresses. While the 802.5 specification recommends that full support for group addressing be provided (a la Ethernet), it does not *require* such support. It is debatable whether or not token ring would have done better in the marketplace had it incorporated true multicast support from its inception.[15]

A functional address has both the I/G and U/L bits set, and the format of such a destination address is as shown in Figure 9.17. The bit that makes this a functional address, rather than just a locally administered group address, is bit zero of byte 2 (the fifteenth bit of the address). If this bit is zero while the I/G and U/L bits are one, then this is a functional address.

Table 9.1 lists all 31 functional addresses,[16] several of which have uses which are specified in the 802.5 standard. An interesting property of functional addresses is that stations that are "members" of a functional address "group" actually incorporate the functional address into the token ring NIC, behaving as if it were one of the station's unicast address.

Many of the functional addresses have been assigned to various tasks, for instance the IETF has been assigned a single functional address that all IP multicast groups on a single ring must share. Due to the limited number of these addresses, it may be the case that more than one protocol is assigned to the same functional ad-

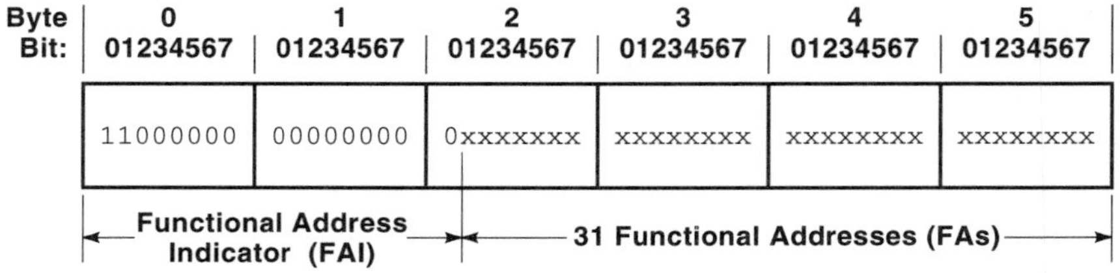

Byte Bit:	0 01234567	1 01234567	2 01234567	3 01234567	4 01234567	5 01234567
	11000000	00000000	0xxxxxxx	xxxxxxxx	xxxxxxxx	xxxxxxxx

Functional Address Indicator (FAI) ◄———► 31 Functional Addresses (FAs) ———►

FIGURE 9.17　Functional address format.

TABLE 9.1 Token ring's 31 functional addresses

Canonical Form	Noncanonical	Description
03-00-00-00-00-80	**C0-00-00-00-00-01**	**Active Monitor**
03-00-00-00-00-40	**C0-00-00-00-00-02**	**Ring Parameter Server**
03-00-00-00-00-20	C0-00-00-00-00-04	reserved for future standardization
03-00-00-00-00-10	**C0-00-00-00-00-08**	**Ring Error Monitor**
03-00-00-00-00-08	**C0-00-00-00-00-10**	**Configuration Report Server**
03-00-00-00-00-04	C0-00-00-00-00-20	reserved for future standardization
03-00-00-00-00-02	C0-00-00-00-00-40	reserved for future standardization
03-00-00-00-00-01	C0-00-00-00-00-80	reserved for future standardization
03-00-00-00-80-00	C0-00-00-00-01-00	available for general use
03-00-00-00-40-00	C0-00-00-00-02-00	available for general use
03-00-00-00-20-00	C0-00-00-00-04-00	available for general use
03-00-00-00-10-00	C0-00-00-00-08-00	available for general use
03-00-00-00-08-00	C0-00-00-00-10-00	available for general use
03-00-00-00-04-00	C0-00-00-00-20-00	available for general use
03-00-00-00-02-00	C0-00-00-00-40-00	available for general use
03-00-00-00-01-00	C0-00-00-00-80-00	available for general use
03-00-00-80-00-00	C0-00-00-01-00-00	available for general use
03-00-00-40-00-00	C0-00-00-02-00-00	available for general use
03-00-00-20-00-00	**C0-00-00-04-00-00**	**IP Multicast (all groups share this functional address)**
03-00-00-10-00-00	C0-00-00-08-00-00	available for general use
03-00-00-08-00-00	C0-00-00-10-00-00	available for general use
03-00-00-04-00-00	C0-00-00-20-00-00	available for general use
03-00-00-02-00-00	C0-00-00-40-00-00	available for general use
03-00-00-01-00-00	C0-00-00-80-00-00	available for general use
03-00-80-00-00-00	C0-00-01-00-00-00	available for general use
03-00-40-00-00-00	C0-00-02-00-00-00	available for general use
03-00-20-00-00-00	C0-00-04-00-00-00	available for general use
03-00-10-00-00-00	C0-00-08-00-00-00	available for general use
03-00-08-00-00-00	C0-00-10-00-00-00	available for general use
03-00-04-00-00-00	C0-00-20-00-00-00	available for general use
03-00-02-00-00-00	C0-00-40-00-00-00	available for general use

dress. If a station receives functionally addressed frames that do not correspond to a function it is actually performing, it ignores the frame.

Another interesting fact about functional addresses is that they may be combined, in that the address C0-00-00-00-00-0A would be received by both the Ring Error Monitor and the Ring Parameter Server, because 0x02 + 0x08 = 0x0A. This might be more obvious in binary:

```
  0000 0010   (0x02)
+ 0000 1000   (0x08)
-----------
= 0000 1010   (0x0A)
```

Token Ring LAN Interconnection

Normally, token rings are interconnected with source route bridges. In a pure token ring (or token ring + FDDI) environment, source route bridges serve to interconnect extended LANs with diameters of up to 14 bridge hops. Token ring has many features that are very different from Ethernet, which makes interconnecting token rings and Ethernets at the MAC layer very tricky.

There are several proprietary techniques for performing "gateway" functions between the two worlds. Probably the most straightforward way to interconnect token ring with Ethernet is to use a router in between them. Of course, this only works when routable protocols are involved! As part of its normal duties, the router localizes the media-specific details to each of its [LAN] interfaces, thereby eliminating the challenging tasks involved in attempting to directly interconnect the very different worlds of Ethernet and token ring. If a router is not a suitable LAN interconnection device, then an 802.5-to-Ethernet gateway must be chosen that accommodates the requirements of the protocols that are in use. The software documentation for a bridge/router will indicate what token ring-to-Ethernet gateway function(s) it supports.

FDDI VERSUS TOKEN RING

The FDDI frame format is similar to the token ring frame. The frame structure omits an AC field; FFDI's FC does the job of token ring's AC and FC combined. From there, the frames are identical. FDDI has one interesting capability in that an FDDI endstation may have both a 16-bit and a 48-bit MAC address at the same time.

FDDI does not use differential Manchester coding, because that would require hardware that could operate at, effectively, 200 Mbaud (the worst case is that every bit has a transition in the middle (it must) and at the beginning, totaling two state transitions per bit; clearly there are up to two baud for every data bit). Instead, a more efficient symbol coding is used, in which 5 bits (32 possible patterns) encode 4 bits of data (16 possible patterns for data bits), plus 16 nondata symbols, of which 9 are used as valid nondata symbols and 7 are simply invalid. This is called a 4B/5B code, and requires that the hardware only operate at, effectively, 125 Mbaud to carry 100 Mbps of data. So, FDDI hardware is transmitting 4-bit blocks of data at a time, while token ring hardware sent each bit individually.

FDDI rings may span large physical distances. The maximum fiber path is 100 km, which makes it ideal for metropolitan-area distributed interconnects, such as "native" LAN-interconnection services. The increased distances also make it ideal for a campus backbone—very few campuses are so large that a 100 km ring would be unable to encircle them. Like token ring, FDDI provides deterministic access to the medium, and also like token ring, FDDI may be loaded to nearly 100 percent utilization without bogging down, an excellent property for a shared-medium LAN technology. FDDI's frame format, as shown in Figure 9.18, is similar to token ring's, but a bit simpler.

The obvious differences between FDDI and token ring come from FDDI's higher speed (100 Mbps) and its dual, counter-rotating, ring design. FDDI's MAC layer protocols are more complex in order to support its very important fault-tolerance functionality. Also, FDDI uses the Timed Token Protocol, which enables each station to know when to expect the next appearance of a token; in token ring, a station does not know when to expect the next token. FDDI Station Management (SMT) is a very involved set of protocols which increases the complexity of FDDI, even compared to token ring. Figure 9.19 illustrates FDDI's layered architecture. Despite the complexity, FDDI has been implemented widely by equipment vendors and deployed widely by customers and service providers. It has been thoroughly debugged and battle-hardened.

Preamble	SD	FC	DA	SA	RI	Information	FCS	ED	FS
≥2 Bytes	1	1	6	6	0 – 30		4	2n	

(← ─────────── 4500 ─────────── →, spanning DA through FCS)

FIGURE 9.18   FDDI frame format.

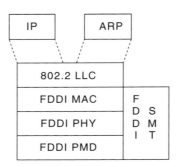

FIGURE 9.19 FDDI's layered architecture.

FDDI is a robust, viable LAN backbone technology. No other LAN technology can match its fault tolerance capabilities. Moreover, FDDI is interoperable with Ethernet and with token ring, in the sense that it is relatively easy to make FDDI-to-Ethernet and FDDI-to-802.5 bridges, which also helped solidify its position as the backbone of choice for LAN interconnection in the early to mid-1990s. In the future, Gigabit Ethernet may erode FDDI's dominance in the LAN backbone, but users will be reluctant to leave behind FDDI's built-in fault tolerance. Perhaps trunking and other enhancements to Ethernet technology will provide solutions to the fault tolerance issue. Any technology that hopes to displace FDDI should offer fault-tolerance capabilities that are at least as robust as FDDI's.

IP OVER TOKEN RING AND FDDI

Token ring does support IP. However, there are a number of major differences from Ethernet; the ARP procedure must accomodate source routing and multicast must use functional addresses. Note that the local/nonlocal decision and other forwarding aspects of IP work just as they do over Ethernet until the very last step of the process—delivery onto the local medium.

The final stage of forwarding is somewhat different, in that the ARP process is not as simple as with Ethernet. Not only must an endstation discover a MAC address of the target (as with Ethernet), but it must also determine the source route to that MAC address. Often, each token ring station will maintain two tables, one mapping neighbor IP addresses into MAC addresses, and another associating these neighbor MAC addresses into source routes. Using all this information, it is then possible to construct a complete set of IP and MAC-layer headers and transmit an 802.5 frame containing an IP packet.

Also, of critical importance for ARP is the fact that the MAC addresses used on the wire are bit-reversed from the way they are expressed in the ARP headers. For token ring, as with *all* other IEEE 802 LANs—even 802.3—the ARP Hardware_Type field is set to "6."

ARP packets are small (and fixed-size packets at that). IP packets are variable size, and therefore must respect the maximum frame size of the medium. Token ring, because it does not have a fixed speed, does not have a fixed MTU. The token ring headers amount to 51 bytes, derived by adding up the fields from SD through FS in Figure 9.4. Since the header is the same size, regardless of the speed at which the ring is operating, the available MTU is very different for IP when operating over a 16 Mbps ring compared to a 4 Mbps ring. In the case of a 4 Mbps ring, the maximum frame size is 4550 bytes, less the 51 bytes for the MAC+LLC+SNAP layer headers,[17] leaving 4499 bytes for a maximum-sized IP packet. A 16 Mbps token ring starts out with a much bigger frame size, 18,200 bytes, leaving up to 18,141 bytes for IP, after allowing for the MAC+LLC+SNAP headers.

Because token rings of differing speeds are often bridged together, an IP implementation cannot transmit an 17,887 byte packet and expect it to arrive intact at any of the local subnet's interconnected rings. Therefore, IP must be conservative and keep the MTU for token ring less than 4499 bytes. Due to limitations in some early token ring bridges, IP's MTU over token ring is recommended to be 2002 bytes, which would be a frame of (at most) 2053 bytes when encapsulated in a full complement of lower-layer headers. This recommendation is from RFC-1042. If your token ring bridges support larger frame sizes, it is safe to set the IP MTU higher on the routers and endstations.

FDDI frames are limited to a maximum of 9000 symbols, each of which represents 4 bits (i.e., half a byte). Thus, an FDDI frame may be up to 4500 bytes long. FDDI's MAC headers consume 49 bytes (see Figure 9.16), with LLC/SNAP consuming their usual eight bytes, for a total of 57 bytes of data link headers. The IETF, in RFC-1390 (a full Internet Standard), recommends an MTU of 4352 bytes, which allowed flexibility for ANSI to add extra MAC headers (i.e., 4500 − 57 = 4443 bytes, so there are 91 extra bytes which could have been used by FDDI extensions.[18]

From ARP's perspective, FDDI is somewhat closer to Ethernet than token ring is, in that the ARP Hardware_Type is "1," which is also Ethernet's Hardware Type code.[19] However, FDDI still uses bit-reversed (noncanonical) MAC source and destination addresses compared to the canonical form found in the ARP header. Most

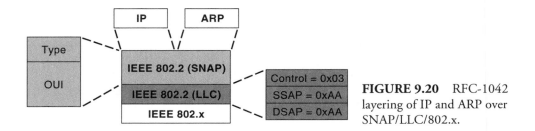

FIGURE 9.20 RFC-1042 layering of IP and ARP over SNAP/LLC/802.x.

FDDI environments are not source-routed, though the FDDI frame format can support source routing, so it is possible that source-routing information may need to be stored alongside the ARP cache. FDDI does support MAC-layer multicast in the same way that Ethernet does (with the small exception that the addresses are bit-reversed), and does not support functional addresses.

Protocol Demultiplexing

As was briefly discussed in Chapter 8, when IP is used over IEEE 802 LANs (including 802.3), it is encapsulated in SNAP/LLC/802.x headers, as diagrammed in Figure 9.20 (cf. Figure 8.5), according to RFC-1042, whch is now a full Internet Standard.

The layering above is used for IP and ARP over both token ring and FDDI, as well as 802.3 Ethernet, token bus (IEEE 802.4), and other technologies such as Frame Relay, ATM Adaptation Layer 5 (AAL5), and Switched Multimegabit Data Service (SMDS).

REFERENCES

International Standard ISO/IEC 10038, 1993. Information technology— Telecommunications and information exchange between systems— Local and metropolitan area networks—Specific requirements, Part 5: Token ring access method and physical layer specifications.

ANSI/IEEE Std 802.1D, 1993. (This edition contains ANSI/IEEE Std 802.1D-1990, ANSI/IEEE Std 802.1i-1992, and IEEE Std 802.5m-1993).

ISO/IEC Final CD 15802-3. Information technology—Telecommunications and information exchange between systems—Local area networks—Media access control (MAC) bridges.

IEEE P802.1D/D15, November 24, 1997. Information technology—Telecommunications and information exchange between systems—Local and metropolitan area networks—Common specifications—Part 3: Media Access Control (MAC) Bridges: Revision (Incorporating IEEE P802.1p: Traffic Class Expediting and Dynamic Multicast Filtering).

Request for Comment (RFC)

1042 Standard for the transmission of IP datagrams over IEEE 802 networks. J. Postel, J.K. Reynolds. Feb-01-1988. (Format: TXT=34359 bytes) (Obsoletes RFC0948) (Status: STANDARD)

1390 Transmission of IP and ARP over FDDI Networks. D. Katz. January 1993. (Format: TXT=22077 bytes) (Status: STANDARD)

1469 IP Multicast over Token-Ring Local Area Networks. T. Pusateri. June 1993. (Format: TXT=8189 bytes) (Status: PROPOSED STANDARD)

"Metropolitan Area Networks: Concepts, Standards, and Services," Gary C. Kessler, David A. Train, McGraw-Hill, 1992. ISBN 0-07-034243-1.

ENDNOTES

1. In fact, token ring technology pioneered operation over [shielded] twisted pair.

2. FDDI uses "concentrators," as opposed to MAUs, but the ring-in-a-box concept is still valid.

3. Originally, token ring could only run over IBM's Shielded Twisted Pair 150Ω cabling, which was the first popular structured wiring system. Now that 10BASE-T has become so popular, token ring has had a new physical layer added so it can run over either shielded or unshielded twisted pair.

4. IBM's Systems Network Architecture (SNA) supports such applications. Token ring was designed by IBM to serve this environment well.

5. A perfectly configured token ring may not have more than 250 endstations.

6. Before FDDI was available, 16 Mbps token ring was invented to act as a backbone for 4 Mbps rings.

7. The speed of a broken 100 Gigabit LAN-of-the-future is 0 bits per second.

8. For those who care about such things, the committee responsible was ANSI X3T9.5. Today, this committee is known as X3.T12.

9. Even though an endstation may transmit more than one frame each time it holds the token, it is not required to do so.

10. FDDI would be extremely inefficient were it not for ETR.

11. Padding is normally needed if the ARP or IP packet is less than 64 bytes long (which is the smallest, legal frame size on an Ethernet). If the packet is at least 64 bytes long, no padding is needed.

12. Symbols = bits. The bits in token ring are expressed as "symbols" at the physical layer. The SD and ED fields contain "code violations" that would never occur in real data.

13. 10 Mbps Ethernet uses plain Manchester bit coding. There are no nondata symbols.

14. Prior to 1992, the IEEE had announced its intention to eliminate support for 16-bit addressing [Metropolitan Area Networks; Concepts, Standards, and Services, pg. 141].

15. It is doubtful that adopting such multicast support—at this late date—is worth the effort.

16. Other IEEE LANs have 2^{24} multicast addresses (16,777,216 addresses), which is somewhat more than the 23 functional addresses which are "available for general use."

17. The 51 bytes include a full-size Routing Information Field of 30 bytes.

18. The author is not aware of any such extensions.

19. This choice facilitates easy operation of IP over mixed Ethernet/FDDI infrastructures, since it means that the bridges need not translate the Hardware_Type values in the headers when copying ARP packets from Ethernet to FDDI or vice-versa.

CHAPTER 10

THE POINT-TO-POINT PROTOCOL

The name "Point-to-Point Protocol" (PPP) represents a set of interdependent protocols working together to support the concurrent operation of multiple higher-layer protocol stacks over a shared[1] point-to-point serial link. PPP supports the encapsulation of higher-layer data, as well as all the necessary negotiation mechanisms that enable the link to be configured to suit the peers. Serial links, also known as lines, or circuits, may be categorized into two main classes: 1) dialup and 2) leased lines.

CLASSIFICATION OF SERIAL LINES

Serial lines, in the context of PPP, connect exactly two points. Although "multidrop" serial line protocols do exist, PPP does not support multidrop leased lines. From the earliest serial line technologies, and up through today, most serial lines provided an equal amount of bandwidth in each direction, though this is beginning to change.

Full duplex, half duplex, simplex

Bidirectional circuits are known as "full duplex," while links where only one end at a time can transmit are known as "half duplex." Finally, another class of circuit is "simplex," which can only transmit in one direction. PPP operates over full-duplex serial links, meaning that data can flow in both directions at the same time. PPP requires full duplex because of the negotiations that occur between the two ends of the link; in order for negotiations to take place, traffic must be able to flow in both directions (though not necessarily at the same speed).

Traditionally, most full-duplex circuits had the same bandwidth in each direction.[2] Bandwidth is a unit of data-carrying capacity and is measured in units of "bits per second" (bps). As in the rest of the metric system, various multipliers can be prefixed onto the unit, such as those in Table 10.1. The asterisks indicate levels in common use today. The double-asterisk at the "tera" level indicates a level that is not yet in use, but that is starting to be heard more often. "Terabit" is heard today in the context of Big F Routers (BFRs)[3], in that their aggregate capacity is measured in up to a small number of Terabits per second.

The author is not aware of any data transmission technology in the terabits per second (Tbps) range, much less the "petabits per second (Pbps)" (or faster) range, at least not for the immediate future. The fastest serial links conceivable today operate at 9,953.28 Mbps, or just under 10 Gbps, and even those are not yet available for mass deployment.[4] Links at one-quarter that speed, or 2488.32 Mbps (2.48832

TABLE 10.1   METRIC PREFIXES RELEVANT TO DATA TRANSMISSION SPEEDS

	yotta	Y	(septillion)	10^{24}	1,000,000,000,000,000,000,000,000
	zetta	Z	(sextillion)	10^{21}	1,000,000,000,000,000,000,000
	exa	E	(quintillion)	10^{18}	1,000,000,000,000,000,000
	peta	P	(quadrillion)	10^{15}	1,000,000,000,000,000
**	tera	T	(trillion)	10^{12}	1,000,000,000,000
*	giga	G	(billion)	10^{9}	1,000,000,000
*	mega	M	(million)	10^{6}	1,000,000
*	kilo	k	(thousand)	10^{3}	1,000

Gbps), are just beginning to be deployed. In fact, Juniper Networks, Inc. is shipping a router that supports links of this speed. For serial lines at the 2.5 Gbps speed, the limiting factor preventing deployment until now has been the lack of routers that could move data around at those speeds. The fiber in the ground certainly has the capacity for Gbps speeds, and much more, but not necessarily zettabits per second (Zbps), or even yottabits per second (Ybps). I have learned never to say never, though.

Figure 10.1 shows a conceptual view of a full-duplex symmetric-bandwidth serial line, indicating the two directions of transmission and the fact that the two directions have the same capacity, in this case 64 kbps. The direction away from one end is usually called its "transmit direction," and similarly the opposite direction is its "receive direction." Each end's transmit direction is connected to the other end's receive direction.

Symmetric versus Asymmetric Bandwidth Circuits

The link in Figure 10.1 is symmetrical in that the bandwidth in each direction is the same. In the late 1990s, Asymmetric Digital Subscriber Line (ADSL) links have begun to emerge, which are characterized by differing transmission rates in either direction. This is well suited to use by many people at home, since it is far more likely for them to be information consumers than information providers. Given that they consume (receive) more data than they originate (transmit), it makes a lot of sense to have more bandwidth toward the home than away from it. V.90 modems (so-called 56-kbps modems also provide for more bandwidth "downstream" than "upstream."

Before mentioning ADSL, we'll observe that the most common pre-ADSL symmetric link speeds are listed in Table 10.2. Symmetric links have typically been used for private telephone networks (corporations and government entities used to build their own phone networks), and they later evolved to carry data between IP routers. These synchronous links have also seen a lot of use in IBM Systems Network Architecture environments, interconnecting front-end processors or removing communications controllers with off-site front-end processors. Typical private telephone and SNA networks did not require speed in excess of T-1/E-1. Telco backbones were the domain of the higher-speed links, and now IP backbones use such circuits between routers—and even faster speeds than these!

FIGURE 10.1 Conceptual view of a serial line.

TABLE 10.2 COMMON SYMMETRIC CIRCUIT BANDWIDTHS

56 kbps		
64 kbps		
1,544 kbps	(T-1)	1.544 Mbps
2,048 kbps	(E-1)	2.048 Mbps
34,768 kbps	(E-3)	34.768 Mbps
44,736 kbps	(T-3)	44.736 Mbps

From the 1960s through the late 1980s a common WAN circuit speed was 56 kbps. High-speed backbones of the time operated at T-1 speeds. Within the last 10 years, deregulation and the explosion of data traffic in general, and the Internet in particular, have created a bandwidth explosion. Internet backbone speeds today are commonly 155.52 Mbps, and even 622.08 Mbps. In 1999, deployment of 2,488.32 Mbps backbone circuits has begun in earnest along with a new generation of ultra-fast routing hardware.

Customer access lines have undergone a similar dramatic growth, starting with 56 kbps being common in the early 1990s.[5] Today, T-1 access lines are very popular for businesses, and T-3 lines, until recently considered a strictly backbone technology, are being sold to customers in ever-increasing numbers. In cases where a customer does not need (or can not afford!), all of a circuit's bandwidth, it is also possible to buy "fractional" T1/E1 or T3/E3 speed circuits.[6] Fractional-speed leased lines allow a customer to buy the bandwidth they need, provided that their local telephone company is selling such services.

As with traditional digital synchronous lines, ADSL links provide a permanent circuit into which data may be sent at any time. ADSL offers "downstream" speeds of up to T-1 (or more, the closer you live to the telephone company central office). The "downstream" direction is the direction toward the customer (i.e., away from the telephone company). The upstream direction is usually much slower, up to the low hundreds of kilobits per second (again, depending on distance). Interestingly, ADSL is designed to work simultaneously with basic phone service, although it is often deployed on a separate pair of wires. Over the same pair of copper wires, ADSL should not disrupt traditional style telephony service.[7] According to the ADSL Forum (web site: <http://www.adsl.com/>):

ADSL provides speeds up to 8 Mbps downstream (to the user) and up to 1 Mbps upstream, depending upon line length and loop[8] and line conditions.

DIAL-UP VERSUS LEASED LINES

The other main class of serial links are dial-up circuits. Permanent circuits are always up (well, they're *supposed* to be . . .), and historically were not only full duplex but also had equal bandwidth in each direction. Generally, these permanent links interconnected routers or other networking devices that require persistent connectivity to each other. Before the advent of packet switching, these circuits interconnected telephone switches and provided for transmission of from 24 to 672 (or even more, in some cases) simultaneous phone calls. The process of digitization of voice calls requires (digitally uncompressed) bandwidth of exactly 64 kbps (64,000 bps).

Dial-up links are established dynamically on demand when data needs to be sent in a manner very similar to making a voice phone call when you need to talk to someone. A modem dials another modem (at the direction of a computer), which can answer a call and negotiate the fastest speed that the line conditions will allow. By far, the majority of dial-up links are regular phone lines with modems at each end. A more advanced form of dial-up technology is Integrated Services Digital Network (ISDN) which provides a standard interface for digital voice and data calls.[9] One advantage of dial-up connections is that they only need to be up while they are being used. If there is no transmission activity, they can be taken down, potentially saving money[10] by reducing total connect time.

Of course, one major disadvantage is that dial-up links are at the very bottom of the bandwidth scale. The fastest modems use a standard known as V.90. V.90 modems are capable of up to 56 kbps in the direction from the telco to the customer, but only up to 32 kbps or so in the opposite direction. For the same reason that ADSL makes sense, these asymmetric modem speeds allow users to achieve the faster speed in the "download direction." Earlier modem standards such as V.32 and V.34 yielded symmetric bandwidths up to 28.8 or 33.6 kbps, respectively.

PPP OVERVIEW

PPP is an IETF Standard protocol, specified in RFC-1661. PPP can carry multiple network-layer protocols and supports many different kinds of serial line standards, both synchronous and asynchronous. PPP is not a "client-server" protocol, in that

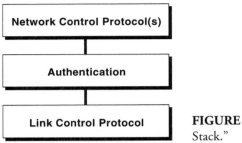

FIGURE 10.2 The PPP "Protocol Stack."

TABLE 10.3 Current PPP network control protocols

RFC-1378	ATCP	AppleTalk Control Protocol
RFC-1638	BCP	Bridging Control Protocol
RFC-1763	BVCP	Banyan Vines Control Protocol
RFC-1762	DNCP	DECnet Phase IV Control Protocol
RFC-1332	IPCP	IP Control Protocol
RFC-2023	IPV6CP	IPv6 Control Protocol
RFC-1552	IPXCP	Novell IPX Control Protocol
RFC-1841	LECP	LAN Extension Control Protocol
RFC-2097	NBFCP	NetBIOS Frames Control Protocol
RFC-1377	OSINLCP	OSI Network Layer[12] Control Protocol (covers CLNP, ES-IS, IS-IS, and IDRP[13])
RFC-1963	SDTP	Serial Data Transport
RFC-2043	SNACP	SNA Control Protocol
RFC-1764	XNSCP	Xerox Network Systems (XNS) Internet Datagram Protocol (IDP) Control Protocol

there is no preferred end of a PPP session. Both ends are equal peers and either end may initiate or terminate a connection.

PPP built upon the implementation and deployment experience of Serial Line IP (SLIP, RFC-1055), which is also an IETF Standard protocol despite its name: *"Nonstandard for transmission of IP datagrams over serial lines: SLIP."* Like PPP, SLIP supported point-to-point serial links, however, only IP could run over SLIP—that is where SLIP got its name, after all. The motivation for PPP stemmed from a desire for multiprotocol support, and for a cleaner, more extensible architecture that was adaptable to many different usage scenarios.

PPP is comprised of three main components, and a slew of ancillary optional extensions. The three main parts of PPP can be viewed as a small protocol stack. First, Link Control Protocol negotiations establish a working physical layer connection over which bits may be successfully transmitted. Next, there is an optional Authentication negotiation phase.[11] Finally, there is a Network Control Protocol negotiation phase (one for each active Network-Layer Protocol). Figure 10.2 illustrates the PPP "protocol stack."

Assuming that the link can be activated, and that the Authentication is completed successfully, the Network Control Protocols (NCPs) individually perform specific negotiations to initialize their respective protocol stack over PPP. Table 10.3 shows the current NCPs that exist at the time of this writing.

LINK CONTROL PROTOCOL (LCP)

The LCP is responsible for establishing, maintaining, and tearing down the physical path between two PPP LCP entities. Once up, LCP also provides for the testing of the link, for the purpose of detecting if the link has gone down.

LCP: Establishing a Link

In the case of a static leased line, the circuit is considered provisionally "up" if a clock is recovered from an otherwise idle link. Typically, serial lines will have some method of supplying a "clocking" signal from the network to the endpoints, which allows the endpoints to transmit their bits at the precise speed of the circuit. Thus, an idle link is not really idle. The clock that is received from the network is used to pace the transmission of frames into the network once LCP has officially declared the link to be up.

What the Heck is a Finite State Machine (FSM)?

Most protocols are defined in the context of FSMs. A protocol has a finite number of states (if it didn't, it might never accomplish anything). The FSM is a compact listing of all the states, along with the events that cause transitions from one state to another. Think of a finite state machine as a flowchart for a protocol.

Excerpted from RFC-1661, Figure 10.3 depicts PPP's high-level states. PPP's complete FSM is much more complex, and is actually represented in the RFC by a matrix, because a diagram such as Figure 10.3 would not fit on one page.

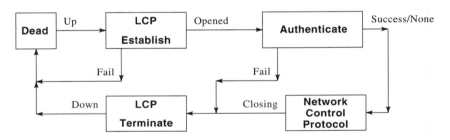

FIGURE 10.3   The PPP high-level finite state machine.

For a more complicated example, I encourage you to look up the IGMPv2 RFC (2236), which has a very impressive-looking FSM on page 16. Neighboring pages in that RFC also have some smaller FSMs.

The clocking signal is a first level, or provisional, indication that the link may be functional, at least as far as the closest telephone company central office, but not necessarily all the way to the other side of the circuit.[14] The only way to tell if the link is working all the way to the other side is to try and get the other side to send you a frame. In order to tell if the other side is reachable, once a clocking signal is seen, a PPP entity begins transmitting PPP Configure-Requests. If the PPP entity on the far end of the circuit hears these frames, it will respond with a PPP Configure-Acknowledgement.

A PPP entity will continue sending Configure-Requests until a Configure-Acknowledgment is seen. Once the Configure-Acknowledgment has been received, the LCP entity can consider the link to be up. The other side, presumably, also saw a clocking signal and also sent its own series of Configure-Requests, and received a Configure-Acknowledgment in return. Both sides should agree on the state of the link, so they both execute the same finite-state machine(s).

PPP's LCP is also used to negotiate link parameters if either side wishes to deviate from the default choices. One such parameter is the Frame Check Sequence, when PPP is used over HDLC framing (RFC-1662). PPP framing defaults to using a 16-bit FCS, but LCP allows the FCS to be negotiated to 32 bits, or to null (zero bits).

Other link parameters include Identification, and the related Magic-Number, Time-Remaining (e.g., sent by a PPP access server to indicate that a client will be disconnected as some specific future time), Callback (facilitates one peer telling the other to call it back, for centralized billing and security), and Compound-Frames (once negotiated, allows multiple LCP negotiation frames to be lumped together instead of having to do each one in turn; also allows grouping multiple data packets in one link-level frame).

The Magic-Number option is especially useful. A PPP entity creates a random 32-bit number somehow, and sends this to the other side during the LCP negotiation. If the other side receives a Magic-Number configuration option that does not match its own, it can deduce that serial line is not in a looped-back condition. Each side may choose its own Magic-Number, which can be used for a link Echo function. Echo-Requests may be sent periodically once the link is up. If a Magic-Number has been negotiated, it is inserted into a field in the Echo-Request. If a PPP implementation ever receives an Echo-Request with its own Magic-Number inside, then it can immediately deduce that the link has transitioned into a looped-back condition. Figure 10.4 shows what we mean when we say "loopback."

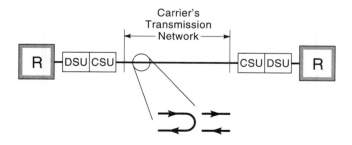

FIGURE 10.4 Serial link loopback.

A loopback occurs whenever a circuit's transmit direction is patched into its receive direction. Loopbacks may be in one direction (as pictured), or in both directions. The left station in Figure 10.4 will see the link status as "loopback" while the right station will see it as "down." Being able to loop a circuit back toward you provides valuable diagnostic information, so virtually every kind of telecommunications equipment supports this function. In Figure 10.4, the Channel Service Unit/Data Service Unit (CSU/DSU) is illustrated, which is the interface between a router or other device's traditional serial interface[15] and the circuit itself, which is generally terminated in a wall jack for sub-T3 speed circuits.[16]

A long time ago, the CSU and DSU were separate boxes, deployed in series, but electronic miniaturization has allowed their two separate functions to be integrated into one box, which is now the typical way you see a CSU/DSU (they are also called DSU/CSUs; either is correct).

Local loopback happens when a device, such as the CSU/DSU, is configured to loop frames back over the serial interface to the router. Loops can be set in either the DSU or the CSU. If the DSU is set to loop all packets back to the router, its correct operation can be verified all the way to the edge of the CSU. Once the DSU has been verified to be correct, the CSU can be set to do the same, thus exercising the entire path from the DSU through the CSU to the edge of the circuit back through the CSU then through the DSU and across the serial interface to the router.

The CSU/DSU usually also supports remote loopback, allowing the entire transmission infrastructure to be tested. Thus, the path from the router through the local DSU and CSU to the remote CSU and back can be verified to be working properly. A CSU sends control messages over the circuit ("loop-up" and "loop-down" codes) to control the remote device. The remote DSU can also loop back frames, thereby exercising the path all the way to the far end serial interface (without actually sending the frames to the remote router). If loopback tests of the circuit prove it to be working, from the CSU/DSU's perspective, then the problem lies somewhere between the two router interfaces and their DSUs.

The CSU/DSU is the main tool that users have with which to configure and test their circuits—independently of the circuit provider. Clearly, if loopback is a useful troubleshooting aid for the customer, it is also useful to the phone company, so virtually every point in the transmission network can be set to loop back a circuit. There are even "smart jacks" that allow a T-1 ciruit to be looped back *from within the wall jack,* at the edge of the patch cable that leads to the CSU/DSU.

Telco loopbacks can be set by a local technician via "craft" interfaces at any of the various add/drop multiplexers and digital cross-connects that a circuit passes through,

A Word on Clocking

Often, multiple devices can be configured to generate a clock signal. In the vast majority of cases, the carrier's transmission network provides a clocking signal to the CSU, which is passed through the DSU and into the router via the serial interface. The router, as noted earlier, uses this clock frequency as a reference when it needs to supply traffic to the DSU, which passes it to the CSU and into the network. Many router serial interfaces and CSU/DSUs can also be configured to supply a local clocking signal.

It is vitally important that only one source of timing exist within a circuit! If two clock signals exist, they are almost certainly not using precisely the same frequency. When these signals overlap imperfectly, the resulting "interference" pattern can look like continuous line-rate data, but it is really only random data due to differences in the clock signals' frequencies. If a circuit appears to be full of random-looking data, there may be multiple active clock sources. Sometimes, the telecommunications network does not supply a clock, in which case most CSU/DSUs can be configured to generate one. Of the pair of CSUs on a circuit, at most one of them needs to generate a clock. The other side will synchronize its clock to the supplied signal.

or via a centralized network management application that can remotely configure the same devices. While a circuit is being provisioned, the carrier may use the loopback functionality to verify that the circuit is properly configured; by the time that they are ready to turn it over to the customer, all the test loops should have been cleared. Unfortunately, sometimes loops remain, which prevents the circuit from operating properly.

The PPP LCP negotiation is designed to work only if the circuit is really connecting two different peers. Negotiation mechanisms, including the Magic-Number, exist to ensure that a PPP device is not talking to itself, as it would be if the circuit were looped back. While the circuit is up, Echo-Requests may be sent periodically so that if a loop condition occurs, it will be detected as soon as possible. Once a loop occurs, the PPP implementation will begin trying to re-establish communications with the other peer.

In the case of dial-up links, the LCP layer is responsible for initiating calls via modems or direct network signaling (as in the case of an ISDN call). Once the call has been completed, and a carrier has been detected, a dial-up link must then be configured by LCP in much the same way that a dedicated link is configured. Once both ends have established that the other exists, the link is finally "up." The "up" indication triggers the next-higher layer (Authentication) to begin its task(s).

LCP: Maintaining a Link

While the link is up, either side may send PPP LCP Echo-Requests in order to ensure that the other side is still reachable. Why do you need an Echo protocol in PPP? Why can't you determine whether or not the link is up based solely on the presence of the clock signal? One reason is that it is entirely possible that the clock may be active on one end, but not the other, due to an equipment outage in the carrier's transmission network. It is also possible that the carrier accidentally reconfigured your line in the middle, and now your packets are being looped back to you instead of passing through to the other side—or even worse, they are simply not reaching their previous destination.

Another all too common failure involves demonic backhoe operators that regularly rip through long-haul backbone fibers. Such a fiber cut in the middle of a circuit may leave both ends of a PPP link receiving a clocking signal from their respective carrier's local equipment, but despite the presence of a clock signal at both ends, there is no end-to-end connectivity. This sort of link-layer "partial" failure is not only possible, but common, so it is clearly prudent to have a link-layer end-to-end "are you still there?" protocol; in this case, the LCP Echo protocol. (Obviously, if one side sees its clocking signal disappear, its PPP implementation should immediately declare the circuit to be down.)

Note that a PPP implementation could choose to interpret incoming data from the other side as an implicit indication that the other side is alive. As an optimization, LCP Echo packets may be sent only when no data has arrived for some time interval. One advantage to sending Echoes all the time is to detect "diode" failures, in which one direction can send data successfully but the other cannot. The LCP Echo protocol has the advantage of being able to test both directions because it requires both ends to be able to both transmit and receive a packet successfully.

LCP: Deactivating a Link

The LCP "layer" also includes messages that PPP uses to tear down the link. Negotiating a link deactivation prior to actually deactivating the link is known as "graceful" termination. Any other form of link deactivation is either due to a failure or misconfiguration between the PPP peers, or the result of one side crashing, or being powered down, or having the serial cable knocked loose from the router or CSU/DSU by a technician that was working in the area. LCP can detect abnormal termination or loopbacks, and attempt to re-establish normal contact with the remote peer.

However, if a router is being rebooted, or if an interface is being "bounced" to get it to restart its PPP state machine, or for any number of other valid reasons, one of the PPP entities may decide to tear down the circuit gracefully. (In the case of dial-up circuits, this will probably involve hanging up the line after the PPP teardown negotiation is complete.) In the case of leased lines, there may be good reasons to tear down the link. For instance, if one of the devices is being rebooted, it may choose to deactivate the link as a courtesy to the other side. This polite behavior will allow the other device to declare the link to be down in the shortest possible time.

AUTHENTICATION

The Authentication layer uses several different protocols to ensure that only a valid device is establishing a connection. When LCP is running over dial-up connections, one of the PPP peers frequently corresponds to a user, e.g., a modem-equipped laptop calling into an Internet Service Provider, or into the user's corporate "1-800" number.[17] When operating over dedicated circuits, the Authentication layer helps ensure that no rogue device has been attached to the other side, or to an intermediate point in the circuit.

Authentication protocols include the Password Authentication Protocol (PAP, RFC-1334), which is now obsolete,[18] the Challenge-Handshake Authentication Protocol[19] (CHAP, RFC-1994), and the Extensible Authentication Protocol (EAP, RFC-2284).

Before delving into the high-level details of each authentication protocol, note that the Authentication layer does not have to use any authentication algorithm—it could simply pass the LCP "up" indication directly to the configured NCPs and not perform any authentication. Most PPP implementations default to null authentication. Authentication is *not* mandatory. Once the physical link has proven to be operational, then an authentication algorithm may be employed that matches the organization's security requirements.

PAP: Password Authentication Protocol

PAP is the simplest—and least secure—authentication method. It is a two-way handshake protocol meaning that one packet from each peer must be exchanged in order to complete the negotiation. PAP's negotiation is depicted in Figure 10.5.

This illustrates only one direction; successful completion of this negotiation only results in B knowing who A is. At that point, A still does not know who it is talking to, so a separate negotiation will be needed, in which B sends its username and password to A. For a little extra security, A and B should use different username/password combinations when talking to other peers. So if A connected to C later, A would use a C-specific username and password.

There are other stronger authentication schemes, but in order to use them, they must be negotiated prior to using PAP. If no other authentication protocol is selected, PAP will be used (if either side requires authentication). Each side of the link has a configured user name and password, which are exchanged in Authenticate-Request packets after LCP declares the link to be "up." The username and password are transmitted repeatedly until the other side acknowledges the message with an Authenticate-Ack packet.

The username and password are both transmitted "in the clear," so they could be trivially intercepted by any interested third party. PAP is also vulnerable to trial-and-error attacks and its use is not recommended. Luckily, most devices that support PAP also support CHAP, which can be more secure.

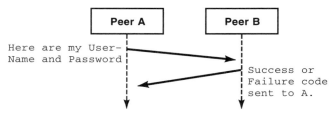

FIGURE 10.5   PAP two-way handshake.

CHAP: Challenge Handshake Authentication Protocol

PAP and CHAP both provide more than simply authentication. By virtue of the fact that they, securely or not, identify a "user" that is connecting, they may use that information to guide the further configurations of the device(s) during the Network Control Protocol phase, which happens after the Authentication phase. PAP represents a two-way handshake, wherein a single PAP configuration request is acknowledged by a single positive or negative response.[20] In a three-way handshake, CHAP completes the steps that are illustrated in Figure 10.6.

After a CHAP negotiation (such as the one in Figure 10.6) has completed successfully, one side of the link knows the identity of the other; the converse is not true after only one three-way handshake. In order for both sides to consider the link up and fully authenticated,[21] each side must challenge the other, thus at a minimum there will be three more packets in this example starting with a Challenge from B. At random intervals, each side challenges the other to re-verify the authentication. These random future challenges need not be synchronized between the two sides.

CHAP differs from PAP in that it uses a three-way handshake. CHAP still depends on there being a "shared secret" that each party knows, but the secret is never transmitted over the wire. The data that is transmitted is enough for the challengee to prove that it knows the secret, given the other information that is provided. The challenger creates a packet that includes the following fields, as in Figure 10.7.

The Length field represents the entire CHAP packet, including the Code and Identifier (and the two byte Length field itself!). The Identifier changes with each

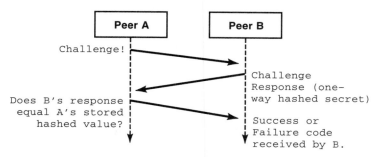

FIGURE 10.6   CHAP three-way handshake.

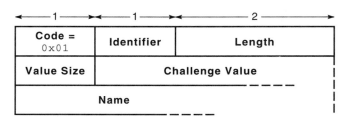

FIGURE 10.7   Challenge format.

new Challenge. The Name field in a Challenge packet is the challenger's name, and the Name field in the Challenge Response contains the responder's name.

Some example hash functionas include "Message Digest 5 (MD-5)," which yields a 128-bit (16-byte) output and is the mandatory-to-implement algorithm specified by the CHAP specification (RFC-1994).[22] The other two defined CHAP hash algorithms are MS-CHAP v1.0 and MS-CHAP v2.0. Another common hash function is the Secure Hash Algorithm[23] (SHA-1), though at the time of this writing there is not a definition of how CHAP could use that algorithm.

CHAP's hash function takes input in the form of the preshared secret sandwiched between a numeric Identifier[24] and a randomly chosen Challenge Value.[25] The Response Value is simply the output of the hash function when acting on those input values. Symbolically, the following is happening (the ◊ symbol indicates concatenation):

Response Value = Hash (Identifier ◊ Shared_Secret ◊ Challenge_Value)

When a Challenge is transmitted, the challenger can precompute the expected Response Value, since it knows all the input independent variables. A Challenge Response is only valid once for one value of the Identifier.[26] Figure 10.8 depicts the Challenge Response when using the MD-5 hash.

The shared secret is persistent over many connections, but the other numbers change with each Challenge. Even though an eavesdropper can see the Identifier and the Challenge Value in the Challenge, and the Response Value in the Challenge Response, she cannot deduce the value of the shared secret. There is something of a chicken-and-egg problem here, in that there must be a way to get the two parties to agree in advance on what pre-shared secret they will use, but it is safe to assume that each peer was able to be configured with the same secret.

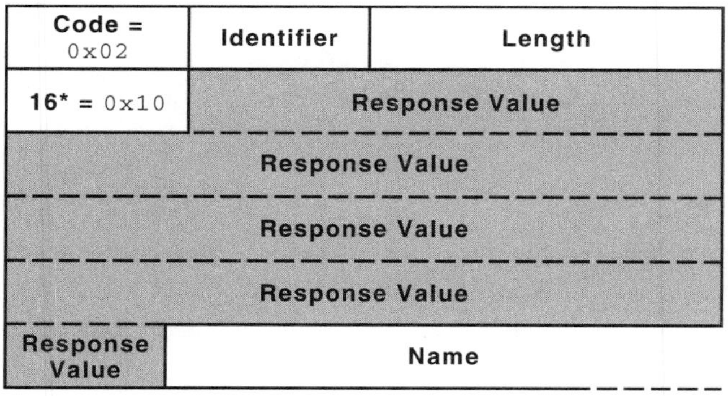

Code = 0x02	Identifier	Length
16* = 0x10	Response Value	
Response Value		
Response Value		
Response Value		
Response Value	Name	

* The [Response] Value size is always 16, regardless of the size of the input to MD-5. Other hash functions may have different [Response] Value sizes.

FIGURE 10.8 Response format.

The hash function must be carefully chosen to be "cryptographically strong," meaning that changing a single bit in the input causes, on average, half the bits in the output to change. By looking at the output of such a function, it is virtually impossible to guess what the input(s) might have been. In this case, the eavesdropper can see two out of three of the independent variables, but the shared secret is protected since it never needs to leave either peer.

For such functions, it is "computationally infeasible" to look at the hash value and determine what input created that value. In this case, far more than 1 bit is changing with each new challenge. Yes, the secret is unaltered with each negotiation, but the Identifier will be a new 8-bit number each time, and the Value field could change length . . . and will certainly change its value. Both sides, because they know the Identifier and Value, can use those numbers together with the shared secret to compute the Response Value. If the challenger sees that its peer has computed the expected Response Value, then the challenger can conclude that the peer is the entity referred to in the Name field.[27]

EAP: Extensible Authentication Protocol

The Extensible Authentication Protocol was created to allow easy future enhancements to PPP's Authentication layer, and is the newest of PPP's authentication protocols. In order to aid the introduction of new authentication technologies, the Extensible Authentication Protocol was created. EAP is really a framework for authentication, allowing future authentication algorithms to be added without needing to make continual changes to LCP. In order to achieve this algorithm independence, EAP changed the basic PPP model in which the authentication algorithm is negotiated during the LCP phase.

This has its benefits, in that a single new LCP option negotiation type opens up an expanding range of authentication techniques. However, before EAP, LCP had negotiated the authentication algorithm itself. These changes will take some time to appear in PPP implementations, but the advantages of EAP will likely compel vendors to support it.

Once EAP has been negotiated, it conducts a set of steps very similar to CHAP (for example), but it also supports non-MD-5 hash algorithms, token cards, one-time-passwords, etc. Each uses EAP to complete a negotiation that satisfies the requirements of the authentication algorithm. Even though it supports many different authentication algorithms, the EAP still generally uses a three-way handshake.

Authentication technology is improving continuously, providing new algorithms and techniques all the time. Previous technologies, like PAP and CHAP, were limited in that the authentication algorithm needed to be negotiated during the LCP phase. EAP only has one code value within LCP, and then EAP performs its own self-contained negotiation.

Another advantage of EAP is that it decouples the authentication from the peer. The peer need not even understand the specifics of the authentication protocol at all! A peer can pass through the authentication data to some backend authentication server, and then receive a success/failure code which is used to activate the link or "hang up" on the other peer. This feature enables users in the field to rapidly adopt new authentication technologies as soon as their PPP stacks support it—without needing to coordinate an upgrade to the Remote Access Servers' software.

Any time a "new" authentication algorithm is negotiated by EAP, the RAS can just 'punt' the request to a backend authentication server (by encapsulating the EAP packet, whose algorithm code the RAS did not understand) in a RADIUS[28] packet. The RADIUS server will respond with an embedded EAP packet containing either a success or failure code, which is all the RAS needs to be able to understand. All the EAP-speaking RAS needs to understand is the success or failure code, which is much simpler than having to understand each and every possible authentication algorithm itself.

EAP already supports similar mechanisms to those in the CHAP, but CHAP was never designed to be extensible with different authentication algorithms. The one kind of authentication that EAP explicitly does not support is PAP-style simple cleartext password authentication. EAP does support One-Time Passwords (RFC-1760) and has provisions for token card-based authentication. (Interestingly, it was always possible to do token card authentication in the context of PAP, simply using PAP as a way to transmit the one-time passwords between the peers.)

NETWORK LAYER CONTROL PROTOCOL(S)

Once the Authentication phase is complete, then the appropriate higher-layer protocols can be initialized. In the PPP model, each higher-layer protocol that is configured to use the PPP link performs its own protocol-specific configuration negotiations. As was noted in Table 10.3, the list of extant PPP Network Control Protocols (NCPs) is quite comprehensive. Essentially every Network layer protocol is supported by PPP. However, the Internet Protocol Control Protocol (IPCP, RFC-1332), is germane to this book, and will serve as a prototypical example of the kinds of negotiations that may occur within an NCP.

IP Control Protocol (IPCP) Functions

IPCP allows IP entities to configure link-specific IP parameters over a PPP link. At the time of this writing, the following text was available at the Internet Assigned Numbers Authority web site, at the following URL:

```
<http://www.isi.edu/in-notes/iana/assignments/ppp-numbers>[29]

PPP IPCP CONFIGURATION OPTION TYPES

The Point-to-Point Protocol (PPP) Internet Protocol Control Protocol
(IPCP) specifies a number of Configuration Options which are distin-
guished by an 8 bit Type field. These Types are assigned as follows:

Type        Configuration Option
---         --------------------
   1        IP-Addresses (deprecated)          [RFC1332]
   2        IP-Compression-Protocol            [RFC1332]
   3        IP-Address                         [RFC1332]
   4        Mobile-IPv4                        [RFC2290]

 129        Primary DNS Server Address         [RFC1877]
 130        Primary NBNS Server Address        [RFC1877]
```

```
131          Secondary DNS Server Address        [RFC1877]
132          Secondary NBNS Server Address       [RFC1877]
```

Configuration options 130 and 132 apply primarily to PC-based networks that use NetBIOS over TCP/IP protocol stack. There is a NetBIOS Name Service (NBNS) that allows PCs to dynamically register themselves and also to look up the names of other PCs. These two IPCP options allow the PC to obtain the address of the primary and secondary NBNS servers so that it may register itself or perform lookups. These options definitely apply to a client PC, as opposed to a router or other device that has no knowledge of the NBNS protocol.

Even the DNS-specific options, namely 129 and 131, are clearly applicable in the case of a client machine, not a router or other such intermediate device. If the client machine can find out the DNS servers' address(es) via IPCP, then it need not be statically configured with this information. Option 4 is specific to Mobile-IP (RFCs 2002, 2003, 2004, 2005, 2006, 2290, and 2234), which is beyond the scope of this book. There are at least two good books on Mobile IP, which can be found in the references. Finally, then there is the IP-Compression-Protocol option and the IP-Address option.

The IP-Compression-Protocol option allows the compression of IP headers and/or data to be negotiated. If this option is not negotiated, the default behavior (i.e., no compression) is in effect. For example, one compression protocol is RFC-1144 Van Jacobson TCP/IP header compression. IP-specific compression protocols can be negotiated, or compression over the entire link can be negotiated, using PPP's Compression Control Protocol (CCP, RFC-1962). Finally, the one thing that IP absolutely needs for it to operate is addressing. The IP-Address option is the one that is likely to be used on virtually every connection.[30]

From RFC-1332, the packet format of the IPCP Configure-Request packet is quite simple. It always consists of a Type, a Length, and the data associated with that Type. In the case of negotiating an IP address, the Configure-Request appears as illustrated in Figure 10.9. The Type is three, and by inspection, the Length of this configuration option is clearly six bytes.

The negotiation of the IP-Address option is very simple. One peer sends a proposal to the other, containing the IP address it would like to use. The address will ei-

Type = 0x03	Length = 0x06	IP-Address...
...IP-Address		

FIGURE 10.9 IPCP Configure-Request format.

ther be positively or negatively acknowledged. If the address is negatively acknowl-edged, the NAK response may include the proper address that the peer should use.

A very important application of the IPCP IP-Address configuration option is when a mobile client machine (e.g., a laptop) is connecting to an ISP. Actually, the client need not be mobile; virtually every time a PPP connection is established to an ISP, the calling machine's IP address is dynamically assigned. This applies equally well to your home PC, or your laptop on the road. If one peer, for instance the calling peer, wishes the other peer to tell it what IP address to use, it sends the Configure-Request with the IP Address field set to 0.0.0.0. The NAK response will include the requested IP address.

Even when a peer does not require dynamic IP address assignment, it will still negotiate the IP address that it wishes to use, so that the two peers can make sure that they are not accidentally using the same IP address. The negotiation allows con-figuration errors to be detected. There is one other case besides dynamic and static addressing. It is possible that the peers do not wish to use any IP addresses on this link, a technique known as an "unnumbered operation."

An "Unnumbered" operation is not strictly a PPP or IPCP feature,[31] but a routing feature. However, it makes sense to talk about unnumbered links in the con-text of PPP, since few subnetwork media can operate without IP addresses. If each end of a link is not configured with actual IP addresses, but with the "unnumbered" code word, then the IP stack won't need IPCP to negotiate any IP Address. So, ne-gotiating the IP Address is simply not performed.

Before VLSM was widely deployed the subnet mask within a network number had to be the same everywhere (a requirement of classful routing protocols). Imagine that a Class B had been subnetted on a /26 boundary. This meant that every active subnet within that Class B had to be a /26. A /26 can hold up to $2^{(32-26)} - 2 = 2^6 - 2$ = 62 addresses. If the network manager wished to assign addresses to the PPP inter-faces (for instance, to allow the interfaces' IP addresses to be "pinged"), then a /26 subnet would have to be used since that is the only available size. Each individual se-rial line would need to be assigned its own /26 subnet address.

Unfortunately (for the network manager), a PPP link only requires two IP ad-dresses—one for each peer. A /30 is the smallest subnet that can be used for a point-to-point link, since a /30 has exactly two unicast IP addresses (plus the subnet-specific broadcast address and the subnet's base address).[32] Despite the well-known fact that a /30 is the best-sized subnet for point-to-point links (since it is the smallest subnet that will do the job), classful technology would not allow one /26 to be carved into 16 /30s. Unnumbered link addressing was created so that network man-agers would have an alternative to wasting valuable IP address blocks on the point-

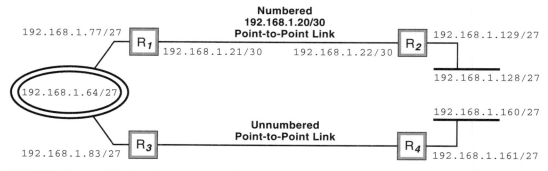

FIGURE 10.10   Numbered versus unnumbered links.

to-point links. Figure 10.10 shows the difference between numbered and unnumbered configurations.

Why would a link's peers need addresses anyway? To discover whether a router is up, it is not necessary to be able to ping all of its interfaces—any one of them will do. But wouldn't it be useful to be able to infer the status of a circuit by pinging that interface's IP address? Not necessarily. One way to implicitly ping the unnumbered interface is to try to ping an address on the far side of the router. Also, if a problem is suspected with a circuit, then the network manager can certainly log in to the router on the near side of that circuit and examine the line status.

For example, if a network manager was using a machine on the 192.168.1.64/27 subnet (the FDDI ring on the left of Figure 10.10), she could ping either 192.168.1.21 or 192.168.1.22 in order to determine the status of the circuit between R_1 and R_2. If she wants to determine the status of the link between R_3 and R_4, she may simply ping the far address of R_4 (192.168.1.161). A ping response confirms that the link is up, but a nonresponse means that either R_3, the circuit, or R_4 could be down.

Backing up a step and pinging R_3's FDDI interface (192.168.1.83) will allow her to determine if the problem is with R_3 or not. If R_3 responds, then the problem is probably with the line or R_4. If R_3 is still up, then logging in to the router will allow examination of link-level statistics, and event logs will enable her to tell what time the circuit went down (if that is, indeed, the problem). The point here is that she was able to discover the link's status without being able to directly ping that interface.

So there are at least two alternatives to directly pinging an interface's IP address. Ultimately, utilizing unnumbered links like other aspects of network design, is a matter of personal preference. Sure, you might not need to have numbered interfaces, but there's nothing wrong with using them if you can afford to spend the address space on them, and if you prefer to use them.

How does a PPP device negotiate unnumbered addressing? First, realize that this is really only applicable to a router implementation of PPP. We saw that attempting to configure yourself with an IP adddress of 0.0.0.0 tells the other peer that you want an address to be assigned to you. If unnumbered links are being used, the routers will simply not bother to negotiate the IP-Address option of IPCP. It is important that they both be configured similarly, so that neither of them tries to negotiate the IP-Address option, thereby ensuring the use of unnumbered addressing for this circuit.

Issues with Unnumbered Links

What about when the router needs to send a packet of its own? What address does it put in the IP SA field?? When using unnumbered links certain bizarre effects can happen when a router transmits a packet—for instance, a ping packet, or telnet, SNMP, etc., any protocol that originates from within the router. The IP header requires that the packet's Source Address field be filled in; otherwise the destination device would not know who the packet came from and would therefore not be able to form a reply. That's all well and good, but if a packet is leaving via an unnumbered link, what address can the router use as the packet's source address?

First, let's briefly examine what goes on in a router's "head" when it has no unnumbered interfaces. A router that needs to send out a packet of its own is exactly like a multihomed host, except that the host was limited to a single default gateway while the router knows about many networked destinations, via many other routers, possibly more than one other router per interface (see Figure 10.11). It can tell that to reach prefix P, or V, the best way to go is via a neighbor router that is reachable via interface 1. For all destinations, it can decide which of its interfaces appears to be in the direction of the destination (within the granularity of its routing protocol information).

So, to send a packet to prefix E, if it needs to use interface 4, it will create the packet with interface 4's IP address as the packet's source IP address. Sending the same packet to a different destination will likely cause the router to choose a different source IP address, one approriate for *that* destination. The source address, for any packet sourced from within the router, is chosen by first finding the best egress interface for the desired destination, then inserting the egress interface's address into the packet's IP Source Address header field. This choice causes the return traffic from

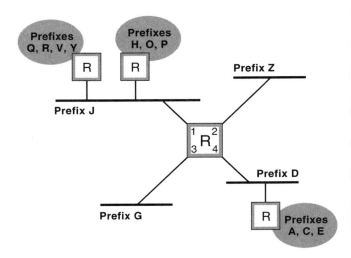

FIGURE 10.11   IP SA set to egress interface's address.

that destination to arrive at the same address (i.e., interface) from which the original packet departed.

Now, if the router has some unnumbered interface(s), it will still look at the destination and look for the best egress interface based on its forwarding table. If the best egress interface is unnumbered, however, there is no interface address! The router still needs to send the packet, however. There is a simple technique that is used in these cases, which is to have the router "steal" an address from another *active* interface. The destination device will reply to that address, and the return packet will still arrive at the router, but addressed to a different interface. This sounds like a perfect solution, but what about when a new site is being activated?

The corporate addressing plan might dictate unnumbered addresses on the PPP links. In this case, it is possible that there will be connectivity problems, caused by the initial usage of unnumbered links. When bringing up a new site, the router may not be reachable, even when the link is up. Generally, the WAN circuit is the main focus of attention when a new router is installed. As soon as the PPP link is established between the central-site router and the new remote site router, the first thing that the remote installer will often try to do is to ping the central-site router or some other IP address at the central site.

For simplicity of configuration, the remote-site router will often have a simple static default route that points at the serial interface. The next hop gateway can't be

TABLE 10.4 Unnumbered next-hop in router's forwarding table

Known Prefixes	Next-Hop Gateway	Metric	Status
0.0.0.0/0	int. 2	1 (static)	Up
192.168.17.96/27	192.168.17.97	0 (connected)	Up

an IP address, because the link is unnumbered, so the "gateway" just tells the router to send packets across the PPP link if it doesn't have a specific forwarding table entry for some destination. Such a configuration is well-suited to a remote site, since traffic at the site is either local to the site or destined for the corporate side; this fake gateway address simply means "over that-a-way." This kind of forwarding table entry is illustrated in Table 10.4.

The remote-site router probably only has two interfaces, the unnumbered one and the LAN interface (usually Ethernet or Token Ring). If the user at the remote site tries to ping any address at all before having connected the new router to the remote LAN, the ping will fail. A lot of time may then be wasted trying to troubleshoot problems with the PPP link (which is actually up and working just fine). Until the LAN interface is up the router will not be able to be the source or sink of any IP traffic.

FRAME FORMAT AND IP ENCAPSULATION

PPP may be carried over a number of framing protocols, including High-level Data Link Control (PPP over HDLC, RFC-1662), Frame Relay (RFC-1973), ISDN (RFC-1618), X.25 (RFC-1598), and SONET/SDH (RFC-1619), as of this writing. PPP can even be tunneled inside IP, e.g., the Point-to-Point Tunneling Protocol (PPTP) and the Layer 2 Tunneling Protocol (L2TP). PPP can run over synchronous framing (all the PPP-over-x protocols listed so far have been synchronous), or asynchronous protocols.[33]

PPP uses HDLC encapsulation by default, which is illustrated in Figure 10.12. In this case, PPP is the higher-layer protocol which is carried in HDLC's Information field.

HDLC uses the Flag character (0x7E) to separate frames, and the [HDLC] Address field is used to identify other reachable HDLC entities on this medium. The [HDLC] Control field is used to indicate what kind of frame this is, whether data or

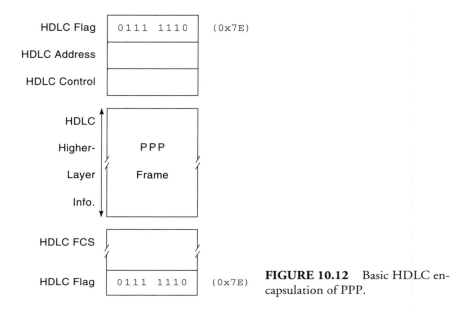

HDLC Flag	0111 1110	(0x7E)
HDLC Address		
HDLC Control		

HDLC

Higher-   PPP

Layer   Frame

Info.

HDLC FCS

| HDLC Flag | 0111 1110 | (0x7E) |

FIGURE 10.12 Basic HDLC encapsulation of PPP.

various HDLC control frame types. After the HDLC Information field (i.e., the PPP frame), there is a Frame Check Sequence, and then the HDLC frame concludes with another Flag character. The same Flag that ends one frame may begin another—if another is ready to be sent when the current frame ends.[34] A series of continuous Flag characters may be transmitted until there is another PPP frame to send.

The PPP header consists entirely of the two-byte "PPP Protocol" field. Figure 10.13 illustrates the PPP encapsulation of IP, also showing the HDLC field values appropriate to PPP. When used for PPP, certain conventions are observed in the HDLC headers. The Flag character is still used to delimit frames, but PPP always uses an HDLC Address of 0xFF, effectively the HDLC broadcast address. Since, in the case of PPP, there is only one other station, the all-1s pattern is an appropriate way to refer to "the other peer." The HDLC Control field is set to 0x03, which means Unnumbered Information.

ARP is Unneeded

As long as a PPP link is "up" state, sending to the other side requires no data-link layer address; packets are simply sent to the other side. The "other side" always has the same HDLC-layer address, namely 0xFF.

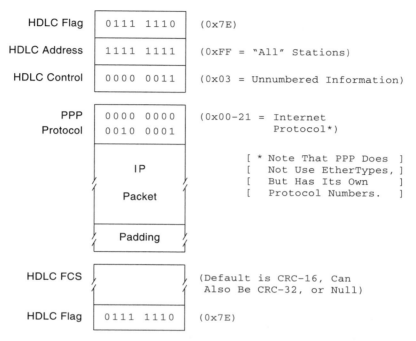

FIGURE 10.13 IP in PPP.

If a PPP implementation receives a packet, it can assume that it came from the other end of the link, unless a loopback condition has been detected. PPP's Echo packets can include a Magic-Number that may optionally be negotiated during the LCP phase. The Magic-Number negotiation results in each side claiming a unique 32-bit identifier[35] that is used for several purposes, one of which is the Echo packet.

If a station receives an Echo-Request that includes its own Magic-Number, then the station can observe that—somewhere along the line—its packets are being reflected back to it. The station should immediately declare the link to be in a "looped back" state and begin a new LCP negotiation once the loopback condition has been cleared. As long as the circuit is looped back, the PPP implementation should know that it cannot be used for data traffic, so it is effectively down. While the circuit is looped back, the PPP station can continue probing the circuit with Echo-Requests until they stop bouncing back at it, at which point a new LCP negotiation can be initiated with the remote peer.

In the case of loopbacks it is not always the case that both sides will see the loop. The other side, if it is sending Echoes, will see the other side stop responding at some point. It can then declare the circuit to be down, and begin sending LCP Configure-Requests. If the other peer detects a loop, it may behave as described above.

REFERENCES

REQUEST FOR COMMENT (RFC)

PPP Base Specification

1661 The Point-to-Point Protocol (PPP). W. Simpson, Editor. July 1994. (Format: TXT=103026 bytes) (Obsoletes RFC1548) (Updated by RFC2153) (Also STD0051) (Status: STANDARD)

PPP Network Control Protocols

1332 The PPP Internet Protocol Control Protocol (IPCP). G. McGregor. May 1992. (Format: TXT=17613 bytes) (Obsoletes 1172) (Status: PROPOSED STANDARD)

1377 The PPP OSI Network Layer Control Protocol (OSINLCP). D. Katz. November 1992. (Format: TXT=22109 bytes) (Status: PROPOSED STANDARD)

1378 The PPP AppleTalk Control Protocol (ATCP). B. Parker. November 1992. (Format: TXT=28496 bytes) (Status: PROPOSED STANDARD)

1552 The PPP Internetworking Packet Exchange Control Protocol (IPXCP). W. Simpson. December 1993. (Format: TXT=29173 bytes) (Status: PROPOSED STANDARD)

1638 PPP Bridging Control Protocol (BCP). F. Baker & R. Bowen. June 1994. (Format: TXT=58477 bytes) (Obsoletes RFC1220) (Status: PROPOSED STANDARD)

1762 The PPP DECnet Phase IV Control Protocol (DNCP). S. Senum. March 1995. (Format: TXT=12709 bytes) (Obsoletes RFC1376) (Status: DRAFT STANDARD)

1763 The PPP Banyan Vines Control Protocol (BVCP). S. Senum. March 1995. (Format: TXT=17817 bytes) (Status: PROPOSED STANDARD)

1764 The PPP XNS IDP Control Protocol (XNSCP). S. Senum. March 1995. (Format: TXT=9525 bytes) (Status: PROPOSED STANDARD)

1841 PPP Network Control Protocol for LAN Extension. J. Chapman, D. Coli, A. Harvey, B. Jensen & K. Rowett. September 1995. (Format: TXT=146206 bytes) (Status: INFORMATIONAL)

1963 PPP Serial Data Transport Protocol (SDTP). K. Schneider & S. Venters. August 1996. (Format: TXT=38185 bytes) (Status: INFORMATIONAL)

2023 IP Version 6 over PPP. D. Haskin, E. Allen. October 1996. (Format: TXT=20275 bytes) (Status: PROPOSED STANDARD)

2043 The PPP SNA Control Protocol (SNACP). A. Fuqua. October 1996. (Format: TXT=13719 bytes) (Status: PROPOSED STANDARD)

2097 The PPP NetBIOS Frames Control Protocol (NBFCP). G. Pall. January 1997. (Format: TXT=27104 bytes) (Status: PROPOSED STANDARD)

IPCP Extensions

1877 PPP Internet Protocol Control Protocol Extensions for Name Server Addresses. S. Cobb. December 1995. (Format: TXT=10591 bytes) (Status: INFORMATIONAL)

2290 Mobile-IPv4 Configuration Option for PPP IPCP. J. Solomon, S. Glass. February 1998. (Format: TXT=39421 bytes) (Updates RFC2002) (Status: PROPOSED STANDARD)

Authentication and other PPP-related Specifications

1334 PPP Authentication Protocols. B. Lloyd, W. Simpson. October 1992. (Format: TXT=33248 bytes) (Obsoleted by RFC1994) (Status: PROPOSED STANDARD)

1663 PPP Reliable Transmission. D. Rand. July 1994. (Format: TXT=17281 bytes) (Status: PROPOSED STANDARD)

1962 The PPP Compression Control Protocol (CCP). D. Rand. June 1996. (Format: TXT=18005 bytes) (Updated by RFC2153) (Status: PROPOSED STANDARD)

1968 The PPP Encryption Control Protocol (ECP). G. Meyer. June 1996. (Format: TXT=20781 bytes) (Status: PROPOSED STANDARD)

1989 PPP Link Quality Monitoring. W. Simpson. August 1996. (Format: TXT=29289 bytes) (Obsoletes RFC1333) (Status: DRAFT STANDARD)

1990 The PPP Multilink Protocol (MP). K. Sklower, B. Lloyd, G. McGregor, D. Carr & T. Coradetti. August 1996. (Format: TXT=53271 bytes) (Obsoletes RFC1717) (Status: DRAFT STANDARD)

1994 PPP Challenge Handshake Authentication Protocol (CHAP). W. Simpson. August 1996. (Format: TXT=24094 bytes) (Obsoletes RFC1334) (Status: DRAFT STANDARD)

2125 The PPP Bandwidth Allocation Protocol (BAP) / The PPP Bandwidth Allocation Control Protocol (BACP). C. Richards, K. Smith. March 1997. (Format: TXT=49213 bytes) (Status: PROPOSED STANDARD)

2153 PPP Vendor Extensions. W. Simpson. May 1997. (Format: TXT=10780 bytes) (Updates RFC1661, RFC1962) (Status: INFORMATIONAL)

2284 PPP Extensible Authentication Protocol (EAP). L. Blunk, J. Vollbrecht. March 1998. (Format: TXT=29452 bytes) (Status: PROPOSED STANDARD)

PPP over . . .

1598 PPP in X.25. W. Simpson. March 1994. (Format: TXT=13835 bytes) (Status: PRO-POSED STANDARD)

1618 PPP over ISDN. W. Simpson. May 1994. (Format: TXT=14896 bytes) (Status: PRO-POSED STANDARD)

1619 PPP over SONET/SDH. W. Simpson. May 1994. (Format: TXT=8893 bytes) (Status: PROPOSED STANDARD)

1662 PPP in HDLC-like Framing. W. Simpson, Editor. July 1994. (Format: TXT=48058 bytes) (Obsoletes RFC1549) (Also STD0051) (Status: STANDARD)

1973 PPP in Frame Relay. W. Simpson. June 1996. (Format: TXT=14780 bytes) (Status: PROPOSED STANDARD)

Mobile-IP Specifications

2002 IP Mobility Support. C. Perkins. October 1996. (Format: TXT=193103 bytes) (Updated by RFC2290) (Status: PROPOSED STANDARD)

2003 IP Encapsulation within IP. C. Perkins. October 1996. (Format: TXT=30291 bytes) (Status: PROPOSED STANDARD)

2004 Minimal Encapsulation within IP. C. Perkins. October 1996. (Format: TXT=12202 bytes) (Status: PROPOSED STANDARD)

2005 Applicability Statement for IP Mobility Support. J. Solomon. October 1996. (Format: TXT=10509 bytes) (Status: PROPOSED STANDARD)

2006 The Definitions of Managed Objects for IP Mobility Support using SMIv2. D. Cong, M. Hamlen, C. Perkins. October 1996. (Format: TXT=95030 bytes) (Status: PRO-POSED STANDARD)

2290 Mobile-IPv4 Configuration Option for PPP IPCP. J. Solomon, S. Glass. February 1998. (Format: TXT=39421 bytes) (Updates RFC2002) (Status: PROPOSED STAN-DARD)

2344 Reverse Tunneling for Mobile IP. G. Montenegro. May 1998. (Format: TXT=39468 bytes) (Status: PROPOSED STANDARD)

RADIUS Specifications

2138 Remote Authentication Dial In User Service (RADIUS). C. Rigney, A. Rubens, W. Simpson, S. Willens. April 1997. (Format: TXT=120407 bytes) (Obsoletes RFC2058) (Status: PROPOSED STANDARD)

2139 RADIUS Accounting. C. Rigney. April 1997. (Format: TXT=44919 bytes) (Obsoletes RFC2059) (Status: INFORMATIONAL)

Books on PPP and Mobile IP

Carlson, James, *PPP Design and Debugging*. Addison Wesley, Reading, MA: 1998.

Solomon, James D., *Mobile IP, the Internet Unplugged*. Prentice Hall, Upper Saddle River, NJ: 1998.

Perkins, Charles with Bobby Woolf, *Mobile IP: Design Principles and Practices*. Addison Wesley, Reading, MA: 1997.

ENDNOTES

1. Not shared in the sense of Ethernet, which shares a medium among many stations, but shared in the sense of multiple protocols being multiplexed over the same link.

2. Newer technologies such as Asymmetric Digital Subscriber Line (ADSL) also support PPP even though the bits are flowing at different speeds in either direction. ADSL is not a dial-up technology—unless there is trouble, it is always up.

3. Some people interpret the F in BFR to mean Fast. That's only one possible interpretation.

4. A one terabit per second (1 Tbps) circuit would be just over 100 times faster than a 10 Gbps circuit!

5. Today's V.90 modems support this speed (albeit in only one direction) over regular phone lines. So today a home user can effectively use nearly the same bandwidth that formerly was used to interconnect entire sites.

6. For example, a fractional T1 operates in units of 64 kbps, so someone may buy part of a T1 line. T3 lines can be broken up along T1 boundaries, or T2 boundaries (one T2 holds four T1s, plus some Physical-layer framing overhead).

7. With the emergence of Voice over IP, how long will it be before we start referring to the "legacy" telephone network?

8. "Loop" is the telephone company term for the pair of wires between their central office and a user device, such as a telephone. The term may also be heard as "local loop."

9. There is also an older digital dial-up technology, known as "Switched 56," which can establish 56 kbps full-duplex synchronous circuits.

10. Some dial-up services may be priced at a flat rate, which does not provide an incentive to conserve connect time by hanging up when the time is idle.

11. Link Quality Monitoring, if implemented, is also at this layer.

12. The OSI Network Layer protocol in this case is the Connection-Less Network Layer Protocol (CLNP). There is also an OSI Connection-Oriented Network Service

(CONS), which operates over a reliable data link layer, and thus cannot operate over PPP.

13. CLNP, as we have already seen, is the Connection-Less Network Protocol. ES-IS is the OSI equivalent of ARP, which stands for the End-System to Intermediate-System protocol. IS-IS, the Intermediate-System to Intermediate-System routing protocol, supports routing for CLNP as well as IP. Finally, IDRP is CLNP's Inter-Domain Routing Protocol.

14. In some cases, a constant stream of "flag" characters, which normally delimit frames, will be continuously transmitted over a link in the absence of any real data to send.

15. Serial interface standards suit a variety of speeds and electrical operating conditions. Some examples are V.35/V.36, RS232, RS449, RS530, High-Speed Serial Interface (HSSI), etc.

16. T3 circuits attach to the CSU with either two coaxial cables or a pair of optical fibers. All faster circuits use fiber, and may plug straight into the router with no intervening CSU/DSU (this scenario requires that the router interface provide adequate alarm indications, provisioning and monitoring signals, and other functions that are normally in the realm of the CSU/DSU).

17. Other toll-free prefixes are 1-888 and 1-877. It is also possible that the user may make a local or long-distance call to reach the corporate Remote Access Server (RAS).

18. PAP is obsolete in that it will not be further standardized. Its use is not recommended due to its poor security, which depends on sending username and password information "in the clear." Many PPP implementations still support PAP, however.

19. Besides "vanilla" CHAP, described in the RFC, a variant was created by Microsoft, now known as MS-CHAP. MS-CHAP is very similar, but not identical, to CHAP. Also note that MS-CHAP 2.0 has been introduced to plug some security holes, and it is not backward-compatible with MS-CHAP 1.0.

20. The state of the peer's response depends on whether or not it recognizes the offered username-password combination.

21. Each side may use a different authentication protocol if both PPP implementations—and their configurations—support that situation. In other words, even when one peer uses CHAP, the other peer need not use CHAP—it could use PAP, EAP, or null authentication.

22. RFC-1994 recommends that the shared secret be at least as long as the MD-5 output (i.e., at least 16 bytes).

23. For the record, SHA-1 has a 160-bit (20-byte) output.

24. The Identifier must be changed for each new Challenge.

25. The Value may be any length, up to 255 bytes.

26. Thereby preventing eavesdroppers from obtaining unauthorized access by replaying a Response at some later time.

27. Of course, it is always possible that the shared secret has been compromised, in which case anyone could masquerade as the peer with that name. Hopefully, CHAP is just the first line of defense against intruders, not the only one.

28. Remote Authentication Dial-In User Service (RFC-2138) is a commonplace protocol used between RAS devices and backend servers (RADIUS servers) that have large databases of usernames and their associated authentication information.

29. If the URL ever changes in the future, start at <http://www.iana.org/> and navigate down to the "Protocol Numbers and Assignment Services." From there, it should be straightforward to find the link to "PPP Number Assignments."

30. If dynamic IP addressing is being used, it is obvious that the IP-Address option must be negotiated, but that option is also negotiated in the static IP addressing case. It enables the peers to ensure that their IP addresses are different.

31. In fact, there is no defined way for IPCP to negotiate unnumbered operation.

32. The dotted-decimal subnet mask for a /30 is 255.255.255.252.

33. Asynchronous communication protocols send a character at a time, delimiting them with start and stop bits.

34. In other words, there is no requirement that one Flag terminate a frame, and then another Flag be sent to initiate the next frame. A Flag could end a frame, followed immediately by the next frame's Address field (0xFF in the case of PPP over HDLC). If there is no data to send, a continuous sequence of Flags may be transmitted until the next frame needs to be transmitted.

35. This unique 32-bit identifier has nothing at all to do with any of the device's IP addresses.

CHAPTER 11

Frame Relay

EVOLUTION OF WIDE-AREA "CLOUD" TECHNOLOGIES

The public switched telephone network (PSTN) pioneered the time-division multiplexing (TDM) style of networking.[1] In TDM, each call or connection is granted a fixed amount of bandwidth for its duration. This works well for the PSTN's main applications, namely phone calls and so-called "leased lines," since each call or connection has fixed bandwidth requirements. PSTN connections are usually full duplex, in that equal bandwidth is available in each direction so that either party may transmit (i.e., talk) at any time.

When the PSTN is used to provide a "nailed up" circuit between two points, no signaling is required before the devices at either end of the circuit may talk to each other—they simply emit data into the link and it pops out the other side after a transmission delay that is proportional to the distance traveled and the bandwidth of the "pipe." Bandwidth is how many bits that may be transmitted over the circuit per second. In the late 1990s, bandwidths in WAN circuits are usually in the range of tens of thousands of bits per second (kbps) to millions of bits per second (Mbps). In the next 10 years, WAN links at gigabit (billions of bits) per second speeds will appear, at first in WAN backbones, then later in access circuits.

There is a hierarchy of TDM bandwidths rooted at the level known as DS-0 (Digital Signal, level 0), or 64 kbps. 8000 times per second, the analog (voice) signal, is measured on a scale from 0–255, as illustrated in Figure 11.1. This process is also known as "sampling" the analog signal at the rate of 8,000 times per second.

Each measurement can thus be represented as an 8-bit binary number. Eight bits times 8,000 measurements per second is 64,000 bits per second, or 64 kbps. This is the bandwidth of a voice call on the PSTN, provided no digital compression is done. Table 11.1 captures all the levels of the traditional telecommunications bandwidth hierarchy. The North American/ Japanese hierarchy is in the left two columns, with the European hierarchy, in italics, in the right two columns.

The next level above DS-0 is DS-1, which packs 24 DS-0 channels (24 times 8 bits, or 192 bits) plus a bit (literally a single bit, for a total of 193 bits in a DS-1 "frame") of overhead into a 1.544 Mbps data stream. DS-1 circuits are also known as "T-1" circuits. Each of the constituent DS-0s is transmitted 8,000 times per second. The 193 bits that comprise the frame are transmitted 8,000 times per second, yielding an overall line rate of 1.544 Mbps, of which 192 times 8,000 (1.536 Mbps) is available to carry "payload." In Europe, 64 kbps is also the base level, but the E-1 level consists of 31 channels of data and one channel of overhead, for a total of 32 times 64 kbps, or 2.048 Mbps, with 1.984 Mbps available for user data (or voice) payload.

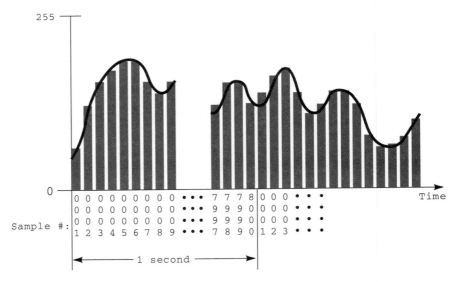

FIGURE 11.1 Digitizing an analog waveform.

TABLE 11.1 SUMMARY OF TRADITIONAL TDM BANDWIDTHS

DS-0	0.064 Mbps		
DS-1	1.544 Mbps		
		2.048 Mbps	*E-1*
DS-2	6.312 Mbps		
		8.448 Mbps	*E-2*
		34.368 Mbps	*E-3*
DS-3	44.736 Mbps		

The next step in the North American Digital Hierarchy is DS-2, which is not sold in the US (it exists only within telephone company central offices)[2] which consists of four DS-1s plus some extra overhead. DS-2 circuits are sold in Japan as "J-2" circuits. The payload capacity of a DS-2 is exactly four times 1.536 Mbps, or 6.144 Mbps. The line rate of a DS-2, including overhead, is 6.312 Mbps.

Beyond DS-2, there is DS-3, at 44.736 Mbps. DS-3 is also known as "T-3." One DS-3 consists of seven DS-2s, plus even more overhead. A DS-3 is typically used in one of two ways, either as a single "fat pipe" between two devices, or as a trunk between telephone switches with a capacity of 672 multiplexed phone calls, or some combination of phone calls, data DS-1s, etc. In Europe, there are also corresponding super-E-1 rates, known as the E-2 (8.448 Mbps) and the E-3 (34.368 Mbps).

Beyond DS-3, there are several proprietary standards such as DS-4NA, as well as the standardized levels of the Synchronous Optical Network (SONET), known in international circles as the Synchronous Digital Hierarchy (SDH). SONET levels, most commonly called "OC-n" (for Optical Carrier, level n), are all multiples of 51.84 Mbps (51,840,000 bits per second). SDH levels are known as "STM-n" (for Synchronous Transport Module, level n), and are multiples of 155.52 Mbps, which corresponds to SONET's OC-3. Table 11.2 summarizes the common bandwidth levels of the SONET/SDH standards.

The SONET base rate was chosen because it could accommodate a DS-3 with not too much room left over (a single DS-3 occupies about 90 percent of the available payload of an OC-1). Because the E-3 is "smaller" than a DS-3, it would only occupy about 70 percent of an OC-1's payload capacity, which is a considerable waste of valuable WAN bandwidth. The SDH STM-1 level was picked to improve packing efficiency for both the DS-3 and E-3 signals. The STM-1 (i.e., OC-3) rate of 155.52

TABLE 11.2 Summary of SONET/SDH bandwidths

OC-1		51.84 Mbps	
OC-3	STM-1	155.52 Mbps	
OC-12	STM-4	622.08 Mbps	
OC-48	STM-16	2,488.32 Mbps	(2.48832 Gbps)
OC-192	STM-64	9,953.28 Mbps	(9.95328 Gbps)

Mbps (exactly triple the OC-1 rate of 51.84 Mbps) fits either three DS-3s (at just under 90 percent efficiency), or four E-3s (at just over 90 percent efficiency).

In the 1950s, researchers began to investigate packet switching, a new style of connectivity that was more suited to computers. Computer communications tend to be brief bursts of data exchange followed by relatively long periods of silence, as opposed to interpersonal communications which last many orders of magnitude longer than a computer "conversation." The earliest packet-switched networks were connection-oriented, in imitation of PSTN calls, but later networks emerged that were "connectionless." The ARPAnet was an experiment in connectionless WAN networking that evolved into the Internet we know today.

There are two ways to use a connection-oriented packet-switched network: 1) Switched "Virtual Circuits" or SVCs, and 2) Permanent Virtual Circuits or PVCs.

SVCs are similar to a phone call, in that some signaling messages are exchanged between the calling party, in this case a computer, and the called party, via the packet-switched network which is also an active participant in call setup. The network establishes a data path and completes the connection. In some cases, it also assigns a short "handle" to the newly-established virtual circuit (VC) that is used by the caller when sending data on this virtual circuit. Other VCs will have different handles to keep them separate. It is up to the calling device to keep track of where these virtual circuits go. Figure 11.2 illustrates the common attributes of various WAN technologies.

PVCs are similar to the "nailed up" leased line connections in the TDM world. A PVC receives a short handle of some kind statically assigned for the length of the service contract. At any time, a user device may send data using this handle. X.25, an early packet-switching technology, uses the term "logical channel number" (LCN) for the handle identifying a VC; ATM calls them Virtual Port Identifier/Virtual

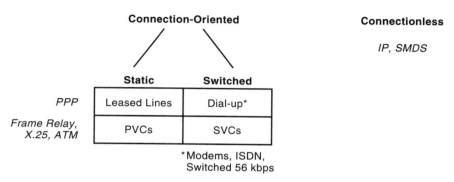

FIGURE 11.2 Comparing key aspects of WAN connections.

Channel Identifiers (VPI/VCIs), and Frame Relay calls them Data Link Connection Identifiers (DLCIs). Generically, they are sometimes known as Virtual Circuit Identifiers, or VCIDs.

The big difference between nailed-up TDM circuits and virtual circuits, as shown in Figure 11.3, is that each site on a TDM-based network needs a physically separate line to each of its neighbor sites. In the virtual circuit world, each site has just one physical access link to the cloud, with the virtual circuits to and from that site *all sharing that single "access link."*

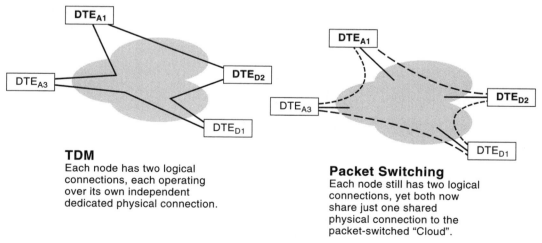

FIGURE 11.3 Logical equivalence of PVCs and leased lines.

Connectionless versus Connection-Oriented

Since connectionless networks have no call setup phase, they just place the destination's entire address in the packet header, letting the packet switches in the network figure out how to deliver it to that destination. The packet switches[3] use routing protocols to learn their location in the topology, allowing them to determine the proper outgoing interface to all reachable destinations.

Note that in connection-oriented networks, packet switches still must have a detailed understanding of their topology, otherwise they would not be able to route the call to the correct destination during the call setup phase! The main advantage of the short handle in connection-oriented schemes is that it somewhat simplifies the forwarding process in the intermediate packet switches. The tradeoff here is that a longer call setup pays for more efficient fowarding for the duration of the call.

Despite the more complex forwarding logic required by connectionless techniques (in the case of the Internet Protocol, a more complex routing table lookup is required for each packet, since the router needs to find the "best" matching destination IP prefix, while lookups in a virtual circuit table are based on the simpler "exact" match), it is possible to accelerate the process greatly by employing special purpose hardware. Thus, extremely fast connectionless forwarding performance is possible, even though more steps are indeed required to process each packet. In the early days of packet switching development, the connection-oriented versus connectionless debates were quite fierce, but at the link speeds of the day (slow compared to the I/O bandwidth of the day's microprocessors) both achieved comparable performance.

A key advantage of connectionless technologies is that they are more resilient to link outages. In a connection-oriented network, once a virtual circuit is built, it is not necessarily maintained. If a packet needs to go out a port, but that port is dead, then the packet goes into a "black hole" and the virtual circuit is dead until the link is fixed.

In a connectionless protocol, each packet switch makes an independent forwarding decision for each packet, so if an interface goes down, it may still have a path to a destination, albeit a less optimal path. However, some path is better than no path![4] This resilience feature of connectionless networks is what made the U.S. military interested in connectionless networking; it had the potential to be more useful in wartime conditions when the infrastructure would be under attack.

Connectionless technologies do not set up a "call" in advance. In connection-oriented technologies, the purpose of the call setup was to specify parameters of the communication, at a minimum identifying the endpoints and allowing the switches to determine the "best" path between them, but also perhaps requesting a certain bandwidth or other call handling options. The output of this negotiation with the network (and with the other party!) was the short "handle," discussed above, which was used as a locally significant "address" referring to the other party.

While other packet-switched WAN "cloud" technologies predated Frame Relay (some are its contemporaries), none are as popular today as Frame Relay.

Scalability Issues for TDM WANs

Until the early 1990s, most data networks were built using TDM technology. Despite the availability of X.25, that technology was not widely used in the U.S., but it was very popular in Europe and elsewhere in the world. One of the problems with using TDM-based leased lines between multiprotocol routers, for example, is that the bandwidth is always there, no matter how much data needs to be transmitted. During peak working hours, the utilization of the network is likely to be fairly high, but during the evening and on weekends the network is probably utilized far less. There may be late night backups, or weekend or month-end traffic that would consume bandwidth during nonbusiness hours, but in general, the bandwidth is unused. This is unfortunate in at least two ways: 1) The phone company cannot sell its underused capacity to anyone else, and 2) The customer must pay the same rate whether or not they are actually using the circuit.

An important practical issue in building large WANs based on leased lines is that connectivity is an n^2 problem, in that the number of circuits required increases proportionately to the number of sites *squared*. Figure 11.4 is a construction that will convince you that the number of circuits required to interconnect n sites is *n(n-1)/2*.

While a rigorous mathematical proof is beyond the scope of this book, we can get an intuitive feel for why the formula must be true. Imagine how many links must leave each of the n sites: There are $n - 1$ other sites, so the answer is that *n-1* links must leave each site in order to directly reach every other site. So, the total number of links should be *n(n − 1)*, right? No, because that formula counts each link twice (once from each end). To eliminate this double-counting, we must divide by two, so the formula is *n(n − 1)/2*. Since *n(n − 1)* is always an even number, the formula will never yield a fractional answer.

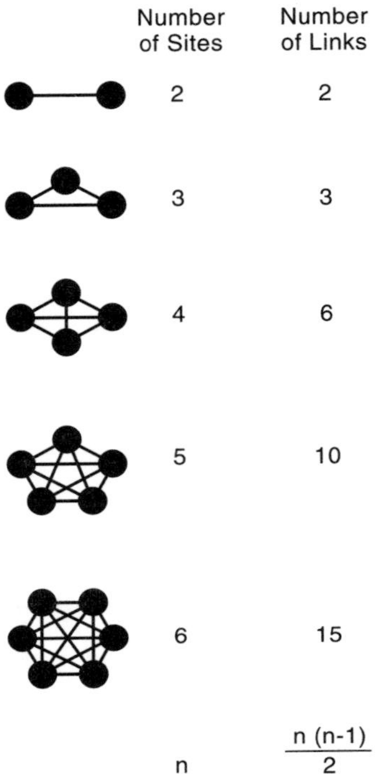

Number of Sites	Number of Links
2	2
3	3
4	6
5	10
6	15
n	$\dfrac{n(n-1)}{2}$

FIGURE 11.4   Number of links to interconnect *n* sites (full mesh).

What is the impact of this formula? In Figure 11.4, there was no room to draw large numbers of sites. Imagine a corporation with 47 sites. If the corporation wished to have full-mesh connectivity, meaning that each site would be directly connected to every other site, it would have to pay for 47(46)/2 = 1081 links. At an average cost of $500 per month for a DS-1 circuit over a reasonable distance, this is $540,500 per month in recurring service costs! Clearly, for even moderate numbers of sites, full-mesh connectivity is prohibitively expensive.

For this reason, network builders turn to "partially-meshed" or "nonmeshed" topologies to reduce the monthly service charge. It is not necessary to have each site be directly connected to every other site in most cases. Typically, there is a data center or other core site to which the remote sites must reach. If each remote site only had one connection to the central site, there would be a star topology, as depicted in Figure 11.5. A pure star topology requires *n* links, which is the cheapest way to reach *n* remote sites, but offers no alternate-path routing; also, each link is a single point of failure.

FIGURE 11.5 Star topology.

In order to improve the robustness of a star topology against single-link failures, one must add just enough extra links such that each site has at least two links toward the central site. Then if the primary link fails, traffic may still reach the central site by using another site as an intermediate "transit" site.

In some cases it is not a requirement that the network operate as well with a link missing as it does with all links functional. Some organizations may be happy with degraded service that allows network managers at the central site to log in to remote hardware to help diagnose the problem. Such an organization may use a mix of higher-speed links (as primaries) and lower-speed links (as backups). If the network is supporting sufficiently mission-critical applications that can not tolerate a reduc-

Applications drive Topologies

While the natural tendency for corporate networks is to have a small number of main sites, and perhaps one or two hot backups, not all WAN applications have the characteristics of a well-defined central site. A good example of a case that needs richer connectivity might be an ISP, which needs to make sure that there are no obvious single points of failure, and that each point-of-presence (POP) has enough exit links—not all their customers at a given POP are likely to want to go in the same direction all the time! Rich connectivity allows the traffic to take routes that are best suited to the users' current set of destinations. Even this scenario, though, does not warrant full-mesh connectivity; careful observation of traffic patterns can allow the ISP to tailor their backbone such that it has adequate capacity and resiliency without needing to purchase all possible interconnections.

tion in bandwidth, that network will require higher recurring costs because of the extra circuits that will be needed; in no case is a full mesh required, however. There is a clear tradeoff between recurring cost and the level of redundancy in the topology. Logically, any topology, even a star topology, provides full-mesh connectivity between any two sites (provided all the links are up), since any site needing to reach another site may do so through some set of other "transit" sites.

When corporate networks become widely geographically distributed, there are often natural opportunities to take advantage of hierarchical topologies. In such cases, a WAN may be subdivided into regions, which are interconnected with an interregional backbone. In each region, a partial mesh may be used, but the backbone may be more densely meshed, even fully meshed if there are not too many regions.

For very large numbers of sites, a two-level hierarchy can greatly reduce the expenses, since line charges tend to be proportional to distance. Within a geographic region, intersite distances are bounded by the size of the region. Figure 11.6 is an example of a hierarchical topology that localizes most of the circuits to their own local regions. TDM-based networks are priced primarily based on circuit bandwidth and distance, but even virtual circuit networks may have some distance-sensitivity in the pricing model.

The number of interregional links would scale with the number of regions, not the number of sites, which greatly reduces the number of required links (the number will always be greater than in a pure star topology, which always has the absolute minimum number of links), but a regional topology trades off a few additional shorter links against forcing all of the links to span the entire distance back to the central site(s).

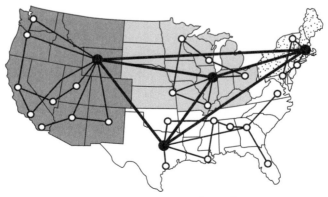

FIGURE 11.6 Hierarchical regional topology.

What would be nice is if there were a way to have a logically full-mesh topology without needing such a large investment in circuit-terminating equipment. A router can only accommodate a fixed number of WAN links. Various router models have different limits, but they are all limited to some finite value. Thus, after a certain number of sites is reached, another router chassis must be purchased. Each link into a router requires a WAN interface capable of accommodating the circuit bandwidth. (Interfaces that handle higher speed links cost more.) Router WAN ports do not usually attach directly to the circuit but require an intervening CSU/DSU. The Channel Service Unit (CSU) half of the device connects to the circuit, while the Data Service Unit (DSU) attaches to the WAN port over a serial interface of some kind (V.35, RS-449, EIA-232-D, High-Speed Serial Interface (HSSI), etc.).

Note that the number of CSU/DSUs and WAN interfaces required scales as $n(n-1)$, not $n(n-1)/2$, because there must be one CSU/DSU at each end of the circuit as well as one WAN interface at each end, so the double-counting of the $n(n-1)$ formula is appropriate in this case. Again, this formula assumes a full-mesh topology (the maximum number of links). In any case, the number of CSU/DSUs and WAN interfaces required will be double the total number of circuits in the topology, whatever its shape.

The price of the CSU/DSUs and routers (chassis and WAN ports) is bounded—you only pay for them once (ignoring the relatively minor additional costs of service contracts, spare parts, software upgrades, etc.). However, the telephone company will be sending you a new bill every month. If your network is in place long enough, the cost of the circuits will exceed the one-time cost of the capital equipment.

Packet switching allows for *logical* any-to-any connectivity without needing a physical link to everyone you might ever want to talk to. Imagine if you had to have a separate pair of wires in your home that reached to all the other phones on earth (or in your country, or in your city). You wouldn't be able to move! The fact that the phone network is "switched" means that your single pair of wires can be used to make a call to any other phone (with the limitation that you can only make one call at a time!). In packet switching, each DTE similarly has one attachment point to the "cloud," which allows it to make data "calls" to other DTEs as needed. Packet-switched clouds also enable each site to have more than one call active at the same time. Thus, the physical scaling issues are removed while preserving the logical any-to-any connectivity.

As the first standardized form of packet switching, X.25 was an example of just such a service. It accommodated both on-demand "calls" as well as permanent virtual circuits (virtual leased lines). The monthly cost varied, but some telephone companies charged by the number of bytes transmitted and received, some on the number of calls (virtual circuits established), some on a flat-rate basis (as long as usage was below some threshold), etc.

The up-front capital cost for packet-switched networking is much lower for customers since each site needs only one DTE (e.g., a router) with a single WAN interface and a single CSU/DSU. Unfortunately, in the 1980s X.25 service was rather slow, usually offering access links of 9.6 or 19.2 kbps. "High-speed" links were 56 kbps! As time went by, the access rates improved to DS-1 and E-1.

Other important trends were under way in the 1980s, in that the phone companies were all rapidly upgrading their transmission infrastructures to be optical fiber based, with the result that bit error rates for all circuit types were much lower than in the past. The cleaner that WAN links became, the less necessary X.25's careful switch-by-switch store-and-forward error checking and retransmission became—it was reasonable to assume that any errors could be handled directly by the DTEs. Another by-product of the deployment of fiber was that higher-speed WAN links became more economical. In the mid-1980s, a 56 kbps WAN backbone was considered fast, but within seven years, backbone speeds had reached (and in some cases exceeded) DS-3 speeds a thousand-fold increase.

As bandwidth was becoming cheaper and cleaner, there was a parallel explosion of corporate connectivity requirements. As LANs began to be deployed, it became more and more important to tie all parts of a corporation into its information technology infrastructure. Before the advent of LANs, there had been wide-area connectivity, but the bandwidth demands of the the terminal-host applications of the day were modest. LAN interconnection drove the increased demand for bandwidth, continuing to this day.

The emergence of LANs drove the development of WAN and MAN (Metropolitan Area Networks) that were more suited to the low-bit-error and higher-bandwidths that were emerging. Two of the most important protocols were Frame Relay and the Switched Multimegabit Data Service (SMDS), which at one time were vying for dominance in the LAN interconnection arena. SMDS was not as successful as it could have been, despite the fact that it had many features that made it much better suited to LAN interconnection than Frame Relay.

Frame Relay became the dominant WAN and MAN protocol for LAN interconnection. To a lesser extent, Asynchronous Transfer Mode (ATM) has been used in WANs, but it is being used mostly in carrier data backbones (frame relay and ATM services may be offered over a common ATM-switched backbone). The early vision for ATM as the universal answer (what was the question, again?) has not yet manifested itself.

FRAME RELAY SPECIFICS

Frame Relay is a streamlined version of X.25. First published in 1976, X.25 was an industry response to IBM's perceived dominance of the emerging field of packet switching. When X.25 was defined, the error rates on typical telecom circuits were much higher than today. X.25 compensated for this by using store-and-forward techniques—each switch had to receive the entire frame and verify that it was error-free before forwarding it, any detected errors were corrected by requiring the previous-hop to retransmit the packet. X.25 was extremely successful in Europe and elsewhere around the world, but not so much in the United States.[5]

As phone companies began aggressively deploying fiber-optic transmission networks, the quality of circuits tended to increase over the years. Eventually, the error checking and recovery that X.25 was capable of were no longer so acutely needed—in fact, as link speeds increased, X.25's careful hop-by-hop forwarding and error-checking now severely impeded performance rather than enhancing it! A more efficient protocol design was called for. Frame Relay is the result of the slimming down of X.25. One implicit assumption was that the lower error rates meant that the edge devices (DTEs) could handle retransmission on their own in the rare event of an error. Frame Relay switches begin forwarding a frame immediately once they have received the destination address (DLCI), without waiting for the entire frame to arrive.

One feature that was initially absent from Frame Relay was signaling support, which means that rather than establishing Virtual Circuits on demand, they were set up statically by the service provider. Eventually, specifications were defined to allow Frame Relay signaling, but the new dynamic method has yet to take the world by storm (it is available from some providers, but most still default to providing PVC-based service).

FRAME FORMAT

The Frame Relay header is very simple. It usually consists of two bytes, the format of which is illustrated in Figure 11.7. Note that there is only one address field, the DLCI, which is 10 bits long. The address only indicates the frame's destination; *there is no explicit source address in the Frame Relay header.*

As in other HDLC-derived protocols, the frame begins and ends with the usual 0x7E flag sequence. The C/R bit, inherited from LAPD,[6] after which the Frame Relay header is specifically modeled, is not used in Frame Relay.

The Extended Address (EA) bit is used to indicate whether or not extended addresses are in use. The header depicted in Figure 11–6 displays the two-byte form

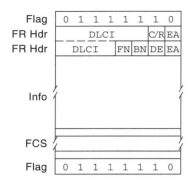

Flag	0 1 1 1 1 1 1 0
FR Hdr	DLCI C/R EA
FR Hdr	DLCI FN BN DE EA
Info	
FCS	
Flag	0 1 1 1 1 1 1 0

DLCI: **Data Link Connection Identifier**
   –akin to X.25's Logical Channel Number (LCN)
C/R: **Command/Response**
   –Not used in Frame Relay
EA: **Extended Address** format indicator
   –Last Occurance is 1, otherwise 0
BN: **Backward Explict Congestion Notification** (BECN)
FN: **Forward Explict Congestion Notification** (FECN)
DE: **Discard Eligibility**

FIGURE 11.7 Frame relay frame format.

(the most common), though three- and four-byte forms have also been defined. In each header byte except the last one, the EA bit is set to 0, which means that more address bits will follow. The final header byte will have the EA set to 1, indicating that the address is complete. In the two-byte case, the EA bit is set to 1. In the common, two-byte case, EA = 1.

The next two bits are used to indicate frame-relay intracloud congestion to other switches and to the DTEs. If a frame is received with the Forward Explicit Congestion Notification (FECN) bit set to 1, then an intermediate Frame Relay switch experienced congestion on this Virtual Circuit and set the FECN bit so that other switches along this frame's path will know that congestion was experienced along the way. The FECN bit is not especially useful for end-devices, except to count them—persistently high FECN rates may indicate that the provider's backbone is underprovisioned. This condition would indicate that an unusually large number of frames arrived having experienced congestion.[7] As a reaction to this condition, a DTE receiving FECN bits on a given DLCI may elect to slow transmission in the reverse direction on that DLCI until the congestion passes.

The BECN bit can be very useful for DTEs. If a frame is received with the BECN bit set to 1, it should elect to reduce its transmission rate back onto that DLCI until the transmission rate is low enough that frames begin to be received with BECN set to 0. If the traffic over a DLCI is primarily TCP-based, another strategy would be to intentionally drop some portion of the TCP packets destined to cross that DLCI. All the TCP packets need not be dropped, just enough that TCP's congestion-detection will cause it to reduce its sending rate. In the event of TCP traffic, this can be an effective technique since it directly conveys the congestion state to the endpoints. If the traffic is not TCP-based, the intermediate device has no choice but to try to buffer the traffic and send it at a slower rate, or just send it into the void if memory is at a premium. Once enough time has elapsed with BECN = 0, the transmission rate can be eased up to "normal."

Finally, frames may be marked as "Discard Eligible" by the transmitting DTE. Each DLCI has a certain bandwidth associated with it (the Committed Information Rate, or CIR). A provider's network should be engineered such that all DLCIs may receive traffic at their full CIR rates at all times, however, due to the burstiness of data traffic, this is impossible in practice. Congestion will always occur. A well-engineered network will have enough interswitch "backbone" capacity that congestion should be rare,[8] as long as all subscribers send data at or below their CIRs. If a DTE knows that it is exceeding the CIR, it may tell the switches that certain traffic can be dropped if congestion is experienced. In times of congestion, frames with the DE bit set are supposed to be dropped before frames which have the DE bit clear.

Sophisticated networks also may associate a "committed burst" rate (B_c) and a "burst exceeded" rate (B_e). These allow a provider to more finely provision their DLCIs. They may commit to a certain burst rate, i.e., a rate in excess of the CIR; similarly, they may inform the customer that there is a traffic threshold above which traffic is very likely to be dropped (B_e). The DTE may use this information to set the DE bit for traffic that is sent above the B_c rate. If resources exist within the switches, the traffic will get through, but if congestion is experienced, the DE bit will allow the DTE to indicate which traffic it considers most important; as long as the congestion is not too severe, the DE=0 traffic will probably get through.

Reserved Addresses

Normally, 10 bits of address space would accomodate precisely 1024 addresses, ranging from 0 to 1023. In the case of Frame Relay, 32 of the addresses are reserved, leaving 992 available for use in addressing users' Permanent or Switched Virtual Circuits (i.e., SVCs or PVCs). The Frame Relay DLCI address space is described in Table 11.3.

This may seem like a small number of addresses for a service that might have many thousands of subscribers; however, the addresses are only locally significant on each link. This means that *each* access link may have up to 992 peer DTEs across the cloud. In the next section, we will see that there are practical limits which keep the number of usable DLCIs at each access link under 500 in most cases.

The DLCI is only a local identifier, which means that it could—it almost certainly will—change along its path through the cloud. The sending DTE may know that to reach a certain remote DTE it must use, for instance, DLCI 577. Each switch

TABLE 11.3 FRAME RELAY ADDRESSES

RANGE	SIZE	DESIGNATION
0	1	Reserved (Call Control Signaling)
1–15	15	Reserved
16–1007	**992**	**Assignable to VCs**
1008–1022	15	Reserved
1023	1	Reserved (Local Management Interface)

along the way may use a different DLCI to indicate that destination. Figure 11.8 is a sample cloud in which we will examine Frame Relay addressing.

Strictly speaking, frame relay is just an access technology. It is possible that the frame relay interfaces that connect switches to users may be interconnected by an Asynchronous Transfer Mode (ATM) backbone, or some other technology. We

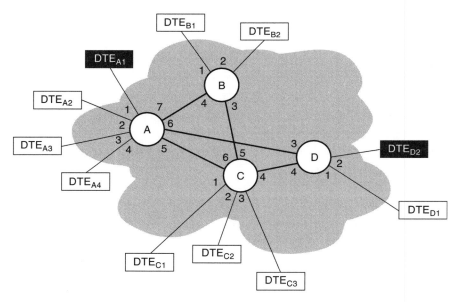

FIGURE 11.8 Example frame relay cloud.

will discuss frame relay as if the entire cloud used frame relay inside and out, but realize that everything applies equally well if frame relay is only used between the customers' DTEs and the service provider's switches, but not in between the provider's switches.

Frame Relay forwarding is table-driven. Each switch verifies that a frame is received on the expected port. For example, switch A may have a forwarding table such as that in Figure 11.9.

Each switch along the way may similarly change the DLCI on the outgoing frame. As long as it is set to the value that the next hop expects to see on an incoming frame on that port, then it can be forwarded properly by the next switch. Frames may only be forwarded if they arrive on the expected interface with a valid destination DLCI. For example, a frame that arrives on port 4 with a DLCI of 22 will be discarded since port 4 is not expecting frames with that DLCI. On the other hand, if a frame arrived on port 3 with a DLCI of 12, it would be transmitted out port 2 with a new DLCI, namely 500. Eventually, the final switch will transmit the frame onto the destination's access line, and the destination will use the DLCI to map it into the proper IP address.

Two observations are in order. First, this discussion assumed that the entire cloud used Frame Relay internally, as well as an access protocol. In reality, many Frame Relay clouds are built over Asynchronous Transfer Mode (ATM) infrastructures, with Frame Relay being used only at the very edge to pass data to and from the DTEs. Second, note that this "label swapping" method of forwarding may seem strange, changing the destination address at each hop, but it is much like driving from point A to point B. If you need to drive from Atlanta, GA, to Memphis, TN, you could first take Interstate 20 West to Birmingham, AL, then Interstate 65 North to Nashville, TN, then Interstate 40 West to Memphis. The different highway numbers that one must take when traveling by car are just like the DLCIs that can change along the path between Frame Relay switches.

Dest. DLCI	In Port	Dest. DLCI	Out Port
42	1	→ 645	6
31	1	→ 33	5
22	1	→ 757	7
33	2	→ 442	5
12	3	→ 500	2
11	3	→ 321	1
21	4	→ 952	7
23	4	→ 111	7

FIGURE 11.9 Switch A's forwarding table.

Local Management Interface (LMI) Protocol

Besides the Frame Relay protocols that enable frames to be transmitted synchronously and addressed properly, there is a control protocol that provides information to the attached DTEs about the accessibility of their remote neighbors. The Local Management Interface (LMI) protocol is a partner protocol that gives periodic status updates to the DTEs on each DLCI. If a DLCI is active, LMI will say so. If a DLCI is not connected end-to-end, it may be reported as down. New DLCIs may be configured by the service provider, and when they are activated they are added to the list of valid DLCIs. Because LMI traffic should be present on a link, even if all the DLCIs are down, a router implementation may use the presence of LMI as an indication that the Frame Relay link is up. LMI is sometimes referred to as a "heartbeat" protocol, since its presence confirms that the switch is still alive, even if no traffic is being received from any peer DTEs.

LMI allows even a PVC-based Frame Relay service to offer some rudimentary form of dynamic "signaling" to the DTEs. Usually, signaling involves the DTE asking the network to connect a call or to otherwise allocate some resource. LMI lets the network inform the DTEs about the health of the PVCs that matter to them. What LMI is advertising to the DTE is a list of reachable destinations.

If a link-level problem prevents the DLCI from being fully operational end-to-end, then the DLCI is reported as "down;" its status will change to "up" after the problem is fixed. Without LMI, the DTE would have to wait for higher-layer protocols, such as routing protocols, to notice that a neighbor has become unreachable, which could take on the order of 40 seconds to three minutes depending on which routing protocol is in use.

In the scenario of directly-attached endstation DTEs, it would be up to the transport layer protocol to attempt retransmissions and eventually declare the neighbor dead. With LMI, the link may still retain some capriciousness, but at least the cloud is directly informing the DTEs of its health on a moment-by-moment basis.

IP makes use of LMI to help identify new peers and trigger an ARP variant designed especially for Frame Relay.

Limitations of LMI

Unfortunately, each PVC's LMI status report occupies several bytes. If a 1500-byte MTU is being used on the Frame Relay interface, then LMI reports are limited to about 440 DLCIs, far less than the theoretical maximum of 992 DLCIs that could be defined on each Frame Relay access link. All the status for a given access link must be reported in a single LMI frame. In practice, this limit is still plenty big enough, since most access links are not fast enough to support that many virtual circuits at the same time.

In the case of specialized applications that involve accessing a large number of relatively low-bandwidth remote DTEs, e.g., in a telemetry application such as reading electric meters from a central site, it might be possible to forgo LMI. An application-specific DTE-based heartbeat protocol may be designed in such cases so the main data collection site could always verify connectivity to all remote sites.

As noted earlier, routers often use LMI as an indication of link status. A Frame Relay link is considered up when two things happen. First, the router must receive a physical layer clock signal. This indicates that the *physical* access link, which is supposed to lead to a Frame Relay switch, is operating correctly. Second, the router needs to hear LMI "heartbeat" frames from the switch. Clearly, heartbeat frames may not be received unless the physical transmission channel is working. So, if a WAN interface is configured to speak Frame Relay, both of those conditions must be met before the link is considered to be up. If LMI were not received, the link would be declared to be down, even if the physical layer had detected a valid clock signal. Setting a router to ignore LMI is equivalent to instructing it to always believe that the link is up, as long as the physical layer clock is received.

IP ENCAPSULATION

The encapsulation of IP packets over Frame Relay is very straightforward, as depicted in Figure 11.10. Besides the expected two-byte Frame Relay header, there is an extra encapsulation layer that provides a "Control" byte (set to 0x03, meaning Un-numbered Information), and possibly padding (not necessary in this case), ending with a Network Layer Protocol IDentifier (NLPID), which indicates which protocol is encased within the frame. The NLPID value for IP is 0xCC. The IP packet is appended immediately following the NLPID. The frame concludes with a Frame Check Sequence and a closing Flag character.

In real Frame Relay networks, the subtleties lie in the means of IP address to DLCI binding. There are two ways to do this; namely, static or dynamic. In LANs, we saw that the dynamic method (i.e., ARP) was preferred. In Frame Relay, and WANs in general (where broadcast capabilities are not normally available), a combination tends to work best. In a network that is growing gradually, a mixed address resolution technique can work quite well.

For sites that are known to be up and operating, it makes little sense to learn their DLCIs dynamically—their addresses typically remain fixed for long periods of

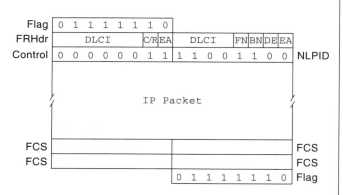

FIGURE 11.10   Encapsulation of an IP packet within a frame relay frame.

time. When a new site is being brought up (visible at each of its peer sites as a new DLCI), it may make sense to allow its addressing to be learned dynamically—this allows the other sites to immediately exchange data with the new site with no additional configuration. Once it is up and stable, the address mappings can be added to the static lists in all its peers. In Figure 11.11, DTE$_{A1}$ has four peers, with the two in gray having recently been learned dynamically by Inverse ARP, a protocol which will be discussed shortly.

DTE$_{A1}$ may have an address translation table (ARP cache) similar to that depicted in Figure 11.12. This table means that should a packet need to be sent to 10.87.152.133 (i.e., DTE$_{C3}$), it would be sent out destined for DLCI 126. Each row is interpreted similarly.

The advantage of static address mapping information is stability. Since each Frame Relay site's address is unlikely to change, it is wasteful for a router (or any DTE) to have to relearn the same old information time after time.

The familiar ARP protocol is designed to map **known target IP** addresses to **unknown target MAC** addresses. When operating over LANs, ARP's operation depends on the LAN's broadcast capability. In a Frame Relay environment, a DTE will know a peer's DLCI (via LMI), which is the peer's "hardware address," *without knowing its IP address*. This is exactly the opposite of the information that is known in the LAN case. Also, there is no broadcast mechanism within the cloud. Inverse

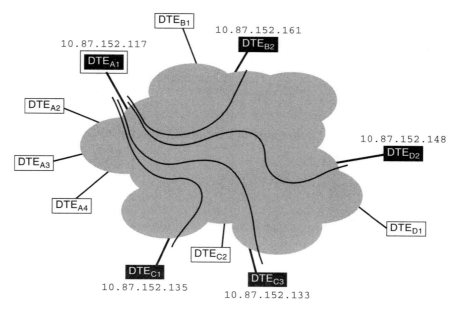

FIGURE 11.11 Frame relay address mapping example.

ARP was designed to perform a form of address resolution within the Frame Relay environment.

Frame Relay Network Addressing Considerations

Addressing Convention

Frame Relay networks are set up so that the DLCI that a frame arrives on is the same one used to return to that neighbor. If this were not the case, InARP would not

Address	Intf	Type	Media Address	Header Format	Address Source
10.87.152.161	1	External	@75	Frame Relay	Static
10.87.152.148	1	External	@81	Frame Relay	Static
10.87.152.133	1	External	@126	Frame Relay	InARP
10.87.152.135	1	External	@101	Frame Relay	InARP

FIGURE 11.12 IP-to-DLCI address translation table (ARP cache).

know which of its active DLCIs to return its Response on—all configuration would need to be static if this were the case! This convention is an artifact of the fact that Frame Relay frames have no embedded Source Address field. Networks must be provisioned such that if some DTE uses DLCI 777 to reach site A, then frames *returning from* site A will also be sent back to the switch on DLCI 777.

Stated another way, when LMI announces that DLCI 777 is active, it means not only that frames to that site must use DLCI 777, but also that frames from that site will arrive on DLCI 777. All frames should arrive on DLCIs that have been previously announced by LMI.

Frame Relay Cloud Addressing Styles

Frame Relay clouds may have their DLCI values assigned in two ways that "make sense" to humans, or in an essentially random way that only must meet the simple uniqueness criteria that each site is represented by exactly one DLCI value. A human-friendly system is probably more manageable!

PVC-Specific Addressing.   First-time users of Frame Relay often focus on the PVCs as the most important entities worthy of "naming." If such a customer has 5 PVCs, arranged as in Figure 11.13, they may call them DLCIs 40, 50, 60, 70, and 80.

Isolating the PVC between sites A and C (see Figure 11.14), notice that both sites use the same DLCI value (50) to reach the other side. Similarly, in this addressing scheme, each pair of sites uses the same DLCI number at each end to represent the other side. The DLCI numbers are equal to the PVC number.

While this scheme is fine to use, it has limitations. The biggest limitation is that the number of addressable entities (the PVCs) scales proportional to the square

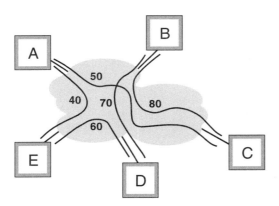

FIGURE 11.13 Example of DLCI-specific addressing.

FIGURE 11.14 PVC between sites A and C.

of the number of sites. A dense enough mesh will have way more PVCs than sites. This observation would seem to suggest that it might be better to investigate associating addresses with the sites instead. If just the sites were numbered, the addressing scheme would scale with the number of sites. Also, it may be possible to relate the site numbers to their IP addresses (a convenience that is irrelevant to the cloud, but one that eases human comprehension of the network).

Endpoint-Specific Addressing. This addressing style is also known as "site-specific" addressing. Using Figure 11.13 as a template, we may choose numbering such that Site A is 701, B is 702, C is 703, D is 704, and E is 705. Figure 11.15 displays the same topology, with the sites numbered as stated.

Each site uses the appropriate value to reach the appropriate site. Figure 11.16 focuses on Sites A and B and examines their logical connectivity.

Note that sites A and B both use DLCI 703 to reach site C. Also, sites C and E both use DLCI 701 to reach site A. In general, every site uses the same DLCI value to reach a given remote site. A is always reached as 701 in this example. If we added a site F, and if this new site had a PVC to site A, the Frame Relay cloud would also be

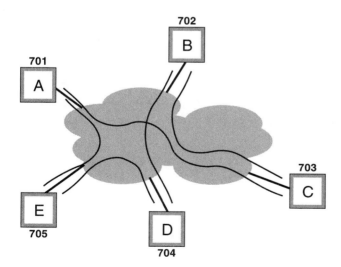

FIGURE 11.15 Example of site-specific addressing.

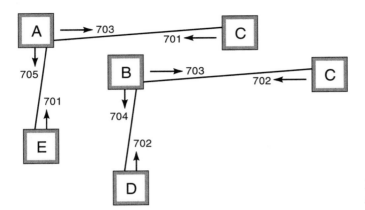

FIGURE 11.16   Isolation of
sites A and B.

configured such that DLCI 701 reached site A. Site F would likely receive DLCI
number 706.

Mapping Site Numbers to IP Addresses

If our Frame Relay WAN will never grow beyond 30 sites, we can use a prefix as small as /27 to cover all these sites. This mapping is purely for human convenience; it eases administration and eases verification of static mappings in router
configurations. One such mapping might be that depicted in Figure 11.17. Let's
choose the following prefix for our example: 10.87.152.96/27. The chosen algo-

IP Address Index	IP Address Value	Frame Relay Site Address Value
1	10.87.152.97	701
2	10.87.152.98	702
3	10.87.152.99	703
4	10.87.152.100	704
5	10.87.152.101	705
6	10.87.152.102	•
7	10.87.152.103	•
8	10.87.152.104	•
9	10.87.152.105	•
10	10.87.152.106	•
•	•	•
•	•	•
•	•	•
30	10.87.152.126	730

FIGURE 11.17   Mapping IP addresses to remote sites.

rithm is to map site 1 (A; DLCI 701) to IP address 1 (10.87.152.97), and increment from there.

The Frame Relay DLCIs need not be tightly packed into a short range of addresses. We need not have 26 sites with DLCI numbers 653–678. The only criteria is that each site use the same number to reach a given remote site. So the 26 DLCIs *could* be chosen arbitrarily from within the range 16–1007 (see Table 11.2). Given that the customer may be in control of these parameters, it makes more sense to keep the numbers consecutive if at all possible. It may even be desirable to choose DLCI numbers that map easily to the desired IP prefix to be used on this frame relay cloud.

Uncorrelated Addressing. In this scheme, each site uses a locally unique value to reach every other site, but the DLCIs are not tied to either the PVCs or the remote sites. One site may be reached as DLCI 491 from one peer, and DLCI 38 from another. The router would have no trouble in this case, because InARP would work just fine, but there is no "help" for the administrator built into the scheme. Since the DLCIs are usually chosen to suit the customer (if a preference is expressed), there is no reason why a customer wouldn't want to set up the addresses in a way that makes their life easier. A cloud with a large number of sites will be much more manageable if a sensible, consistent mapping exists between sites and DLCIs (and the associated IP addresses).

Summary. Numbering the PVCs themselves works well only for small numbers of sites, but it wastes DLCI numbers and does not scale well. The number of PVCs needed in a partial mesh will explode as the number of sites increases. A logical full mesh of only 45 sites will need 990 PVCs, which essentially exhausts the DLCI address space, which is limited to 992 addresses. This same example, using site-specific addressing, would only need 45 DLCI numbers at each site (the same 45 numbers, not 45 different numbers at each site!) Given that the DLCIs are chosen for the customer's convenience, it makes good sense to lay out a plan that ties the DLCIs to the IP addresses.

InARP Protocol Description

InARP may be used by any Frame Relay DTE. Routers are a very common type of InARP-speaking DTE so this discussion will be in their context, though the operation of the protocol is independent of the type of DTE using it. The only real restriction is that, perhaps obviously, InARP supports IP, so the DTE and its peer must both be using IP.

Imagine that an IP router is initializing a Frame Relay interface. Once it receives its first LMI packet, it learns which DLCIs are active and which are inactive. Knowing a DLCI allows the router to send a packet to the other side. InARP provides a "who's there?" function. The router sends an InARP request on each active DLCI; the InARP packets include its own source IP address. The packet is eventually delivered to the peer router, which records the last-hop DLCI and the original source's IP address.

InARP, as seen in Figure 11.18, does not have an assigned NLPID value. Instead, it is encapsulated within a SNAP header, because SNAP does have a NLPID value (0x80). Note that the [Ether]Type field of the SNAP header is filled in with ARP's usual Type value, 0x0806. The SNAP OUI field is set to all-0s (0x00-00-

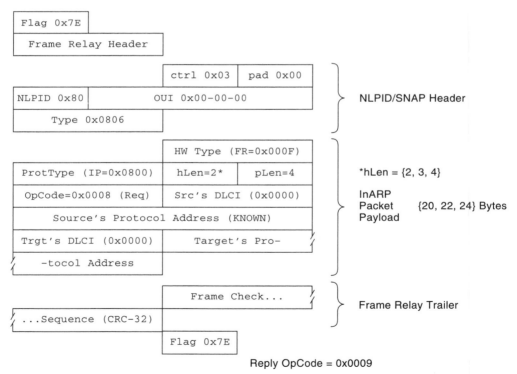

FIGURE 11.18 Encapsulation of inverse ARP.

00) which indicates that the final two bytes of the SNAP header contain a Type field.

The InARP packet format is directly inherited from the [LAN] ARP packet, but the source's and target's hardware addresses (in the Frame Relay context, these may also be known as the source's and target's DLCI) are irrelevant. Since a given site does not have a single DLCI value that uniquely represents itself, it has no choice but to fill in 0x0000 in this field. Similarly, even though the source knows the target's DLCI, this number will not be the same on the target's access link, so it does the target no good to know which DLCI the source uses to reach it. All InARP is trying to do is get each side to reveal its IP address to the other.

Returning to our example from Figure 11.10, we can describe how DTE_{A1} learned DTE_{C3}'s IP address. In order to simplify the description, we will focus on just that part of the diagram that is relevant to this discussion, as shown in Figure 11.19.

First, LMI informed DTE_{A1} that a new DLCI was active, namely DLCI 126 (this is step 1 in Figure 11.20). DTE_{A1} now must attempt to determine the IP address of this new peer by sending an InARP Request[9] destined for DLCI 126, the newly discovered DLCI, which is step 2, indicated by the bold, dashed line pointing toward DTE_{C3}.

If the network is operating properly, the InARP request is delivered at the other end on some different DLCI, possibly 55 (the exact value is irrelevant). DTE_{C3} re-

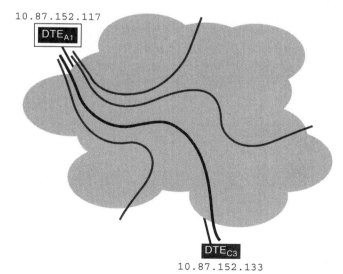

10.87.152.117

DTE_{A1}

DTE_{C3}

10.87.152.133

FIGURE 11.19 InARP protocol in action.

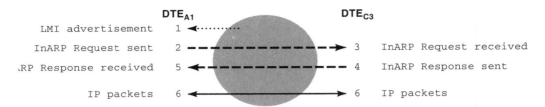

FIGURE 11.20   InARP step-by-step.

ceives the InARP Request packet in step 3, noting which DLCI it was addressed to at the Frame Relay layer (the DLCIs within the InARP packet, as we have already seen, are useless in practice). Along with the inbound DLCI, DTE_{C3} records the source IP address contained in the InARP packet, so it builds up a local mapping that DTE_{A1} (10.87.152.117) is reachable via DLCI 55. Step 3 is comprised of all these items.

In step 4, indicated by a bold, dashed line pointing back toward DTE_{A1}, DTE_{C3} creates an InARP Response by changing the InARP Request packet's Op-Code from 8 to 9, and filling in DTE_{C3}'s IP address (10.87.152.135) in the target IP address field. DTE_{C3} also swaps the values in the target and source address fields. The InARP Response is addressed back onto the same DLCI from which the original request was received (i.e., DLCI 55).

Once DTE_{A1} receives the InARP Response from DTE_{C3} in step 5 (on DLCI 126!), it can map the InARP packet's source IP address field's value (10.87.152.135) to DLCI 126. DTE_{A1} may now safely infer that DTE_{C3} knows how to reach it. In the future, denoted by step 6, either end may send IP packets to the other side, since they both know which DLCI to use to reach the other's remote IP address.

REFERENCES

REQUEST for COMMENT (RFC)

2427 Multiprotocol Interconnect over Frame Relay. C. Brown, A. Malis, September 1998. (Format: TXT=74671 bytes) (Obsoletes RFC1490, RFC1294) (Status: STANDARD)

2390 Inverse Address Resolution Protocol. T. Bradley, C. Brown, A. Malis, August 1998. (Format: TXT=20849 bytes) (Obsoletes RFC1293) (Status: DRAFT STANDARD)

Kessler, G., Train, D., *Metropolitan Area Networks: Concepts, Standards, and Services.* New York: McGraw-Hill, 1992. ISBN: 0-07-034243-1.

ENDNOTES

1. The PSTN also used Frequency-Division Multiplexing, which has largely been supplanted by TDM. In FDM, calls still got a fixed resource, in this case a slice of radio frequency spectrum, primarily in the microwave area.

2. Specifically, within an M13 multiplexer, which mixes 28 DS-1s, in seven groups of four (i.e., seven DS-2s), into a single DS-3.

3. In IP, the packet switches are traditionally called "routers," though it is lately fashionable to call some of them "layer-3 switches," if they achieve high-performance forwarding by employing special-purpose hardware. Layer-3 switches still make the same forwarding decision, minimally based on the IP destination address, and they still must run routing protocols so they know how to reach other parts of the topology.

4. To be fair, modern connection-oriented protocols sometimes support link monitoring and virtual circuit rerouting functions.

5. If I had to guess why this was, I would suggest that there may have been two factors. In the first place, US telephone companies don't have a long history of understanding the "data" world; it is entirely possible that early X.25 tariffs were cost-prohibitive. Secondly, massive infrastructure improvements were under way to build out fiber backbones in the U.S., which greatly improved the quality of long-haul circuits, which gradually made X.25's error checking and retransmission features less relevant. Once American phone companies discovered the rapidly growing data transmission market, the high-quality backbones were mostly in place and frame relay was much more appropriate.

6. LAPD, "Link Access Procedures on the D-channel," is the data link layer of ISDN's Q.931 signaling protocol. LAPD is formally known as CCITT Q.922, which explains the notation in RFC-2427, "Multiprotocol Interconnect over Frame Relay." Frame Relay only uses the so-called "core aspects" of LAPD.

7. Since many virtual circuits may all terminate at a given site, it is useful to keep FECN statistics on a per-DLCI basis. This information will allow you to give specific complaints to the service provider about which parts of their backbone may be underprovisioned.

8. Congestion is inevitable, even if all the DTEs respect their CIRs. If enough of them coincidentally transmit at nearly the same time, some links within the network could be temporarily overloaded.

9. LAN-based ARP uses OpCodes 1 and 2 for Request or Reply, respectively. To avoid any possible confusion, InARP uses different OpCodes, namely 8 and 9, respectively, for Request and Response

PART III

Standards—based IP Routing Protocols

INTRODUCTION
TO ROUTING

I n any network-layer protocol, there is a close relationship between the protocol's routing function and its addressing structure. After all, each individual "network number" is an island. Routing is the process that routers employ in order to figure out how to get to all the other network numbers. Regardless of the network-layer protocol, its routing function is composed of two independent, but highly interdependent, subfunctions, as depicted in Figure 12.1.

Component 1 is of paramount importance; without the information derived from routing protocols, a router can not forward traffic. Routing protocols involve both advertising routing information to (and receiving it from) neighbors, as depicted in Figure 12.2. Each solid line below represents a bidirectional exchange.

Each routing protocol represents its routing information differently, and each follows different rules in distributing and processing that information. The output of the routing protocol calculations is the router's forwarding table. Component 2 depends on the existence of that forwarding table. Each packet that arrives at the router will have its destination address compared against the "routing" table then forwarded to the best next hop.

As depicted in Figure 12.2, routers usually—but not as a general rule—converse with other "neighbor" routers that are attached to the same subnetwork; in this way, routing information spreads from neighbor to neighbor, until it is has been

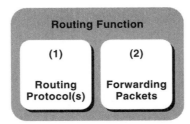

FIGURE 12.1 Components of the routing function.

distributed across the entire Routing Domain. The figure shows the worst case, in which each router sends an update to each neighbor individually, requiring *n(n-1)* messages, where n is the number of neighbor routers on a LAN. It is possible to streamline this process by employing MAC-layer broadcast or multicast packets so that each router need only send its routing update data out once allowing all the neighbors to receive it "simultaneously."

In order for the exchanged routing information to be intelligible, the routers must have an unambiguous way of referring to the subnetworks that they are attached to. In Figure 12.2, or whenever routers have interfaces attached to a common subnetwork, all the routers must be configured such that they agree on the network number of the attached common LAN. The routers' network-layer addresses serve this function by being individually associated with exactly one subnetwork per network number. By extension, the implication is that all the subnetworks in an entire "Routing Domain" have unique network numbers.

So, addressing (in particular, the use of unique network numbers for individual subnetworks) enables deterministic routing. Routers, on the other hand, define the boundaries of network numbers. Routers share the locations of the subnetworks by exchanging data regarding the relative location of the network numbers.

What do we mean by the term "Routing Domain"? Network-layer protocols each have at least one associated routing protocol. Table 12.1 lists the routing protocols associated with several network-layer protocols.

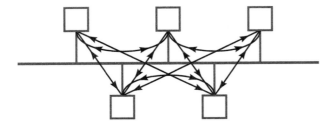

FIGURE 12.2 Neighbor routers exchange routing data.

TABLE 12.1 ROUTING PROTOCOLS

AppleTalk	RTMP	Routing Table Maintenance Protocol
	AURP	AppleTalk Update-based Routing Protocol
IP	RIPv1	Routing Information Protocol, version 1
	RIPv2	Routing Information Protocol, version 2
	OSPF	Open Shortest Path First
	I-IS-IS	Integrated Intermediate System to Intermediate System
	BGP-4	Border Gateway Protocol, version 4
	EGP	Exterior Gateway Protocol
	IGRP	Cisco's Interior Gateway Routing Protocol
	E-IGRP	Cisco's Enhanced-IGRP
Novell IPX	RIP	Routing Information Protocol
	NLSP	Netware Link Services Protocol
Xerox XNS	RIP[1]	Routing Information Protocol

For those network-layer protocols that only have one associated routing protocol, the entire internetwork is one Routing Domain. However, when more than one routing protocol is available, there may be "bubbles" that execute different routing protocols, as in Figure 12.3. The bubbles are Routing Domains, which are interconnected by routers (black dots) with interfaces in multiple Routing Domains.

For example, in IP-based networks, there may be a RIP bubble and an OSPF bubble, or any of the protocols listed in Table 12.1 under "IP." A collection of routers that speaks the same routing protocol for a given network-layer protocol constitutes a Routing Domain. For the sake of simplicity, it is safe to think of Routing

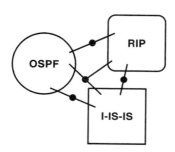

FIGURE 12.3 Three routing domains.

Domains as being disjoint, but it is possible for them to overlap, either by design or by misconfiguration.

Administrative Domains are a set of routers that share a common administration. It is possible that a single Administrative Domain might represent exactly one Routing Domain, if that administration's routers all run one routing protocol. Alternatively, an Administrative Domain may contain a set of interconnected Routing Domains, as shown in Figure 12.4.

Finally, note that many different administrative entities may choose to run the same routing protocol. An obvious example of this situation is the Internet "backbone," where BGP-4 is the norm. Just because each Administrative Domain runs the same routing protocol doesn't make the whole collection a Routing Domain. Each individual Administrative Domain has its own policies about who it will accept traffic from, for which destinations. Such "routing policies" are represented by which route prefixes are advertised to each peer, and which prefixes may be received from each peer.

Administrative Domains are usually interconnected via a "demilitarized zone," or DMZ, a LAN that is in neither domain. Whereas Routing Domains internal to an Administrative Domain may be connected by multi-homed routers with some interfaces in each Routing Domain, this is not a suitable way to interconnect Administrative Domains—who would manage the router? In order to ensure that each side has a point of administrative control, each extends a router interface to a common LAN, as in Figure 12.5.

The DMZ is a special purpose miniature Routing Domain, with two routers, one from each Administrative Domain. The two administrations agree in advance on what routes they will exchange with each other, via which routing protocol. Pragma-

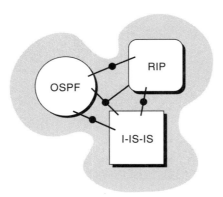

FIGURE 12.4 Administrative domains versus routing domains.

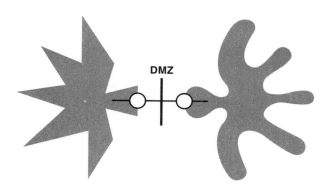

FIGURE 12.5 Interconnecting administrative domains.

tism may dictate that each router be configured with "route filters" to allow only the prenegotiated routes to be received, discarding all others.

THE RELATIONSHIP BETWEEN ADDRESSING AND ROUTING

One of the most important factors determining the linkage between Addressing and Routing is the structure of the protocol's network-layer address space. The high-level structure of a network-layer address is nearly always (network-number.node-number). The address' network-number portion is used as a unique label across the Routing Domain. These labels are used to enable the forwarding of packets; they must be uniquely mapped to subnetworks in order for routing to be deterministic.

Each protocol varies only by the size of the respective portions of the address, and by how much (if any) hierarchical structure there is in the network-number portion. Table 12.2 summarizes the network-layer addressing structure for some representative protocol families.

Routers exchange information about the relative locations of all reachable destinations (represented by their associated network numbers along with some "metric" that is usually distance-sensitive) in the Routing Domain. Given this information, the routers can locate themselves relative to any known destination. Some routing protocols allow a router to see the whole topology, while others provide coarser information (e.g., "network 13 is that way"). Within each network-number there is a set of node-numbers, each of which must be unique within the network-number. Figure 12.6 shows a simple Routing Domain.

As you can see, each subnetwork has a different network-number. Also, note that even though two nodes have node-numbers equal to 209, their addresses are

TABLE 12.2   NETWORK-LAYER ADDRESSING STRUCTURES

Protocol	Network Number	Node Number	
AppleTalk Phase II	16 bits	8 bits	
DECnet Phase IV	6 bits	10 bits	
IPv4	variable	variable	(total = 32 bits)
IPv6	variable	variable	(total = 128 bits)
Novell IPX	32 bits	48 bits	
OSI CLNP	variable	variable	(total = up to 160 bits)

still distinguishable because their network numbers are different: e.g., `14.209` versus `26.209`.

What do we mean when we say that some network-layer protocol's address space is hierarchically structured? As a case study, we can consider IPX versus IP.

- IP forwarding is not based on an exact match, but a "longest match," in which the best forwarding entry is the one that has the most leading bits in common with the packet's destination address. Other protocols that do not have hierarchical addresses can use exact match forwarding. In a nonhierarchically-addressed protocol such as IPX, a packet's destination network number is either in the forwarding table or it is not.

- In the IPX environment, the `network-numbers` are just numbers. One is as good as another. They are all the same size, in that each of them accommodates 2^{48} possible nodes within itself (since the `node-numbers` are

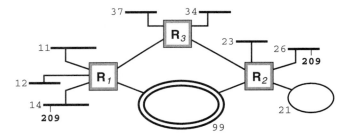

FIGURE 12.6   Example routing domain.

48-bit quantities). IP addresses are all 32 bits, just as IPX network numbers, but there is no fixed `network-number` size.

- In IPX and other local-use-only protocols, the protocol's entire address space is available for use within each independent Administrative Domain, while IP each organization is allocated a prefix of a size that meets their needs.

- Another important distinction is that the IP address space is, for the most part, globally unique. If I have the IP prefix 192.156.136.0/24, then no one else can have that prefix.

  We saw that all the `network-numbers` in a Routing Domain had to be unique, so that the routing protocol(s) could positively identify all the different potential destinations. This rule is true even beyond the local routing-domain level. Within the Internet, all the network numbers (i.e., network prefixes) must be unique in order for the Internet's routing protocols to work correctly.

If there are 4,096 active subnetworks in an IPX Routing Domain, then each IPX router will need 4,096 entries in its forwarding table if it wants to know how to get everywhere. It is not possible to use one network number to represent more specific network numbers, as in IP. (IPX does have a "default" route, which can be used in some topologies to help control the size of the overall routing table.)

For instance, in an IP Routing Domain with 4,096 active subnetworks, there could be as many as 4,096 entries in the forwarding table, or as few as 16, . . . or 4, or 1. Based on our practice with IP addressing in Part I, we saw that a prefix of 201.64.0.0/10 may represent 4,096 "/22" prefixes. 201.64.196.0/22 is just one component of 201.64.0.0/10, whose components are 201.64.0.0/22, 201.64.4.0/22, 201.64.8.0/22, and so on, up to 201.127.248.0/22, and finally 201.127.252.0/22.

IP addresses are like Russian "matryoshka," the nesting dolls. A larger (i.e., shorter) prefix can contain a smaller (i.e., longer) prefix, which can itself contain yet a smaller prefix, and so on. The dolls can all be nested inside the large one and carried around together, as in Figure 12.7.

In IPX, the network numbers are just numbers with no inherent hierarchical structure. So, `network-number 0x7C04FDBC` is not more specific than `0x7C04FDB0` or `0x7C040000`. There is no inherent relationship among them; they are all just different numbers, as different as `0x00000001`, `0x10101010`, and `0xFEDCBA98`. In IPX, the total address is effectively 80 bits long (32-bit network number plus 48-bit node address), but the "mask" is always /32. There is no way to

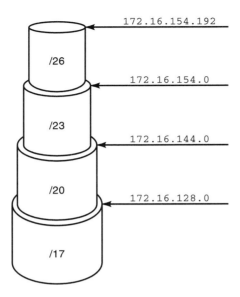

172.16.154.192

/26

172.16.154.0

/23

172.16.144.0

/20

172.16.128.0

/17

FIGURE 12.7   Nesting IP prefixes.

make the mask more or less specific, as in IP, where the address/mask notation indicates the fluid boundary between the extended-network prefix and the "host" portion.

ROLE AND TYPES OF ROUTING PROTOCOLS

What does it mean to advertise a prefix? Another way of asking the same question is: What is a router saying when it advertises a prefix? It is saying: "I know how to reach this destination." Advertising a prefix also carries with it an implicit offer to help carry traffic toward that destination.

Once routing information has been acquired it is processed according to the routing protocol's rules and then represented as a forwarding table, also commonly called a "routing" table. The packet's destination address is searched for in the forwarding table, and the packet is then forwarded to the "best" neighbor router.

Routing is far more important to the Internet than anything else.[3] It is the key underlying technology without which the whole shebang would fall in to a useless blinking mass of idle long-haul circuits. Routing is how routers figure out where "everything" is. Because the routers tell each other what they're attached to, the Internet can grow in a decentralized way.[4] New networks come on line continually, at which time their presence is advertised, enabling traffic to reach them. Routing pro-

IMPOSING HIERARCHY ON A FLAT Address Space

A flat address space is more demanding on the routers since all the reachable subnetworks' network numbers must be stored in each router. However, because of the complete freedom to assign addresses (each independent network manager "owns" the entire address space), the network manager can create a pseudo-hierarchy that makes sense for their network.

For instance, a fictitious IPX Administrative Domain might have the following structure imposed upon it: 0xCC00BBxx. The CC portion is the campus code. Eight bits worth of campus space yields up to 256 campuses. The next byte is reserved for growth, with the next level of hierarchy, BB, representing any of up to 256 possible buildings in each campus. Finally, the xx representing any of 256 possible subnetworks per building. So, IPX address 0x99001342 represents campus 0x99, building 0x13, subnetwork 0x42. A different campus, perhaps 0xE3, may also have a building 0x13 with a subnetwork 0x42 (also, 0xE3001342).

Again, it is not possible to represent everything in campus 0x99 as the address 0x99000000 or every subnetwork in building 0x17 of campus 0x76 as 0x76001700. Thus, all the routers must know about all reachable subnetworks; aggregation is effectively impossible. The structure was created purely for administrative convenience and has no basis in simple arithmetic (as does IP).

Even when the addresses themselves have no mask and cannot represent blocks of more specific addresses, it is still possible to create useful structure within the address space in an Administrative Domain. Each Administrative Domain manager is free to define a pattern that makes sense locally.

tocols make every effort, within their individual mechanisms, to maintain a complete and correct picture of the topology.

When an outage happens, there is inevitably a window between the outage occurring and the routers finding out about it.[5] During this window, some routers will still think that the destination is reachable and will therefore send any such traffic in

Imposing Flatness on a Hierarchical Address Space

Just as it is possible to assign meaning to the digits of a flat address space's network numbers, it is also possible to assign addresses within IP such that aggregation is impossible. The natural aggregation boundaries become virtually meaningless if addresses are not assigned with binary boundaries mapping to natural physical boundaries.

As an example, if one had a /16, and made the common choice to implement a fixed /24 subnet mask, there are 256 available subnets. It is natural to use byte-aligned subnet boundaries, since this mask choice creates nice decimal subnet numbers in the third byte (from 0 to 255). This human convenience can have a cost within the network, however. Figure 12.8 shows two possible arrangements of IP prefixes across four buildings.

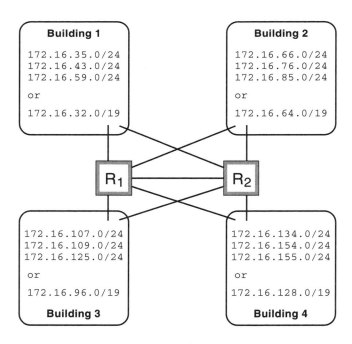

FIGURE 12.8 Aggregatable address assignment.

continued

If the hierarchical scheme above is deployed, then the routers will only need to have one forwarding table entry for each building. There will be up to 32 /24s within each building, so any intrabuilding routers will need to know about the intrabuilding /24s. However, outside the building, only the aggregate needs to be advertised.[2]

If the very same prefixes were assigned without regard to any hierarchical structure in the third byte of the address, then all the routers, both inside and outside of the buildings, will need to know about all the reachable prefixes. Figure 12.9 shows the relative sizes of the forwarding tables in either case.

Routing Tables with Aggregation		Routing Tables without Aggregation	
Dest. Prefix	Metric	Dest. Prefix	Metric
172.16.32.0/19	0	172.16.35.0/24	0
	1		1
172.16.64.0/19	0	172.16.43.0/24	0
	1		1
172.16.96.0/19	0	172.16.59.0/24	0
	1		1
172.16.128.0/19	0	172.16.66.0/24	0
	1		1
		172.16.76.0/24	0
			1
		172.16.85.0/24	0
			1
Note: Metric = 0 indicates		172.16.107.0/24	0
a direct path into a			1
building.		172.16.109.0/24	0
			1
		172.16.125.0/24	0
Metric = 1 indicates			1
an indirect path via		172.16.134.0/24	0
another router.			1
		172.16.154.0/24	0
			1
		172.16.155.0/24	0
			1

FIGURE 12.9 Address allocation impacts forwarding table size.

that direction of where the destination *used to be* . . . and straight into a "black hole" that they are not yet aware of. Some routing protocols are very good at avoiding black holes, but they can never be eliminated completely since the updates take a finite amount of time to propagate. The best that can be done is to make the update process as efficient as possible.

Another problem that can arise during topology changes is that "forwarding loops" may form.[6] Not all routing protocols are equally good at loop avoidance. The router topology surely always contains loops of various sizes, but the routing protocols normally compute a logical tree over the topology. A forwarding loop is a degenerate condition in which some set of routers cannot successfully deliver a packet toward some destination, but keep sending it around in circles. A set of routers may be a loop for only certain destinations, or perhaps for all destinations, depending on the way the loop formed and which routing protocol in use.

If a loop has formed, a packet may enter it at any point. The first router forwards the packet (toward the destination, to the best of its knowledge) to the second router (which also forwards it toward the destination, again, to the best of its knowledge). Each router thinks it knows how to reach the desired destination, but the set of them does not actually know. There may be more than two routers involved in the loop. There are well-known failure scenarios in certain simple protocols (e.g., RIP) that can result in the formation of persistent long-lived loops. If the loop has n routers in it, the packet will have its TTL decremented by n on each pass through the loop, until the TTL reaches zero and an ICMP error message is sent back to the packet's source.

Once a topology change has happened, whether the change was the addition of a new network, the removal of a network, or a router outage that changes the set of available pathways, the routing protocol transmits messages to help it "converge" on a new stable state, reflecting the actual topology. The convergence time is a key differentiator between various routing protocols, because some converge very slowly (especially in certain difficult topologies), while some converge very quickly, without much regard to different topologies. There are two basic classes of routing protocols, namely, distance-vector and link-state.

DISTANCE-VECTOR ROUTING PROTOCOLS

Distance-vector is a complicated sounding name, but in fact these protocols are the easiest to understand. If we dust off our old high school Math or Physics textbooks, we remember that a vector is a one-dimensional array, an ordered set of quantities. A vector is distinguished from a scalar, which is a single number. Vectors are used to represent things like velocity, which has both a magnitude (the speed) and an associated direction. What, then, does a vector have to do with routing?

Distance-vector protocols transmit vectors of distances. At the simplest, each vector represents one [destination][7] prefix and may be written (prefix, mask, distance). In certain protocols, the mask may be implicit, whereas in others the mask may be part of the vector. If a router knows 103 destinations, it may transmit the following 103 vectors as indicated in Figure 12.10.

Note that multiple vectors may be transmitted together in a single packet, or carried in multiple packets if need be. This amounts to one representation of its routing table. It is unlikely (but not impossible) that a router is directly connected to 103 subnetworks. At least a few of these vectors will in fact represent direct connections whose distance equals zero (from its perspective), and remote subnetwork prefixes, which have larger values for the distance parameter. The distance represents the hop-count, or the number of routers that must be crossed to reach the destination. Some distance-vector protocols use a more general "metric" than simple hop count.

In order to ensure that the routing protocol converges in a reasonable amount of time, an arbitrary diameter is imposed on the distance-vector Routing Domain. In RIP, the maximum number of routers that may be crossed in the domain is 15. Other distance-vector protocols may have different limits,[8] but all do impose a limit.

A router advertises the vectors it knows with its own locally perceived distance, allowing each neighbor the freedom to add 1 (or more than 1) hop to the route vector when it is received. Each router transmits its routing update periodically (in the case of RIP-IP, every 30 seconds; the Novell IPX version of RIP uses a 60 second update period). The specific behavior of which vectors are advertised, and whether or not the advertising router increments the hop count, or the receiving router does, are specific to each individual protocol. Distance-vector protocols exist that have more detailed vectors. The same core (prefix, mask, distance) elements usually appear, but other factors could be advertised as part of a longer vector, such as administrative weights, delay, utilization factors, etc.

$$\begin{aligned}
\text{vector}_1: &\quad (\text{prefix}_1, \text{mask}_1, \text{distance}_1) \\
\text{vector}_2: &\quad (\text{prefix}_2, \text{mask}_2, \text{distance}_2) \\
\text{vector}_3: &\quad (\text{prefix}_3, \text{mask}_3, \text{distance}_3) \\
&\qquad\qquad \bullet \\
&\qquad\qquad \bullet \\
&\qquad\qquad \bullet \\
\text{vector}_{103}: &\quad (\text{prefix}_{103}, \text{mask}_{103}, \text{distance}_{103})
\end{aligned}$$

FIGURE 12.10 Vectors representing 103 prefixes.

For efficiency reasons, there are techniques that are often used to limit the size of the periodic routing updates. For instance, if you receive a set of routes on an interface, you need not re-advertise them back out onto that interface—the router can assume that its neighbors also heard that update. This technique is known as "split horizon," and serves to reduce the size of routing updates by eliminating information that other neighbors on an interface should already know.

The prefixes received on all interfaces are part of the forwarding table, but they don't all need to be advertised out every interface. Figure 12.11 shows what split horizon is, and why it makes sense.

When R_2 needs to advertise routes onto the common prefix$_A$ LAN, it will omit all the routes it learned over that LAN (e.g., prefixes B, C, and D). It will only advertise routes that it has not learned via the common LAN (e.g., X, Y, or Z), as shown in Figure 12.12. Router R_1 has learned about prefixes B, C, and D from within the cloud at its left, and likewise Router R_2 has learned about prefixes X, Y, and Z from within the cloud to its right. The circles show what each router's internal forwarding table looks like.

It would be silly for R_2 to advertise B, C, or D back to R_1. For example, if R_2 advertised D to R_1, it would effectively be saying "You, R_1, can get to D in four hops by going through me." However, R_1 knows already that it can get to D in two hops without any help from R_2. R_2 also knows this; hence, there is no need to advertise a prefix back onto an interface from which it was learned. The advantage of split hori-

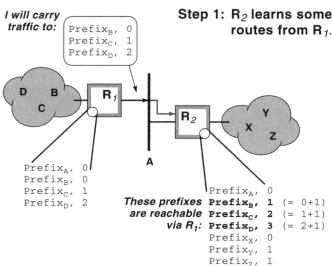

FIGURE 12.11 Split horizon in action—Step I.

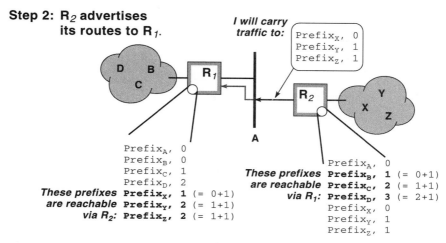

FIGURE 12.12 Split horizon in action—Step II.

zon is that it reduces the number of prefixes that need to be advertised, which reduces the amount of time that the routers must spend processing routing updates.

There is another optimization that is similar to split horizon, known as "poison reverse." If R_2 has learned routes from R_1 via A, it advertises them back over A with a cost of "infinity," which tells R_1 that those prefixes are definitely not reachable in R_2's. When topology changes happen, poison reverse actually helps improve the return to a stable state, or the convergence time. The down side of poison reverse is that each router must advertise its entire routing table, marking those prefixes that were received over an interface with a cost of infinity when transmitting them back out over that same interface. Using the same topology from Figures 12.11 and 12.12, we see the effect of poison reverse in Figure 12.13.

In the figure, we use a common value for "infinity," i.e., 16. Distance-vector protocols may choose bigger values in some cases, but the way infinite-cost routes are treated is the same. When Router R1 receives, for example, prefix B with a cost of 16 (infinity), it discards it upon receipt. Distance-vector protocols can encounter an error condition known as "count-to-infinity," which is beyond the scope of this book. However, it is worth noting that using poison reverse limits the impact of the count-to-infinity problem by having the cost on known-unreachable prefixes cranked immediately to infinity by their originating routers. The prefixes will then age out of the other routers' forwarding tables much more quickly, at the cost of forcing the every routing update to contain every prefix that each router knows. Any

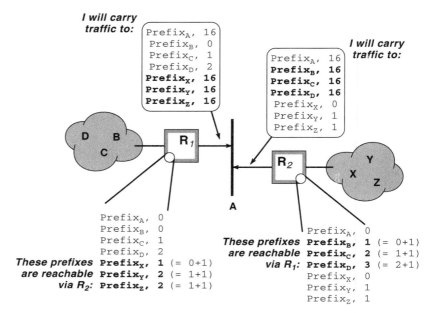

FIGURE 12.13   Poison reverse.

prefix that would have been suppressed by split horizon is advertised with a cost of
infinity in the poison reverse scheme.

The final technique to help improve the efficiency of distance-vector protocols
is the triggered update. In the event that a router sees an interface go down, it can
immediately transmit a route advertisement indicating that the prefixes that it formerly provided a path to are now an infinite distance away (as far as it is concerned).
Other routers in the Routing Domain may still have connectivity to these prefixes,
and this router will eventually learn this via the normal route update process. The
triggered update permits a router that has seen a topology change to immediately notify that either a route has disappeared (issue a new update with the distance set to
15), or that a new route has appeared (issue a new update that may just include this
one route; then incorporate it into the next regular update).

Summary of Distance-Vector Protocol Techniques

1. Periodic updates
2. Limited Routing Domain size (max. hops = infinity − 1)
3. Advertisements derived directly from forwarding table

4. Advertisements are multicast or broadcast onto every LAN wherever the protocol is active

5. Received updates can be easily incorporated into local forwarding table with a minimum of computation

6. Split Horizon can limit the size of routing updates

7. Poison Reverse can improve the convergence time, at the expense of larger routing updates

8. Triggered updates allow changes to be propagated as soon as they are detected, without possibly waiting up to [at least] 30 seconds until the next route advertisement happens

Link-State Routing Protocols

Link-state protocols are a bit more difficult to understand but about equally easy (or difficult, depending on your perspective) to configure. In distance-vector protocols, routers tell each other about essentially everything they know about—in the entire Routing Domain. Without split horizon or poison reverse, each router will hear lots of prefixes that it already has in its routing table. Unfortunately, each router only knows how far it is from each destination, with no idea of what the topology looks like.

Distance-vector routing updates are spread one link at a time using link-layer multicast or broadcast so that all the attached routers will hear routing updates. Link-state protocols also spread topology information only to neighbors on a link, but routers only have to advertise "links" that they are directly attached to. Each router tags its advertised links with its own routerID so that the routers build up a Link State Database which lists all the routers in the Routing Domain and tells what links each router is attached to.

Rather than being based on simply hop count, which is not always the best metric to use, link-state protocols associate a numerical "cost" with each link. Commonly, the cost is inversely proportional to the speed of the link—low-speed links have high cost, while high-speed links have low cost. In OSPF, a common link-state protocol, routers divide the link speed into 10^8 in order to compute the link's default cost. Network managers are free to override the router's default cost computation with their own chosen value. Figure 12.14 shows why hop count is not always the best way to judge which path is best. Hop count alone, in this case, will select the "slowest" path, while cost will select a path with more hops, but faster links.

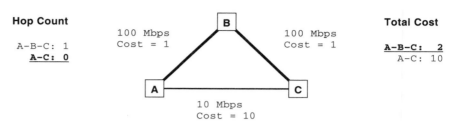

FIGURE 12.14   Hop count versus cost.

All routers in a Routing Domain must have a common view of the Link State Database (LSD). In order to achieve that goal, there is a reliable "flooding" mechanism in place that allows all the routers to quickly and accurately share their individual link status so they all know what all the other routers are attached to.

On LANs, link state updates are multicast (for efficiency). Routers pick up changes received on one interface and readvertise them onto other interfaces. The current LSD is downloaded by new routers, and then only changes need to be transmitted. In the absence of changes to the topology, the routers keep track of each others' presence by some kind of "Hello" protocol. If a neighbor stops transmitting Hellos, then you wait a while and delete it (and all its links) from the LSD. Periodically, the link state entries age out and must be flushed from the LSD.

Given the topology database, each router executes a graph-processing algorithm, perhaps[9] the one published by E. W. Dijkstra,[10] in 1959. In Dijkstra's algorithm, the router places itself at the root of a tree and works out from there until it has walked through all the links in the Link State Database. A router will build a forwarding table that tells it how far every other link is from itself, and which neighbor is the best next-hop to reach each destination.

One big distinction from distance-vector protocols is that the link-state routers form explicit "adjacencies" with each other to facilitate the reliable flooding procedure. This is extremely useful in practice, and well worth the extra effort to understand and deploy these protocols. For instance, on a router that is running OSPF, you can ask it to show you its current "neighbor status." At a glance, you can see which other routers are healthy and which are "down." The adjacencies are formed and maintained by a simple "Hello" protocol, which is how they detect when something is wrong with a neighbor. If several Hello_intervals go by without hearing any Hellos from a neighbor, then that neighbor is considered to be "down." Adjacencies are more than a neighbor state maintenance technique. Routers are adjacent when they have detected each other's presence *and* have synchronized their Link State Databases.

When a router boots, it issues a Hello message, which is seen by the other neighbor routers (that it does not yet know about). Hellos are usually multicast at the link layer, but they could be broadcast. The neighbors see the Hello, and they all issue Hellos in return that list all the routers that they see. Especially critical is the new router seeing itself listed in the Hellos of the other neighbors. That means that its Hello has been seen by them.

Once it has received a bunch of Hellos from neighbors, it reissues its Hello, this time listing all the neighbors whose Hellos it has seen. Now, when the neighbors receive the new neighbor's updated Hellos, they will know that 1) they could hear the new neighbor, so there is a valid communications path from the new neighbor to them, and 2) the neighbor heard them, so there is a valid communications path from them to the new neighbor. Once each side has seen its routerID in the other's Hellos, it knows that there is a valid two-way communications path between them.

Adjacencies can only form when there is a two-way path in place, and they are maintained by continuing the Hello protocol indefinitely. An adjacency is fully established once a router has exchanged (i.e., synchronized) its complete Link State Database with a peer router (on a LAN this would be the Designated Router). Whenever there is a change in the Link State Database, a router must spread the changed data to all its "fully adjacent" peers so that all routers are always up-to-date on which parts of the topology are active.

On a LAN, every router hears every other router's Hello packets. There would be a major traffic explosion if every router had to synchronize its Link State Database with every other router. This problem would only get worse if the network were larger, a very unfavorable scaling characteristic. In order to prevent this massive explosion of traffic, and to minimize the state that routers must keep, link-state protocols elect a Designated Router (DR) on a LAN. Most link-state routing protocols contain a router_priority variable that can be used to bias the DR election in favor of some preferred router(s).

The DR becomes fully adjacent with all the other routers with which it has established two-way connectivity. Any changes to the Link State Database are flooded to its (fully adjacent) neighbors, which is to say, all the other routers on the LAN. These updates cannot be multicast, since the LSD's integrity must be assured. Any link-state updates are unicast from the DR to all its adjacent peers. With the DR in place, only n copies of the link state updates must cross the LAN. Without the DR, each of the n routers would have sent a total of $n(n - 1)/2$ updates.[11] With the DR, one router on the LAN will tell the DR about some change(s) to the Link State Database, then the DR will repeat the change(s) to the other $n - 2$ routers.[12]

Some protocols (notably OSPF) elect a Backup DR (BDR) which can take over immediately in the event that the DR fails; a new BDR will then be elected

Faking out the Hello protocol

I have seen LAN switches that get into funny states, leading OSPF to believe that all is well when it is definitely not.[13] If a switch has failed in such a way that it is still flooding multicast frames, but is *not* forwarding unicasts, then all the routers on that LAN will think that their adjacencies are all still "up" when in fact no real data can be sent among any of them! Even though the Hello protocol, and the adjacency status it maintains, are normally very reliable and useful, they are not perfect—don't trust them completely.

among the remaining routers on the LAN. In protocols that specify a BDR, link state updates need to be sent to both the DR and BDR, which OSPF accomplishes by having a special multicast address for "all designated routers" (on a LAN). Link-state updates are multicast to that address.

Summary of Link-State Techniques

1. Neighbor discovery via a Hello protocol
2. Only form adjacencies when two-way connectivity exists
3. Reliable flooding algorithm enables all routers to share a common Link State Database
4. More flexible metrics
5. Choice of topology processing algorithm
6. Adjacency status is a very useful troubleshooting hint
7. Designated Router reduces update traffic on LANs, reducing the order n^2 number of updates to only order n

Static routing

Dynamic routing protocols are useful because they use the network itself to discover available paths within the network. However, there is a cost associated with operating a dynamic routing protocol: it uses some of the network's bandwidth to do its job. In some network scenarios, where bandwidth is extremely scarce, it may be possible, even desirable, to use static routing.

For an initial example, as in Figure 12.15, we can look at a small five-router network, with nine subnetworks. Each router will need to have a set of configuration commands to tell it which next-hop router serves every possible destination.

If we select router C, its routing commands must be something akin to the following (syntax borrowed from the Unix® operating system so as to remain nonrouter-vendor-specific):

```
route add A1 BB.A 1
route add A2 BB.A 1
route add B1 BB.B 1
route add D1 BB.D 1
route add D2 BB.D 1
route add D3 BB.D 1
route add E1 BB.D 2
```

The syntax above is "route add prefix/mask next-hop metric". In this example, we have used the network's label (from Figure 12.16) instead of inventing a bunch of prefix/mask combinations. Also, the IP addresses of the routers are represented as BB.C, etc., which means the IP address of router C's backbone interface. Using actual network numbers would only obfuscate the real lesson here, which is that a specific static route had to be added for each nonlocal network.

Each router needs to be configured so that it is aware of all valid destinations. If a new subnetwork is added, its prefix/mask, next-hop, and metric will need to be entered into the configurations of every router. If you have *m* routers and *k* subnet-

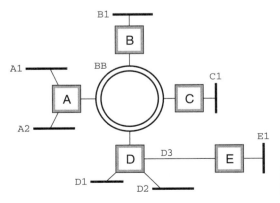

FIGURE 12.15 Basic static routing example.

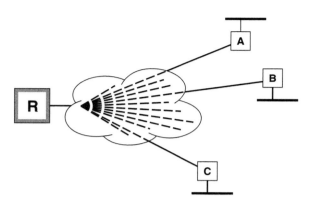

FIGURE 12.16 WAN static routing.

works, there will be on the order of $m*k$ configuration commands (it is actually always less than that, because you need not tell a router about networks that it is directly connected to).

That was a rather contrived example, just to familiarize ourselves with the concepts of static routing. Now, consider a WAN that is built from channelized T-1 circuits at a central site, with each remote site having a single 56/64 kbps circuit. In this case, the line speeds are slow enough that we might be concerned about running a dynamic routing protocol. Consider the following example, as shown in Figure 12.16.

The central-site T-1 circuit is partitioned into 24 independent channels at either 56 or 64 kbps. Sites A, B, and C have been drawn to illustrate the inherent asymmetry that makes static routing ideal in this scenario (and other similar ones, such as low-speed frame relay or X.25 PVCs). A remote site, for instance site B, needs only a very simple route statement:

```
route add 0.0.0.0 ~B 1
```

This command adds a "default" route to router B, which roughly translates into the following English statement: "Send all traffic that I don't explicitly know how to reach to the central-site router. Just send it out interface ~B, the unnumbered PPP link that leads to the central-site router." The central-site router will have a similar statement:

```
route add Bx v.B 1
```

This translates as: "Send all traffic destined for B's prefixes (e.g., Bx) out interface v.B, the unnumbered PPP link that leads to site B's router." What if the circuit is down? The PPP link status will be "down," so the router should mark interface v.B as being unusable. In such a case, if the router receives a packet destined for one of B's prefixes, it can send back an ICMP "destination unreachable" error message.

It is a shame, however, that the packet had to get all the way over to the last-hop router before the WAN link only to find the remote prefix(es) unreachable. It would be nice if there were a way for all the routers in the core to know whether or not some destination were reachable. If not, the packet could be discarded efficiently (the nearer to the source, the better). Static routing has no way to "advertise" changes—it is not really a routing protocol. Sometimes it makes sense to import some static routes into a dynamic routing protocol, for a hybrid static/dynamic solution.

Given the tedious, error-prone, and daunting task of explicitly telling every router about the existence of each prefix, static routing obviously does not scale for large installations.[14] But if "interior" routers do not know about these destinations, they will never forward traffic here. Generally, the remote prefixes are imported into whatever interior routing protocol is in use.[15] Once the prefixes have been imported into the dynamic routing protocol, they are advertised throughout that Routing Domain as if they had been learned via the dynamic protocol itself. Chapter 14 will explore several techniques for interconnecting Routing Domains that are executing different routing protocols.

REFERENCES

Huitema, Christian, *Routing in the Internet,* Englewood Cliffs, NJ: Prentice Hall, 1995.
Dijkstra, E. W., "A Note on Two Problems in Connection with Graphs," *Numerische Mathematic*, Vol. 1, pp. 269–271, 1959.

ENDNOTES

1. The fact that "RIP" appears with more than one network-layer protocol does not mean that each RIP is the same. They are all similar, but differ in various aspects, e.g., the size of the network number fields, the encapsulations, etc.
2. The interbuilding router can simply advertise a default route into the building. The default route allows intrabuilding routers to reach active subnets in other buildings without explicit knowledge of which remote subnet prefixes exist.

3. The second most important part is the Domain Name System (DNS), but DNS can't work if routing is broken.

4. There is a zeroth-order problem of how to assign addresses to organizations to use in identifying their unique parts of the global Internet. The address assignment function does require central coordination, though the job is split among various continental-scale "Internet Registries."

5. The routers that are the furthest away (topologically speaking) will take the longest to find out about the outage, whereas routers that are nearby will know about the outage much more quickly.

6. Loops may also be the result of misconfiguration, or of noninteroperable implementations of the same routing protocol specification.

7. Saying "destination" prefix is redundant. However, it is useful to reinforce the fact that routing protocols are concerned with two problems: 1) finding out about what places exist, and 2) determining the best way to get to them.

8. The Distance Vector Multicast Routing Protocol (DVMRP) is a RIP derivative which has a maximum hop count of 31.

9. Link-state protocols are defined by the fact that routers report their immediate link status and reliably "flood" the data into a distributed topology database; the algorithm that processes the topology data isn't required to be Dijkstra's.

10. Dijkstra is pronounced dike-stra.

11. If there are n routers, why not just send the update to the $n-1$ other routers? Well, $n(n - 1)$ counts all the updates, but it actually double-counts them, since each update need only be sent from one end of an adjacency. The other end need not send the update back to it. Thus, we actually need $n(n - 1)/2$ updates.

12. It will also propagate the changes to other neighbors on its other interfaces, if any.

13. No, I won't tell you what vendor's switch did this, since it was a bug. The point isn't that some vendor's switch did a weird thing, it is that the Hello protocol can be fooled.

14. Even if it did, a router seven hops away only knows what direction a destination is . . . it does not know if the destination is actually reachable.

15. It is even possible to have the advertisement of a prefix be contingent on the status of the circuit that leads to that prefix. This achieves a modicum of dynamism without wasting any bandwidth on the WAN link.

CHAPTER 13

RIP and OSPF

Dynamic routing protocols allow the routers to use the network to learn the shape of the network. The information that they start with is just their interfaces' defined address/mask pairs. By using the network to share this information with each other, they learn what destinations are active, or reachable. Moreover, not only do the routers learn what destinations exist, but they also learn enough information to decide which of their neighbor routers provides the best (i.e., shortest, fastest, cheapest, etc.) path to each destination.

Each router needs to know which of its neighbors is one step closer to all possible (i.e., currently reachable) destinations. When forwarding a packet, a router is either directly attached to the physical subnetwork that has been assigned a prefix that matches the packet's destination IP address, or it has not. When it is not directly attached to the destination's prefix, the router must forward the packet to another router, hopefully one that is closer to the packet's destination.

Dynamic routing protocols are resilient in the face of topology changes, such as:

- a router is disconnected from a LAN
- a link goes down (WAN or LAN)
- a new router is added to the internetwork
- new prefixes are added to the existing internetwork

When any topology change occurs, the other routers will detect this change and recompute their forwarding tables to reflect the new topology. In the case of an outage, there may be other paths around the outage that had not been chosen in the past because they were less preferred for some reason (e.g., slower links, more hops, etc.). In the case of new routers or prefixes being added, they are integrated into the existing forwarding tables. It is also possible that there is no way around the outage, in which case the routers on both sides of the outage will eventually forget about the destinations on the other side of the outage (until it is fixed).

RIP and OSPF are IP's most commonly deployed standards-based dynamic routing protocols. Understanding RIP and OSPF is a critical prerequisite to being able to design and operate modern IP networks. This chapter will cover the high-level functionality of both protocols, as well as describe a technique for migrating from RIP to OSPF. Advice will also be provided on the configuration of routers for maximum robustness, such as static, overridable routes that should be used as a backup in case the dynamic routing protocol is temporarily out of service.

RIP and OSPF are both classified as "Interior Gateway Protocols" (IGPs), as opposed to BGP and its ilk, which are "Exterior Gateway Protocols" (EGPs). The term EGP is confusing, because there was a protocol called EGP, which was the Internet's first backbone routing protocol, and EGP is also the name for the entire class of exterior routing protocols. If you hear the term EGP today, it probably refers to Exterior Gateway Protocols in general, not EGP, the obsolete exterior routing protocol.

ROUTING INFORMATION PROTOCOL

IP's Routing Information Protocol (RIP) was originally developed on Unix® systems, and several slightly different implementations predated its specification. RIP for IP imitated a very similar protocol within the XNS protocol suite. The Unix® implementations predated dedicated router hardware; in the old days, multihomed Unix® systems acted as routers. RFC-1058, written in June of 1988, was an attempt to write down the protocol to enable compliant implementations to interoperate. RFC-1058 represented a nonconflicting superset of several RIP variants' features. At the time, it was only the second routing protocol that had been specified in an RFC.[1]

The fact that RIP is the oldest, and thus the best known, "interior" routing protocol has created a situation in which it is quite prevalent, both in today's network equipment and in today's internetworks. Another factor that has acted in RIP's favor is that it is very simple, and people tend to use protocols that they understand, even though there may be better choices available. Eventually, other routing protocols were born and evolved, such as OSPF, Integrated IS-IS, BGP, etc.

RIPv1

The IETF has deemed RIPv1 to be Historic for a number of reasons, but chiefly it lacks the ability to work in a VLSM environment, including a CIDR environment. Also, the IETF has spent considerable time and effort developing better Interior Gateway Protocols, such as OSPF.[2] RIP is not dead, though; RIPv2 is a variant of RIP that supports VLSM and CIDR, and is now a full Internet Standard (RFC-2453).

Despite the fact that RIPv1 is now Historic, it is not "history" by a long shot. It is almost certainly still the most widely implemented and deployed routing protocol. RIP is a very simple distance-vector protocol. It has all the basic features of a distance-vector protocol, as described in Chapter 12. In this section, we will examine the specific features that make RIPv1 unique, including its packet format, update interval, and other items. We will also document the RIPv1 packet format for future reference.

RIPv1 packets are either requests or responses. A router that has just booted can broadcast a RIP request, which will cause all the other RIP speakers on that LAN to transmit their forwarding tables to the new router. The new router could have just waited 30 seconds for all the neighbors to send their regularly scheduled periodic updates, but sending a request is a quicker way to get itself up and running. Requests are one-time events, while responses are periodic, so the majority of RIP packets will be unsolicited responses.

As alluded to above, most routers update each other every 30 seconds with their current forwarding table. These updates are broadcast, so that all the neighbors on a LAN receive the update at essentially the same time. The updates serve two purposes. Besides the obvious—sharing what destinations each router can reach—the periodic updates are a way to discover a neighbor's existence. On WAN subnetworks that do not support broadcast, it may be necessary to send an update to each neighbor individually. Neighbors may be statically defined in each router, which would allow updates to be sent via unicast to each of them, or neighbors may be dynamically discovered, in which case future updates can be sent to active neighbors. The mechanisms for dealing with nonbroadcast subnetworks tend to be medium-dependent.

In addition to the normal periodic updates, which are effectively "all is well" messages, it is possible that a response may be triggered by a topology change. When a RIP router detects that an interface is going or has gone down, or a neighbor goes away, or a new subnetwork or neighbor is added, etc., it should send a "triggered update," which indicates the prefixes that need to be added or removed. RIP routers send triggered updates so that the new information may be propagated as quickly as possible across the Routing Domain, instead of simply waiting to send the change embedded within their next regular 30-second update. Each router that receives a triggered update will process it and then immediately propagate it away from the originating router so that the new routing information rapidly permeates the entire Routing Domain.

The output procedure in RIPv1 is very simple. In the unrefined default case, it amounts to transmitting the entire forwarding table out each interface. These routing updates are broadcast, so that the other routers get them at essentially the same time. As discussed in Chapter 12, Split Horizon and Poison Reverse are used to limit the size of the transmitted forwarding table, or to improve the protocol's convergence time (respectively). Split Horizon truncates route updates by not mentioning prefixes that were learned from that interface.

Poison Reverse sets these prefixes to a metric of infinity (16 in the case of RIPv1), so that the routing updates are the same size as if they had all been transmitted in full. Each destination prefix that a router is providing a path to is advertised with its local metric. However, when a router is not providing a path to a destination (i.e., for routes that Split Horizon would omit from updates), it advertises those prefixes with a metric of infinity. Poison Reverse can improve convergence time for some kinds of topology changes, but this improvement comes at the cost of transmitting maximum-size forwarding tables on a regular basis.

When a router receives a RIPv1 update, it will add at least one hop to each destination prefix before they are installed in the local forwarding table. This is the normal case. It is also possible that the network manager wants this router to use a different interface to reach some destination, and for such destinations the metric is increased by more than one, making the destination appear to be more hops away when going out this interface. This could be done on a per-interface basis (e.g., all routes received on this interface will be considered to be three hops further away, not one, or a per-neighbor basis, or even a per-prefix basis (i.e., certain routes received on this interface are *n* hops further away, not one).

Once a router has learned about a destination, it starts a timer for that destination. Future routing updates that are received and contain this destination reset the timer to zero. However, if time expires and that destination is not mentioned in routing updates, the router will eventually age that destination's entry out of the forwarding table.

In RIP (both versions 1 and 2), the maximum time that a prefix is valid—without it being refreshed by a new update—is 180 seconds (three minutes). If a forwarding table entry ever reaches the age of 180 seconds, it is moved into the "garbage collection" state for 120 seconds. During garbage collection, that destination is advertised as being unreachable (i.e., its hop count is increased to 16 in routing updates). If the garbage collection period expires and the router *still* has not heard a routing update regarding this destination, then the destination is removed from the forwarding table. Thus, the maximum lifetime of a RIP forwarding table entry is 300 seconds (five minutes), which is ten times the route advertisement interval. This is more than generous; most protocols consider the "lifetime" to be just three or four times the update interval.

The operation of RIP may be modified by the imposition of "routing policies." Perhaps the most obvious, and most useful, is to list the valid neighbors from which a router will accept routing updates. This policy can prevent routers from being misled by misconfigured routers that are placed on the network without permission of the network management staff. Beyond listing which neighbors are valid, it is possible to define a list of expected routes that should be received (or should *not* be received) on each interface. This is further protection and limits the scope of damage that may result from temporarily misconfigured routers.

The network manager knows the shape of the topology, and she may know that certain destinations should always be reachable via certain interfaces. Such rules are easiest to implement near the edges of a Routing Domain, since there are probably fewer alternate paths out at the edge. However, in the interior of the Routing Domain, it is likely that a topology change could result in a destination being reachable via a different interface than the most direct one. Suppose that there were a rule that said "destination X may only be learned on interface 8," and the topology changed such that destination X would validly be reachable via interface 11. Such a rule would have the result that the router would never learn the new path to destination X, and destination X would age out of the forwarding table.

One path that is very important to keep track of is the "default route," (the path that represents all destinations that are not explicitly in the forwarding table) and it is important to tell the routers where the default route should or, more importantly, should not be learned from. At the edge, a safety rule might be to say that the default route should not be learned from the "edge side" of the router. It is safe for the router to learn the default route via one of its core-facing interfaces as in Figure 13.1.

Policy rules may be either positive (i.e., "just this list of destination prefixes may be learned") or negative (i.e., "any destination prefixes *except* this list may be learned"). The rules may be interface-specific or even neighbor-specific (e.g., a separate inclusion and/or exclusion list per neighbor). Besides controlling what the router learns, policy rules can also be used to control what destinations the router advertises, and moreover to which interface(s) or which neighbor(s) certain destinations are advertised. If the Routing Domain's configurations are carefully protected by routing policy rules, then it will be much more stable. The policy rules give the routers a real-

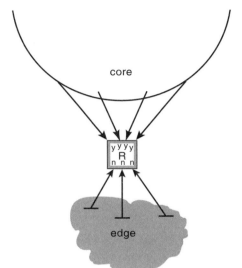

FIGURE 13.1   Controlling the default route.

time sanity check that makes them resilient against malicious, misconfigured, or misbehaving routers.

RIPv1 is encapsulated in UDP packets and transmitted on LANs as an IP limited-broadcast packet.[3] Each RIP update can contain up to 25 route objects, each of which occupies 20 bytes of the packet. The packet format of a RIP over UDP packet is shown in Figure 13.2. The IP header is omitted to conserve space, and also because it has been shown before (Figure 1.10).

The byte numbers above are based on a maximum-sized IP header (60 bytes), and would be reduced by 40 in the case of an IP header with no options.

The UDP header has both its source and destination port set to 0x0208 (520 in decimal), and the length field would be 0x0200 (512) in the case of a maximum-sized packet since the UDP length includes the eight-byte UDP header as well as the four-byte RIP header and the 500 bytes of route objects (25 objects at 20 bytes each).

The RIP header specifies a "version" field of 0x01 (1), and a "command" field that indicates whether this packet is a request (0x01) or a response (0x02). RIP updates are responses. The purpose of a RIP request is to ask for a route to some particular destination, or to ask for the entire current forwarding table. The latter is useful when a router has just booted, which saves it from waiting up to 30 seconds for all its neighboring routers to send it their regular routing updates.

```
                          1                   2                   3
Byte#   0 1 2 3 4 5 6 7 8 9 0 1 2 3 4 5 6 7 8 9 0 1 2 3 4 5 6 7 8 9 0 1
        +=+=+=+=+=+=+=+=+=+=+=+=+=+=+=+=+=+=+=+=+=+=+=+=+=+=+=+=+=+=+=+=+
   64 I      Source Port = 0x0208 (520)    I    Dest. Port = 0x0208 (520)   I UDP
        +--------------------------------------+-------------------------------+
   68 I   Len. [UDP+RIP = 0x0200 (512)]    I        UDP Checksum              I UDP
        +=+=+=+=+=+=+=+=+=+=+=+=+=+=+=+=+=+=+=+=+=+=+=+=+=+=+=+=+=+=+=+=+
   72 I    Command      I    Version       I         Must Be Zero            I RIP
        +----------------+-----------------+-------------------------------+
      I    Address Family Identifier       I         Must Be Zero            I Dest.01
        +----------------------------------+-------------------------------+
      I                        IP Address                                    I Dest.01
        +--------------------------------------------------------------------+
      I                        Must Be Zero                                  I Dest.01
        +--------------------------------------------------------------------+
      I                        Must Be Zero                                  I Dest.01
        +--------------------------------------------------------------------+
   92 I                           Metric                                     I Dest.01
        +--------------------------------------------------------------------+

                                      o
                                      o

        +------------------+-----------------+-------------------------------+
      I    Address Family Identifier       I         Must Be Zero            I Dest.25
        +------------------+-----------------+-------------------------------+
      I                        IP Address                                    I Dest.25
        +--------------------------------------------------------------------+
      I                        Must Be Zero                                  I Dest.25
        +--------------------------------------------------------------------+
      I                        Must Be Zero                                  I Dest.25
        +--------------------------------------------------------------------+
  572 I                           Metric                                     I Dest.25
        +--------------------------------------------------------------------+
```

FIGURE 13.2 RIPv1 over UDP packet format.

Each route object contains an Address Family Identifier, which is 2 for IP. This field could conceivably allow destinations from multiple address families to be mixed within a single RIP update. Routers are supposed to skip route objects with address families that they do not support. To the author's knowledge, most RIPv1 implementations only support IPv4 addresses. Finally, each route object contains a metric, which is a 32-bit field, but can only take on values of 0x00-00-00-00 through 0x00-00-00-10 (0 through 16, inclusive). A metric value of 0x00-00-00-10 (i.e., 16) means that a route is unreachable. Observe that the metric could clearly have been expressed within an 8-bit field.[4]

If a router were advertising a destination prefix of 10.147.98.0 (0x0A.93.62.00) at a metric of 9, the route object would appear as in Figure 13.3. Remember that the prefix's mask is interpreted based on the mask of the interface that receives the advertised prefix. So, if the receiving interface is inside network 10 and has an interface mask of 255.255.254.0, then that interface's mask will be assumed to be the mask of the received route. If, however, the receiving interface is not in network 10.0.0.0, then the destination will be interpreted as a route to 10.0.0.0/8, and the non-zero values in the second and third bytes will be ignored.

```
      +-----------------------------------+-----------------------------------+
0x00.02'00.00 |0 0 0 0 0 0 0 0 0 0 0 0 0 0 0 1 0|0 0 0 0 0 0 0 0 0 0 0 0 0 0 0 1|
      +-----------------------------+-----------------------------------------+
0x0A.93.62.00 |0 0 0 0 1 0 1 0.1 0 0 1 0 0 1 1.0 1 1 0 0 0 1 0.0 0 0 0 0 0 0 0|
      +-----------------------------+-----------------------------------------+
0x00.00.00.00 |0 0 0 0 0 0 0 0 0 0 0 0 0 0 0 0 0 0 0 0 0 0 0 0 0 0 0 0 0 0 0 0|
      +-----------------------------------------------------------------------+
0x00.00.00.00 |0 0 0 0 0 0 0 0 0 0 0 0 0 0 0 0 0 0 0 0 0 0 0 0 0 0 0 0 0 0 0 0|
      +-----------------------------------------------------------------------+
0x00.00.00.09 |0 0 0 0 0 0 0 0 0 0 0 0 0 0 0 0 0 0 0 0 0 0 0 0 0 0 0 0 1 0 0 1|
      +-----------------------------------------------------------------------+
```

FIGURE 13.3   Example route object (10.147.98.0, metric = 9).

Only 25 destinations may be advertised in one RIP packet, at 20 bytes for each destination. A maximum-sized RIP packet can therefore have up to 500 bytes of route data. The RIP packet has a four-byte header, which is itself encapsulated in the eight-byte UDP header. So the UDP + RIP portion of a maximum-size RIP packet is up to 512 bytes long. An IP header may be up to 60 bytes long, though it is usually 20 bytes long when it has no options. The RIP length was chosen to be short enough so that the RIP route data, plus all the necessary headers (including a worst-case maximum-sized IP header) will still be less than IP's required minimum MTU of 576 bytes.

If a router needs to advertise 672 routes, RIP requires that 27 packets be transmitted. The first 26 of these will carry 25 routes each, making them all 532 byte packets (because there probably won't be any IP options). The final RIP update will only carry 22 routes, so the packet will be 60 bytes shorter (since three route objects consume 60 bytes), or 472 bytes. Thus, a total of [26 * 532) + 472 =] 14,304 bytes of bandwidth has been consumed.

Curiously, RIP does not use link MTUs when transmitting its updates. An Ethernet frame, whose MTU is 1500 bytes, could contain a maximum-sized IP header (60 bytes), a UDP header (eight bytes), the RIP header (four bytes), and 71 route objects (1420 bytes, at 20 bytes each), for a total of 1492 bytes, which just fits into an Ethernet frame. If RIP could do this, it would reduce the number of packets that it would need to transmit. In the example above, only 10 packets would need to be transmitted (instead of 27). The first nine would be full-sized, each with 1452 bytes[5] and 71 routes inside, and the last one would have only 33 routes, at 692 bytes. The 10 packets will have consumed 13,760 bytes of bandwidth, 544 bytes less than before.

The big win isn't the 3.8 percent reduction in bandwidth usage, but the fact that we are sending 17 fewer packets. Some routers have RIP implementations with a difficulty receiving lots of back-to-back packets, which can prevent them from learning about certain routes. Reducing the number of packets sent would tend to ameliorate that problem. Unfortunately, RIP does not allow the transmission of "large" link-MTU-sized packets, so RIP domains maybe limited in their scalability by the number of back-to-back packets that its routers can receive.

The worst aspect of RIP's strategy of always transmitting the entire forwarding table is that *it always transmits the entire forwarding table!* A way to classify RIP is as a "no news is bad news" protocol. The first received RIP update says "I can get to this set of destinations: { . . . }." The next update says the same thing, and the one after that as well, and so on. The only way to detect a change is to keep comparing received updates against the local forwarding table (triggered updates help a bit by allowing immediate notification of changes). RIP is often called "chatty," partially because its updates are broadcast to all stations, but mostly because it repeatedly transmits redundant information.

A "no news is good news" protocol would not worry about a destination being unreachable unless it was explicitly told that a change had occurred. In OSPF, which we will examine shortly, once the Link State Database is synchronized, a router has learned the entire topology. Thereafter, only changes need to be transmitted, saving enormous amounts of bandwidth compared to RIP. In stable networks very few updates will be necessary, and the routers only need to keep track of their immediate neighbors to ensure that there have not been any changes. Apple's AppleTalk Update-based Routing Protocol (AURP) is an example of a "no news is good news" distance-vector routing protocol.

RIPv1 SUMMARY

* Widely used, despite its official "Historic" status
* A classful routing protocol
* If a network number is being subnetted, the mask must be uniform throughout
* Periodically broadcasts routing updates (every 30 seconds)
* Prefixes live for 180 seconds after the last update was heard
* Prefixes then enter the Garbage Collection state for 120 seconds
* RIP Routing Domains are limited to a diameter of 15 hops
* Split Horizon can be used to limit the size of routing updates
* Poison Reverse can be used to improve RIPs convergence time
* Triggered updates allow information about changes to spread quickly

- Routing policies can control what routes get advertised or received
- RIP is encapsulated in UDP, using port 520 (0x208)
- Updates are up to 572 bytes (to stay within IP's minimum MTU, 576 bytes)
- Each RIP update reports on the presence of up to 25 destinations at a time, each of which consumes 20 bytes of the RIP packet

RIPv2 ENHANCEMENTS

In order to allow RIP to support VLSM and CIDR, it has been updated as RIPv2 (RFC-2453). This RFC is now a full Internet Standard (STD-56). The impetus for improving RIP was the fact that it did not support VLSM; the initial work came when CIDR and supernetting were just beginning to be discussed. A classless version of RIP seemed to be a requirement for it to remain useful in the future Internet.

In the course of updating RIP, other features were added so that RIPv2 not only supports subnet mask information but also route object tags, allowing external routes to be processed differently than internal ones. Routing updates can also be authenticated in RIPv2, which is another tool to help ensure the correctness of routing information.

The final important feature is the inclusion of support for a "next-hop" attribute on certain routes. This feature allows a router to advertise a route as being reachable by some other router that is not currently speaking RIPv2. Previously (i.e., in RIPv1), when a router advertised a destination, the advertising router itself was considered to be the next-hop toward that destination. In some cases, notably on the boundaries between Routing Domains where all the routers may not be speaking the same routing protocol, it is useful to be able to advertise a route saying, "here is destination N, but don't send traffic destined for N to me, instead send it to router X." This scenario will be described in detail below, as it is also a feature of OSPF and it is important to understand when and why this is a useful feature.

RIPv2 copies most of the mechanisms and packet formats directly from RIPv1. RIPv2 domains are also limited to 15 hops; destinations are transmitted and received in very similar manners. How does RIPv2 carry the extra information necessary to implement its new features? One clever trick is that RIPv2 supports a multicast address: 224.0.0.9. If the RIPv2 routers speak to each other using this multicast address instead of the broadcast address, their messages will not be heard by RIPv1 speakers on the same LAN.[6] The RIPv2 specification recommends that implementations use the broadcast address by default, making the use of multicast optional.

The new RIPv2 packet format is the same as RIPv1, in that the basic structure of the packet and the meaning of most fields is identical to that specified in RFC-1058. Figure 13.4 illustrates the RIPv2 packet format.

As in Figure 13.1, the IP header has been omitted. Moreover, Figure 13.3 also assumes that the worst-case 60-byte IP header precedes the UDP header. Reduce all the byte counts by 40 to get the numbers for the common case of a 20-byte IP header.

The structure of the RIPv2 packet, including that of the route objects, is the same as RIPv1 in that they are the same size and all the fields are the same size. The Address Family Identifier is still going to be two for IPv4. The new "Route Tag" field could be used for an Autonomous System (AS) number from an Exterior Gateway Protocol, but the exact usage of this field is not defined in the RIPv2 specification. The IP Address field is unchanged from RIPv1, but the two succeeding fields that used to be eight bytes of all 0s are now the "subnet mask" and the "Next Hop" attributes. The subnet mask is represented in binary, so a mask of 255.192.0.0 is 11111111.11000000.00000000.00000000. Other mask values are similarly converted from decimal to binary and stuffed into this four-byte field. If you prefer

```
                      1                   2                   3
Byte#   0 1 2 3 4 5 6 7 8 9 0 1 2 3 4 5 6 7 8 9 0 1 2 3 4 5 6 7 8 9 0 1
      +=+=+=+=+=+=+=+=+=+=+=+=+=+=+=+=+=+=+=+=+=+=+=+=+=+=+=+=+=+=+=+=+
 64 I     Source Port = 0x0208 (520)    I   Dest. Port = 0x0208 (520)   I UDP
      +-------------------------------+-------------------------------+
 68 I  Len. [UDP+RIP = 0x0200 (512)]  I           UDP Checksum         I UDP
      +=+=+=+=+=+=+=+=+=+=+=+=+=+=+=+=+=+=+=+=+=+=+=+=+=+=+=+=+=+=+=+=+
 72 I    Command     I    Version      I              Unused           I RIP
      +-----------------------------------------------------------------+
    I     Address Family Identifier    I           Route Tag           I Dest.01
      +-------------------------------+-------------------------------+
    I                         IP Address                              I Dest.01
      +-----------------------------------------------------------------+
    I                        Subnet Mask                              I Dest.01
      +-----------------------------------------------------------------+
    I                         Next Hop                                I Dest.01
      +-----------------------------------------------------------------+
 92 I                          Metric                                 I Dest.01
      +-----------------------------------------------------------------+
                                    o
                                    o
      +---------------+---------------+-------------------------------+
    I     Address Family Identifier    I           Route Tag           I Dest.25
      +-------------------------------+-------------------------------+
    I                         IP Address                              I Dest.25
      +-----------------------------------------------------------------+
    I                        Subnet Mask                              I Dest.25
      +-----------------------------------------------------------------+
    I                         Next Hop                                I Dest.25
      +-----------------------------------------------------------------+
572 I                          Metric                                 I Dest.25
      +-----------------------------------------------------------------+
```

FIGURE 13.4 RIPv2 over UDP packet format.

to write masks as /n, then simply set the first 'n' bits to 1 and leave the remaining 32-n bits set to 0.[7]

Earlier we mentioned that Authentication of routing updates was a new feature in RIPv2, yet Figure 13.4 shows no place for such a feature. The implementation of Authentication is quite clever. A special value of the Address Family Identifier is reserved that serves to extend the four-byte RIP header, as in Figure 13.5.

Authentication data occupies what would otherwise be the first route object, leaving room for only 24 total route objects instead of 25. The packet's overall size is unaffected by the use of Authentication. The Address Family Identifier value of 0xFFFF means that this first sequence of 20 bytes is not a route object but Authentication data. RFC-2453 only specifies simple password authentication, but RFC-2082 describes a way to use MD-5 to authenticate RIPv2 routing packets. OSPF has a similar mechanism that uses MD-5 to protect the Hello protocol.[8]

The Next Hop attribute is interesting and useful, so we will examine it in detail. Consider the topology in Figure 13.6.

Router B has learned a set of destinations from Router A via OSPF, but Router C does not speak OSPF. Router B knows that Router C does not speak OSPF (otherwise it would be an OSPF neighbor). Rather than readvertise all of the OSPFF-learned prefixes to Router C without the Next Hop attribute, Router B tags each of

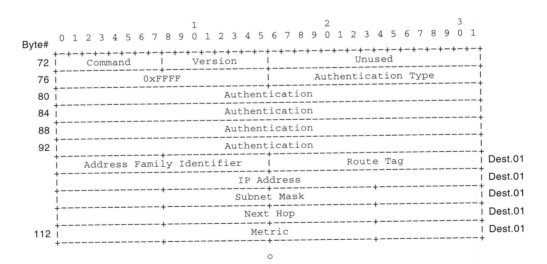

FIGURE 13.5 Authentication in RIPv2.

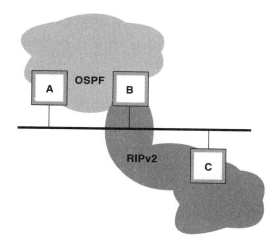

FIGURE 13.6 Applicability of the next hop attribute.

the OSPF-learned prefixes with Router A's IP address. Now Router C will learn that these destination prefixes are reachable via Router A and will send packets to those destinations via Router A, which is the most direct path. (Some of the prefixes in the OSPF domain may be more directly reached via Router B, in which case it would not place any IP address on their Next Hop field.)

If the Next Hop attribute had not been used, then Router C would have considered Router B to be the next-hop gateway for those destinations, and then Router B might end up forwarding some of the traffic back over the LAN to Router A, as in Figure 13.7.

Not all the traffic would flow this way. Any destinations for which Router B is the best next-hop will not have the Next Hop attribute set, so that Router C will use Router B to get to those destinations. The Next Hop attribute enables all the packets to Router A's prefixes to only cross the link once. Figure 13.8 shows the what happens when the Next Hop attribute is used.

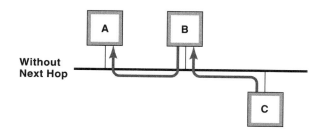

Without Next Hop

FIGURE 13.7 Forwarding without the next hop attribute.

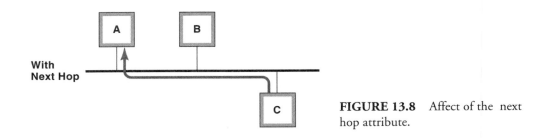

FIGURE 13.8   Affect of the next hop attribute.

Another way to work around this issue would be for A and B to both run RIPv2, so that A could advertise its reachable destinations to Router C directly. The Next Hop attribute allows only one of the OSPF speakers to advertise all the routes, and still have the non-OSPF routers pick the correct next-hop OSPF routers to reach all the known OSPF destinations.

RIPv2 SUMMARY

- Now a full Internet Standard
- A classless routing protocol (supports both VLSM and CIDR)
- Updates are broadcast every 30 seconds as in RIPv1
- New feature: Optionally updates can be multicast to 224.0.0.9 (also every 30 seconds)
- Prefix lifetimes as in RIPv1
- RIP Routing Domains [still] limited to a diameter of 15 hops
- Split Horizon, Poison Reverse, and Triggered updates, as in RIPv1
- Routing policies as in RIPv1
- RIP is encapsulated just like RIPv1
- New feature: Authentication of routing update packets
- New feature: Next Hop optimizes forwarding over exchange LANs
- New feature: Tagging of routes as external to the RIPv2 Routing Domain

OPEN SHORTEST PATH FIRST

OSPF, now a full Internet Standard (STD-54, RFC-2328), is the IETF's recommended Interior Gateway Protocol per RFC-1371 ("Choosing a Common IGP for the IP Internet"). It is much more complex to write an OSPF implementation than a

RIP implementation. At the time that OSPF was designed, RIP was the only routing protocol in common use, and RIP was less than optimal, as described above. OSPF was an attempt to build an improved Interior Gateway Protocol for the Internet. Luckily, there had been extensive experience with link-state routing protocols in the Internet community (see RFC-1074, "NSFNET Backbone SPF-Based Interior Gateway Protocol").

OSPF was originally developed by John Moy, then of Proteon. Proteon allowed their internally-developed routing protocol to be standardized within the IETF. The first OSPF RFC was published in October of 1989. The final, full Internet Standard version, RFC-2328, was published in April of 1998, after eight and a half years of hard work by John and the rest of the OSPF Working Group.

OSPF is comprised of two major interrelated components: its Hello protocol and its "reliable flooding" mechanism. The Hello protocol enables OSPF to detect neighbors and to confirm their continued exsitence.[9] The Hello protocol operates on each active OSPF interface, and it uses multicast addresses so that the traffic does not bother non-OSPF speakers. The reliable flooding algorithm ensures that all the routers (in an OSPF area) always have a consistent Link State Database.

Forwarding table entries are derived from the OSPF Link State Database using a slightly modified version of Dijkstra's graph-processing algorithm. If all the routers did not share a common Link State Database, then they would not all calculate the same forwarding table, thereby causing forwarding loops or black holes to form. OSPF operates over IP, so it supports all LAN and WAN technologies that are supported by IP. Figure 13.9 separates the various technologies into their respective categories. The NBMA technologies can also be modeled as "Point-to-MultiPoint" domains.

Since OSPF is encapsulated in IP, using protocol number 0x59 (89), it can run over anything that IP runs over. The main difference between subnetwork types

Broadcast-Capable	Point-to-Point	Non-Broadcast, Multiple-Access (NBMA)	Point-to-Multi-Point
LANs – Ethernet – FDDI – Token Ring – etc.	WAN – PPP	WANs – Frame Relay – X.25 – ATM PVCs – ATM SVCs	WANs – Frame Relay – X.25 – ATM PVCs – ATM SVCs
WAN – SMDS			

FIGURE 13.9 Subnetwork topologies supported by OSPF.

is how the neighbors are discovered. OSPF's Hello protocol is always used for neighbor discovery, but the way the subnetworks are represented in the Link State Database is different.

OSPF has a common 24-byte packet header that precedes all of its different packet types. Figure 13.10 shows this common header, which immediately follows the IP header (again, the IP Protocol field is set to 0x59 in all OSPF packets). The format of the data that follows this header depends on the value of the Type field, which has its five defined OSPF Types (listed in the figure).

Hello Protocol

The Hello protocol's packets are multicast onto those router interfaces on which OSPF is enabled. Per RFC-2328 and RFC-1700, the destination address for Hello packets is 224.0.0.5 (all OSPF routers). This multicast address is represented on Ethernet LANs as 0x01-00-5E-00-00-05. It is always the case that packets sent to multicast addresses from the range 224.0.0.0 – 224.0.0.255 (i.e., 224.0.0.0/24) are supposed to be transmitted with the packet's TTL set to one. (If a sender mistakenly uses a TTL greater than one, the receivers are supposed to know that these multicast destinations are not to be forwarded.) These packets are multicast on LANs, rather than broadcast, so that non-OSPF speakers will not be bothered with OSPF's Hello (keepalive) traffic.[10]

```
                        1                   2                   3
    0 1 2 3 4 5 6 7 8 9 0 1 2 3 4 5 6 7 8 9 0 1 2 3 4 5 6 7 8 9 0 1
   +-+-+-+-+-+-+-+-+-+-+-+-+-+-+-+-+-+-+-+-+-+-+-+-+-+-+-+-+-+-+-+-+
   |    Version    |     Type      |         Packet Length         |
   +-+-+-+-+-+-+-+-+-+-+-+-+-+-+-+-+-+-+-+-+-+-+-+-+-+-+-+-+-+-+-+-+
   |                          Router ID                            |
   +-+-+-+-+-+-+-+-+-+-+-+-+-+-+-+-+-+-+-+-+-+-+-+-+-+-+-+-+-+-+-+-+
   |                           Area ID                             |
   +-+-+-+-+-+-+-+-+-+-+-+-+-+-+-+-+-+-+-+-+-+-+-+-+-+-+-+-+-+-+-+-+
   |           Checksum            |            AuType             |
   +-+-+-+-+-+-+-+-+-+-+-+-+-+-+-+-+-+-+-+-+-+-+-+-+-+-+-+-+-+-+-+-+
   |                        Authentication                         |
   +-+-+-+-+-+-+-+-+-+-+-+-+-+-+-+-+-+-+-+-+-+-+-+-+-+-+-+-+-+-+-+-+
   |                        Authentication                         |
   +-+-+-+-+-+-+-+-+-+-+-+-+-+-+-+-+-+-+-+-+-+-+-+-+-+-+-+-+-+-+-+-+

      Version: 2

        Type          Description
       ------    --------------------------
          1      Hello
          2      Database Description
          3      Link State Request
          4      Link State Update
          5      Link State Acknowledgment
```

FIGURE 13.10   OSPF's common header.

OSPF's Hellos are, by default, transmitted every 10 seconds, Hello Interval. The continued presence of Hello packets from a router tells the other routers that it is still alive. If four Hello Intervals pass without hearing a Hello from a neighbor, that neighbor is declared to be "down." Using the default value for the Hello Interval (10 seconds), the router dead time is 40 seconds.

The OSPF Hello protocol has multiple functions:

1. It advertises a router's "aliveness"
2. It verifies two-way connectivity
3. It avoids one-way connectivity
4. It elects Designated and Backup Designated Routers
5. It maintains OSPF Adjacencies, once they are etablished

When a router first initializes OSPF on an interface, it begins transmitting Hello packets. The first Hello tells the other routers (if any) that there is a new neighbor present. If this router is the only neighbor on the LAN, it won't know that for up to 10 seconds. If it is the only router present, then it declares itself to be the Designated Router (DR) for that subnetwork. Before describing the DR election procedure, we will examine the concepts of one-way and two-way connectivity.

RIP cannot detect one-way links. In a RIP environment, if a link, such as the one in Figure 13.11, were one-way, then Router A will receive a set of routes from Router B, but any traffic forwarded from Router A to those destinations will not be able to cross the link (since the link is broken such that traffic can only flow from B to A, *but not from A to B*). Such a one-way link is represented by the electrical symbol for the diode, which only allows current to pass in one direction, blocking it in the opposite direction.

Note that Router B never hears Router A's advertised routes. Therefore, Router B cannot send traffic to destinations reachable via Router A, even though the path from B to A would allow packets to pass through.

OSPF's Hello protocol allows detection of one-way links (not an uncommon failure mode). To accomplish this goal, OSPF routers simply list neighboring routers' RouterIDs in their Hello packets. Consider the case in which there are only two routers, $Router_1$ and $Router_2$. If either router is alone on their common subnet-

FIGURE 13.11 One-way (diode) link.

work, then there will not be an active neighbor. If Router$_1$ had been alone, and then Router$_2$ joins it, Router$_2$'s initial Hello will just serve to identify its existence.

Then Router$_1$'s next Hello will list Router$_2$'s RouterID. When Router$_2$ receives this Hello from Router$_1$, Router$_2$ know that Router$_1$ has seen Router$_2$'s Hello packet. Similarly, once Router$_2$ has received a Hello from Router$_1$, it will also report Router$_1$'s RouterID in Router$_2$'s Hellos. Router$_1$ will then know that Router$_2$ has seen its Hellos. Figure 13.12 shows the sequence of events between these two routers.

As long as both routers are up, and OSPF continues to be enabled on their common subnetwork, they will each keep transmitting Hellos that lists all their neighbors, every Hello Interval. We make the common sense assumption that if Router$_1$ sees its own RouterID in Router$_2$'s Hellos, that Router$_2$ will also be seeing its own RouterID in Router$_1$'s Hellos; i.e., if one neighbor sees the medium as two-way, the other will too. This property of broadcast media is known as transitivity, meaning that if A and B have a two-way communications path, and so do B and C, then A and C should also have a two-way communications path.[11] OSPF routers will not attempt to form an adjacency (i.e., synchronize Link State Databases) until they see themselves as sharing a two-way data link.

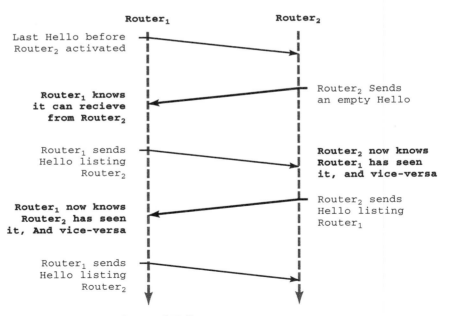

FIGURE 13.12 Exchange of Hellos.

Figure 13.13 shows the format of the OSPF Hello packet. The common OSPF header is not shown, in order to save space. As indicated above, the router's neighbors are listed at the end of the packet.

OSPF does not do fragmentation, so the link MTU limits how many neighbors an OSPF router may have. Given a 60-byte IP header (worst-case), a 24-byte OSPF header, and the 20-byte Hello header, we have consumed 104 bytes of the 1500 byte Ethernet MTU, leaving 1496 for listing our neighbors' RouterIDs. 1496/4 = 374, which is probably more than enough for a LAN environment, but on a frame relay WAN, with a 1500-byte MTU, this limit could be a significant scaling constraint.

The Hello packet's Network Mask field is set by the transmitting router to be the mask of the interface on which the Hello is being transmitted. A /18 would be represented as 0xFF-FF-C0-00, a /13 as 0xFF-F8-00-00, and so on. This information is used by its neighbors, in conjunction with the transmitting router's source IP address, to enable them to decide whether or not they are within the same prefix as the transmitting router. (Two routers will not form an OSPF adjacency unless they are both members of the same IP prefix).

The Hello packet format contains several fields on which all routers attached to a common subnetwork must agree. The HelloInterval must be the same on all the routers, as well as the RouterDeadInterval. OSPF's specification says that the HelloInterval is 10 seconds, and the RouterDeadInterval is 40 seconds, but these values can be adjusted by network managers, and the ratio between the two need not be 1:4. The OSPF common header also has a field that all the routers must set identi-

```
                    1                   2                   3
  0 1 2 3 4 5 6 7 8 9 0 1 2 3 4 5 6 7 8 9 0 1 2 3 4 5 6 7 8 9 0 1
  :                               :                             :
  +-+-+-+-+-+-+-+-+-+-+-+-+-+-+-+-+-+-+-+-+-+-+-+-+-+-+-+-+-+-+-+-+
  |                          Network Mask                         |
  +-+-+-+-+-+-+-+-+-+-+-+-+-+-+-+-+-+-+-+-+-+-+-+-+-+-+-+-+-+-+-+-+
  |         HelloInterval          |     Options     |   Rtr Pri  |
  +-+-+-+-+-+-+-+-+-+-+-+-+-+-+-+-+-+-+-+-+-+-+-+-+-+-+-+-+-+-+-+-+
  |                        RouterDeadInterval                     |
  +-+-+-+-+-+-+-+-+-+-+-+-+-+-+-+-+-+-+-+-+-+-+-+-+-+-+-+-+-+-+-+-+
  |                        Designated Router                     |
  +-+-+-+-+-+-+-+-+-+-+-+-+-+-+-+-+-+-+-+-+-+-+-+-+-+-+-+-+-+-+-+-+
  |                    Backup Designated Router                  |
  +-+-+-+-+-+-+-+-+-+-+-+-+-+-+-+-+-+-+-+-+-+-+-+-+-+-+-+-+-+-+-+-+
  |                            Neighbor                          |
  +-+-+-+-+-+-+-+-+-+-+-+-+-+-+-+-+-+-+-+-+-+-+-+-+-+-+-+-+-+-+-+-+
  |                            Neighbor                          |
  +-+-+-+-+-+-+-+-+-+-+-+-+-+-+-+-+-+-+-+-+-+-+-+-+-+-+-+-+-+-+-+-+
  :                               :                             :
```

FIGURE 13.13   OSPF hello packet format.

cally, namely, the AreaID field. Before two OSPF neighbors will become adjacent these parameters must either exactly agree or be consistent with each other.

When the Hello protocol is operating over a broadcast medium, such as a LAN, we can trivially generalize the two-party example to the situation where a router initializes and there are already 'n' OSPF routers present on a LAN. On a stable LAN, each of the Hellos will list all of the active neighbor routers (as well as the LAN's DR and BDR). Therefore, the new router immediately learns about all its neighbors after hearing just one Hello packet. By the principle of transitivity, if the router knows that it has a two-way communication path to one neighbor, then it has two-way connectivity to all of that neighbor's neighbors. A way to paraphrase this is "a neighbor of my neighbor is also my neighbor." When the new router sends its next Hello packet, it will list all of its neighbors' RouterIDs in its Hello packet. After it has established two-way connectivity to all its new neighbors,[12] it will form adjacencies (i.e., synchronize link state databases) with the DR and BDR.

Forming Adjacencies

All OSPF routers on a subnetwork do not necessarily form adjacencies. By "forming an adjacency" we mean that a pair of routers exchanges and then maintains the common Link State Database. If each possible pair of routers on a LAN had to exchange their Link State Databases with each other, an excessive amount of traffic would be consumed by the protocol. But, if we could live with the excessive amount of traffic, the protocol would be very robust since there would be no single point of failure.[13]

In order to limit the amount of data that needs to cross a LAN, the concept of a Designated Router was introduced. Now, if there are 'n' routers, we only need 'n − 1' adjacencies (instead of $n(n − 1)/2$), but the DR is a now a major single point of failure. In order to help make the protocol more robust, a Backup Designated Router (BDR) is elected so that it can take over immediately in the event of the failure of the DR. The nondesignated routers all form adjacencies with *both* the DR and BDR, and the DR and BDR become adjacent with each other.

When a new router comes up, it does not know about any of its neighbors (unless it is statically preconfigured with a list of several neighbors). It learns about them by hearing just one Hello packet, which not only lists all the neighbors on that LAN, but also the addresses of the Designated Router and Backup Designated Router. Once the new router has established the set of routers with which it shares two-way connectivity, it will become adjacent with the DR and BDR (those two routers must be among the set of two-way-capable routers before the adjacencies can form).

So, clearly the DR and BDR must become adjacent with every router on the LAN to which a two-way communication path exists. In order for a router to form an adjacency with another router, it must first verify two-way connectivity. Once two-way connectivity has been established, one of these conditions must also apply in order for an adjacency to form:

1. The underlying network type is either:
   a) broadcast,
   b) point-to-point,
   c) point-to-multipoint, or
   d) NBMA
2. The router itself is either:
   a) the Designated Router, or
   b) the Backup Designated Router
3. The neighboring router is either:
   a) the Designated Router, or
   b) the Backup Designated Router

The OSPF Link State Database is a distributed database that all the OSPF routers share. If the OSPF Routing Domain is broken into Areas, then the Link State Database is partitioned, and each Area has its own unique Link State Database. The Area Border Routers (ABRs) must maintain a collection of Link State Databases, one for each area to which they belong. Refering to Figure 13.14, the two routers between Areas A and B, and between Areas B and C, are Area Border Routers (ABRs). The lower router and the left router are the Autonomous System Border Router (ASBRs).

If nothing ever changed, the OSPF routers would all exchange the Link State Database once and that would be that. Unfortunately, things are always changing. New routers are added, links go up and down, suicidal squirrels eat through power lines, backhoes chomp long-haul fiber backbones, etc. In order to maintain accurate forwarding to the remaining parts of the network, i.e., those parts that we can still reach, we need a reliable way to pass information about Link State Database changes across the area, or if there are no areas, then across the entire OSPF Routing Domain.

Returning to the problem of reliable forwarding of topology changes across an OSPF Area, we will simply note that OSPF forms a spanning tree of routers across the Area. Any changes that happen need to be flooded across the spanning tree so that all the routers in the Area will know about the change as soon as possible. Each update must be acknowledged so that the routers are sure that the change has been reliably handed off to the next router. On a LAN, the change is flooded to the DR and BDR by sending it to the all-OSPF-designated-routers multicast address: 224.0.0.6.

OSPF Topological Entities

In OSPF the overall Routing Domain is referred to as an Autonomous System. This is somewhat confusing since BGP interconnects Autonomous Systems, too. A BGP Autonomous System can include multiple, disjoint, OSPF Autonomous Systems, or other routing protocol domains. In order to avoid confusion, I will only use the term "OSPF Autonomous System" when it is absolutely required, but will normally refer to an OSPF Routing Domain instead, reserving the term Autonomous System for BGP. Figure 13.14 illustrates OSPF Areas, OSPF autonomous systems (Routing Domains), and BGP Autonomous Systems.

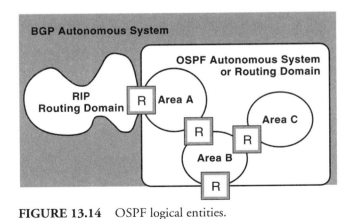

FIGURE 13.14   OSPF logical entities.

Since multicast is unreliable (heck, even unicast over a subnetwork isn't necessarily reliable), the sending router retransmits the update until it has been acknowledged. Once the DR and BDR have the update, they issue a copy of the update to each neighbor with which they have an adjacency. Again, each of their adjacent peers must acknowledge receipt of the update or it will continue to be retransmitted. In normal circumstances, the update is acknowledged very quickly and it spreads across the Area in a very short time. The entire process of spreading the update reliably over a spanning tree that includes all the Area's routers is known as OSPF's reliable flooding algorithm.

The reliable flooding algorithm is absolutely essential to OSPF's ability to build consistent forwarding tables. Since each router has the same Link State Database, which is an abstract representation of the logical topology, they will all build a loop-free and black-hole-free set of forwarding tables. Also, the convergence happens virtually immediately, allowing the routers to offer steady service in the face of topology changes.

[B]DR Election

We have mentioned the concepts of the Designated and Backup Designated Routers several times already, and it is important to understand how they are elected. Because the DR and BDR have such an important job, it is critical that there be as much stability as possible over time. If the DR and BDR were changing often, the routers on the LAN would be spending too much time updating each other and too little time forwarding packets. To ensure the stability of the DR and BDR, they remain in their roles once they are elected, even if a "better" choice comes along.

The first router that is active on a LAN declares itself to be the DR after a suitable waiting period[14] to make sure that there are no other active routers on that LAN. The DR's Hello packets will reflect that it is the DR, by filling in its own RouterID in the Designated Router field. The second router will become the BDR since the only other router on the LAN will already be the DR and it (the DR) will not list a BDR in its Hello packets.

After waiting a sufficient time[15] to ensure that no BDR is active, the second router will elect itself as the BDR. The BDR will send Hellos listing its own RouterID in the Backup Designated Router field, and so will the DR. Any future routers that join this LAN will receive the DR and BDR RouterIDs from either the DR or the BDR's Hello packets.

If several routers all come on at the same time, and there is no previous DR or BDR on that LAN, the router with the numerically largest RouterID will become the DR, and of the remaining routers, the one with the next highest RouterID will become the BDR. There is also a RouterPriority field that can be used to control which routers tend to win the election. The RouterPriority is an 8-bit field within the OSPF Hello packet and so can be any value from zero to 255, with higher values being more preferred. An administrator who sets the RouterPriority value to zero on a router's interface never wants this router to become the DR or BDR (on that particular interface). Most routers default to have their RouterPriority set to one. On a LAN with no prior [B]DR, if several routers initialize at about the same time, the one with the highest RouterPriority will become DR. If more than one router has the same elevated RouterPriority then the one with the highest RouterID will become DR.

In order to stabilize the protocol, once the DR and BDR have been elected they are not changed for any reason, except the failure of one or the other. Even if both the DR and BDR have RouterPriorities of 1, and then a new router with a RouterPriority of 200 joins the LAN, there will be no change. If the DR dies, then the BDR will become DR (that's why it was elected BDR, so it could take over immediately if necessary). The new router, with the RouterPriority set to 200, would then become the BDR after waiting for RouterDeadInterval seconds. If the original DR ever comes back up, it does not jump back into its role as DR. Again, the only time that the active DR and BDR will change is if one of them dies.

What is in the Link State Database?

The entries in OSPF's Link State Database are known as "Link State Advertisements." There are several types of LSAs that are very common and seen regularly in any OSPF network. Before delving into the descriptions of all these LSAs, we need to understand what an LSA looks like. There is a common LSA header, which serves to identify the kind of LSA that follows. Each LSA type has its own structure. Figure 13.15 illustrates the common LSA header.

Each LSA can live for up to one hour (3600 seconds, 0x00-0E-01-00) and has a set of Options associated with it (see below). The LS Type determines which kind of LSA follows this common header; the types are listed in the figure. The LSA is tagged with the RouterID of the router that originated it, and there is a sequence number so that more recent versions of the LSA can overwrite older ones. Once a router emits an LSA it normally lives until its age expires, but there is a method to prematurely remove an LSA from the Link State Database. Finally, each LSA has a checksum that helps to ensure that it has not been altered from its original contents.

```
                       1                   2                   3
 0 1 2 3 4 5 6 7 8 9 0 1 2 3 4 5 6 7 8 9 0 1 2 3 4 5 6 7 8 9 0 1
+-+-+-+-+-+-+-+-+-+-+-+-+-+-+-+-+-+-+-+-+-+-+-+-+-+-+-+-+-+-+-+-+
|            LS Age              |    Options    |    LS Type    |
+-+-+-+-+-+-+-+-+-+-+-+-+-+-+-+-+-+-+-+-+-+-+-+-+-+-+-+-+-+-+-+-+
|                         Link State ID                         |
+-+-+-+-+-+-+-+-+-+-+-+-+-+-+-+-+-+-+-+-+-+-+-+-+-+-+-+-+-+-+-+-+
|                      Advertising Router                       |
+-+-+-+-+-+-+-+-+-+-+-+-+-+-+-+-+-+-+-+-+-+-+-+-+-+-+-+-+-+-+-+-+
|                      LS Sequence Number                       |
+-+-+-+-+-+-+-+-+-+-+-+-+-+-+-+-+-+-+-+-+-+-+-+-+-+-+-+-+-+-+-+-+
|          LS Checksum          |            Length             |
+=+=+=+=+=+=+=+=+=+=+=+=+=+=+=+=+=+=+=+=+=+=+=+=+=+=+=+=+=+=+=+=+

    LS Age:     0x0000 - 0x0E10   (i.e., 0-3600) seconds

    LS Type     Description
    --------    -----------------------
       1        Router-LSA
       2        Network-LSA
       3        Summary-LSA (IP network)
       4        Summary-LSA (ASBR)
       5        AS-External-LSA
```

FIGURE 13.15 Common LSA header.

LSAs represent the important elements of an IP topology, namely routers, and networks. Router-LSAs identify a router and contain a list of all its attached networks. Network-LSAs contain a list of all the network's attached routers. (The DR is responsible for originating a LAN's Network-LSA.) Using these two different views of the logical connectivity, a router can knit together a forwarding table that lists all the networks (in an Area), and that lists all reachable destinations. Figures 13.16 and 13.17 show the format of the Router-LSA and the Network-LSA, respectively.

In the case of the Router-LSA, each of the networks to which the router is attached are represented by separate Link IDs. The Link Data for each link depends on the Link Type that is being represented. For stub networks[16] (Link Type = 3), the Link ID is the network/subnet prefix and the Link Data is the mask for that prefix. For transit networks[17] (Link Type = 2), the Link ID is the DR's RouterID, and the Link Data is the router's interface IP address within that prefix. The other Link Type values (1 and 4) are beyond the scope of this book, as is the procedure used to convert this raw data into a forwarding table (i.e., Dijkstra's algorithm). This information is being provided to give you an idea of the kind of data that OSPF routers exchange to inform each other about what networks they are attached to, or to take a network-centric point of view to see which routers are attached to which networks.

In the Router-LSA's LSA header (see Figure 13.15), the Link State ID is set to the originating router's RouterID, as is the Advertising Router field. Also note that when any LSA is first issued, its "LS Age" field is set to zero. Each LSA's age is incremented individually by every router (in the Area), until the one hour mark is

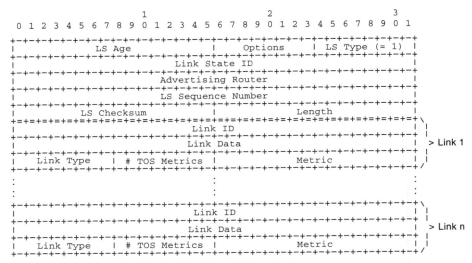

FIGURE 13.16 Router-LSA.

reached, at which time the LSA is purged from the collective Link State Database. OSPF does not rely on routers to all have synchronized clocks; the stale LSA is re-flooded by the originating router with the LS Age set to 0x00-0E-10-00, which causes the other routers to purge that LSA from the Link State Database. The LSA can be reintroduced with a new sequence number to preserve connectivity. Only the

```
                 1                   2                   3
 0 1 2 3 4 5 6 7 8 9 0 1 2 3 4 5 6 7 8 9 0 1 2 3 4 5 6 7 8 9 0 1
+-+-+-+-+-+-+-+-+-+-+-+-+-+-+-+-+-+-+-+-+-+-+-+-+-+-+-+-+-+-+-+-+
|           LS Age               |    Options    | LS Type (= 2) |
+-+-+-+-+-+-+-+-+-+-+-+-+-+-+-+-+-+-+-+-+-+-+-+-+-+-+-+-+-+-+-+-+
|                         Link State ID                         |
+-+-+-+-+-+-+-+-+-+-+-+-+-+-+-+-+-+-+-+-+-+-+-+-+-+-+-+-+-+-+-+-+
|                       Advertising Router                      |
+-+-+-+-+-+-+-+-+-+-+-+-+-+-+-+-+-+-+-+-+-+-+-+-+-+-+-+-+-+-+-+-+
|                       LS Sequence Number                      |
+-+-+-+-+-+-+-+-+-+-+-+-+-+-+-+-+-+-+-+-+-+-+-+-+-+-+-+-+-+-+-+-+
|         LS Checksum            |            Length            |
+=+=+=+=+=+=+=+=+=+=+=+=+=+=+=+=+=+=+=+=+=+=+=+=+=+=+=+=+=+=+=+=+
|                         Network Mask                          |
+-+-+-+-+-+-+-+-+-+-+-+-+-+-+-+-+-+-+-+-+-+-+-+-+-+-+-+-+-+-+-+-+
|                       Attached Router 1                       |
+-+-+-+-+-+-+-+-+-+-+-+-+-+-+-+-+-+-+-+-+-+-+-+-+-+-+-+-+-+-+-+-+
:                             :                                 :
+-+-+-+-+-+-+-+-+-+-+-+-+-+-+-+-+-+-+-+-+-+-+-+-+-+-+-+-+-+-+-+-+
|                       Attached Router n                       |
+-+-+-+-+-+-+-+-+-+-+-+-+-+-+-+-+-+-+-+-+-+-+-+-+-+-+-+-+-+-+-+-+
```

FIGURE 13.17 Network-LSA.

router that originates a LSA can remove it, except in the case of LSAs that reach MaxAge (e.g., those that are one hour old).

Network-LSAs are only originated by the DR (for those media that elect a DR). In this case, the listed routers will be those that the DR is adjacent to. The RouterID is used, in conjunction with the Router- and Network-LSAs, to determine the subnet prefixes that are attached to each router. In a Network-LSA, the Link State ID is set to the originating router's interface address, interpreted with the mask in the data portion of the Network-LSA. The rest of the Attached Router fields are the other routers' interface addresses within that prefix.

Router-LSAs and Network-LSAs are restricted to use within an OSPF Area. Outside of the Area, the exact interconnections[18] are invisible, but the networks in the Area are advertised so that routers outside this Area can reach them. The Summary-LSA enables this information to be externalized and is depicted in Figure 13.18.

In practice, the nonzero Type of Service (ToS) and ToS Metric fields are not used, so the packet usually ends after ToS zero's Metric field. The end of the packet is determined by the Length that was specified in the LSA's header. An Area Border Router needs to originate one Summary-LSA for each of its Areas' reachable network prefixes. Aggregation can be used to reduce the number of Summary-LSAs that need to be injected into the Backbone Area, but only when an Area boundary aligns with an IP address prefix. OSPF Area Border Routers must be explicitly configured to perform "area range aggregation."

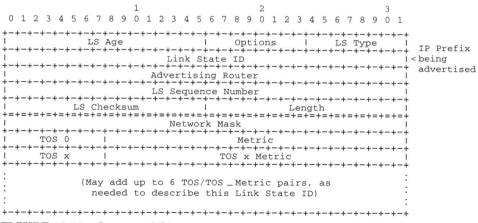

FIGURE 13.18 Summary-LSA.

This is true in general. Automatic proxy aggregation is not possible in BGP either. The routers closest to an address prefix must originate the aggregate; they are the most qualified to do so *accurately*, but only under the network manager's direction. Figure 13.19 illustrates the concepts of the Backbone Area and ABR.

OSPF Areas (Hierarchical Routing)

We have seen several references to OSPF Areas already. Each network medium (and its associated prefix) is in only one Area. The routers on each subnetwork tag their Hello packets with the AreaID (routers must be preconfigured with that information), and only become adjacent with other routers if their AreaID's match. Network-LSAs and Router-LSAs are only flooded within an Area. We will now take a moment to examine OSPF Areas in more detail.

OSPF uses Areas to implement hierarchical routing. If Areas were not available, the amount of information, measured by the size of the Link State Database, would increase rapidly as the OSPF Autonomous System grows. This is because the Link State Database does not only list the destination prefixes, but also how all the routers attach to those prefixes. When Areas are deployed, each Area has its own Link State Database. This implies that each ABR needs to maintain some number of independent Link State Databases, one for each Area to which it is attached.

At a minimum, the Summary-LSAs reduce the number of LSAs that are visible outside the Area because the large number of Network- and Router-LSAs are hidden

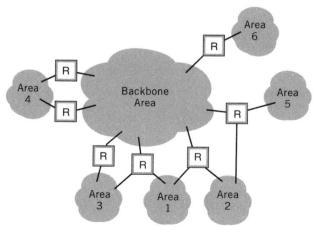

FIGURE 13.19   Interconnecting OSPF Areas.

within the Area's boundary. While the Summary-LSAs still lists all the reachable network prefixes in an Area, they do not have to also list all the routers that are attached to each of those networks.

OSPF's inter-Area topology is not completely arbitrary. One OSPF Area, with the reserved AreaID value of 0.0.0.0 (although the Area ID is a 32-bit number, it is not necessarily an IP address), is defined as the "Backbone Area." All the Area Border Routers (ABRs) in the OSPF Autonomous System must have an interface in the Backbone Area. Areas come in three flavors at present, namely, Transit, Stub, and Not-So-Stubby. The backbone is a transit Area, which means that it allows AS-External[19] LSAs in its Link State Database. Because all the ABRs have interfaces in the backbone area, they all know about all the inter-Area Summary-LSAs, whether or not they are being aggregated. The ABRs all know the intimate topological details of the areas to which they attach, which enables them to forward packets optimally inside their attached areas.

Stub areas are the least sophisticated of all Area types in that they cannot carry AS-External routing information, and by default do not carry any inter-Area Summary-LSAs either, (though inter-Area Summary-LSAs can be imported into Stub Areas if the ABRs are specifically configured to do that). Stub Areas' Link State Databases are limited to containing their internal LSAs, plus an optional Default-Summary LSA, which may be injected by the ABR(s) at a configured StubDefault cost.

Transit Area's ABRs may import inter-Area Summaries, as well as AS-Externals, into a Transit area. Generally, the network manager decides which routes to import into the Transit Area. The Backbone Area is a Transit Area, and has all the same properties, with the additional restriction that it must be present if an OSPF Autonomous System is broken into multiple Areas. Not-so-stubby Areas (NSSAs) are a hybrid between Transit and Stub that allows a "stub" Area to house an ASBR, something that a normal Stub Area cannot do.

There is a hierarchy of routers in addition to the hierarchy of areas. Intra-area routers are at the bottom of the functionality ladder. Each of these has only one Link State Database. The ABRs are the next step up in functionality. They have to maintain a separate Link State Database for each area to which they attach, as well as being responsible for introducing Summary-LSAs or aggregated Summary-LSAs between the Areas. ABRs are also responsible for flooding AS-External LSAs into Transit Areas. An Area may have multiple ABRs.

The highest functionality router is the OSPF Autonomous System Border Router (ASBR), which is a special purpose ABR. This router speaks at least one non-OSPF routing protocol. Just as an Area may have multiple ABRs, an Autonomous

System may have multiple ASBRs. An ASBR may be located in any transit area, not just the backbone area. ASBRs may also reside in Not-So-Stubby Areas (NSSAs), but *not* in plain Stub Areas. ASBRs can optionally specify a "Forwarding Address" for an AS-External LSA, which can be used to optimize routing on exchange LANs where all the routers do not speak both protocols. The forwarding behavior is the same as RIPv2's "Next Hop" behavior,[20] though of course they are implemented completely differently.

An ASBR is responsible for exporting an administratively determined list of reachable prefixes from the OSPF Autonomous System into the neighboring Routing Domain. Conversely, it is also responsible for importing administratively selected prefixes into the OSPF Autonomous System. External routes only need to be imported into the OSPF routing system if there are multiple exit points, or perhaps if the OSPF domain is a transit domain for other Routing Domains. Chapter 14 discusses Routing Domain interconnection in detail.

External destination prefixes are represented by AS-External LSAs, of which there are two types. Type-1 externals are treated like a Summary-LSA, in that the cost to reach a Type-1 external is cumulative across the OSPF Autonomous System; the further it is propagated, the higher its accumulated cost. Type-2 externals have a fixed cost, regardless of how far they propagate away from the originating ASBR. Both types of AS-External LSAs have their uses, which will be discussed in Chapter 14.

In certain situations it may be desirable to want to have a Stub Area within a Transit Area, as in Figure 13.20. In my case, I was doing some testing of "OSPF over Demand Circuits" (RFC-1793) support, and it was time-consuming to have my remote ISDN router be forced to download all of the AS-External LSAs in the Transit Area, plus all the intra- and interarea LSAs. The remote router spent several seconds synchronizing its Link State Database before it could begin forwarding data, which was inconvenient for my testing.

The configuration was simple, though, and my remote router had only one way out, so a single default route would have been sufficient to represent all that information. Rather than reconfigure the Transit Area to reduce its Link State Database, I wanted to isolate the pair of test routers in their own Stub Area, which would keep all those bulky AS-External LSAs away.

Unfortunately, I was forgetting a cardinal rule of OSPF: All ABRs *must* have an interface in the Backbone Area. Router R_1 and R_2 were cut off from the world in this configuration. The logical topology in the figure was deceptive—it looked so promising. In order to see clearly what is broken, we need to look at a diagram of the Area topology, as in Figure 13.21.

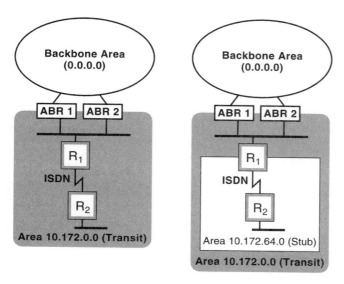

FIGURE 13.20 Stub area within a transit area.

In this figure it is clear that Area 10.172.64.0 is an orphan, with no connectivity to the backbone area. OSPF has a mechanism known as "Virtual Links" to enable logical inter-Area connectivity where physical connectivity is either not desirable or not possible. Figure 13.22 shows the correct Area and Logical Topologies, including the required Virtual Link.

Virtual Links must be configured statically by the network administrator. With the Virtual Links in place, the configuration works as desired. Router R_1 still knows all the AS-External LSAs, plus the LSAs from its other attached Area, namely 10.172.0.0. However, because Area 10.172.64.0 is a Stub Area, this extraneous in-

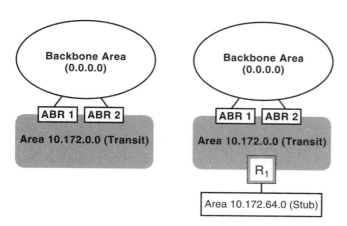

FIGURE 13.21 Equivalent area topology.

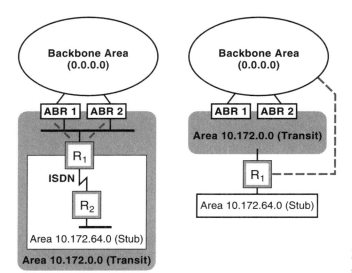

FIGURE 13.22 Correct topologies.

formation is *not* passed down to R_2, which makes the R_1-R_2 adjacency come up almost instantaneously; the Link State Database for that area consists of two Router-LSAs, two Network-LSAs, and a Default-Summary-LSA for the default route. This Link State Database only took a small fraction of a second to synchronize, allowing the adjacencies to be formed and data to flow almost immediately after the PPP link came up.

OSPF SUMMARY

OSPF is a link-state routing protocol that uses the Dijkstra algorithm to build a forwarding table from its distributed Link State Database. The elements of the Link State Database are known as Link State Advertisements, and they are reliably flooded to all the routers that need them. The reliable flooding algorithm ensures that all the routers have the exact same Link State Database, from which they all compute a set of consistent, loop-free, forwarding tables. OSPF supports hierarchical routing via the concept of Areas, each having its own Link State Database. OSPF converges much more quickly than RIP. It seems to be the case that link-state protocols converge much more quickly than distance-vector protocols, especially as the network size increases.

Despite the complexity of the OSPF protocol itself, it need not be much more complicated to configure than RIP. In simple topologies, it must simply be enabled on

CONVERGENCE

In 1992, a colleague and myself had just converted a small wide-area network from RIP to OSPF.[21] The improved convergence times of OSPF were one of the reasons we wanted to switch. As a test, we had logged in to two routers. Each router's telnet session was in its own terminal window. One router was local, at NASA's Goddard Space Flight Center, just outside of Washington, DC, and the other was in Alaska. The test we planned to do was to disable an Ethernet interface in Alaska and then watch the local router to see how long it took before its forwarding table reflected the change.

The command to disable the interface in Alaska was typed and entered, a hand was moved from the keyboard to the mouse, which clicked in the local router's window. At that point, the command was typed to show the local router's forwarding table and . . . the destination was already gone! We even tried the test by pretyping the command to show the local router's forwarding table so that all we had to do was hit return in the Alaska router's window, click the mouse in the local router's window, and hit return there. Even with this streamlined test, OSPF still beat us.

all desired router interfaces. As the network grows, or if it is big to start with, then some care must be taken in defining the best Area boundaries for the internetwork. For the few routers that are ABRs, the AreaID must be configured on their different interfaces. Intra-area routers must have all their interfaces' AreaIDs set to the local Area's AreaID, which is only a minor additional configuration burden. Of course, as with any routing protocol, the interfaces of each router need to be configured with unique IP addresses, and each interface needs to reside in a unique IP address prefix.

By default, most OSPF networks will use the default cost-as-a-function-of-interface-bandwidth[22] heuristic, and will also use the default HelloInterval and all other timers. While most OSPF implementations allow these timers to be tuned, there is usually little reason to do so since the defaults work well in a wide variety of situations. The interface cost, on the other hand, is often tweaked to allow the network administrator some control over which interfaces are more or less preferred. Also, in situations where a large number of links in the network operate at speeds of 100 Mbps or more, their costs are all one, and that is probably not the desired value. Increasing the cost of an interface has the effect of making it less preferred than it would be by default.

General OSPF Guidelines

Control of Aggregation

When designing a new network, it is wise to attempt to match a network's area boundaries to its addressing boundaries. If an existing network would require renumbering to have aggregatable addresses, then it is unlikely to be worth the effort to renumber the network just to support aggregation. In cases where the addressing and area boundaries don't line up well, or at all, the scalability of OSPF will be more limited compared to similar-sized networks that have been designed to take advantage of aggregation. When used effectively, aggregation reduces the necessary information that the routers must keep track of in order to generate an accurate forwarding table; moreover, the forwarding table itself may be considerably smaller, offering additional savings. If the OSPF area boundaries do line up with an internetwork's addressing boundaries, then OSPF "area address range" aggregation may be configured, thereby reducing the amount of routing information that must be carried by routers in the backbone.

For instance, if Area 51[23] consists of the prefix 192.168.0.0/19, which could be arbitrarily subnetted (e.g., 192.168.8.0/21, 192.168.16.0/21, 192.168.24.0/21, 192.168.26.0/23, and 192.168.25.0/24,[24] then the Backbone Area's routers need only be made aware of Area 51's single prefix: 192.168.0.0/19, and they would all have one forwarding table entry showing that this prefix is reachable via the ABR(s) that advertised the aggregate (an Area may have more than one ABR).

The aggregate prefix is advertised by the ABR as a "Summary-Net" LSA (LS Type = 3). The router, on its own, can not infer that no part of 192.168.0.0/19 will be used anywhere else in the network in the future, so it can not automatically generate a shorter-mask aggregate that minimally covers the five forwarding table entries above.[25] Lacking the network manager's knowledge of the network design, the ABR has no choice but to advertise each of the Area's reachable prefixes as an individual Summary-Net LSA, even though they may appear to be aggregatable. For another example, if an Area consisted of 192.168.8.0/22, 192.168.12.0/22,

192.168.13.0/23, and 192.168.14.0/23, is it necessarily 192.168.8.0/21? It could be ... but it could also be part of 192.168.0.0/20, or 192.168.160.0/19, or any number of other possibilities with shorter masks than /21.

Any time aggregation is performed, it must be controlled by the network manager(s). A router cannot be sure that it has complete information about the addressing plan of the network; some parts of the network may be unreachable due to maintenance or an outage, some parts may be planned but not yet active, or there may be corrupted, incorrect or incomplete data in the routing protocol's topology database. In general, it is impossible for routers to do automatic "proxy aggregation." This applies to aggregation between OSPF Areas all the way up to inter-ISP aggregation using the Internet's Border Gateway Protocol (BGP-4).

On the other hand, if Area 51 consists of five non-aggregatable prefixes (e.g., 192.168.17.0/24, 192.168.18.0/23, 192.168.20.0/24, 192.168. 58.192/26, and 192.168.61.128/25) then the routers in the backbone must all be made aware of those five prefixes. If area address range aggregation has not been configured, five Summary-Net LSAs will be sent into the Backbone Area's Link State Database, instead of just one. This will create five forwarding table entries in all these routers, instead of only one forwarding table entry (i.e., the aggregate). An Area's ABRs will generate these individual Summary-Net LSAs without needing any special configuration commands.

Limiting the Workload of Specialized OSPF Routers

The A(S)BRs[26] have more work to do than other, non-specialized, OSPF routers. In order to minimize the processing load on the A(S)BRs, it is wise to limit the number of interfaces on which they become the (B)DR.[27] Remember that each interface connects to a unique subnetwork, and each subnetwork elects its own DR and BDR. Without explicit control, the A(S)BR could become (B)DR on enough interfaces that its OSPF implementation would be overworked.

Consider ABRs: They must process updated Link State Advertisements in each of the separate Link State Databases of each of the Areas to which they are attached. By definition, ABRs have complete visibility into each attached Area, so all topology changes in all attached Areas must be processed by the ABR. Also, each attached Area's internal prefixes (or configured aggregate(s)) must be advertised into the Backbone Area, and optionally into other attached Transit Areas.

Consider ASBRs: They must keep track of reachable prefixes in an external routing domain and import these reachable external prefixes as AS-External (Type 5) LSAs, according to the policy rules with which it has been configured. Conversely, it must advertise the OSPF autonomous system's reachable prefixes (or its configured aggregate(s)) into the external routing domain. An ASBR may also be an ABR (subject to all the ABR constraints listed above), or it may simply be an ASBR. If there are several routers on a common subnetwork, it is wise to ensure that the A(S)BRs do not become (B)DR—it is better to force two of the other non-A(S)BRs to handle the (B)DR duties.

In order to limit the stress on the A(S)BRs, use the RouterPriority to prevent an internetwork's A(S)BRs from becoming (B)DR on more interfaces than necessary. For router interfaces on which (B)DR status is undesirable, the OSPF RouterPriority may be set to zero. A(S)BRs should be configured this way on as many interfaces as possible. If some A(S)BR must also be a (B)DR on some set of interfaces, try to minimize the number of areas/AS's served by that router, and also minimize the number of (B)DR interfaces.

Actually, what really matters is the total number of active neighbors on those interfaces on which a router is a (B)DR. If one router has 20 interfaces, and is either DR or BDR on each of them, but each subnetwork only has at most four routers, then the maximum number of Full adjacencies that this router must maintain is 60. Another router might be (B)DR on "only" three interfaces, but these subnetworks may attach to up to 38 neighbors each. This router, then, may have to maintain up to 114 Full adjacencies. So, the number of (B)DR interfaces is not so important as the total number of Full adjacencies that the router must maintain. It is important to minimize the number of interfaces, but also keep in mind the total number of Full adjacencies that may need to be established over those interfaces.

Each LAN[28] needs a DR and BDR. NBMA-style subnetworks also elect (B)DRs. (It is worth noting that Point-to-Multipoint mode may be a better choice for WAN subnetworks than NBMA mode, since p-t-mp mode eliminates the requirement of electing a (B)DR.) The normal (B)DR election procedure is based solely on the routers' OSPF RouterID . . . the two numerically highest addresses become DR and BDR, respectively.[29]

A network manager need not let the routers determine the (B)DR haphazardly, based solely on the ranking of their RouterIDs. It is best if a subnetwork's (B)DRs could be chosen as the least busy routers, in terms of having the fewest total interfaces, and fewest total neighbors. This will place the least processing burden on them, enabling them to effectively flood the network's changing LSAs to its fully adjacent neighbors. Also, as stated above, it is best to avoid routers that are doing other specialized OSPF duties (i.e., A(S)BRs). If such specialized routers do exist in a subnetwork, it is a very good idea to set their RouterPriorities equal to zero, which will ensure that the (B)DR duties are performed by other, less-busy, routers.

OSPF Scaling: Areas per ABR

An ABR might be able to support between 10 and 20 attached areas, provided it is not (B)DR on too many interfaces, and provided the attached Areas are not too large or dynamic. Some OSPF implementations may be able to support more Areas per ABR than others. As noted above, in order to force an A(S)BR to not be a (B)DR on an interface, simply set the RouterPriority to zero on that interface. If there are only one or two routers on a subnetwork, it is clearly pointless to try to prevent them from becoming either DR or BDR on that subnetwork.

There should be minimal operational impact on an ABR if it is a (B)DR on an interface where there are very few neighbors. The real stress on a (B)DR occurs during the reliable flooding algorithm, when it must make sure that each adjacent neighbor has the most current version of some set of updated LSAs. Clearly, the more adjacencies that the (B)DR must maintain, the more difficult its job will be during topology changes.

OSPF Scaling: Neighbors per Router Interface

Theoretically, OSPF's Hello protocol could support 349 neighbors on a LAN with a 1500-byte MTU. The following allowances are made, which will allow you to calculate the number of neighbors on other media with different MTUs. As you can see, the total headers of an OSPF Hello packet, including the IP, OSPF, and Hello headers, amount to at most 104 bytes.

IP Header:	60 bytes (max)
OSPF Header:	24 bytes (fixed)
Hello Header:	20 bytes (fixed)
Neighbor Entries:	4 bytes each

If we take away these headers from the MTU of an Ethernet, we are left with 1396 bytes for data. Since each Neighbor entry is simply four bytes long (the neighbor's RouterID), we divide 1396 by 4 and are left with 349, which is the maximum number of neighbors that can fit in a single OSPF Hello packet when it is transmitted over Ethernet. If the IP header were assumed to be its normal length of 20 bytes, then there would be room for an additional 10 neighbor routers on an Ethernet subnetwork.

Most OSPF implementations should have little trouble with 15 or so neighbors per interface, for a reasonable number of interfaces. Depending on the topology, and whether the router is very busy, it may be possible to have more neighbors, even up to 40 or more on an interface, but only if the router does not have too many total neighbors and also is not a (B)DR on too many interfaces. Also, this assumes that the router is not an A(S)BR.

OSPF Scaling: Routers per Area

50 routers per Area is likely to be a safe target. When OSPF was originally published, the recommended maximum number of routers per Area was 200. The limits here stem from the fact that each Area's Link State Database gets bigger as more routers (and their associated subnetwork prefixes) are added to the Area. Depending on the Area's topology, it may be possible to have more than 50 routers . . . or even more than 200—provided the network has been designed to take maximum advantage of aggregation.

Some Areas may be "bushy" with dense interconnections between routers, while others may be sparse trees, with few redundant links. Since Network-LSAs expand when there tend to be larger numbers of routers per subnetwork, and Router-LSAs also tend to expand when there are more subnetworks per router, it is clear that the network topology drives the size of the Link State Database.

An Area with a sparse, almost tree-like topology might be able to support 200 or more routers, while one with about the same number of routers, but many more interconnections between them, may have difficulty safely approaching 100, or even 50 routers in an Area. It is a good idea to monitor the size of each Area's Link State Database to ensure that the routers are not being drowned in information. Good OSPF implementations should gracefully handle database overflow (see RFC-1765); also, if an implementation is nearing the limits of internal memory or CPU resources, it should notify the network manager through some management interface (log file, SNMP trap, etc.).

Finally, if an Area tends to have stable links, such as campus LAN segments that are not subject to the forces of Nature to the same extent that long-distance circuits are, then several such areas may be able to co-exist in an ABR. If, however, an Area is largely comprised of WAN links that tend to go up and down a lot, there will be a drain on the CPU due to performing the Dijkstra algorithm more frequently. Remember that all the routers in an Area have to keep their common Link State Database in sync via OSPF's reliable flooding algorithm, meaning that each router has to process each updated LSA.

OSPF DEPLOYMENT CONSIDERATIONS: SUMMARY

If the following guidelines are observed, your OSPF network will be able to scale to very large sizes, and will tend to be more stable than networks of similar size that have not followed these guidelines.

1. For networks that are large enough to require OSPF Areas, use aggregatable addresses and configure OSPF "area address range" aggregation in the ABRs.
2. Choose (B)DRs, such that the total number of fully-adjacent neighbors is minimized across the subnetworks that they interconnect.
3. For networks that are large enough to warrant the use of Areas, use stub areas, if possible, to minimize the size of the Area's Link State Database.
4. Whenever possible, try to make sure that A(S)BRs are not too busy being (B)DRs. Set the interface RouterPriority to zero on as many A(S)BR interfaces as possible.
5. For non-broadcast subnetworks, use point-to-multipoint subnetwork type (if your router vendor supports it), since point-to-multipoint does not employ a (B)DR, contrary to the NBMA subnetwork type.

OSPF is a highly capable routing protocol, that is suitable for use in very large networks. These guidelines will help to ensure that the network will be more stable and more scalable. Even without these guidelines, however, OSPF is still capable of handling very large, complex topologies. It also has the advantage of converging much faster than RIP[30] after a topology change.

OSPF-Assisted Troubleshooting

Because OSPF maintains explicit neighbor relationships, it is a valuable troubleshooting tool in its own right. All OSPF implementations have a way of displaying the OSPF neighbors that a router is adjacent with, or that it has seen. If a router has just had OSPF enabled, the first thing to check is that it has learned all the appropriate neighbors on each of its interfaces. In the future, if a router has a problem reaching some destination (e.g., a traceroute shows that packets to some destination stop at this router), all one has to do is look at its neighbor list and see which neighbor is "Down." OSPF's statistics also provide a wealth of troubleshooting information. Figure 13.23 is a short list of some of the statistics that may be collected. I have made every effort to make this book nonrouter-vendor-specific,

```
ACCUMULATED VALUES
------------------------OSPF Statistics------------------------
SPF Calculations                                        0
Resource error                                          0
--OSPF Statistics-----------1--------2------------------------
Hello Rcvd                      0        0
Hello Xmit                      0        0
DD Rcvd                         0        0
DD Xmit                         0        0
LSR Rcvd                        0        0
LSR Xmit                        0        0
LSA Rcvd                        0        0
LSA Xmit                        0        0
LSU Rcvd                        0        0
LSU Xmit                        0        0
Number of DR Election           0        0
Adjacency UP  Events            0        0
Errors:
    Xmit fail                   0        0
    Rcv bad packet header       0        0
    Mismatch HelloTime          0        0
    Mismatch RouterDeadTim      0        0
    Mismatch subnet/mask        0        0
    Mismatch area ID            0        0
    Unknown packet type         0        0
    authentication Error        0        0
    Packet Checksum Error       0        0
    LSA Checksum Eror           0        0
```

FIGURE 13.23   Some OSPF statistics.

but the only router I had handy for this display was a 3Com NETBuilder.[31] None of these statistics are proprietary; similar displays in other implementations would have equivalent contents, but the display would vary.

Now, if we are on a LAN with, for example, five total routers, then on each router the Hellos received should outnumber those transmitted by about four to one. If not, there might be a problem. If the number of SPF calculations is increasing rapidly, that indicates that either some link is transitioning between the up and down states, or that perhaps some router's OSPF implementation is mistreating some LSAs, making it appear as if there is an unstable link.

If an adjacency is not forming as we think it should, then probably the statistics on Mismatched HelloInterval, RouterDeadTime, Subnet/mask, or AreaID will give a strong clue as to what is misconfigured. Any nonzero values here will pinpoint exactly what needs to be reconfigured to make the adjacency happen properly. Another subtle block to adjacencies forming is when you forget that you are using OSPF Authentication on a LAN. Nonzero values of the Authentication Errors counter are a positive indicator of this condition.

Another sign of trouble would be if there are an excessive number of DR elections on an interface. This should be very stable over time; if it isn't, there is either a Physical- or Data-Link layer problem on that LAN, or one or both of the DR or BDR routers is flaky and should have its RouterPriority demoted. Similarly, if there are large numbers of AdjacencyUp or AdjacencyDown events, it is worth looking at the LAN itself and at the routers to determine the likely culprit.

A very cool feature of OSPF is that the Link State Database allows a form of remote troubleshooting. Since the reliable flooding algorithm ensures that the Link State Database is the same on all routers in an Area, it is possible to find a broken router by looking for bogus LSAs that were orignated by its RouterID. Most OSPF implementations allow the Link State Database to be viewed at many levels of detail.

MIGRATING FROM RIP TO OSPF

Migrating from RIP to OSPF is not hard to do, provided all the routers in your internetwork support OSPF, and moreover prefer OSPF-derived destinations over RIP-derived destinations. The steps are as follows:

1. Define area boundaries; match to addressing boundaries if at all possible (this step is optional)
2. Configure OSPF on all interfaces according to the result of step one, and enable it
3. Verify that all OSPF routers have formed the expected adjacencies
4. Verify that the forwarding table shows all of the RIP-derived forwarding table entries that have been superseded by OSPF-derived forwarding table entries
5. Watch for stability (at least one day, preferably a week)
6. Disable RIP
    a) You may still use RIP at the edge, on stub networks, to advertise a default route to Unix® and other hosts that listen to RIP (if possible, you should try to use ICMP Router Discovery Protocol (RFC-1256) instead of RIP)

RIP AND OSPF SUMMARY

OSPF (RFC-2328, STD-54), as the IETF's recommended Interior Gateway Protocol (RFC-1371) is never a bad choice over RIP (either version) if it is available. RIPv2 (RFC-2453) at least supports VLSM, CIDR, and Next Hop, but it is still a distance-vector protocol, and will still converge slowly in large networks. In small networks, there is probably no compelling reason to choose OSPF over RIPv2. RIPv1 should only be used when there is no other choice, i.e., when the available equipment supports neither OSPF nor RIPv2.

REFERENCES

Moy, J., *OSPF, Anatomy of an Internet Routing Protocol,* Addison Wesley, Reading, MA, 1998.

Request for Comment (RFC)

RIP

1058 Routing Information Protocol. C.L. Hedrick. Jun-01-1988. (Format: TXT=93285 bytes) (Updated by RFC1388, RFC1723) (Status: HISTORIC)

1387 RIP Version 2 Protocol Analysis. G. Malkin. January 1993. (Format: TXT=5598 bytes) (Obsoleted by RFC1721) (Status: INFORMATIONAL)

1388 RIP Version 2 Carrying Additional Information. G. Malkin. January 1993. (Format: TXT=16227 bytes) (Obsoleted by RFC1723) (Updates RFC1058) (Status: PROPOSED STANDARD)

1581 Protocol Analysis for Extensions to RIP to Support Demand Circuits. G. Meyer. February 1994. (Format: TXT=7536 bytes) (Status: INFORMATIONAL)

1582 Extensions to RIP to Support Demand Circuits. G. Meyer. February 1994. (Format: TXT=63271 bytes) (Status: PROPOSED STANDARD)

1721 RIP Version 2 Protocol Analysis. G. Malkin. November 1994. (Format: TXT=6680 bytes) (Obsoletes RFC1387) (Status: INFORMATIONAL)

1722 RIP Version 2 Protocol Applicability Statement. G. Malkin. November 1994. (Format: TXT=10236 bytes) (Status: DRAFT STANDARD)

1723 RIP Version 2 - Carrying Additional Information. G. Malkin. November 1994. (Format: TXT=18597 bytes) (Obsoletes RFC1388) (Updates RFC1058) (Status: DRAFT STANDARD)

1923 RIPv1 Applicability Statement for Historic Status. J. Halpern & S. Bradner. March 1996. (Format: TXT=5560 bytes) (Status: INFORMATIONAL)

2082 RIP-2 MD5 Authentication. F. Baker, R. Atkinson. January 1997. (Format: TXT=25436 bytes) (Status: PROPOSED STANDARD)

2091 Triggered Extensions to RIP to Support Demand Circuits. G. Meyer, S. Sherry. January 1997. (Format: TXT=44835 bytes) (Status: PROPOSED STANDARD)

2092 Protocol Analysis for Triggered RIP. S. Sherry, G. Meyer. January 1997. (Format: TXT=10865 bytes) (Status: INFORMATIONAL)

OSPF

1074 NSFNET backbone SPF based Interior Gateway Protocol. J. Rekhter. Oct-01-1988. (Format: TXT=10872 bytes) (Status: UNKNOWN)

1131 OSPF specification. J. Moy. Oct-01-1989. (Format: TXT=268, PS=857280 bytes) (Obsoleted by RFC1247) (Status: PROPOSED STANDARD)

1245 OSPF Protocol Analysis. J. Moy. Jul-01-1991. (Format: TXT=26160, PS=33546 bytes) (Also RFC1247, RFC1246) (Status: INFORMATIONAL)

1246 Experience with the OSPF Protocol. J. Moy. Jul-01-1991. (Format: TXT=70441, PS=141924 bytes) (Also RFC1247, RFC1245) (Status: INFORMATIONAL)

1247 OSPF Version 2. J. Moy. Jul-01-1991. (Format: TXT=433332, PS=989724 bytes) (Obsoletes RFC1131) (Obsoleted by RFC1583) (Also RFC1246, RFC1245) (Status: DRAFT STANDARD)

1370 Applicability Statement for OSPF. Internet Architecture Board, L. Chapin. October 1992. (Format: TXT=4303 bytes) (Status: PROPOSED STANDARD)

1371 Choosing a Common IGP for the IP Internet. P. Gross. October 1992. (Format: TXT=18168 bytes) (Status: INFORMATIONAL)

1583 OSPF Version 2. J. Moy. March 1994. (Format: TXT=532636, PS=990794 bytes) (Obsoletes RFC1247) (Obsoleted by RFC2178) (Status: DRAFT STANDARD)

1586 Guidelines for Running OSPF Over Frame Relay Networks. O. deSouza & M. Rodrigues. March 1994. (Format: TXT=14968 bytes) (Status: INFORMATIONAL)

1587 The OSPF NSSA Option. R. Coltun & V. Fuller. March 1994. (Format: TXT=37412 bytes) (Status: PROPOSED STANDARD)

1765 OSPF Database Overflow. J. Moy. March 1995. (Format: TXT=21613 bytes) (Status: EXPERIMENTAL)

1793 Extending OSPF to Support Demand Circuits. J. Moy. April 1995. (Format: TXT=78728 bytes) (Status: PROPOSED STANDARD)

2154 OSPF with Digital Signatures. S. Murphy, M. Badger, B. Wellington. June 1997. (Format: TXT=72701 bytes) (Status: EXPERIMENTAL)

2178 OSPF Version 2. J. Moy. July 1997. (Format: TXT=495866 bytes) (Obsoletes RFC1583) (Obsoleted by RFC2328) (Status: DRAFT STANDARD)

2328 OSPF Version 2. J. Moy. April 1998. (Format: TXT=447367 bytes) (Obsoletes RFC2178) (Also STD0054) (Status: STANDARD)

2329 OSPF Standardization Report. J. Moy. April 1998. (Format: TXT=15130 bytes) (Status: INFORMATIONAL)

2370 The OSPF Opaque LSA Option. R. Coltun. July 1998. (Format: TXT=33789 bytes) (Also RFC2328) (Status: PROPOSED STANDARD)

Exterior Gateway Protocol

0827 Exterior Gateway Protocol (EGP). E.C. Rosen. Oct-01-1982. (Format: TXT=68436 bytes) (Updated by RFC0904) (Status: UNKNOWN)

0888 "STUB" Exterior Gateway Protocol. L. Seamonson, E.C. Rosen. Jan-01-1984. (Format: TXT=53227 bytes) (Updated by RFC0904) (Status: UNKNOWN)

0890 Exterior Gateway Protocol implementation schedule. J. Postel. Feb-01-1984. (Format: TXT=5899 bytes) (Status: UNKNOWN)

0904 Exterior Gateway Protocol formal specification. D.L. Mills. Apr-01-1984. (Format: TXT=65226 bytes) (Updates RFC0827, RFC0888) (Status: HISTORIC)

1092 EGP and policy based routing in the new NSFNET backbone. J. Rekhter. Feb-01-1989. (Format: TXT=11865 bytes) (Status: UNKNOWN)

1093 NSFNET routing architecture. H.W. Braun. Feb-01-1989. (Format: TXT=20629 bytes) (Status: UNKNOWN)

1105 Border Gateway Protocol (BGP). K. Lougheed, Y. Rekhter. Jun-01-1989. (Format: TXT=37644 bytes) (Obsoleted by RFC1163) (Status: EXPERIMENTAL)

1163 Border Gateway Protocol (BGP). K. Lougheed, Y. Rekhter. Jun-01-1990. (Format: TXT=69404 bytes) (Obsoletes RFC1105) (Obsoleted by RFC1267) (Status: HISTORIC)

1164 Application of the Border Gateway Protocol in the Internet. J.C. Honig, D. Katz, M. Mathis, Y. Rekhter, J.Y. Yu. Jun-01-1990. (Format: TXT=56278 bytes) (Obsoleted by RFC1268) (Status: HISTORIC)

1265 BGP Protocol Analysis. Y. Rekhter. Oct-01-1991. (Format: TXT=20728 bytes) (Status: INFORMATIONAL)

1266 Experience with the BGP Protocol. Y. Rekhter. Oct-01-1991. (Format: TXT=21938 bytes) (Status: INFORMATIONAL)

1267 Border Gateway Protocol 3 (BGP-3). K. Lougheed, Y. Rekhter. Oct-01-1991. (Format: TXT=80724 bytes) (Obsoletes RFC1163) (Status: HISTORIC)

1268 Application of the Border Gateway Protocol in the Internet. Y. Rekhter, P. Gross. Oct-01-1991. (Format: TXT=31102 bytes) (Obsoletes RFC1164) (Obsoleted by RFC1655) (Status: HISTORIC)

1322 A Unified Approach to Inter-Domain Routing. D. Estrin, Y. Rekhter, S. Hotz. May 1992. (Format: TXT=96934 bytes) (Status: INFORMATIONAL)

1338 Supernetting: an Address Assignment and Aggregation Strategy. V. Fuller, T. Li, J. Yu, K. Varadhan. June 1992. (Format: TXT=47975 bytes) (Obsoleted by RFC1519) (Status: INFORMATIONAL)

1364 BGP OSPF Interaction. K. Varadhan. September 1992. (Format: TXT=32121 bytes) (Obsoleted by RFC1403) (Also RFC1247, RFC1267) (Status: PROPOSED STANDARD)

1397 Default Route Advertisement In BGP2 and BGP3 Version of The Border Gateway Protocol. D. Haskin. January 1993. (Format: TXT=4124 bytes) (Status: PROPOSED STANDARD)

1403 BGP OSPF Interaction. K. Varadhan. January 1993. (Format: TXT=36173 bytes) (Obsoletes RFC1364) (Status: PROPOSED STANDARD)

1517 Applicability Statement for the Implementation of Classless Inter-Domain Routing (CIDR). Internet Engineering Steering Group, R. Hinden. September 1993. (Format: TXT=7357 bytes) (Status: PROPOSED STANDARD)

1518 An Architecture for IP Address Allocation with CIDR. Y. Rekhter & T. Li. September 1993. (Format: TXT=72609 bytes) (Status: PROPOSED STANDARD)

1519 Classless Inter-Domain Routing (CIDR): an Address Assignment and Aggregation Strategy. V. Fuller, T. Li, J. Yu, & K. Varadhan. September 1993. (Format: TXT=59998 bytes) (Obsoletes RFC1338) (Status: PROPOSED STANDARD)

1520 Exchanging Routing Information Across Provider Boundaries in the CIDR Environment. Y. Rekhter & C. Topolcic. September 1993. (Format: TXT=20389 bytes) (Status: INFORMATIONAL)

1654 A Border Gateway Protocol 4 (BGP-4). Y. Rekhter & T. Li, Editors. July 1994. (Format: TXT=130118 bytes) (Obsoleted by RFC1771) (Status: PROPOSED STANDARD)

1655 Application of the Border Gateway Protocol in the Internet. Y. Rekhter & P. Gross, Editors. July 1994. (Format: TXT=43664 bytes) (Obsoletes RFC1268) (Obsoleted by RFC1772) (Status: PROPOSED STANDARD)

1656 BGP-4 Protocol Document Roadmap and Implementation Experience. P. Traina. July 1994. (Format: TXT=7705 bytes) (Obsoleted by RFC1773) (Status: PROPOSED STANDARD)

1745 BGP4/IDRP for IP—-OSPF Interaction. K. Varadhan, S. Hares, Y. Rekhter. December 1994. (Format: TXT=43675 bytes) (Status: PROPOSED STANDARD)

1771 A Border Gateway Protocol 4 (BGP-4). Y. Rekhter & T. Li. March 1995. (Format: TXT=131903 bytes) (Obsoletes RFC1654) (Status: DRAFT STANDARD)

1772 Application of the Border Gateway Protocol in the Internet. Y. Rekhter & P. Gross. March 1995. (Format: TXT=43916 bytes) (Obsoletes RFC1655) (Status: DRAFT STANDARD)

1773 Experience with the BGP-4 protocol. P. Traina. March 1995. (Format: TXT=19936 bytes) (Obsoletes RFC1656) (Status: INFORMATIONAL)

1774 BGP-4 Protocol Analysis. P. Traina, Editor. March 1995. (Format: TXT=23823 bytes) (Status: INFORMATIONAL)

1863 A BGP/IDRP Route Server alternative to a full mesh routing. D. Haskin. October 1995. (Format: TXT=37426 bytes) (Obsoletes RFC1645) (Status: EXPERIMENTAL)

1965 Autonomous System Confederations for BGP. P. Traina. June 1996. (Format: TXT=13575 bytes) (Status: EXPERIMENTAL)

1966 BGP Route Reflection An alternative to full mesh IBGP. T. Bates & R. Chandrasekeran. June 1996. (Format: TXT=14320 bytes) (Status: EXPERIMENTAL)

1997 BGP Communities Attribute. R. Chandra, P. Traina & T. Li. August 1996. (Format: TXT=8275 bytes) (Status: PROPOSED STANDARD)

1998 An Application of the BGP Community Attribute in Multi-home Routing. E. Chen & T. Bates. August 1996. (Format: TXT=16953 bytes) (Status: INFORMATIONAL)

2283 Multiprotocol Extensions for BGP-4. T. Bates, R. Chandra, D. Katz, Y. Rekhter. February 1998. (Format: TXT=18946 bytes) (Status: PROPOSED STANDARD)

2385 Protection of BGP Sessions via the TCP MD5 Signature Option. A. Heffernan. August 1998. (Format: TXT=12315 bytes) (Status: PROPOSED STANDARD)

Related RFCs

0940 Toward an Internet standard scheme for subnetting. Gateway Algorithms and Data Structures Task Force. Apr-01-1985. (Format: TXT=6881 bytes) (Status: UNKNOWN)

0985 Requirements for Internet gateways - draft. National Science Foundation, Network Technical Advisory Group. May-01-1986. (Format: TXT=59221 bytes) (Obsoleted by RFC1009) (Status: UNKNOWN)

1009 Requirements for Internet gateways. R.T. Braden, J. Postel. Jun-01-1987. (Format: TXT=128173 bytes) (Obsoletes RFC0985) (Obsoleted by RFC1812) (Status: HISTORIC)

1136 Administrative Domains and Routing Domains: A model for routing in the Internet. S. Hares, D. Katz. Dec-01-1989. (Format: TXT=22158 bytes) (Status: INFORMATIONAL)

1142 OSI IS-IS Intra-domain Routing Protocol. D. Oran. Feb-01-1990. (Format: TXT=425379, PS=1204297 bytes) (Status: INFORMATIONAL)

1195 Use of OSI IS-IS for routing in TCP/IP and dual environments. R.W. Callon. Dec-01-1990. (Format: TXT=187866, PS=362052 bytes) (Status: PROPOSED STANDARD)

1256 ICMP Router Discovery Messages. S. Deering. Sep-01-1991. (Format: TXT=43059 bytes) (Also RFC0792) (Status: PROPOSED STANDARD)

1264 Internet Engineering Task Force Internet Routing Protocol Standardization Criteria. R.M. Hinden. Oct-01-1991. (Format: TXT=17016 bytes) (Status: INFORMATIONAL)

1477 IDPR as a Proposed Standard. M. Steenstrup. July 1993. (Format: TXT=32238 bytes) (Status: PROPOSED STANDARD)

1478 An Architecture for Inter-Domain Policy Routing. M. Steenstrup. July 1993. (Format: TXT=90673 bytes) (Status: PROPOSED STANDARD)

1479 Inter-Domain Policy Routing Protocol Specification: Version 1. M. Steenstrup. July 1993. (Format: TXT=275823 bytes) (Status: PROPOSED STANDARD)

1584 Multicast Extensions to OSPF. J. Moy. March 1994. (Format: TXT=262463, PS=426358 bytes) (Status: PROPOSED STANDARD)

1585 MOSPF: Analysis and Experience. J. Moy. March 1994. (Format: TXT=29754 bytes) (Status: INFORMATIONAL)

1716 Towards Requirements for IP Routers. P. Almquist, F. Kastenholz. November 1994. (Format: TXT=432330 bytes) (Obsoleted by RFC1812) (Status: INFORMATIONAL)

1812 Requirements for IP Version 4 Routers. F. Baker. June 1995. (Format: TXT=415740 bytes) (Obsoletes RFC1716, RFC1009) (Status: PROPOSED STANDARD)

1860 Variable Length Subnet Table For IPv4. T. Pummill & B. Manning. October 1995. (Format: TXT=5694 bytes) (Obsoleted by RFC1878) (Status: INFORMATIONAL)
1878 Variable Length Subnet Table For IPv4. T. Pummill & B. Manning. December 1995. (Format: TXT=19414 bytes) (Obsoletes RFC1860) (Status: INFORMATIONAL)

ENDNOTES

1. The first was the Exterior Gateway Protocol (EGP, RFCs 827, then 904), which is now classified as "Historic," as is RIPv1.

2. OSPF is the preferred IGP for the Internet, according to RFC-1371.

3. The subnet-specific broadcast format may also be used.

4. RIP does not need to support metrics as large as 4,294,967,295 hops, which is the largest number that would fit in the route object's metric field (i.e., 0xFF-FF-FF-FF).

5. We save 40 bytes if there are no IP options.

6. Some RIPv1 implementations may be confused by RIPv2's newer packet formats. The use of the multicast address avoids confusing older routers by "hiding" the newer traffic from them.

7. Note that a 32-bit field is an inefficient way to describe a subnet mask. The subnet mask could have been shoehorned into a single byte, in which the value of the field expresses the number of left-aligned 1-bits in the subnet mask.

8. There is even a specification (RFC-2154) that describes how to cryptographically sign potentially every object in the Link State Database, for the ultimate in routing protocol integrity.

9. In some cases, notably PPP and Frame Relay, link-layer mechanisms allow detection of a dead neighbor well before the Hello protocol would have pronounced the neighbor to be dead.

10. As an aside, multicast is also used for sending Link-State Updates to the Designated Routers. For this purpose, a different address, 224.0.0.6 (all OSPF designated routers) is used, so that each update packet can inform both the Designated Router and the Backup Designated Router simultaneously.

11. Many media do *not* have this property! If the medium is nonbroadcast, it may be non-transitive.

12. A router may decide to wait at least HelloInterval seconds to make sure that a Hello is heard from every neighbor whose existence was inferred by virtue of their being mentioned in the first Hello.

13. At least as far as the routers are concerned. Of course, a failure of the subnetwork medium itself would either partition or disable the inter-router connectivity.

14. The waiting period is set to the RouterDeadInterval, as specified in the Hello packets.

15. Again, the delay is the RouterDeadInterval.

16. A stub network is not used to reach destinations beyond the network itself.

17. Transit networks interconnect multiple OSPF routers.

18. The details being exactly which routers are attached to which networks, and which networks touch which routers.

19. AS-External LSAs represent reachable prefixes that are outside of the OSPF Autonomous System.

20. The OSPF Forwarding Address predated RIPv2's Next Hop attribute.

21. The network was NASA's Earth Observing System, Data and Information System, version zero, or EOSDISv0 for short.

22. Most routers use a value of 100,000,000 (i.e., 10^8) divided by the interface speed. So a 10 Mbps Ethernet would be a cost of 10, an FDDI (100 Mbps) would be a cost of 1, and a T-1 line (1.536 Mbps) would be a cost of 65, and so on.

23. Technically, AreaIDs are 32-bit numbers; like IP addresses, they are written as a "dotted quad." In many cases, the AreaIDs are abbreviated, so Area 17 is actually Area 0.0.0.17. Similarly, the Backbone Area is also called Area 0, short for Area 0.0.0.0. Area IDs may also be taken from their enclosed prefix block; an area that encloses prefix 172.16.18.192/26 might be called Area 172.16.18.192.

24. Note that these subnet prefixes do not use up all of the 192.168.0.0/19 prefix. The network manager has decided that she will not assign addresses from this /19 in any other OSPF Area.

25. Remember, these prefixes are all part of 192.168.0.0/19, but they are also part of 192.168.0.0/18, or 192.0.0.0/3 for that matter! An ABR cannot know how much space has been allocated to its Area, just based on the prefixes that exist at some point in time. Only the network manager knows that a certain prefix has been allocated to an Area, and can ensure that part of that prefix will not be used in another Area.

26. Stands for either an Area Border Router (ABR) or an Autonomous System Border Router (ASBR).

27. Stands for either the Backup Designated Router (BDR), or the Designated Router.

28. OSPF classifies LAN subnetworks as the "broadcast" interface type.

29. If there is only one router on a LAN, it is the DR. The second router to appear is the BDR, regardless of the new router's RouterID or RouterPriority. Subsequent routers defer to the (B)DRs. Only when the first two routers are being activated at about the same time (within 4*RouterDeadTime of each other) will the highest RouterID become DR—otherwise the DR is simply the first router with a non-zero RouterPriority.

30. Convergence time for RIPv1 and RIPv2 should be identical.

31. As a matter of fact, the NETBuilder's OSPF implementation was the first from the specification (i.e., not ported from Rob Coltun's code that he wrote while at the University of Maryland).

CHAPTER 14

INTERCONNECTING DISSIMILAR UNICAST ROUTING DOMAINS

Interconnecting different Routing Domains is essential in order to build IP-based networks. Given the range of choices in the routing protocol department,[1] it is not surprising that different Administrative Domains will choose to use different routing protocols. Within an Administrative Domain, there will almost certainly be different Routing Domains. The choices of routing protocols are often driven by the personal preferences of network managers,[2] but just as often are dictated by the capabilities of the equipment being used in a particular Routing Domain. If your favorite routing protocol is not supported well, or at all, you have to make do—and you still have to interconnect that Routing Domain with the rest of your network.

The use of a variety of routing protocols across different Routing Domains is manifested at the macro level in the Internet's routing system, as illustrated by Figure 14.1. The Border Gateway Protocol, version four (BGP-4), is used to attach the various Administrative Domains to their ISP(s). Each attached Administrative Domain represents at least one Routing Domain,[3] and it uses BGP-4 to advertise its list of reachable prefixes (a.k.a., its "routes") to its ISP(s).

Figure 14–1 is a simplified representation of the way ISPs attach to each other; ISPs also exchange routes via a BGP peering session across a common DMZ network. Public DMZs where many ISPs interconnect are known as Network Access Points (NAPs). ISPs that need to exchange significant amounts of traffic may set up

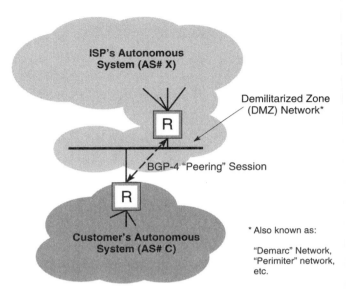

FIGURE 14.1   BGP-4 Autonomous systems.

a private DMZ, known as a "private peering" point. For increased robustness, ISPs usually attach to each other at several geographically dispersed locations.

In BGP-4 parlance, an Administrative Domain is called an "Autonomous System," or AS, which is usually defined as a collection of routers under a single administrative authority.[4] Each BGP AS is identified by a unique 16-bit number (i.e., AS numbers lie between 0 and 65,535). The figure shows the customer having their own AS number, which is not a requirement—in fact, most customers are attached to their ISP as an extension of one of the ISP's AS numbers. Even in this case there is always a clean point of demarcation across the Administrative Domain boundary.

Only those customers that want to be attached to multiple ISPs (for extra capacity, increased resiliency, etc.) *need* their own AS number. Multihoming—i.e., connecting your AS to multiple ISPs—is not easy (you can only truly control how packets *leave* your network) and should not be attempted lightly. BGP-4 is really beyond the scope of this book, but I can recommend the excellent Networld+Interop two-day tutorial "Building Scalable and Resilient Internetworks Using OSPF and BGP-4" by Eural Authement and Marten Terpstra. Also, a book entitled *"Internet Routing Architectures"* by Bassam Halabi covers this subject in some detail.

Whether or not the customer has their own AS number, the customer's internal internetwork is still a separate Administrative Domain; the ISP isn't necessarily operating the customer's network for them.[5] Within a customer's Administrative Domain, selected subsets of their routers may be organized into Routing Domains of their own. One might ask why everyone just doesn't pick one routing protocol and use that across their entire Administrative Domain, making it a single Routing Domain. There are many valid technical, political, or practical reasons for using multiple routing protocols, as outlined here.

1. **Technical:** Topological complexity may dictate that a "more sophisticated" protocol be used. Some regions of the network may require faster convergence times than others (e.g., core versus edge). Features such as equal-cost multipath routing, or efficient operation over low-speed WAN links may also drive the choice of one protocol over another in some topological region(s).

2. **Political:** When one company purchases or merges with another, it may be the case that the two networks, including their MIS staffs, are not tightly integrated.[6] There is a spectrum of possibilities, from a very disjoint case, similar to an ISP-to-ISP attachment, to a case in which the two networks are eventually integrated. On the more disjoint end of the spectrum, the choices of routing protocol within a Routing Domain will probably be driven by history as much as any other factor. Interconnecting the formerly independent networks need not impact their internal structure.

3. **Practical:** Each router (or routing-capable networking device, e.g., a dial-in remote access concentrator, a layer-three switch, a terminal server, etc.) will support a different set of routing protocols. In order to enable all the devices to communicate, one must choose a routing protocol that they all support. The choice of routing protocol must be from the intersection of all the products' feature sets. Suppose that Product A supports routing protocols {A, B, D}, and Product B supports {B, C, D}. Clearly, the choice is between protocols B and D, since only those two protocols are supported by both products. If some class of device only supports one routing protocol, then that device effectively dictates the choice of protocol for that Routing Domain. In practice, the intersection is never the empty set, because nearly every device that supports IP routing also supports RIP (and static routing, too).

Given that multiple routing protocols and multiple Routing Domains are a fact of life, we need to have a set of techniques for gluing them together. The goal is that all the Routing Domains know about all the reachable prefixes within the entire Administrative Domain. All the following techniques support the achievement of this goal, but they are not all equally applicable to all situations.

OVERVIEW OF INTERCONNECTION TECHNIQUES

The following three techniques require that at least one router implementation includes the required set of routing protocols. If one Routing Domain is using routing protocol X and another is using Y, then at least one router, somewhere on the Routing Domain border, needs to be able to participate in, or "speak," both routing protocols. The techniques proceed from the simplest to the most complex. Objectively speaking, it is difficult to rank these, since there are actually many criteria that could be used to compare them.

Simple Aggregation may be the most attractive from an architectural perspective, but actually deploying it might require readdressing a Routing Domain (probably not an attractive option in practice). On the other end of the scale, internal router functions can be used to directly import and export prefixes between routing processes within the router. This is conceptually simple, but can become tricky if one needs to integrate classful and classless Routing Domains. Most people immediately think of this technique, which is unfortunate because it is not necessarily the cleanest solution. These techniques can be combined to match the needs of the relevant routing protocols.

Finally, it is also possible to deploy DMZ networks between Routing Domains, so that no single router (or set of routers) on the Routing Domain boundary needs to be under the simultaneous administrative control of two separate parties. Politically, this may be the most appealing solution. However, when problems crop up—as they inevitably will—it will be more difficult to verify that *two* routers have nonconflicting configurations than to check a single router's configuration for errors. Moreover, it is slightly more challenging to get two routers working correctly in the first place. It is not impossible for this solution to work well, but it may be more of a challenge than is initially expected.

One advantage of using a DMZ network is that multiple routers, in parallel, can share the role of a domain's border router. The use of redundant routers could increase the robustness of the interconnection, but redundant routers alone cannot compensate for a DMZ failure.[7] If the LAN goes down, it would take out the backup router as well as the primary. To combat this possibility, it is also possible to use parallel exchange LANs. Figure 14.2 shows several possible interconnection scenarios (to be discussed in more detail below). The chosen solution will balance cost,

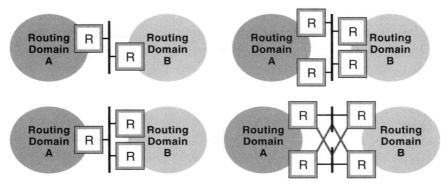

FIGURE 14.2 Several ways to use a DMZ.

management complexity, and the required degree of robustness. The level of redundancy may also dictate the choice of routing protocol in use across the DMZ.

Many people focus on the network as the only source of outages when trying to make it more robust. It would be unwise to overlook items such as power distribution as well. If an interconnect is highly mission-critical, its power should come from an uninterruptable power supply (UPS). There are numerous stories of people designing highly redundant networks and plugging all the routers into the same power source. If the power source fails, then all the routers, primaries and backups, as well as both DMZs, could be taken out. An excellent resource for war stories about poorly designed systems is Dr. Peter G. Neumann's book *"Computer-Related Risks."*

SIMPLE: AGGREGATION

When using aggregation, a Routing Domain is represented by a single IP prefix and a router sits at the aggregation point (there can be more than one router and more than one aggregation point). For an illustrative example, we can use the old 1997 InteropNet architecture. Aggregation was built into the network design, and addresses were carefully assigned so that aggregation was maintained.

The InteropNet is blessed with a Class A network number (45.0.0.0/8). An aisle in a convention center basically mapped to a "rib" that connected all its exhibitors. The subnet mask was /22, which applied to the rib itself and to any prefixes that had been assigned to any exhibitors. All of a rib group's /22s were drawn from its common /16 prefix. Figure 14.3 depicts an imaginary Rib 77.

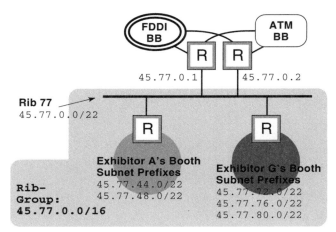

FIGURE 14.3   InteropNet Rib 77.

The fixed /22 subnet mask within the rib group facilitates the use of RIPv1 on the rib, which is virtually universally supported among router vendors. RIPv1 support was important since no one could predict what vendor's router would be used by a given exhibitor to connect their booth to the rib. Also, in an event that promotes standards and interoperability, there is no good reason to impose arbitrary restrictions that would impede an exhibitor's easy attachment to the InteropNet.

While the ribs used RIPv1 due to its ubiquity, the routing protocol in use over the FDDI and ATM backbones had been OSPF for several years. The primary and secondary routers on the ribs also spoke OSPF, allowing them to actively maintain an adjacency over the rib. The rib's OSPF AreaID was 45.77.0.0 (each rib's AreaID was simply its /16 prefix), and each rib was a stub area. Also, if any exhibitor wanted to join the OSPF routing system, they could do that if their router supported OSPF.

The primary and secondary routers both advertised the default route onto the rib via RIP,[8] which provided the rib-attached routers with a way out to destinations beyond the rib. It was unnecessary to advertise any other routes onto the rib. The primary and secondary routers knew that they were attached to 45.77.0.0/22, and they were configured to learn RIP routes on their rib-77 interfaces. All routers on the rib would learn RIP routes from each other, as well as learning the default routes from the backbone routers.

As a safety measure, the backbone routers were configured so that they could only learn valid RIP routes—i.e., only those /22s within 45.77.0.0/16. Since there are always 64 ($2^{(22-16)} = 2^6 = 64$) /22 prefixes within any /16 prefix, there can be no more than 64 RIP-learned routes per rib. For this rib, the valid prefixes were: 45.77.0.0/22, 45.77.4.0/22, ..., 45.77.248.0/22, and 45.77.252.0/22. So, for those exhibitor intrabooth networks that were alive at any point in time, the backbone routers will know about all the valid more specific routes inside 45.77.0.0/16, having learned of their existence via RIP. Any /22 routes that were not within this /16 prefix should not be learned (via this rib). For example, it would be an indication of a problem if a route to 45.101.88.0/22 were ever learned via Rib 77. Obviously, this /22 prefix should have been learned on Rib 101 (since the supposed subnetwork prefix is part of 45.101.0.0/16).

Since aggregation was in use, the backbone routers did not need to import each specific active /22 prefix into the backbone. Instead, they were configured to use OSPF's Area-Range Aggregation feature,[9] so that they only advertised a single aggregate prefix (i.e., 45.77.0.0/16) into the backbone. Advertising this single aggregate prefix tells all the other backbone routers that these two routers should receive any traffic destined for 45.77.*.*. When such a packet arrived at either router, the router would look at its set of RIP-learned routes (from its attached ribs) to make a decision about how to forward the packet. For example, the primary router may have a forwarding table as shown in Figure 14.4.

Several observations are in order. First, note that this imaginary router had learned, via OSPF, several /16s via its 45.0.4.0/22 interface (i.e., the FDDI backbone). These OSPF-learned /16s are other rib-group aggregates (there were many more than this in the real InteropNet). Note that the other rib-groups' internal structure is invisible to us, just as the internal structure of our local Rib 77 group is invisible to them.[10] Finally, observe that because this router had the interface address 45.77.0.1, it must be the primary router on Rib 77.

Known Prefixes	Next-Hop Gateway	Metric	Source
0.0.0.0/0	45.0.4.1	10	OSPF
45.0.4.0/22	45.0.4.1	0 (connected)	direct
45.60.0.0/16	45.0.4.60	6	OSPF
45.61.0.0/16	45.0.4.60	6	OSPF
45.62.0.0/16	45.0.4.60	6	OSPF
45.63.0.0/16	45.0.4.60	6	OSPF
45.77.0.0/22	45.77.0.1	0 (connected)	direct
45.77.16.0/22	45.77.0.7	1	RIP
45.77.20.0/22	45.77.0.7	2	RIP
45.77.32.0/22	45.77.0.11	1	RIP
45.77.44.0/22	45.77.0.21	1	RIP
45.77.96.0/22	45.77.0.35	1	RIP

FIGURE 14.4 Forwarding table showing route sources.

The primary router has learned five routes via RIP, of which four are one hop away, which means that they are just on the other side of an exhibitor's booth router that is attached to Rib 77. Obviously, all the next-hop gateways, for subnetworks that are reachable via this rib, have addresses in the 45.77.0.0/22 prefix. However, the fifth prefix is two hops away, which would imply a network inside of an exhibitor's booth, advertised onto the rib by the exhibitor's router. The two-hop route and one other route have the same next-hop router, which is more evidence that they are both in the same exhibitor's booth. Figure 14.5 is a graphical illustration of the forwarding table in Figure 14.4.

If the router received a packet destined for 45.77.96.171, it will be forwarded to 45.77.0.35 as directed by its forwarding table. If that destination is actually reachable (presumably somewhere inside the exhibitor's booth), then the exhibitor's router will deliver it. On the other hand, if that router has no luck reaching that destination IP address, then an ICMP Destination-Unreachable message may be generated.

Aggregation-Induced Routing Loops

What if the primary router in Figure 14.5 had received a packet destined for 45.77.251.99? Based on its forwarding table, it has not learned the 45.77.248.0/22 prefix, so what should it do? There is actually a slight required modification to the router's forwarding logic due to the fact that the router is generating an aggregate for 45.77.0.0/16. The router must <u>not</u> forward this packet—which it does not have a

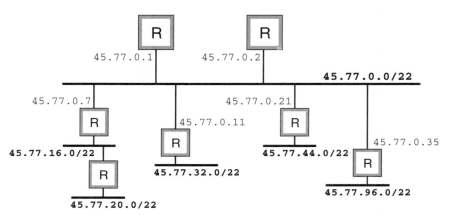

FIGURE 14.5 Logical view of Rib 77 per Figure 14.4.

specific forwarding table entry for—to its default gateway, as it would do with other packets that are addressed to unknown destinations that lie outside its aggregate(s). The router must realize that since it is creating the aggregate for 45.77.0.0/16, it *must* know all the more specific routes within that prefix. If the router does not know how to deliver a packet addressed within one of its aggregates, then no other router could possibly know how to deliver it.

Consider what would have happened if the router had forwarded the packet to 45.0.4.1 (its default gateway). 45.0.4.1 would have received it, looked up the destination in its forwarding table, found 45.77.0.0/16 (reachable via 45.0.4.70), and forwarded the packet right back, after decrementing the TTL by one. If we again insist on following our default route—forwarding the packet back to our default gateway—it will politely return it to us once again. The net result will be that the TTL has been decremented by two each time the packet bounces back and forth. The routing loop is happening because the router that is generating the 45.77.0.0/16 aggregate is not taking responsibility for the entire aggregate. If it cannot reach some destination within the aggregate, then no other router can. Figure 14.6 illustrates this situation.

This is a fundamental issue that arises whenever a router performs aggregation. The proper behavior is for this router to have realized that it was the aggregator for this prefix, and then for it to have immediately generated an ICMP Destination-

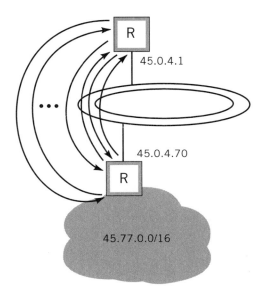

FIGURE 14.6 Aggregation-induced routing loop.

Unreachable error message. The routing loop causes a lot of excess traffic (over 200 copies of the packet), but eventually the packet's TTL will expire. Whichever router received the packet when its TTL equaled one will have to generate a ICMP Time-Exceeded error message and send it to the packet's source.

Either way, the packet's source eventually finds out that the packet was undeliverable, but one way is much more efficient than the other. Also, one way is much more descriptive of the problem than the other. If you ever spot a tight routing loop between a router that is doing aggregation and its default router, you can start with a working hypothesis that the aggregator has a bug in its forwarding logic, in that it does not treat intra-aggregate destinations as a special case.

SUMMARY

The InteropNet was (and still is) custom designed, so there was substantial freedom to force the addressing to match the network topology. In a corporate network, it is often the case that addressing is not topologically significant, which may limit the applicability of aggregation in the real world. Had the networks' addressing plans taken aggregation into account from the start, aggregation would be possible.

To be fair, most of today's networks were deployed before VLSM was widely understood, or even before it was available in routers. There is no shame in having a network that has been up and running since before VLSM came along! The earliest applications of aggregation were in the interdomain routing world, with CIDR-based address assignment and "CIDR-ized" classless routing protocols, such as BGP-4. This serves to reinforce the assertion that the easiest time to deploy aggregation is in new installations.

The best opportunity to take advantage of aggregation is when new networks are being designed. If an addressing plan is created that is topologically significant, then aggregation will be possible at any addressing boundary in the internetwork. Discipline is required to stick to the addressing plan once it has been designed and deployed. The benefits of aggregation are many; namely, it minimizes routing table size in core; it's natural—no "protocol" exchange is required; and it gives the user lots of practice with binary math.

Aggregation lets us collapse an entire chunk of the network topology into a single prefix that we advertise "up" the hierarchy, i.e., toward the backbone. The aggregating router needs to participate in some routing protocol within the aggregate, and must be configured to summarize that aggregate into the backbone. It is not required that the router should be running RIPv1 and OSPF. In fact, it would be possible for

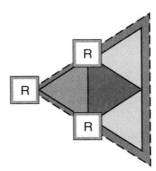

FIGURE 14.7 Recursive aggregation.

a router to be running RIPv2 on both sides, or RIPv1 inside the aggregate and RIPv2 outside it.[11] The key requirement is that whichever routing protocol is being used, the router must be able to learn all the reachable intra-aggregate routes.

Finally, note that aggregation may be recursive, as illustrated in Figure 14.7. It is possible that multiple routing protocols may be used within an aggregate, depending on how large a Routing Domain is represented by the aggregate.

COMPLEX: EXPLICIT IMPORT/EXPORT OF ROUTES

Any router that supports more than one routing protocol, and moreover supports the simultaneous use of more than one routing protocol, usually supports the exchange of routing information between the active routing protocol processes. This capability is known by several names, including "routing policies," "route redistribution," and "route leaking," among others. Before discussing this technique, we need a bit of background in order to understand what goes on inside a router.

Each routing protocol is implemented as a separate process. The router includes an "operating system," which supports the operation of these different routing protocol processes. The operating system provides necessary infrastructure, such as drivers for all the supported interfaces, message-passing, interrupt handling, user interface(s), interprocess communication, etc. The routing processes implement their routing protocols and use the router's "operating system" to send messages, e.g., routing updates, etc., over the router's interfaces.

For IP, and most other Network-layer protocols, what matters is the forwarding table; *how* it is built does not affect packet handling. Each routing process can contribute prefixes that it has learned into the forwarding table, if permitted by the router's "routing policies." If multiple processes have learned a route to the same destination, there are precedence rules that control which forwarding table entry will actually get used. For example, if OSPF and RIP both learn a route to prefix A, most router implementations will prefer to use the OSPF-learned route over the one that RIP learned. Routers may allow these default precedence rules to be overriden. Figure 14.8 illustrates the relationship among the processes within a router.

For example, under Unix®, one may run `gated` and `routed`[12] at the same time. The `gated` process may implement OSPF and RIPv2 subprocesses, while the `routed` process implements RIPv1. In Figure 14.8, multiple processes per routing protocol are depicted. There are actually two ways that multiple processes may be implemented. One way, as drawn in the figure, shows all the routing protocols contributing to one forwarding table, which represents a single logical router. It is also conceivable that a vendor could support multiple logical routers within a box, each with its own forwarding table and its own set of associated routing protocol processes, but this capability is not necessarily a mainstream requirement.

The router's routing policies are the rules that control which of each routing protocol's prefixes get installed into the forwarding table (on the left). The interface's IP process can create the necessary headers when the router needs to transmit its own packets, or when it needs to simply forward packets on behalf of other systems. The

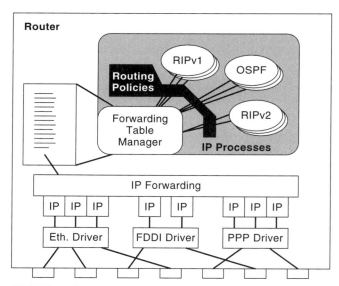

FIGURE 14.8　Routing processes.

IP forwarding process only requires the forwarding table in order to operate. It is not cognizant of the various routing protocols.

A router may need to participate in two Routing Domains that each run the same protocol, as in Figure 14.9, but may also want to carefully control the import/export of routing information across the boundary.

If the two Routing Domains were simply attached to the same router they would create one large Routing Domain, which may not be the intended result. Running multiple instances of the same routing protocol within a router can facilitate such an interconnection in a "one-box" solution. In the case of two companies merging, each with their own substantial OSPF networks already in place, it is usually not advisable to just interconnect the two networks' backbone areas and hope for the best.

Now that we have a framework for discussion, we can work through some concrete examples that will illustrate how challenging the import/export of prefixes is in practice, especially between classless and classful routing protocols.

RIP-OSPF

Subnetted RIP is obviously classful, so if the RIP Routing Domain has any internal subnetting it will have a fixed mask-length across each network number in each domain. (Each network number may have a different extended-network-prefix length.) On the other hand, OSPF, being classless, can have variable mask-lengths on its side. Any routes that are passed from the OSPF side to the RIP side will lose all their masks and revert to their classful interpretation.

Any RIP-derived routes can be passed into the OSPF domain, but care must be taken so that those same routes are not reintroduced into the RIP domain from a different location. This might result in traffic from one part of the RIP domain needing to traverse the OSPF domain to get to another part of the RIP domain. This is not as hard to imagine as you may think. Any two Routing Domains that are worth inter-

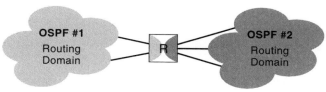

FIGURE 14.9   Multiple routing protocol processes.

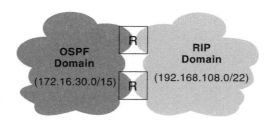

FIGURE 14.10   Route leaking example topology.

connecting are worth interconnecting robustly, but multiple interconnection points create opportunites for just such "interesting" misconfigurations.

RIP-OSPF Interconnection Example

We will examine the issues with "route leaking" in the context of Figure 14.10, in which each Routing Domain consists of only one classless network prefix, but the RIP domain is four classful network numbers, and the OSPF domain is two classful network numbers.

Importing RIP Routes into OSPF.   Routers allow routes to be leaked with a level of precision that can be matched to the needs of the network topology. We will examine the two ends of the spectrum, which are to import an entire aggregate representing the whole RIP domain, or to import all the individual reachable subnetworks in the RIP domain. In the real world, you might need to support a configuration that is somewhere in the middle, which will make more sense once you understand the extremes.

When importing from RIP into OSPF, there are four choices, as drawn in Figure 14.11. We will consider the positive and negative aspects of all the quadrants of the figure.

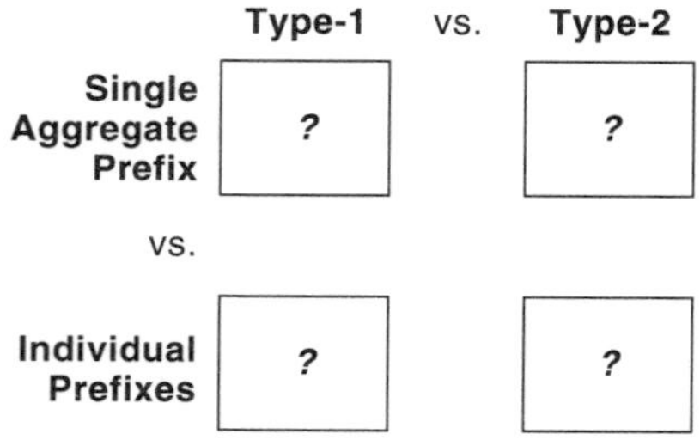

	Type-1 vs.	**Type-2**
Single Aggregate Prefix	?	?
vs.		
Individual Prefixes	?	?

FIGURE 14.11   Importing RIP into OSPF.

TYPE-1 VERSUS TYPE-2 AS-EXTERNAL LSAs

When an ASBR imports an external prefix into the OSPF Autonomous System, it may assign either a Type-1 or Type-2 metric to the AS-External LSA. Type-1 metrics are treated as are intradomain intra- and inter-Area metrics; they are added to the accumulated intra-domain metric. So, if an AS-External LSA is imported with a metric of 1000 and there are two routers, one at a cost of 107 and the other at 193 away from the ASBR, the AS-External LSA will be seen as having a cost of 1107 from the former and 1193 from the latter. This means that the former router is "closer" to the prefix represented by the AS-External LSA imported by the former ASBR in some sense.

Type-2 metrics are a constant. If an AS-External LSA is generated with a cost of 450, every router in the Autonomous System will see that prefix as being at a cost of 450.

Importing the entire aggregate as one prefix (in this example, 192.168.108.0/22) will cause an AS-External LSA to be injected from each border router (ASBR) into the OSPF domain. Now, we have a second-order issue to understand, which is how to choose what type of AS-External LSA to inject, and if a Type-2, what should the cost (i.e., metric) be from each router?

If we choose to import the entire RIP domain as a single aggregate, injecting a single AS-External LSA from both of the ASBRs, we might want to use Type-2 AS-External LSAs. In this case, we just pick one router that we believe will be more reliable, or that is better connected, or the one you like better, then set that router's injected Type-2 external metric to 1 (or some other low number). On the other router, for the RIP domain's AS-External LSA, set the metric to 2 (or a number higher than that used by the primary ASBR). With this choice of metrics, all the routers in the OSPF domain will prefer to reach the prefix representing the RIP domain via the primary ASBR, i.e., the one that is injecting the RIP domain's prefix with the lower metric.

If the primary ASBR fails, the rest of the routers in the OSPF domain will be able to fail over to the secondary ASBR. After all, they already know about the secondary ASBR, which is importing the aggregated AS-External LSA with a less preferred (i.e., higher cost) Type-2 metric. The OSPF domain's routers will be left with only this single entry in their forwarding tables for 192.168.108.0/22, reachable via the secondary ASBR. When the primary ASBR comes back up, the other routers will see the lower metric Type-2 AS-External LSA, which will cause them all to recalculate their routes to the RIP domain via this freshly undead router.

If we chose to import the entire RIP domain as a single Type-1 AS-External aggregate, we would probably choose to have both ASBRs use the same initial metric for the aggregate's LSA, e.g., 100.[13] Then the individual routers in the OSPF domain will calculate their individual distances to the aggregate representing the RIP domain. One OSPF intradomain router may have an accumulated cost to the upper ASBR of 176, and to the lower ASBR of 231. Such a router would prefer to reach the RIP domain via the lower-cost route,[14] which for this router is the upper ASBR.

Each router in the OSPF domain will see a different accumulated cost to each ASBR for the aggregate prefix's Type-1 AS-External LSA, and so there will be a crude form of load sharing across the ASBR. The OSPF routers that see themselves as "closer" to the RIP domain via the upper ASBR will send their traffic that way. Similarly, the routers that see themselves as "closer" to the lower ASBR will send their traffic to the RIP domain toward that router.

To recap: Injecting the RIP domain's aggregate as two different Type-2 external metrics will create a primary/secondary traffic flow across the two ASBRs. If the primary is up, only it will ever carry traffic to the RIP domain. Alternatively, injecting the aggregate prefix's AS-External LSA with a Type-1 external metric will split the traffic between the two ASBRs. OSPF routers will use the ASBR that is topologically closest to them to reach the RIP domain. In the Type-1 case, traffic will still fail over properly should one of the ASBRs fail, since there will only be one LSA for this prefix in the Link State Database.

Importing only the aggregate prefix has the advantage of minimizing the impact on the forwarding tables in the OSPF domain. In this case, we add only one extra forwarding table entry in each intradomain OSPF router, and a slightly larger Link State Database size (again, each OSPF router must carry this AS-External LSA, at least those routers in the backbone and transit areas). The disadvantage of importing just an aggregate is that we treat all destinations within the RIP domain as if they were equally reachable via either ASBR. Said another way, the OSPF intradomain routers will all consider all parts of the RIP domain to be the same distance away.

In reality, it might be better to know that certain parts of the RIP domain are actually closer to one ASBR than the other, allowing a better-informed forwarding decision to be made. Unfortunately, in order to make this decision, the OSPF routers need more information about the internal structure of the RIP domain. That added information comes in the form of an enlarged Link State Database (more AS-External LSAs) and an enlarged forwarding table, which includes specific entries for all the relevant (i.e., reachable) prefixes within the RIP domain.

Taken to the extreme, we can configure the ASBRs to inject every one of the the RIP domain's reachable prefixes into the OSPF domain. Using Type-2 metrics in this case doesn't make much sense, since we want to know which ASBR is closest to some part of the RIP domain. The Type-2 metric is a constant and thus will not allow a router deep in the OSPF domain to tell which ASBR it should use, since all parts of the RIP domain would look like they were, for example, a metric of 1 via the upper ASBR, or a metric of 2 via the lower ASBR. (Of course, we could assign different metrics to various prefixes depending on which ASBR was closer to that part of the RIP domain—but this static configuration could not adapt to topology changes, so this is not a good interconnection strategy.)

Using Type-1 externals with a fixed initial value such as 200, each router in the OSPF domain will know which ASBR is closest to each external prefix. We can even do better than this—by not injecting all the Type-1s with the same metric; but if we do this, we should follow the same rules at each ASBR. For example, if the upper ASBR is three hops from a particular subnet in the RIP domain, it might inject the external LSA for that subnet's prefix with a Type-1 cost of 230. The lower ASBR may be only two hops from that subnet, and may then inject that subnet's external with a Type-1 cost of 220. This will create a bias within the OSPF domain, allowing the intradomain routers to choose the egress ASBR that is closer to the destination subnet in the RIP domain.

You can pick any formula for the import metric, depending on the cost structure within the OSPF domain. For instance, you may want to multiply a RIP hop count by eight before adding it to a fixed base Type-1 cost, such as 200. You don't want to pick a multiple that is so small that it will not be a useful discriminator between routes. By the same token, if you pick a multiplier that is too large, you may end up with the hop count in the RIP domain totally dominating the cost structure in the OSPF domain. This wouldn't necessarily achieve the goal of having the OSPF domain's internal routers choose the ASBR that is closest to each subnet within the RIP domain.

To recap: Injecting all of the RIP domain's subnet prefixes with two different Type-2 metrics doesn't offer any real advantage over just importing the entire RIP domain as a single aggregated Type-2 external. However, injecting the individual subnets with Type-1 metrics (optionally with variable costs; lower meaning closer) will split the traffic between the two ASBRs more intelligently than in the case where only a single aggregate prefix was imported as a Type-1.

When we import the individual subnet prefixes, we retain the beneficial aspect of Type-1 metrics, in that the OSPF routers will choose the closest egress ASBR within the OSPF domain to get to each destination. We may choose to add extra hop-count-dependent cost to help the OSPF routers determine which ASBR is closer to which external destination. OSPF routers will use the ASBR that is topologically closest to them to reach the RIP domain . . . *and* they will know that they are minimizing the cost all the way to the destination.

Again, this improved routing comes at a cost; the OSPF Routing Domain needs to carry more external information than in the case where we only imported a single aggregate prefix to represent the entire RIP domain as a monolithic entity. If the traffic levels are such that it makes sense to use the "best" egress ASBR, then it is worth importing the extra AS-External LSAs. If there is relatively little traffic across the boundary, then it probably doesn't make sense to carry extra routing information in the OSPF domain. It is a general rule that a router can make better forwarding decisions when it has more detailed routing information on which to base a decision.

Importing OSPF Routes into RIP.   We now will shift our focus and imagine that we are inside the RIP domain. From here, we need to reach the OSPF domain. What information do the RIP domain's routers need in order to make this happen? RIP does not have many "knobs" that can be tuned, making this case much simpler than the view from the OSPF domain.

Referring back to Figure 14.10, we recall that the prefix in the OSPF domain is 172.16.30.0/15. Regardless of how the OSPF domain is subnetted, the RIP domain will see it as two Class B network numbers: 172.16.30.0 and 172.16.31.0. RIP has no facilities to manipulate external routes differently than internal ones, so these Class Bs must be assigned a hop count metric, then be advertised into the RIP domain.

If both ASBRs have about the same connectivity, then it may make sense to start the two Class Bs off with a hop count of 1, from each ASBR. If the RIP domain is not too large, it is possible to prefer one ASBR over the other by biasing the import metric. For example, if the lower ASBR were better connected within the OSPF domain, we might choose to import the Class Bs there with a hop count of 1, and at the same time import them from the upper ASBR with a hop count of 3 (or more).

If the lower ASBR disappears, RIP-domain routers will still have a route to the Class Bs, as long as the RIP domain is smaller than 13 hops across (if it were more than 13 hops across, then some routers would never even see a route to these Class Bs, since the total metric would be >15, so they would effectively be an infinite distance away as far as RIP is concerned).

Each router in the RIP domain will choose to forward traffic to these Class Bs over the path with the smallest hop count. Once the traffic arrives at the ASBR, the packet will be forwarded optimally to its destination within the OSPF domain. The ASBR is in the OSPF domain, and it has a detailed, OSPF-derived forwarding table with which to make an informed forwarding decision.

COMPROMISE: EXCHANGE LAN, STATIC ROUTES, USE DEFAULT

When using a router to interconnect two Routing Domains, one must dedicate a separate chassis as the border router with at least one interface per Routing Domain. In such an interconnection scheme, the interdomain boundary is actually inside the router. As such, Routing Domain interconnection is the province of proprietary import/export features. Using an intermediate exchange LAN, e.g., a DMZ or an inter-domain "demarc net," externalizes the interdomain boundary from the interior of the router to the LAN. Besides moving the boundary outside of the router, there are other benefits, in that multiple routers can more easily back each other up. Also, it is easier to make the system as resilient as the application demands. For interconnects requiring ultra-high reliability, one might use dual DMZ nets, with dual routers that are dual connected (each router to both DMZs). Refer back to Figure 14.2 for an illustration of some of the possible interconnection topologies.

There are a few simple choices that one can make when using a DMZ to interconnect Routing Domains. One can use a combination of static and default routing, which requires no protocol exchanges, or one can use a protocol to exchange reachability information across the exchage LAN.

Static and Default Routing

In order to understand how this works, we need to define the terms "transit domain" and "stub domain." A stub domain is one that is attached to only one other domain. It may be attached to the other domain at more than one location, but the routing is set up so that no "through traffic" uses this domain. By "through traffic," we mean traffic that has neither its source, nor its destination, in the stub domain. If a stub domain has multiple exit points, or egress points as they are sometimes called, the routing may be tuned so that intradomain routers can have enough information to make well-informed choices.

Carrying external[15] routing information does not automatically make a domain into a transit domain, but for practical purposes that is a necessary minimum criterion. Transit domains are attached to multiple other domains for the express purpose of carrying traffic between them. In the InteropNet example, the OSPF-based backbone was interconnecting many stub domains (i.e., the RIPv1-based rib groups). Routers inside a transit domain have a critical need for detailed information about which external prefixes may be reached through which egress routers. This information cannot be restricted to the egress routers alone, as it is in a stub domain.

The default route, 0.0.0.0/0, is all about information hiding—so is aggregation. They are different sides of the same coin. Inside a stub domain, a dynamic default route is a way for the egress routers to advertise themselves as the way out. If there are multiple exit points, then the natural question is "what is behind door number 1? or 2? or 6?" A default route is less useful with multiple exit points. In situations where the network designer knows that "most" of the network is reachable via some router, they may choose to have that router advertise a default route. The other routers that attach to the domain may then advertise the hopefully short list of specific destinations that they provide service to, so that the intradomain routers will have just the right amount of information. Their default route will cover those destinations for which they have no explicit forwarding table entry.

A static default route is one that is hard-coded into a router's configuration, rather than being learned dynamically by the stub domain's routing protocol. Often, a dynamic and static default are used together. The network manager knows where the default route is *supposed* to be coming from, so she sets up a router with a static default route as a backup. Most routers support the option of adding static routes (to any destination, not just 0.0.0.0/0), with an override option of some kind. Some routers may do this as an explicit "override" command in the "add a static route" command. Others may associate an administrative metric[16] with the static routes, which has the effect of making the static forwarding table entry less preferred than a dynamically-derived route to the same destination.

The static-override default route can be very handy when transitioning from one routing protocol to another, since it provides a router with some basic forwarding information that it can use while the transition is happening. I have personally transitioned a routing domain from RIP to OSPF without losing any connectivity during the process. These routes can also be handy when changing the OSPF area structure, since as soon as an interface has its AreaID changed, it will invalidate all of its adjacencies, resulting in a loss of all forwarding table entries that were formerly reachable via those now-unreachable neighbors. Just because OSPF can't speak to those neighbors doesn't mean that the router can't deliver packets to them—after all, the LAN isn't down. If the router knows its neighbors' addresses, and what prefixes they lead to, then it can temporarily operate without a dynamic routing protocol. This is an important observation: The default route is not the only static route that may be useful to install in your routers.

Figure 14.12 shows a simple topology that illustrates three intradomain routers in each domain, and one domain border router in each domain.

Figures 14.13 and 14.14 summarize the forwarding tables of these routers. Any of the forwarding table entries may be static, but the point of this example is that packets can get from one domain to the other, even though the intradomain routers have no forwarding table entries that specifically mention the other domain. Even the border router need not know about the internal prefixes in the other domain, though this configuration is somewhat dangerous.

What can we learn by examining these forwarding tables? First, the default route helps routers the most the deeper they are inside the Routing Domain.[17,18] Second, a domain border router needs to know about everything that is inside its own domain. Third, the intradomain routers don't need to know about any prefixes that are not inside their domain, including the DMZ's prefix D. Why is it "dangerous" to have the border routers both[19] configured with a default route, pointing at the other?

If they both think that any unknown prefix is reachable via the other domain border router, then a major routing loop will form whenever a new destination appears. Keep in mind that these static configurations aren't magically updated as the

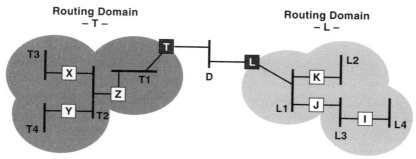

FIGURE 14.12 Static routing sample topology.

Router X

Dest .	Next-Hop
0.0.0.0/0	Router Z
Prefix T2	n/a (Self)
Prefix T3	n/a (Self)

Router Y

Dest .	Next-Hop
0.0.0.0/0	Router Z
Prefix T2	n/a (Self)
Prefix T4	n/a (Self)

Router Z

Dest .	Next-Hop
0.0.0.0/0	Router T
Prefix T1	n/a (Self)
Prefix T2	n/a (Self)
Prefix T3	Router X
Prefix T4	Router Y

Router T-"Dangerous"

Dest.	Next-Hop
0.0.0.0/0	Router L
Prefix D	n/a (Self)
Prefix T1	n/a (Self)
Prefix T2	Router Z
Prefix T3	Router Z
Prefix T4	Router Z

Router T-"Safe"

Dest.	Next-Hop
Prefix D	n/a (Self)
Prefix L1	Router L
Prefix L2	Router L
Prefix L3	Router L
Prefix L4	Router L
Prefix T1	n/a (Self)
Prefix T2	Router Z
Prefix T3	Router Z
Prefix T4	Router Z

FIGURE 14.13 Forwarding tables for routing domain T.

Router I

Dest.	Next-Hop
0.0.0.0/0	Router J
Prefix L3	n/a (Self)
Prefix L4	n/a (Self)

Router J

Dest.	Next-Hop
0.0.0.0/0	Router L
Prefix L1	n/a (Self)
Prefix L3	n/a (Self)

Router K

Dest.	Next-Hop
0.0.0.0/0	Router L
Prefix L1	n/a (Self)
Prefix L2	n/a (Self)

Router L-"Dangerous"

Dest.	Next-Hop
0.0.0.0/0	Router T
Prefix D	n/a (Self)
Prefix L1	n/a (Self)
Prefix L2	Router K
Prefix L3	Router J
Prefix L4	Router J

Router L-"Safe"

Dest.	Next-Hop
Prefix D	n/a (Self)
Prefix L1	n/a (Self)
Prefix L2	Router K
Prefix L3	Router J
Prefix L4	Router J
Prefix T1	Router T
Prefix T2	Router T
Prefix T3	Router T
Prefix T4	Router T

FIGURE 14.14 Forwarding tables for routing domain L.

network topology grows, so if a new network appears on the left, say, T5, it will be unreachable in the absence of any dynamic routing protocol information. So, what if a packet happens to be addressed to an address within T5's prefix, starting from within the L domain?

Clearly, the routers within the L domain will all have the routing tables in Figure 14.13; they never knew anything about specific networks on the T side. Any router over there would forward the packet toward the default route. Once the packet reaches Router L, it will forward the packet to Router T, which will look in its forwarding table for the destination's prefix. Since the router doesn't yet know about T5, it will follow its default route and send the packet back to Router L (by the same logic that led Router L to send the packet to Router T). Router L receives the packet and, like Router T, has no specific prefix that matches this packet's destination so it (again) follows its default route, sending the packet back to Router T. This cycle repeats until the packet's TTL expires, and either Router T or L will then have to send an ICMP Time-Exceeded error message back to the packet's source.

The exact same situation would occur if the packet started within the T domain. If we continue with the presumption that none of the routers have been updated with the new prefix (except, obviously, the one that is directly attached to the new prefix!), then the routers within the T domain will all dutifully forward the packet toward the default route. Ultimately, the packet will reach Router T, which will then also follow its default to Router L, thereby beginning the loop all over again.

This loop happens for two reasons. First, the forwarding tables are not up to date; second, the domain border routers do not have "complete" routing information. If either one of them did *not* have a default route, the loop would be broken. For example, imagine that Router L has the "safe" configuration (with no default route), and router T has a default route that points at Router L. If the packet originates in the L domain, it will follow the intradomain static default routes until it reaches Router L. At this point, Router L will be able to send back an ICMP Destination-Unreachable error message, because the router cannot forward the packet further. If the packet originated in the T domain, it would follow the T domain's default route until it reached Router L, and the same result would occur. No routing loop would happen, because one router knows "everything," and it is logically at the top of the tree of default routes.

If both routers had the "safe" (i.e., default-free) configuration, then the packet would never leave either domain. The packet still will cross the entire domain as the routers follow the intradomain default routes. The only way to limit the packet's travel would be to have no default route at all in any of the intradomain routers. In general, if static routing were to be done, among *m* subnetworks connected by *n* routers, then the network manager needs to make approximately $n*m$ static routing entries in total across the Routing Domain.

$n*m$ is the absolute worst-case scenario. If there are any aggregation boundaries, then some routers may be able to forward packets into a subdomain by only knowing about its aggregate, instead of needing to know about all of its constituent prefixes. For instance, if L3 and L4 are both /27 prefixes, e.g., 172.16.19.64/27 and 172.16.19.96/27, respectively, then all Router L would need to know was that 172.16.19.64/26 was reachable by going through Router J. If such a packet ever did arrive at Router J, it would know that it was directly attached to L3, and also that Router I was on the way to L4. Within the aggregate, the routers need to know how to get around (i.e., they need complete reachability information), but no router outside the aggregate needs to know the aggregate's internal structure in order to function properly.

If each routing domain is an aggregate, then the routing tables become considerably simpler for the domain border routers T and L, as shown in Figure 14.15. This figure does not reflect any intradomain aggregation, which would further reduce the size of the domain border routers' forwarding tables.

Negative Aspects of Static (-Override) Routing

- Significant administrative overhead in maintaining approximately $n*m$ correct static entries in routers (worst case, no aggregation)[20]
- Routing loops happen easily, but only if there is no dynamic forwarding information present in a router

Router T-"Safe"

Dest.	Next-Hop
Prefix D	n/a (Self)
Prefix L	Router L
Prefix T1	n/a (Self)
Prefix T2	Router Z
Prefix T3	Router Z
Prefix T4	Router Z

Router L-"Safe"

Dest.	Next-Hop
Prefix D	n/a (Self)
Prefix L1	n/a (Self)
Prefix T	Router T
Prefix L2	Router K
Prefix L3	Router J
Prefix L4	Router J

FIGURE 14.15 Safe aggregate-based forwarding tables for domain border routers.

Positive Aspects of Static (-Override) Routing

- Enables easier network reconfiguration if routers can fall back on static forwarding tables (provided the static information is maintained accurately by the network manager!)
- Improves network stability during unintended routing protocol outages

Clearly, static routing is a tool that has its uses, but it really shines as a backup scheme, not as a primary routing technique. As a Routing Domain interconnection technique, it can be quite effective. At a minimum, a tree of static default routes will carry intradomain traffic toward the egress router, which can then use its knowledge of the other domain's prefix(es) to forward the packet(s). The tree of default routes need not be static; they may be derived from a default route that the domain border router advertises and is propagated within the domain. Because the static information in the domain border routers is likely to be stable over long periods of time, the use of static routes is appropriate. Why bother to keep sending "dynamic" routing protocol messages across the DMZ which really just serve to announce, "The following set of prefixes { . . . } is still over here." "The following set of prefixes { . . . } is still over here." "The following set of prefixes { . . .} is still over here," and so on. The routing protocol is really not passing any information that is likely to be time-variable. What it is doing in that case is providing the other side with a heartbeat message, indicating that it is still alive (and that it is still providing a path to that set of prefixes . . .).

By the same token, without the use of a dynamic interdomain routing protocol, the domain border routers always think that the other domain is reachable—the forwarding table entry is *static* after all! If they only have some statically configured forwarding table entries on which to base a decision, then there is no way to detect whether or not (some portion of) the other domain is actually reachable. The point is that the defined prefixes in the other domain are likely to be stable over long periods of time, but the immediate time-varying reachability is not guaranteed.

This is why static-override routes come in handy, since they capture the other domain's long-term prefixes but are overridden by whatever dynamic protocol is in use. The static routes serve as a safety net so that dynamic routing protocols can be reconfigured—or changed to entirely different protocols—without interfering with packet forwarding. As long as the network manager periodically verifies that the forwarding table has a static-override route for every dynamically-learned route, then the safety net has no holes. This check can be automated by periodcially processing the domain border router's forwarding table with an automated script. Any dynamic forwarding table entries without a corresponding static-override entry could be indicated to the network manager.

Actually, in low-bandwidth WANs, it makes a heck of a lot of sense to use static routing instead of a dynamic protocol, which wastes bandwidth. For example, if we had a remote site, as shown in Figure 14.16, all the central site needs to do is import the statically-defined remote-site prefix into the central-site's routing protocol.

In the DMZ-based interconnection scenario, we needed the dynamic routing protocol to convey "liveness" information between the domain border routers, whereas in the case of a point-to-point WAN link, we can use the PPP LCP status (up or down) to directly infer whether or not the remote site is reachable. We can do a similar thing in frame relay environments, because the LMI protocol tells us which DLCIs are active and which are down.

The remote site needs only a static default route pointing toward the central site. There is only one way out—if the link is down, then the remote site router can immediately issue an ICMP Destination-Unreachable error message in response to packets that attempt to leave the remote site. Similarly, the central-site router probably can conditionally import the static route based on the "liveness" of the circuit. As long as the circuit is up (reflected by the status of WAN interface 9 in Figure 14.16), the central-site router will advertise the remote site's prefix R into the corporate network, enabling the corporate network to reach this remote site. If the WAN link goes down, prefix R may then be withdrawn from the corporate network.

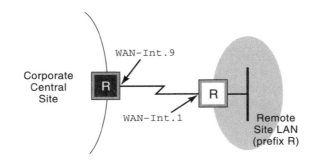

Central Site			Remote Site	
Dest.	Next-Hop		Dest.	Next-Hop
Prefix R	WAN-Int.9		0.0.0.0/0	WAN-Int.1
			Prefix R	N/A (Self)

FIGURE 14.16   Static routing in WAN Environments.

At the remote site, if there is only one LAN, as shown in the figure, then the router need only send error messages whenever an endstation attempts to send a packet to the corporate network. If its WAN interface 1 is down, then it should invalidate its default route, since the WAN interface is the next hop.[21] If there are multiple LANs at the remote site, then the remote site router should inject a default route only if its WAN interface 1 is up. Intrasite static-override default routes will provide for packet forwarding in the absence of a dynamic default route (in cases where there are multiple LANs attached to the remote site router).

Usage Constraints for the Default Route

Care must be taken in using the default route. As mentioned above, default routing is easily applied in stub domains, but only safely when the stub domain has one egress point. It is possible to have multiple routers providing egress, logically backing each other up. However, if a domain can be exited via two or more truly distinct locations, then the default route should only be advertised from one location. If the default route were advertised from multiple locations, then some intradomain router may see itself as perhaps four hops away from it, while another router may be three hops away from default, but from a different egress point. Is this bad? Not if the egress points have equivalent connectivity outside the domain.

The real problem with multiple sources of default is in troubleshooting. Some parts of your routing domain may be working just fine, and others may be broken. All of them are following the default route, but some of them may be closer to a source of default that is mishandling their traffic, while other traffic is going to well-behaved sources of default. To see what is going wrong, one has to log in to a router that is attached to a subnetwork that is experiencing difficulty. Examining the router's default route in its forwarding table will point you in the direction of the offending router. The `traceroute` debugging tool can also prove to be very valuable, since a traceroute performed to a destination that is outside of the domain will include the misbehaving router. The misbehaving router is the one that will terminate the traceroute.

As we saw above, domains that are dual-connected and that want to make the best internal forwarding decisions need to have some external routing information. This extra information allows the best egress point to be chosen, i.e., the egress point that looks to be nearest to the ultimate destination. For example, within a domain it might be the case that to reach prefix C, egress router R_3 needs to be taken, and that prefixes D and E are reachable via router R_5. Besides those two specific exceptions, all other prefixes are reachable by router R_1. In this case, router R_1 should originate a default route, but routers R_3 and R_5 must only advertise their specific destination prefixes, C, D, and E, respectively. Figure 14.17 illustrates this scenario.

A domain with external routing information can still be a stub domain, but if the routing policies are such that the domain is providing connectivity between other domains, then it has become a transit domain. The domain in Figure 14.17 will certainly provide transit among C, D, and E. Default routes do not necessarily work well within transit domains, since there is probably not a preferred direction for traffic to take when leaving the domain. The direction each individual packet should take, and its best egress point, depends on its destination, not on where it came from.

The Internet backbone is often referred to as "default-free," often in the same breath as someone bragging that they have all 55,000, or however many routes in their forwarding tables. Those two statements do go hand in hand—if you don't have a default route, then you had better know how to get *everywhere*.

Dynamic Routing

Interconnecting two (or more) routing domains across a LAN DMZ really does require a dynamic routing protocol; otherwise, black holes are guaranteed to form. If static forwarding table entries are the only information that a router has, and it needs to send a packet to a prefix in another domain, it just needs to ARP for the appropriate domain border router's DMZ IP/MAC address pair. Once it knows the other domain border router's MAC address, it can send traffic to it at any time.

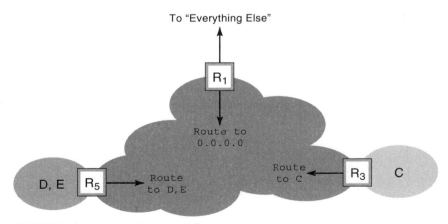

FIGURE 14.17 Stub domain with extra externals.

However, if that other router is ever disconnected from the DMZ—or is rebooted, or crashes, or if the DMZ hub/switch loses power, or crashes, or has its forwarding table corrupted, or any number of other failure scenarios occur—then the router will still send the traffic toward that MAC address. (If the hub or switch loses power, the router might see its link go down, which would take that interface down. Other failures may not be detectable by the router.) In order to protect against such outages, and to allow operation during topology changes in general, a dynamic routing protocol must be used.

Choosing an Inter-Domain Routing Protocol

We have seen that static routes have their uses, especially static-override routes, and we know that they don't provide a complete solution by themselves, so we need to decide on an appropriate dynamic routing protocol. At a minimum, we are conveying reachability information of prefixes, and also neighbor status information. Protocols like BGP-4 and OSPF do a good job for both reachability and neighbor status. Protocols like RIPv1 and RIPv2 are good at advertising reachability, but aren't necessarily good at keeping track of which neighbors are alive. The problem with RIP (either version) is that the routing information takes a long time to age out of the routing table once a neighbor has stopped transmitting. This time represents a black hole for the other routers, since they will have forwarding table entries but the router or destination prefix is actually not there anymore.

Many people choose RIP for this role because it is simple and it is widely supported across many vendors' routers, but its lack of detailed neighbor state maintenance is a real liability when a neighbor becomes unreachable. RIP can take up to three minutes to remove a router and the prefixes formerly reached through it from the forwarding table. If RIP must be used, at least try to use RIPv2, since it is a classless routing protocol. If you are integrating two different parts of the same classful prefix, RIPv1 can't do the job, but if the two routing domains are two different classful network numbers, than RIPv1 can work.

BGP-4 and OSPF, on the other hand, maintain explicit neighbor status. BGP-4 maintains its peering sessions, and OSPF its adjacencies. Beyond being applicable when talking to an ISP,[22] BGP-4 is also a strong candidate for use between Routing Domains *within* an Administrative Domain. The limiting factor will be whether or not it is supported in the routers you are using.

OSPF is not a great choice for interdomain use in the common case where OSPF is in use inside one or both of the Routing Domains. The DMZ, if it runs OSPF, will join the two OSPF Autonomous Systems, plus itself, into one big OSPF domain, which may not be desirable. If a router can run multiple instances of OSPF, it could keep the three OSPF networks separate (each Routing Domain is one OSPF network, plus the DMZ is the third).

REFERENCES

Halabi B. *Internet Routing Architectures,* Cisco Press, New Riders Publishing, Indianapolis, IN, 1997.

Neumann, P.G. *Computer-Related Risks,* Addison-Wesley, Reading, MA, 1997.

ENDNOTES

1. Standards-based: Static routing, RIPv1, RIPv2, OSPF, I-IS-IS, BGP-4, EGP. Proprietary: Cisco's IGRP and E-IGRP, and many others (not as popular).

2. These preferences are often, but not always, based on solid technical reasoning. Past experience also plays a strong role.

3. BGP-4 does not care what routing protocol(s) is (are) in use within that Administrative Domain.

4. There may actually be several cooperating management entities within the AS, but as far as BGP is concerned, the AS is under a single administrative entity.

5. It is worth noting that outsourcing is becoming more common. However, even if the management of the customer's network is being outsourced, the ISP would probably still manage it as a separate Administrative Domain.

6. Here is a case where BGP-4 might see only one AS for the whole merged company, but internally there may be not only different Routing Domains, but also different Administrative Domains. (It may be the case that both companies will retain their own Internet connections, but they will not necessarily advertise each other's networks to the Internet, which would commit each of them to carry the other's Internet traffic, whenever the other's Internet connection was down.)

7. LANs with built-in fault tolerance, such as FDDI, make especially good DMZ subnetworks. A more robust DMZ technology may reduce the need for the ultimate "redundant routers dual-connected to redundant DMZs" scenario. It is also the case that extremely high-availability environments may require both the dual DMZs to be fault-tolerant.

8. The primary and secondary routers also injected an OSPF stub-area default, for the benefit of any OSPF participants.

9. This implies that the rib is an OSPF Area. The InteropNet design convention was to set the AreaID equal to the rib-group's subnet prefix (i.e., 45.77.0.0 in this case). The InteropNet's ribs are all stub areas, since there is no reason to introduce external routing information into them.

10. For clarity, each forwarding table entry's companion entry, the same prefix reachable via the ATM backbone, is not shown. Also for clarity, this router has only two interfaces shown in the forwarding table, the zero-cost "direct" entries. (In the real InteropNet, backbone routers attached to 4–7 ribs.)

11. Clearly, it is impossible to run RIPv1 on both sides of an aggregate, since a prerequisite of using RIPv1 with subnets is that the extended-network-prefix must be uniform across the Routing Domain. Aggregates clearly have a different mask-length, so RIPv1 can only be used *within* an aggregate. The only exception to this rule would be the case where the two RIPv1 domains were two different classful network numbers.

12. Pronunciation key: `gated` = gate-dee, `routed` = route-dee.

13. We may still wish to give a slightly lower Type-1 metric for the externals from the ASBR that we believe to be "more reliable."

14. The lower-cost path is the topologically shortest path.

15. "External" here is used in the sense of 'external to this domain,' not necessarily an external route from an exterior gateway protocol, such as BGP-4.

16. Such administrative metrics are only used inside the box.

17. In the sense that their forwarding table size is minimized (or at least reduced).

18. Deep, in this context, means further away from the domain border router.

19. If only one domain border router is configured this way, then no damage is done.

20. Out-of-date entries are not a problem as long as the dynamic routing protocol is working. Network administrators should periodically review their forwarding tables and make sure that every dynamically-learned entry has a corresponding, and less preferred, statically-defined entry.

21. The router need not be using unnumbered links for this to work. If the serial line is a /30 prefix, then the link being down would indicate that the next-hop gateway was unreachable, which further indicates that the default route is unusable. If unnumbered links are in use, the link itself is the next hop; if it is down, the default route is directly unusable.

22. Just because ISPs use BGP-4 to talk to each other does not mean that customer networks must use BGP-4 to talk to their ISP—RIP is often used. The ISP needs to advertise a default route to the customer, and the customer needs to advertise its prefix(es) to the ISP. RIPv1 has been used in the past, but RIPv2 is superior because it is classless.

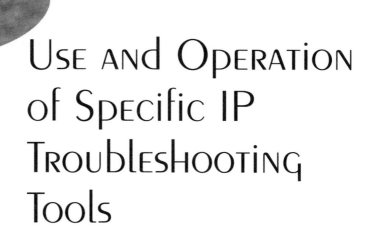

Use and Operation of Specific IP Troubleshooting Tools

INTRODUCTION

The Internet Control Message Protocol (ICMP) is a critical ingredient in two of the most important IP troubleshooting tools: ping and traceroute. ICMP deserves a bit of analysis before ping and traceroute are described. Ping and traceroute use ICMP in different ways, with ping using specific ICMP messages designed for the ping "application," while traceroute typically uses ICMP's error reporting features to do its job.

Because both tools use ICMP to some extent, they share some failure modes, which are most easily explained in the context of ping.

ICMP IS INSEPARABLE FROM IP

The Internet Protocol (IP, RFC-791) could not operate without its companion protocol, the Internet Control Message Protocol (ICMP, RFC-792). Per this quote (punctuation unaltered) from the introduction to RFC-792—now a Full Internet Standard—ICMP must be implemented on any device which implements IP:

ICMP, uses the basic support of IP as if it were a higher level protocol, however, ICMP is actually an integral part of IP, and must be implemented by every IP module.

Figure A.1 shows ICMP in the context of the IP protocol stack. ICMP serves several critical purposes, notably error reporting and troubleshooting. All the error reporting ICMP Types implicitly support troubleshooting by telling you both what is wrong, and where it happened. Explicit troubleshooting is also supported via a "probe" packet known as the Echo. The "ping" application uses Echo packets to discover if a destination is reachable. Table A.1 summarizes the many ICMP packet Types, each of which reports various error conditions, or, as in the case of the Echo, actively probes a destination.

Figure A.2 shows a default IP header with an ICMP header immediately following. The fields in uppercase are most important from ICMP's perspective. The other IP header fields are not unimportant, but they aren't critical to ICMP's normal operation. For instance, the identification, flags, and fragment offset are all related to IP packet fragmentation mechanisms. The identification field provides a way for the sender to label its packets so that the receiver may easily correlate any fragments as being constituents of the same original packet. The flags and fragment offset are used with the identification field to implement the mechanics of IP packet fragmentation. IP fragmentation should be transparent to protocols that are based on IP, except for the fact that intermediate routers are delayed in forwarding traffic if it needs to be fragmented.

To achieve the highest performance in data transfer, most IP implementations try to avoid sending packets that will require fragmentation by intermediate routers. To accomplish this, end-stations want to send the largest packets that the end-to-end path can carry without fragmentation. This so-called "Path MTU" can be discovered using the techniques described in RFC-1191, which involve setting the IP "don't fragment" bit and sending packets as large as the local link will accept. If link-MTU-sized packets

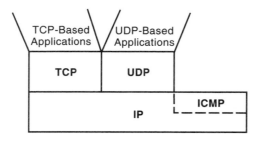

FIGURE A.1   ICMP's logical relationship to the IP protocol suite.

TABLE A.1 Selected ICMP Message Types

Type	Ref	Name
0	[ICMP]	Echo Reply
3	[ICMP]	Destination Unreachable
		Codes for ICMP Type 3
		0 Net Unreachable
		1 Host Unreachable
		2 Protocol Unreachable
		3 Port Unreachable
		4 Fragmentation Needed but Don't Fragment was Set
		5 Source Route Failed
		6 Destination Network Unknown
		7 Destination Host Unknown
		8 Source Host Isolated
		9 Communication with Destination Network is Administratively Prohibited
		10 Communication with Destination Host is Administratively Prohibited
		11 Destination Network Unreachable for Type of Service
		12 Destination Host Unreachable for Type of Service
	[RREQ]	13 Communication Administratively Prohibited
	[RREQ]	14 Host Precedence Violation
	[RREQ]	15 Precedence cutoff in effect
5	[ICMP]	Redirect
		Codes for ICMP Type 5
	0	Redirect Datagram for the Network (or subnet)
	1	Redirect Datagram for the Host
	2	Redirect Datagram for the Type of Service and Network
	3	Redirect Datagram for the Type of Service and Host
8	[ICMP]	Echo
9	[RDSC]	Router Advertisement
10	[RDSC]	Router Selection
11	[ICMP]	Time Exceeded
		Codes for ICMP Type 11
	0	Time to Live exceeded in Transit
	1	Fragment Reassembly Time Exceeded

```
 0           1           2           3
 0 1 2 3 4 5 6 7 8 9 0 1 2 3 4 5 6 7 8 9 0 1 2 3 4 5 6 7 8 9 0 1
       +-+-+-+-+-+-+-+-+-+-+-+-+-+-+-+-+-+-+-+-+-+-+-+-+-+-+-+-+-+-+-
IP  | VERSIONI IHL Itype of Service |      TOTAL LENGTH     |
       +-+-+-+-+-+-+-+-+-+-+-+-+-+-+-+-+-+-+-+-+-+-+-+-+-+-+-+-+-+-+-
IP  |   Identification      |Flags| Fragment Offset |
       +-+-+-+-+-+-+-+-+-+-+-+-+-+-+-+-+-+-+-+-+-+-+-+-+-+-+-+-+-+-+-
IP  | TIME TO LIVE |  PROTOCOL  |  Header Checksum   |
       +-+-+-+-+-+-+-+-+-+-+-+-+-+-+-+-+-+-+-+-+-+-+-+-+-+-+-+-+-+-+-
IP  |              SOURCE ADDRESS              |
       +-+-+-+-+-+-+-+-+-+-+-+-+-+-+-+-+-+-+-+-+-+-+-+-+-+-+-+-+-+-+-
IP  |            DESTINATION ADDRESS           |
       +=+=+=+=+=+=+=+=+=+=+=+=+=+=+=+=+=+=+=+=+=+=+=+=+=+=+=+=+=+=+=
ICMP |   TYPE   |   CODE   |     Checksum     |
       +-+-+-+-+-+-+-+-+-+-+-+-+-+-+-+-+-+-+-+-+-+-+-+-+-+-+-+-+-+-+-
ICMP |   Identifier   |   Sequence Number    |
       +-+-+-+-+-+-+-+-+-+-+-+-+-+-+-+-+-+-+-+-+-+-+-+-+-+-+-+-+-+-+-
ICMP |   Data...
       +-+-+-+-+-+
```

version	If the version field is 4 (0x0100), the IP header is as depicted above. In the future, IPv6 may supplant IPv4 as the Internet's network-layer protocol.[1]
IHL	Internet Header Length (multiply IHL by four to get the real header length in bytes)
	5 (0x0101) is the minimum value of this 4-bit field, when there are no IP options. This is the most common value, indicating a 20-byte IP header. 15 (1111) is the maximum, indicating a 60-byte IP header.
	If IP options are present, they are added after the IP Destination Address, and they must be padded to a 32-bit boundary, (so the IP header length is maintained as a multiple of four).
	Note that the Total Length header field expresses the exact number of bytes in the packet (including the header). It can be any length up to 65,535 (11111111 11111111) bytes; only the IP header's length must be a multiple of four.
TOS	This field has never really been used for its original purpose. Now, in early 1999, there are many plans to use this field to implement "better-than-best-effort" or "differentiated" classes of service.
TTL	A packets' initial TTL can be as large as 255 (11111111).
Protocol	ICMP is IP Protocol number 1 (0000 0001).

FIGURE A.2   IP+ICMP packet format.

are successfully delivered to the destination, then the sender knows it need not send smaller packets. Otherwise, an error message is received—ICMP Destination Unreachable, Type 3, Code 4 (Fragmentation Needed but Don't Fragment bit was set)—indicating that the full-sized packet couldn't reach the destination. In this case, there is a prescribed set of smaller MTUs to try. The worst case is that the IP required minimum MTU would be used, in which the IP Total Length field is 576 bytes (`0x0240` in hex, or `00000010 01000000` in binary).

Despite initial efforts to send packets that won't need fragmentation, there may be a topology change during the connection that forces packets over a path with a smaller minimum MTU. In this case, an intermediate router will want to fragment packets to this destination. If Path MTU Discovery is enabled, fragmentation will not be allowed to occur, and the sender will receive an error message as described above. Upon receiving this error message, the sender will retransmit its packets with a smaller MTU.

Table A.1 shows a list of some of the more common ICMP Types, including Types 8 (Echo) and 0 (Echo Reply) which are used to implement `ping`. The Internet Assigned Numbers Authority's web site should be consulted for a complete and up-to-date listing of the ICMP message types. The IANA's URL is: <`http://www.iana.org/`>.

PING: AN APPLICATION OF ICMP

ICMP rides on top of IP as IP Protocol number 1. All ICMP packets begin with the same 4 bytes—the Type field (1 byte), the Code field (1 byte), and the Checksum field (2 bytes). `Ping` uses two of ICMP's 256 possible Type values, the Echo (Type 8) and the Echo Reply (Type 0). Another possible design would have been to use one ICMP Type with one sub-Code for Echo and another for Echo Response. The method using two distinct ICMP Types was chosen.

The format of the remainder of any ICMP packet depends on its ICMP Type. In `ping` packets, the packet continues with two 2-byte fields, namely "Identifier" and "Sequence Number." These may be used to aid in matching Echo Replies to Echoes. These fields are not required to have nonzero values, but regardless of their values, the target must preserve them when sending an Echo Reply.

Before we delve into ways that `ping` can be thwarted in its mission, I'll note that "`ping`" is an appropriate name in that it connotes the SONAR concept of "pinging" another object in the water. In a SONAR system, a burst of sound is emitted and an echo is listened for. In the context of the Internet, `ping` has a similar functionality of emitting something (an ICMP Echo packet) and waiting for its reflection (an ICMP Echo Response packet). Interestingly, the letters p-i-n-g form a somewhat contrived acronym, standing for "Packet INternet Groper."

Using Ping

Assuming that all is well in the network, an IP packet is sent containing its ICMP payload, with the ICMP Type field set to 8. Some time later, an IP packet returns with an identical ICMP payload, now with the ICMP Type set to 0. Responding to an ICMP Echo consists of reversing its IP source and destination addresses, changing the ICMP Type from 8 to 0, and recomputing the ICMP and IP checksums. The rest of the packet must be returned exactly as it was sent, including any data in the ping packet, and the values in the Identifier and Sequence Number fields. The ability to respond to an ICMP Echo packet is a requirement for all IP implementations.

Most `ping` implementations take the opportunity to measure the round-trip delay between the endpoints. Often three or five echo requests are done in a row; in each case the originating computer starts a timer which runs until the matching Echo Response arrives. Each of the attempts is measured, and the program's output typically includes the minimum, maximum, and average round-trip times. `Ping`'s primary function, however, is to determine if a given IP address is reachable. A successful `ping` also implicitly indicates that a working path exists both to and from the target. `Ping` is actually telling you three things when it works:

1) there is a functioning path from the source to the target
2) the machine with the target IP address is "up"
3) there is a functioning path from the target back to the source.

Figure A.3 illustrates how, even in a simple situation, the paths to and from a target may be different. PC_1 has its default gateway set to Router A (R_a), which fowards the packet received from PC_1 to PC_2 on the other LAN interface. PC_2, on the other hand, is configured to use Router B (R_b) as its default gateway, so Router B handles the return traffic from PC_2 to PC_1.

While Figure A.3 illustrates a fairly simple scenario, it is only slightly contrived. As indicated in the title of the figure, situations such as this are termed "asymmetric routing." Asymmetric routing means that the path taken from A to B may be different than the reverse path from B to A. In smaller networks, routing may tend to be largely symmetric, but the longer the path between the endpoints, the more likely the "to" and "from" paths are to diverge, especially if the packet needs to cross the Internet to reach its destination. This asymmetry is not necessarily a bad thing: As

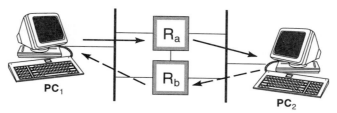

FIGURE A.3   Simple example of "asymmetric routing."

long as packets flowing in each direction experience about the same delay and probability of packet loss, the user will not be able to tell that the packets are traveling over different paths.

Asymmetric routing is quite common in today's Internet. ISP routers conspire to deliver a packet to some target. A completely different set of ISPs will probably deliver the packets back to the source. Even if the same ISPs are involved, it is probable that a different set of routers will carry the packets in the reverse direction. Figure A.4 illustrates this commonplace situation of asymmetric routing found today.

One big reason that the paths are different is the fact that many ISPs use a technique known as "early-exit" routing. In this scheme, if a packet is headed for a destination that is served by another ISP, it is handed off to the next-hop ISP as soon as possible. The thinking is that the packet should be delivered to its "home" ISP as soon as possible so *that* ISP can bear the cost of carrying the packet over its own

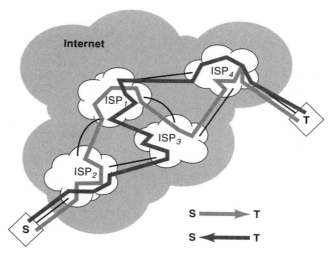

FIGURE A.4   Asymmetric routing in the Internet.

wide-area backbone. Transit ISPs often carry the packet for as short a distance as possible before handing it off to the next transit ISP toward the destination prefix's ISP, or to the penultimate ISP that is advertising the destination's prefix.

Ping of Death

Any ICMP packet may carry arbitrary data up to the maximum possible size of an IP packet. An IP packet can be at most 65,535 octets, but 20 of those octets (at a minimum) are needed for the header, leaving at most 65,515 bytes of IP payload for carrying upper-layer protocol data, e.g., ICMP. ICMP Echo packets also have an 8-octet fixed header, leaving a maximum of 65,507 bytes for data within the Echo packet. The so-called "ping of death" (or "ping-o'-death") is a malicious exploit that was implemented by crackers in 1997. It took advantage of the fact that some systems (notably Windows 95) were capable of sending ICMP packets with more than 65,507 bytes of data.

Since few data links can carry a packet longer than about 1500 bytes, the sending station must split the IP packet into fragments according to the link's MTU. Besides being a packet fragment, each of these fragments is an individual packet on its own. Each [fragment] packet's IP Total Length only applies to it, not the whole [original] packet. Therefore, as each fragment is received, the receiver can't tell how big the whole packet is—until it has collected all the fragments. Once all the fragments have arrived, the combined length of all the fragments will—in the case of the Ping of Death—exceed the maximum possible size of an IP packet (65,535 bytes). This unexpected error condition may often cause the receiver to overflow some internal data structure, which may result in a system crash, or the error may just crash the IP stack.

Note that this is not really just a "ping" of death. The bug that is being exploited has to do with IP fragmentation, whereby an IP stack is not written to handle the error condition of oversize fragmented packets. Even applications based on TCP or UDP, if they could be forced to send similar illegal IP packets, would cause the receiver to suffer the same fate. After the Ping of Death was widely publicized, many operating system vendors' IP stacks were patched to gracefully handle this error condition.

How Can a Ping Fail?

An unsuccessful ping may have failed because 1) there is no available path to the target, 2) the target really is down, or 3) there is no return path from the target. Thus, *an unsuccessful ping does not always mean that the destination is down.* With no evidence other than an unsuccessful ping, it would be a rush to judgment if one were to draw a conclusion that the target was dead. It is at least as likely that there is a network problem that is interfering with traffic between you and the target.

Note that in case #1 we should receive an ICMP Destination Unreachable error packet (Type 3, Code 0, 6, or 7). If there is a path back to the source, then this error message will be received; however, if there isn't a path back to the source (case 3), then neither an ICMP Echo response or destination unreachable error message packet will be able to reach the original source.

Routing loops or misconfigurations of network equipment may make it impossible to get a packet to a destination. While routers are not the only culprits, we'll concentrate on them because the `ping` (and `traceroute`) tools are designed for network-layer troubleshooting, and thus are particularly sensitive to routers being off balance. By the same token, `ping` and `traceroute` are also useful tools to help determine the location of router problems. In fact, routers are frequently the targets of `ping` packets.

Generally, it doesn't take a troubleshooting tool to discover that there is a network outage. Some server becomes unreachable, or people can't get to their favorite web sites, or you can't access your e-mail. Once this happens, you know at least one thing that you can't get to . . . there may also be other things! If you have a topology map either on paper or in your head, you probably know a few of the routers on the way to whatever it is that you can't reach.

A good way to find the broken link in the chain is to ping a router that is about halfway to the thing you can't reach (in terms of hops). If that succeeds, then move half again closer to the target, or else move half again back toward yourself. This procedure will help you home in on the farthest router that you can reach. You might also just ping routers from your end on out, or from the other end on in, until you get either a non-response or a response, depending on whether you are moving away or toward your location. If there are less than a dozen or so routers between you and the outage, either technique will likely converge on the outage rather quickly, but there is another tool that will automate the search process: `traceroute`. Depending on the nature or the outage, it may pinpoint your problem very quickly. Before we talk about how `traceroute` works, let's discuss a few common outage scenarios to see why they broke our attempted ping.

Routing Loop Among Intermediate Routers

Routing loops typically effect certain destinations, not all destinations. A routing loop is when several routers are confused about how to reach a particular destination and end up forwarding packets in a circle among themselves. They keep circulating among this group of routers, never making any real progress toward destinations. Each router decrements the packet's TTL until it eventually expires, causing an ICMP Time Exceeded error message (Type 11, most probably Code 0) to be issued toward the packet's source.

There are a number of reasons why a routing loop could form:

1. misconfiguration
   • border routers import a prefix but disagree on what its metric should be
   • bad static configuration (default route?)
2. two different implementations of the same routing protocol compute different paths to a destination
3. transient effect during a topology change; cleared when routers "converge" upon a stable, accurate forwarding table

The loop could affect your traffic in at least two ways: 1) client traffic for a network service never gets to the target server, or 2) traffic from the server never makes it back to the client. In case 2, the client never gets an ICMP Time Exceeded message (the ICMP error message would also get caught in that loop!), but in case 1 you can tell a loop has occurred because you get the error message and you know that there are nowhere near 255 routers between you and the server!

Once you identify the nearest router to you that you can reach, log into it and look at its routing table. How can you decide where to start? Well, if you ping the destination and there is a routing loop en route, one of the routers in the loop will eventually send you an ICMP Time Exceeded error message. That router would be a good place to continue the investigation, because it would have to be in the routing loop to send you this error message.

After logging in this router you should examine its forwarding table. You will need to look at the routes to the target prefix, and the route back to your source prefix. If all looks well, then telnet to the next-hop router toward the targets destination's prefix (extract this next hop address from the forwarding table). At the next router you can examine the same information in its forwarding table. By looking up the targets prefix in each router's forwarding table, successively telneting from router to router, you will be able to hop around the routing loop. In this process of checking out each router, you should find the cause of the loop—a router that is zigging when it should be zagging.

Intermediate Router Loses Route to Source or Target

When a router loses a route to a destination prefix, any less-specific (shorter-mask) prefix will now be used to forward traffic to a destination. Often, there is no less-specific prefix other than the default route (which is the least-specific route, having zero bits in its mask). If there is no default route, then the router must return an ICMP Destination Unreachable error message (Type 3, either Code 0 or 6).

Again, you can iteratively determine the router farthest from you that you can still reach. Once you have telneted to that router, you can try to discover why it can't get to the destination in question. If the answer isn't obvious as to why the destination prefix isn't in this router's forwarding table, you may have to log into each of its neighbors to see how they see the world.

Aggregation gone Astray

Normally, the forwarding decision is rather straightforward: find a prefix in your forwarding table that is the best match of this packet's destination; if no specific prefix exists then send the packet along the default route. When routers advertise a shorter-mask aggregate to their neighbors, they must remember that they have done this, since it should influence the forwarding decision. The aggregating router needs to check if a packet's destination lies within an aggregate prefix that is has generated.

For example, the router may be advertising 10.192.0.0/16, so any constituent parts of that prefix should be reachable via this router (and are thus invisible to routers that tie outside the aggregate). So if a packet arrives for 10.192.17.35, and the router has no more-specific route to that destination (e.g., a prefix like 10.192.16.0/22, or 10.192.17.0/24, or 10.192.17.32/29, etc.), then the router must send an error message. After all, if *it* doesn't know how to get an element of 10.192.0.0/16, what other router would?

If the router were to forward such a packet to its default next-hop gateway, its default gateway would look at its routing table and decide that the packet needs to head back to the aggregator that is sending it the 10.192.0.0/16 prefix. These two routers will continue playing a very fast game of ping-pong with the packet until its TTL expires.

If a router has done aggregation and doesn't know how to deliver the packet, then it must send an ICMP Destination Unreachable error message. Only this router can send this message, because the internal structure of 10.192.0.0/16 is invisible to the other routers—it has been aggregated away!

One-Way (Diode) Links and other Strange Errors

Occasionally, a normally two-way LAN will become effectively one-way. There are several ways this can happen:

1. A neighbor's LAN interface goes "deaf" (either it can't hear anyone or, less probably, it just can't hear you)
2. A neighbor's LAN interface goes "dumb" (either it can't talk to anyone or, less probably, it just can't talk to you)
3. A hub or switch port forgets that you exist
4. A neighbor's hub or switch port forgets they exist
5. A software error in a switch or bridge prevents you from reaching a MAC address that was formerly reachable
6. etc.

The point is that LANs have many active devices (MAUs, repeaters, transceivers, bridges, switches, etc.) and there are many ways that they can fail (substandard or misaligned cabling, hardware failures like corroded, dirty, or loose parts, software errors including bugs, lost packets, exceptional conditions that the code was not designed for, etc.). A total failure might be easy to detect and fix, but partial failures are far more common. (As an example of an attempt to be robust in the face of marginal connectivity, OSPF's adjacency establishment procedure was designed so that OSPF routers won't become adjacent with a potential neighbor unless they are sure that they have a two-way communication path between them.)

Figure A.5 illustrates the situation where intermediate Router A needs to deliver a ping, but is unaware that the link is a diode link. Any packet that Router A transmits to Router B will die on the link, which may be comprised of multiple switches, repeaters, bridges, hubs, and other layer-1 and layer-2 devices.

The outage may not affect the entire LAN, but one unreachable router interface may seriously degrade reachability within your network. This router is considered a valid next-hop for certain destinations, but in fact it is a black hole for any traffic sent to it. Should a diode link occur between the routers, the source will never receive an Echo Reply or an error message, and the ping attempt will time out. Router A will think the packet was successfully transmitted, so which device could send an error message? Router B never got the packet, so it certainly could not send an error message.

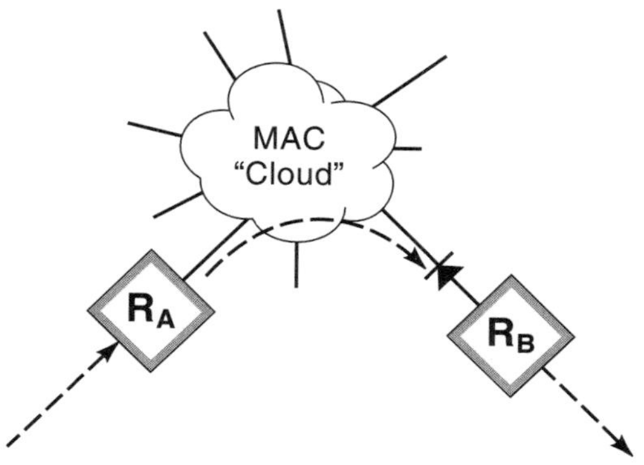

FIGURE A.5 A diode link between two routers.

Depending on the nature of the diode link, the next-hop router (Router B) may age out of its neighbors' routing tables (i.e., if they have stopped hearing its routing protocol updates). After enough time has passed, Router A may no longer have a path to the ping target's destination prefix, or its path to that prefix may be through a router that it can actually send traffic through. In the first case, Router A could send a Destination Unreachable (ICMP Type 3, Code 0 or 6) error message back to the source, while the second case requires no error message.

One other problem that I have seen involves switches that go into a degraded state, in which the switches continue to forward multicast and broadcast packets but block unicast packets. In this case, OSPF adjacencies continued to be kept alive by OSPF's multicast-based Hello protocol. Each router on that link still believed that all the others were still reachable because their Hellos continued to be received.

When OSPF is in use, a common troubleshooting technique involves looking at the OSPF neighbor status display, or "grep"-ing the IP routing table to see if any destination prefixes are reachable via a suspect neighbor on this LAN. If the LAN has stopped carrying unicast traffic, both these tests will show that the router thinks everything is okay. (Even if RIP were in use, the routers would be fooled by this situation because all RIP messages are broadcast.) No actual [unicast] data packets would cross that link, even though all the routing updates kept getting through. This situation can be confirmed by trying to ping a router's neighbors. If the routing table looks fine, yet pings fail, then some intervening switch(es) may need to be rebooted.

Data-Sensitive WAN Links

It is possible that certain patterns in a packet's data could make a link fail temporarily. These data patterns may be interpreted as a command by the telephone company's switches, muxes, and/or cross-connects that comprise the digital circuit. Perhaps the data pattern is interpreted as a command that tells some device in the midst of the circuit to turn on clock generation, or enables an intracircuit loopback, or resets some line card, etc. Whatever the action, the result is to temporarily disable the circuit, which may require telephone company intervention to restore. (This type of failure is less common in modern transmission networks that employ out-of-band signaling.)

One way that such links have been discovered is when performing file transfers. For most files, the data flows to or from the server perfectly well, but for some files, the data transfer begins fine but then always stops at the same spot. Your knowledge of the contents of the file can be used to isolate the suspect data packet. Once the bad data packet has been identified, you can use it to test the link. After the phone company has worked on the line, you can quickly tell them if the link is now working properly, just by resending the entire "bad packet" as the data within a ping packet. (If the whole packet won't fit, due to MTU restrictions, it may be broken up—the resulting smaller packets should still cause the outage.)

TRACEROUTE

Ping is sort of a one-dimensional tool. It provides valuable information, but it does not give especially detailed results. We use it to determine that there is a path to a given destination, that the destination is up, and that there is a return path from the destination to us. Besides this coarse topological information, we also typically learn how long the round-trip takes to the destination. Traceroute was initially developed for the Unix operating system(s), but has been ported widely and is now available for many operating systems. It is also available as a command in most router implementations.

Necessity is the mother of invention, and traceroute was invented to help map the entire path from the source to a target. In the early days of the Internet, the routing system often experienced instabilities. A tool was desperately needed to discover the identities of misinformed or misbehaving routers. Similar to ping, traceroute also measures time, but we get a measure of how long it takes to get to each router hop along the way to the target instead of ping's coarse measurement of the entire time for the round trip.

Before describing how traceroute works, let's look at what traceroute does. Figure A.6 shows an example of the output of the traceroute command from my local router (IP addresses modified):

What does this output in Figure A.6 show? Each line labeled TTL shows a different IP address. These are the addresses of the router interfaces along the way to the target. Each row represents three different attempts at that TTL, with the round-trip times (RTTs) being reported for each attempt.

One expects to see the RTTs increasing as the packet moves farther away from the source. In this case, the initial RTT is large because of the relatively slow (128 kbps during this test) ISDN link from my home to the office. Once there, all the links are either switched-10 or -100 Mbps Ethernet or FDDI links. This is why the RTTs barely increase after the first TTL (the average only increases from 25 1/3 to 29 1/3 ms).

Traceroute can often be used to pick out other information based on the timing changes from one TTL level to the next; for instance, Figure A.7 shows a traceroute from within 3Com to NASA Goddard Space Flight Center's domain name server (ns.gsfc.nasa.gov, 128.183.10.134).

The sudden jump in RTT values from TTL 8 to 9 reflects a long-distance WAN link (within the first-hop ISP, InterNex, a link is being crossed from San Jose, California to Washington, D.C.). Even though this link is undoubtedly a T-3, which runs at just under 45 Mbps, it still takes some time for the electrical signals to propagate across the country. From this output, it looks like the one-way trip time from the Bay Area to Washington is about 40 ms. Beats flying!

```
[1]maufer # tr 10.7.192.1

TraceRoute to 10.7.192.1 using TOS 0
TTL   Next Hop Address    RTTs
1     10.7.172.3          26 ms   25 ms   25 ms
2     10.7.172.1          27 ms   26 ms   25 ms
3     10.7.175.253        30 ms   28 ms   26 ms
4     10.7.48.107         30 ms   27 ms   28 ms
5     10.7.192.1          31 ms   27 ms   30 ms

[2]maufer #
```

FIGURE A.6 Sample traceroute output to a machine on my campus network.

```
[2]maufer # tr 128.183.10.134

TraceRoute to 128.183.10.134 using TOS 0
TTL   Next Hop Address    RTTs
1     10.7.172.3          26 ms   26 ms   24 ms
2     10.7.172.1          27 ms   26 ms   25 ms
3     10.7.175.253        29 ms   27 ms   27 ms
4                          *       *       *
5                          *       *       *
6     192.156.136.2       34 ms   29 ms   31 ms
7     205.158.1.225       36 ms   31 ms   31 ms
8     205.158.0.4         34 ms   32 ms   31 ms
9     207.88.3.2         117 ms  113 ms  114 ms
10    192.41.177.125     119 ms  115 ms  116 ms
11    192.43.240.34      122 ms  115 ms  163 ms
12    128.183.10.134     122 ms  117 ms  119 ms

[3]maufer #
```

FIGURE A.7   Sample traceroute output to a machine on the east coast.

Note TTLs 4 and 5 do not show a router IP address. This is probably because their firewall filters prevent them from sending ICMP packets. What does ICMP have to do with `traceroute`? The answer to that question is addressed next, when we describe how `traceroute` works.

Mechanisms Employed by Traceroute

From the examples above, it should be clear that `traceroute` tries to give us a list of all the routers along the path to some target. There are many ways that such a tool could have been designed, but a goal of `traceroute`'s design was that it should work with existing, unmodified router and endstation software. A protocol could have been designed that actually interacted directly with the routers, but the method chosen requires no special support in the routers, other than that they support ICMP, which they have to do anyway. The chosen method was very clever: A series of packets are sent toward some target in such a way that each one generates an error message from a different router.

The way this is done is that the initial packet to the target is sent with the minimum TTL, which is 1. The first router receives that packet and decrements the TTL, making it 0. The router must now send an ICMP Time Exceeded (Type 11) error message back to the source, indicating the problem. The router will send this message from the interface on which the packet arrived. The fact that the source has gotten an error message is not really a problem, though—that is what the source was hoping for! Now the source knows the address of the first router interface on the way to the destination. Typically, three packets are sent at each TTL and the RTT is measured for each trial.

Now the TTL is incremented by one, and an otherwise identical packet is sent toward the target. The first router will get the packet, decrement the TTL, and forward it, since this time the remaining TTL is non-zero. The next-hop router will receive it and decrement the TTL, but at this point, the next router will notice that the packet's TTL has reached 0. Now this next router will send a Time Exceeded error message back to the source. Again, this is just what we wanted. Now we know the address of the second router's interface that is crossed along the way to the ultimate target.

This procedure is continued, incrementing the TTL by one each time, until we reach the target. Each router along the way will have identified itself by means of ICMP Time Exceeded error messages, and we will have collected RTT data in triplicate at each hop. What then? How do we know we have reached the target?

We need to send a packet that the target won't recognize, one that is not likely to find an open socket. If, by some unbelievably wild coincidence, the packet happens to be accepted by some open socket within the target, then the traceroute procedure will never terminate. The three attempts at the target's "correct" TTL will time out, yielding one of those " * * * " entries at this TTL. Then the `traceroute` program will increment the TTL and try to move on. This next attempt will again terminate at the destination IP address; however, this time with one more tick remaining in the TTL field when it reaches the target. Most `traceroute` implementations will keep working until they have gone 30 hops.

We need a method that will hit the target and yield an error message that the target will send back to us. Then we'll know we have reached it. The choice that has been made is to use a packet destined for a "high" UDP port number, something above 32,768. Many Unix implementations start with the UDP port number at 33434 when the TTL = 1 and increment the UDP port number each time they increment the IP TTL. Thus, the formula would be UDP port = 33434 + TTL - 1. In this rarefied port range, no actual programs are likely to be actively listening for data. (The highest registered TCP/UDP port that had been assigned as of early 1998 was 17,007, with many large gaps below that point.) Another choice is to use an ICMP Echo packet instead of a high-port UDP packet, though not all `traceroute` implementations support this.

Once the source has incremented the UDP packet's TTL high enough such that the packet can reach the target's IP address, the target will try to deliver it up the

UDP/IP stack and find no process that it can deliver it to. In other words, there will be no matching open socket for this UDP packet. At that point, the target will send a Destination Unreachable error message (ICMP Type 5) with the Code set to 3 (Port Unreachable). As soon as we get this ICMP "Port Unreachable" packet from the target, we know that this packet was in response to the message we had sent to that port, not some other packet that just happened to arrive from that target while we were tracing the route to it.

Tracing Routes that Don't Start with You

Traceroute tells us how the routers will forward traffic between us and some destination. The tool does not tell us how the packets get back from there. The longer the path, the more likely it is that the reverse path will be different from the forward path. If you want a picture of the complete bidirectional path, you can use the tool in a special mode to see it. In the Unix implementation of traceroute there is a "-g" option that allows you to specify that your packets will contain the "Loose Source Record Route" IP option. (Not all implementations of traceroute support this option.)

A "loose" source route is one that requires that a packet's path must include at least the routers listed (it may cross other routers as well), whereas a strict source route forces a packet to cross only the listed routers. The list of routers, in either case, is encoded in the appropriate IP option type. You can use this method after tracing the route to a destination. Once you know the last-hop router before the destination, you can use that as the only router in your "loose source record route" IP option. Then you can ask the traceroute tool to trace the path from that router to any further destination, including back to your local IP address. In order to trace a path starting from a remote router, you'd need to make the initial TTL large enough to get one hop past that router; in other words, the TTL should be the same as the number of hops needed to reach the original target of the traceroute. Incrementing from there will trace the path from that router to the ultimate destination.

Potential "Problems" with Traceroute

Traceroute, by its very design, sets out to exercise the network between two points, so that network managers may probe the current routing behavior of their network(s). In the course of its operation, problems may be encountered which appear to be network outages. The DNS may inadvertently make the traceroute tool pause for long periods in between two hops, but DNS-related problems are not indicative of network outages. In an effort to be more user-friendly, the `traceroute` program tries to look up the IP addresses of the routers it encounters, so that the user may be presented with names in addition to IP addresses. If there are nontrivial delays in accessing the DNS names, `traceoute`'s output will be seen to pause for perceptibly long periods of time, which may lead one to mistakenly believe that the program has encountered a network outage. To see if that is, in fact, the case, one may run the traceroute program with a flag that turns off the DNS lookups. When run in that mode, any delays really are due to routers being slow or unable to respond. This scenario is covered in detail in the following section.

Traceroute Interactions with the DNS

Typically, a `traceroute` implementation will attempt to display more than just the IP addresses of each router interface that is encountered by the tracing process. The Domain Name System (DNS) is often used to store names of router interfaces for the convenience of those operating the network (see Figure A.8). Names like "ethernet-1.boston-south.company.com" or "mktg-LAN.chicago.company.com" are easier to use than IP addresses like 10.53.178.129.

Most `traceroute` clients receive the ICMP Time Exceeded error message and then immediately query the DNS for records that correspond to the received IP address. If the DNS responds quickly, as is usually the case, then the output is barely affected. However, if the DNS for some domain is unreachable, then the `traceroute`

```
Hop    IP Address      Domain Name
---    ------------    --------------------------
1      10.87.174.65
2      10.87.172.3
3      10.87.172.1
4      10.87.175.253
5      <ICMP messages probably suppressed by firewall rules>
6      <ICMP messages probably suppressed by firewall rules>
7      192.156.136.2   3com-inex.3com.com
8      205.158.1.225   us-hq-border1-h5-0.rtr.internex.net
9      205.158.0.4     us-hq-core1-f1-0.rtr.internex.net
10     207.88.0.74     us-dc-wash-core1-a0-3.rtr.internex.net
11     192.41.177.125  mae-east.nsn.nasa.gov
12     192.43.240.34   rtr-wan2-ef.gsfc.nasa.gov
13     128.183.10.134  ns.gsfc.nasa.gov
```

FIGURE A.8 A sample output from a DNS-enhanced `traceroute` client.

output may appear to pause—for a long time—and then continue. This at first appears to be a network outage, unless you wait long enough to see the traceroute resume after what could be 10–15 seconds or more. Many people will be frustrated and cancel the traceroute well before the DNS Query times out, and then begin to troubleshoot a phantom problem at the point where the traceroute left off. However, there is no real problem there at all. In fact, there may be no problem anywhere along that path, just high delays getting to the DNS servers that may be far from the path being traced.

This traceroute situation arises due to some programming shortcuts. Many traceroute application developers expected the DNS to be robust, fast, and reliable. They should stop their timers when the ICMP Time Exceeded message is received, and then work on the DNS Query as a separate operation. To keep from worrying the user, traceroute's output could be continued after two seconds if the DNS Query has yet to be answered. If traceroute, by default, did not try to look up IP addresses in the DNS before continuing to the next hop, then there would be no problem. Most traceroute clients can be invoked in such a way that DNS lookups are disabled.

Firewall Interference

As noted above, firewalls may prevent certain information from being divulged. Most firewalls will not issue ICMP error messages. Many will not even respond to ping! In the traceroute example above (Figure A.8), the packets were leaving my company, so I was allowed to send them out into the Internet. The reverse is definitely not the case: Incoming traceroutes or pings will get only as far as our Internet "front door" and no farther.

If one tries to trace into a corporate network that is protected by a firewall, the traceroute client will work for a while, then begin a pattern of timing out at each higher hop count. This does not mean that the traceroute client is successfully getting, say, 23 hops from you, and that the last six hops have been unable to reply. It just means that the last router to reply was the last-hop router before reaching the ingress firewall router at your traceroute destination's corporation.

Router "Mishandling"

The error processing required by traceroute is not part of the "fast path" forwarding code in routers. The error condition is handed off to the CPU for detailed processing. Certain router vendors almost always drop the second of three `traceroute` attempts at a given hop count. Other router vendors may take a long time to generate ICMP error messages in response to `traceroute`, but could actually be forwarding packets just fine (i.e., the RTT delay may not be indicative of actual packet forwarding delay).

REFERENCES

REQUEST FOR COMMENT

0791 Postel, J., Internet Protocol. September 1981. (Format: TXT=97779 bytes) (Obsoletes RFC0760) (Status: STANDARD)

0792 Postel, J., Internet Control Message Protocol. September 1981. (Format: TXT=30404 bytes) (Obsoletes RFC0777) (Updated by RFC0950) (Status: STANDARD)

1191 Mogul, J.C., Deering, S.E., Path MTU discovery. November 1990. (Format: TXT= 47936 bytes) (Obsoletes RFC1063) (Status: DRAFT STANDARD)

1256 Deering, S., ICMP Router Discovery Messages. September 1991. (Format: TXT= 43059 bytes) (Also RFC0792) (Status: PROPOSED STANDARD)

1393 Malkin, G., Traceroute Using an IP Option. January 1993. (Format: TXT=13140 bytes) (Status: EXPERIMENTAL)

1812 Baker, F., Requirements for IP Version 4 Routers. June 1995. (Format: TXT=415740 bytes) (Obsoletes RFC1716, RFC1009) (Status: PROPOSED STANDARD)

ENDNOTES

1. Of course, an ICMPv6 packet will be preceded by an IPv6 header, which is different from today's IPv4 header. The IPv6 "Next Header" value for ICMPv6 is 1, which is analogous to IPv4's Protocol field for ICMPv4, also equal to 1. Both IPv4's Protocol field and IPv6's Next Header serve to identify the next higher-layer protocol header which will follow the IP header.

    IPv6+ICMPv6 is functionally very similar to IPv4+ICMPv4. ICMPv6 is still part of the IPv6 module, and provides very similar error-reporting functions. In fact, many of the error codes (see Table A.1) are the same. For the purposes of the `ping` and `traceroute` applications, the ICMPv6 Types are still the same: Type 8 is Echo, Type 0 is Echo Reply, and Type 11 is Time Exceeded.

    ICMPv6 incorporates functions that were part of IGMP in IPv4, so there is no separate IGMPv6 protocol; also, error messages pertaining to fragmentation are not applicable in IPv6, since routers no longer do fragmentation; this is an end-to-end function in IPv6

IEEE 802.1Q
AND 802.1p

The IEEE protocols that implement MAC-layer multicast filtering are straightforward. There are actually two related ideas which were standardized at the same time,[1] namely Virtual LAN (VLAN) filtering and MAC-layer multicast filtering. How are these two seemingly different technologies related? Essentially, they both are "pruning" the spanning tree by logically blocking more ports than would normally be blocked.[2]

IEEE 802.1Q and 802.1p[3] both provide additional information that is used during the layer-two forwarding process to enable logical filtering operations to be performed. These new protocols both effectively create a subset of the spanning tree, so only those ports that need to emit a given frame do so. In the case of VLAN filtering, a tagged broadcast packet will only be transmitted out via those ports that actually lead to stations within a particular VLAN. Similarly, multicast packets, rather than being flooded on all ports, are only transmitted out on ports that lead to known group members.

Figure B-1 shows how broadcasts (and multicasts) are normally forwarded by bridges; note that all the nonblocking ports (indicated by dashed lines in the figure) receive all the traffic in either case—the traffic goes everywhere. Each switch floods the traffic on all nonblocked ports—except the port on which the frame arrived—until the frame reaches the root bridge, which continues flooding down the remainder of the spanning

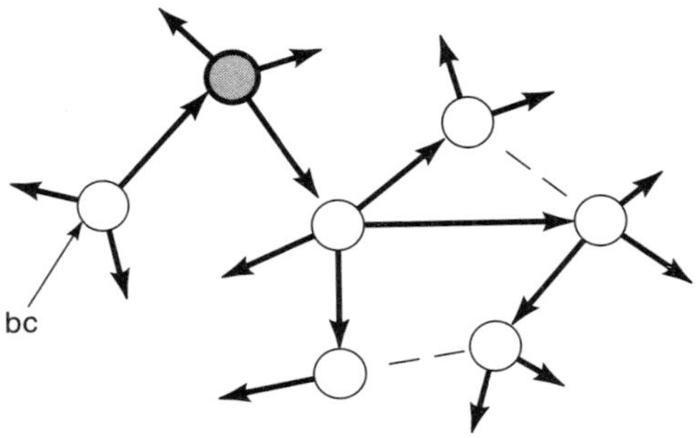

FIGURE B.1   Normal flooding of broadcasts and multicasts.

tree. Actually, the forwarding logic is the same on bridges whether they are upstream or downstream of the root. There is only one rule: Flood a broadcast on all ports except blocked ports (this constrains the broadcast to the spanning tree, which is loop-free by definition). If you imagine a broadcast arriving on any port in Figure B.1, you will see that the broadcast will traverse the entire spanning tree if you follow this rule.

Figure B.2 shows how this same spanning tree might be "pruned" to limit propagation of frames based on their appropriate VLAN ID or multicast group address. Each port may have a list of valid VLAN IDs, or active multicast groups. Figure B.2 shows only a few ports with active group members or VLAN members, so that the limited flooding is more obvious. In each case, the multicast frame or VLAN-tagged broadcast frame, respectively, starts its journey by arriving at the left-hand bridge.

Now the bridges needed to learn in advance which active VLAN(s) or which active multicast group(s) are reachable via each port. Also, the simple forwarding rule

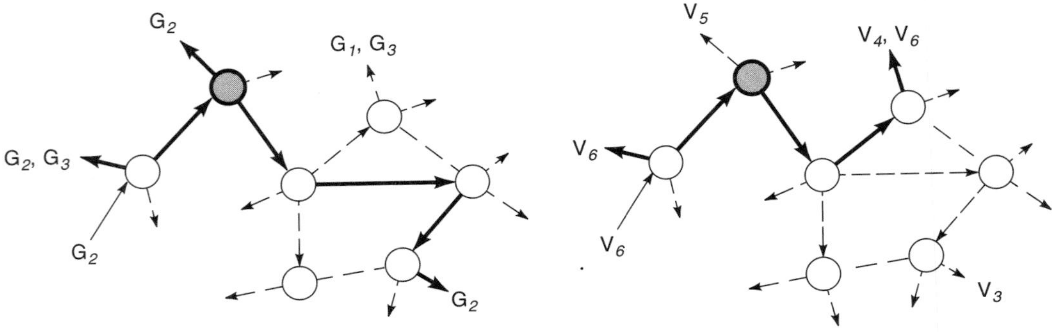

FIGURE B.2   Group address pruning and VLAN filtering.

has been modified. Flood a packet out a port if it is not blocked *and* if the frame's VLAN ID (or its destination multicast group address) matches the appropriate list on each nonblocked port.

A simple protocol has been invented to convey this VLAN or multicast group membership information between switches and endstations, which is called GARP, the Generic Attribute Registration Protocol. GARP, by itself, does nothing. It is really a skeleton for two other "application" protocols: the GARP VLAN Registration Protocol (GVRP) and the GARP Multicast Registration Protocol (GMRP).

GARP provides a common set of messages and finite state machines defining how "arbitrary" attribute information must be conveyed between switches. GMRP and GVRP are different in only one small detail: G*V*RP manipulates VLAN IDs, which are 12-bit quantities, while G*M*RP is concerned with 48-bit MAC-layer multicast addresses. Other than that, the protocols are identical, both serving to propagate information about which ports lead to members of which VLANs, or about which ports lead to active members of which MAC-layer multicast groups.

Both GVRP and GMRP allow the switches to tell each other about their local environments. Since this information is propagated upstream toward the root, all intermediate links acquire the memberships of all their downstream neighbors. GVRP and GMRP, then, allow the VLAN and multicast group memberships to change dynamically, enabling rapid convergence on the new membership trees.

IEEE 802.1Q TAG HEADER

IEEE 802.1Q specifies a two-byte "VLAN" header that is inserted between the end of the MAC-layer header and the higher-layer protocol header. This header is depicted in Figure B.3.

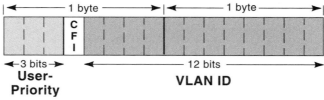

FIGURE B.3   IEEE 802.1Q "Tag Control Information" header.

The 802.1Q specification defines this two-byte header format and how endstations and switches must manipulate it in the context of VLANs. Even though the Tag Control Information (TCI) header is only two bytes long, the 802.1Q header actually ends up consuming four additional bytes of space in the MAC header. An EtherType field, set to 0x8100, along with the TCI header, is inserted between the MAC SA and the rest of the frame, which is then treated as data until the tag is received or stripped. The 0x8100 Type field identifies the fact that this frame has been 802.1Q-tagged.

Previously, switches only needed to look at the MAC DA in order to forward a frame, but now forwarding decisions also depend on the contents of the 802.1Q tag (specifically the VLAN ID), whose presence is indicated by the 0x8100 EtherType. The two-byte Type field plus the two-byte Tag Control Information Header field comprise the 802.1Q tag.

Figure B.4 depicts the location of the 802.1Q tag within an Ethernet frame, showing how it shifts the (unaltered) remainder of the frame four bytes farther behind the MAC SA field. When the 802.1Q tag is stripped, its four bytes are removed, which restores the original frame exactly as it was before the 802.1Q Tag was inserted (of course, the FCS will be different in the tagged version of the frame).

IEEE 802.1Q tags can be used with any protocol, but IP is the subject of this book, so it is used to illustrate this point about how the 802.1Q tag is placed within the header. These extra four bytes mean that the IP MTU must be reduced from

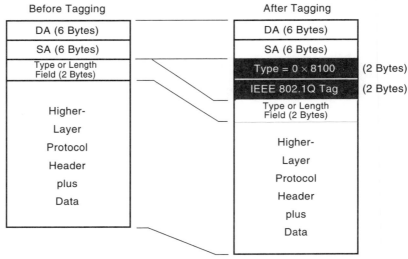

FIGURE B.4   IEEE 802.1Q header placement.

1500 to 1496 when 802.1Q-tagging is being performed (or from 1492 to 1488 if IP over SNAP/LLC/802.3 encapsulation is used). If the MTU were not reduced, then IP could send a maximum-sized packet of 1500 bytes, which becomes a 1518-byte Ethernet frame (the MAC SA and DA are each six bytes, plus there is a two-byte Type field and the four byte FCS, for a total of 18 extra bytes). That is fine, until an 802.1Q tag is inserted into an already maximum-sized frame, which would cause it to exceed the standard maximum frame size.

If an oversized frame did make it onto the wire, it might not cause any problems. Most older Ethernet physical layer chips will probably only record an oversize-frame (i.e., "giant") event in their statistics counters. The danger of using oversized frames is that some devices, possibly older store-and-forward bridges, may decide that these are bad frames and will consequently discard them. Cut-through bridges will probably log this as an oversized frame, since they can't didn't know how big it was until after the whole frame had been received and forwarded. The safest thing to do, in order to ensure maximum compatibility with installed devices, is to sacrifice four bytes from the MTU. There should be no perceptible performance difference (since a 1496-byte frame has only 0.3% less capacity than a 1500-byte frame).

PRIORITY TAGGING

The 802.1p specification is really an extension of the 802.1D bridging standard, which leverages the 802.1Q Tag Control Information header. There are two major features in 802.1p: 1) Class of Service prioritization, and 2) MAC-layer multicast filtering. A new version of the 802.1D specification, including the 802.1p extensions, was ratified by the IEEE 802.1 committee in June of 1998. 802.1p specifies the meaning of the three-bit priority field within the 802.1Q header.[4] These three bits provide up to eight different levels, or classes, of service for the data flowing across LAN switches.

Note that a TCI header may indicate that a frame is associated with VLAN 0x000 but has a non-zero priority field. Such frames are known as "priority-tagged" frames, and they must be handled slightly differently than VLAN-tagged frames. It is likely that priority-tagged frames will be the earliest application of the 802.1Q "VLAN" TCI header. At the time of this writing, the market seems to be craving "Class of Service" (CoS) prioritization more than VLANs. Even if the market eventually embraces VLANs, after initially having embraced CoS, the 802.1Q/p-enabled switches should be able to do any combination of 802.1Q VLANs and 802.1p prioritization, giving customers the flexibility to make their own individual implementation decisions.

Three bits yield eight different CoS priority levels. The three 802.1p "user priority" bits, despite being embedded within the 802.1Q header, are independent of 802.1Q VLANs. Thus, it is possible to use the priority bits without using VLAN tags. The VLAN ID of 0x000 is reserved for these "priority-tagged" packets, which then are only using the 802.1Q tag to indicate the frame's desired MAC-layer class of service. Due to the emergence of high-performance routers (layer three switches), the need for VLANs may not be as acute, but many emerging applications do appear to require CoS and Quality of Service (QoS) features.

GARP

Besides defining the meaning of these three bits, 802.1p also defines several new protocols. We have already discussed the Generic Attribute Registration Protocol. GARP was originally designed with one job in mind: to facilitate multicast filtering at the MAC layer. GARP, at that point, stood for "Group Address Registration Protocol," which was strictly designed to help control MAC-layer multicast filtering.

As GARP was being developed, the IEEE's protocol designers noticed that VLAN registration was very similar[5] and could perhaps use a similar protocol. GARP was generalized a bit to become the Generic Attribute Registration Protocol, and two trivial "applications" were defined on top of the new GARP: the GARP VLAN Registration Protocol (GVRP) and the GARP Multicast Registration Protocol (GMRP). The only difference between these two protocols is that they manipulate different-sized elements of data. GMRP manipulates 48-bit multicast MAC addresses, while GVRP handles 12-bit VLAN IDs.

Curiously, only GVRP is mandatory in the new IEEE standards,[6] so GMRP is not being implemented as quickly as one might hope—despite the fact that GARP was originally designed to solve the multicast flooding problem! Of the two protocols, GMRP is the one that could make the most immediate difference in today's networks, especially as multicast-enabled applications proliferate.

Because the two protocols are so closely related (in order to implement GVRP one must implement GARP) it is trivial to develop GMRP once one has developed GARP—it is as simple as duplicating the source code for GVRP and changing a few variable declarations from VLAN IDs to multicast MAC addresses. All the protocol state machines are identical, since GVRP and GMRP are both instances of GARP. For a programmer who has already implemented GVRP, this process should involve less than one day of work.

VLAN-Augmented Forwarding

In the case of VLANs, one primary goal is to limit the scope of broadcast packets to stations within a VLAN, rather than its normal scope which is every station on the whole bridged (switched) LAN. Instead of copying broadcast frames out all non-blocked ports, the broadcast is only copied onto ports which lead to known members of this VLAN, thereby containing the broadcast to that VLAN. The VLAN ID is logically part of the destination address, because it influences the forwarding decision. There are both "ingress" and "egress" processing stages.

There is no magic here; if a broadcast frame needs to cross the spanning tree backbone to reach a distant port, the VLAN-tagged broadcast still uses up about the same amount of bandwidth on the common backbone link. The savings is at the egress ports of the switches; at that point, the broadcast frame is filtered if its VLAN ID is not in the list of active VLANs reachable via that port.

Multicast-Augmented Forwarding

In the case of MAC-layer multicast filtering, the goal is also to limit the scope of the multicasts to just those ports that lead to known group members. Multicasts are forwarded along the spanning tree the same way that broadcasts are. Now, instead of using VLAN membership to limit the flooding of broadcasts to ports leading to VLAN members, we use group membership to restrict the flooding of multicasts to ports that lead to identified group members. VLAN boundaries serve to restrict the scope of broadcast packets, but these are not terribly frequent packets in a healthy LAN.

Multicast groups, on the other hand, could be pumping out some serious amounts of data. Even if each group, individually, is using only about 1 Mbps, having 37 groups active means there is going to be 37 Mbps worth of data leaving every non-blocked port in your switched LAN. This is very wasteful; obviously, the switches *should* only need to forward the multicast frames to ports that lead to interested group members—the trick is figuring out which non-blocked ports should be used.

Providing multicast group membership information to the switches enables a big improvement in efficiency. In the unfiltered case, even though the nonmember endstations will not actually be extracting these multicasts from their local media (they're not members, after all), the multicast data is still wasting bandwidth that the stations could be using for traffic that they actually *are* interested in! Even in the case where a station is receiving multicast traffic, it is probably only a member of a handful of groups. The remainder of the traffic is wasting its local bandwidth to almost the same degree as in the case of the nonmulticast stations.

An important observation about GMRP is that it does not have a complete view into the exact IP multicast Class D address that is being joined or left. The MAC-layer expression of an IP multicast address contains only the least significant 23 bits of the 32-bit IP multicast address.[7] It turns out that each MAC-layer multicast address can represent any of 32 different IP-layer multicast addresses, because the Class D address has four fixed leading bits (1110), leaving 28 bits for the group ID. So, when GMRP is joining or leaving *one* MAC-layer group address, it is actually joining or leaving *32* IP-layer multicast addresses.

In the event that an endstation has tuned in to multiple overlapping IP multicast addresses, the GMRP software would have to keep enough state information to know that it should not send a GMRP Leave message until all the IP multicast addresses have left. Careful multicast address assignment can greatly reduce the occurrence of IP multicast addresses that all share the same least-significant 23 bits.

REFERENCES

Maufer, Thomas, *Deploying IP Multicast in the Enterprise.* Prentice Hall, Upper Saddle River, NJ. 1997.

Perlman, Radia, *Interconnections.* Addison-Wesley, Reading, MA. 1992.

ISO/IEC Final CD 15802-3, IEEE P802.1D/D15, November 24, 1997. Information technology—Telecommunications and information exchange between systems—Local and metropolitan area networks—Common specifications—Part 3: Media Access Control (MAC) Bridges: Revision. (Incorporating IEEE P802.1p: Traffic Class Expediting and Dynamic Multicast Filtering)

P802.1Q/D9, February 20, 1998. Draft Standard P802.1Q/D9. IEEE Standards for Local and Metropolitan Area Networks: Virtual Bridged Local Area Networks

ENDNOTES

1. Though in different documents. . . .

2. In "classic" spanning tree, ports are only blocked to remove loops in the bridge topology.

3. 802.1p has been integrated into the 1998 revision of the 802.1D MAC-layer bridging specification. It is no longer a separate document, but we will refer to its functionality as if it were.

4. Note that this three-bit field may be used in the absence of VLANs. Also note that GMRP is specified within 802.1p as is GARP itself. GVRP is defined separately, within 802.1Q. Thus 802.1Q depends on 802.1p, since GVRP depends on GARP.

5.   VLANs are all overlaid on the common, underlying, spanning tree. Each VLAN is its own broadcast domain, and VLAN-cpable LAN switches must restrict intra-VLAN broadcasts to only certain ports, lest they leak into VLANs other than the one to which they were transmitted. This filtering based on VLAN ID modifies the switch's forwarding rules in very similar ways to filtering based on group address. All multicast groups also share a common spanning tree, but only ports leading to known group members should see the group's traffic.

6.   In order to claim compliance with 802.1Q, vendors must implement GVRP.

7.   A complete description of multicast is beyond the scope of this book, but the subject is covered in detail in the author's first book, *Deploying IP Multicast in the Enterprise,* which is also published by Prentice Hall

Dynamic Host Configuration Protocol (DHCP)

DHCP has become an indispensable tool for managing IP address assignment to ever larger numbers of client machines. Before DHCP existed, most addresses were assigned manually, being statically configured into each machine's IP stack. There were methods for obtaining addresses dynamically, but they were a patchwork solution (the BOOTstraP protocol [BOOTP], Reverse ARP [RARP], etc.) that did not have a complete feature set that scaled to large installations. DHCP is more manageable than the protocols that came before it, allowing dynamic addressing to be widely deployed in a coordinated fashion.

SOME ADVANTAGES OF DHCP

One improvement that DHCP has over BOOTP is that DHCP can assign an address for a well-defined time interval, whereas BOOTP's assignments were, and are, irrevocable. This is very useful in tailoring the operation of the address assignment protocol to the varying dynamism in each network. Second, DHCP can provide all the configuration information that an IP station needs to operate; default gateways, DNS server addresses, etc., can all be supplied to a client. A client can even be directed to use the ICMP Router Discovery protocol (RFC-1256) rather than being given an explicit (set of) router address(es).

Obviously, in order to function, an IP stack needs an address, and DHCP automates the process of *getting* an address, along with (optionally) other necessary configuration information.[1] An important side effect of easing address assignment is that DHCP also greatly simplifies "moves, adds, and changes."[2] When a station is plugged in to a new network segment it will obtain an address from within the local subnetwork's prefix. This happens "automagically," without having to touch the station's IP stack configuration. In fact, DHCP has become so popular that many new IP stacks default to DHCP upon being installed. In the past, the default was most often to await configuration of a static address.

DHCP clearly facilitates a station getting a new dynamically-assigned address when it moves to a new subnetwork, but a station's IP address may be forced to change even if it has not moved. In situations where there are a large number of machines on a subnetwork, relative to the size of the subnet's allocated IP address prefix, DHCP may not be able to preserve assigned addresses indefinitely.[3] If a subnetwork's prefix is nearly full, then another machine may boot up and claim an address while the original holder of that address is off-line.

For example, if there are more than 200 stations in a /24, or more than 900 in a /22, the probability of address "collisions" increases. DHCP is designed to minimize such addressing capriciousness, but if there are almost as many machines as there are available addresses, then some "churn" within the set of machine-to-address mappings is inevitable. Most client IP stacks can tolerate their IP address changing with little or no trouble; the user will rarely even notice—unless there are no dynamic IP addresses left on that subnetwork. Certain client IP stacks may cause a system to "freeze" during the booting process while waiting fruitlessly for an address to be assigned. (Ideally, the system's search for an IP address would proceed asynchronously relative to the rest of the steps in the boot process.)

A "DISADVANTAGE" OF DHCP

There is one "disadvantage" to DHCP: if it is possible for the address to change, then there is no longer a fixed mapping between the machine's address and its name. DHCP has simply moved the clerical/administrative task of assigning IP addresses to a similar task of keeping the Domain Name Server up to date with all the latest "name-to-IP" and "IP-to-name" mappings. How big a problem is this in practice? The answer is quite subjective, and depends to some extent on the class of machine, whether client or server.

The IETF has developed two solutions to this problem, known as "Dynamic Updates in the Domain Name System (DNS UPDATE)," RFC-2136, and "Secure Domain Name System Dynamic Update," RFC-2137. Even though these dynamic DNS update protocols have been defined, they are not yet widely implemented due to their relatively recent publication.[4]

Dynamic Addressing's Effect on Clients

Since most machines are clients, some would say that it is not a great tragedy if they do not have well-defined names. On the other hand, troubleshooting can be made somewhat simpler if one knows which user to contact when a machine is misbehaving,[5] which implies that meaningful IP-to-domain-name mappings are useful in certain situations. Even if there is a valid IP-to-domain-name mapping present, the user's identity—or the machine's physical location—must somehow be reflected in the machine's domain name or the name won't be a troubleshooting aid. (There could be an auxillary database of user names, listing IP addresses, etc., so that cross-referencing would allow specific troubleshooting information to be obtained.)

For instance, machine names such as space-ghost.3com.com are not necessarily useful for troubleshooting. Names such as maufer-pc-16-1-446.3com.com are more useful for troubleshooting, but really aren't names. RFC-1178, "Choosing a Name for Your Computer," is an interesting tutorial on choosing names for computer systems. The name above is simply a description of the machine and where it is now. If the machine offers any services, and then moves, all the clients of that service will then need to be told about the new name (reflecting the new location). So there is some level of tension between troubleshooting-friendly names and user-friendly names. DHCP adds another dimension to this issue—it did not create the issue.

One way around this is to maintain a separate database that maps user names to DNS names, to physical locations, etc. It can be challenging to keep multiple databases up-to-date, but at least a persistent DNS name helps track the machine through its various locations. Another possibility is to take advantage of the DNS features that allow a single IP address to be referenced by more than one name, which may satisfy both the user's desire for a cool name, plus MIS' desire for a useful name. Of course, a backend database may still be useful to tie all these names together with phone numbers and other user-specific information.

Emerging policy-based networking technology will ease troubleshooting by allowing users to be mapped to either IP or MAC addresses via policy-based network management services, independent of the DNS. It is the author's opinion that using the DNS in this way is an artifact of inadequate network management tools that have been available to date. Ideally, finding users to contact when their machines are misbehaving should be a network management problem. If people want to name their machines "da-boss.company.com" or "cheese.univ.edu," those choices should not impede network troubleshooting.

Dynamic Addressing's Effect on Servers

Servers, on the other hand, *do* need persistent names. If they do not have persistent names, they will not be usable by client machines, because the client software is usually configured statically with the name of all necessary servers for its operation. For example, an e-mail client may be configured to know that its Post Office Protocol (POP) server is pop.company.com. Other static repositories of server names are HyperText Markup Language (HTML) web pages containing embedded URLs pointing to a WWW server such as www.university.edu.

If these names pointed to IP_{pop} and IP_{www}, respectively, and then the servers obtained new addresses, what would be the effect? The names would still point to the old addresses, but the servers would no longer be reachable at those addresses. Luckily, in such situations, the MIS staff will probably have coordinated the necessary updates to the name servers[6] in conjunction with the POP or web server machine move, so that any clients will obtain the correct address when they look up the server name.

DHCP DETAILS

DHCP has three modes of address allocation:

1. Automatic allocation
   * IP address assigned permanently to a particular endstation (as in BOOTP)
2. Dynamic allocation
   * IP address assigned for a limited time, or until the endstation relinquishes it
3. Manual allocation
   * IP addresses statically mapped by network administrator (i.e., inside the DHCP server)
   * DHCP is only used to configure the endstation when it boots

The first mode, the "fully automatic" one, matches the way BOOTP used to work. Addresses are automatically assigned to endstations, and once granted, are never revoked. Mode 2 is also automatic in the sense that the network administrative staff need not be involved in the act of assignment, but the network administrator can control how long each dynamically-assigned address may be held by an endstation. Finally, the network administrative staff can assign static IP addresses, but keep them locally inside the DHCP server. Each time a machine boots it includes its MAC address as a token within the DHCP header, and the DHCP server can look up the proper IP address based on the supplied MAC address.

Routers as DHCP Relays

Booting DHCP clients send out an IP broadcast packet to the limited-broadcast address of 255.255.255.255. The packet's source address must be 0.0.0.0, since the station does not yet have an IP address! Because the packet is sent to the limited-broadcast address, it will only be heard by machines on that same subnetwork. Unless there is a DHCP server on every subnetwork, how can the DHCP server know that there has been a request if it hasn't heard the broadcast?

There is a function in routers, called the BOOTP Relay Function (or the DHCP Relay Function, or DHCP could be configured as part of a generic IP- or UDP-Broadcast Helper Function). If a router is properly configured as a Relay, then when it receives IP broadcast packets that are also UDP packets, and in particular are also destined for the DHCP server port (67), the router will forward the packets to the DHCP server, whose address it knows by virtue of a configuration command. Figure C.1 illustrates the decision flowchart of the DHCP Relay function.

DHCP Protocol Exchanges

The DHCP protocol works as follows. Note that there may be more than one server that could respond to a client's request. First, the client broadcasts a DHCPDISCOVER packet that will be relayed to all the DHCP servers that the DHCP Relay routers know about. Each of the servers will determine the proper configuration for this client, based on where the client is in the topology, as well as other parameters that may be entered into the DHCP server that would apply to any client, such as DNS servers. The servers' DHCPOFFERs (responses to DHCPDISCOVERs) will then be relayed back to the client, which will collect them and decide on the best one (or the first one, depending on the client's DHCP implementation).

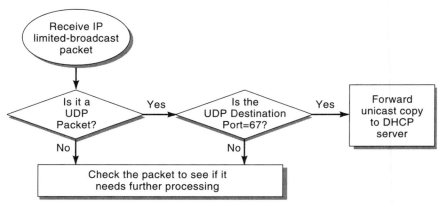

FIGURE C.1   DHCP relay function flowchart.

The selected configuration will result in a new broadcast message from the client, a DHCPREQUEST, which will include a server Internet address (`siaddr`) entry indicating the client's selected server. The request is now explicitly asking for the IP address that the client just received in the "your" IP address (`yiaddr`) field of the DHCPOFFER, from the server whose address is contained within the `siaddr` field. The server, if all is still well, replies with a DHCPACK, which includes all the requested parameters.

Before using the assigned address, the client should broadcast an ARP Request for that IP address to make sure that no other machine on its local subnetwork is accidentally using it. If that is the case, the client will send a DHCPDECLINE message back to the server, and try the whole process again. There are other nuances to the protocol, but this is the basic procedure.

DHCP Packet Format

The DHCP data is itself encapsulated in a UDP header, sent to UDP port 67, the "DHCP server" port. Return traffic is sent to UDP port 68, the "DHCP Client" port. The source ports are chosen at random from the range 1024–65,535. Figure C.2 illustrates the IP/UDP/DHCP packet.

DHCP header fields that end in "iaddr" refer to some kind of "IP address," or "Internet Address." The fields are described in RFC-2131 as follows:

```
                            1                   2                   3
          0 1 2 3 4 5 6 7 8 9 0 1 2 3 4 5 6 7 8 9 0 1 2 3 4 5 6 7 8 9 0 1
          +-+-+-+-+-+-+-+-+-+-+-+-+-+-+-+-+-+-+-+-+-+-+-+-+-+-+-+-+-+-+-+-+
     IP  |0 1 0 0| I HL  |  Type of Service         |       Total Length        | Vers. = 4
          +-+-+-+-+-+-+-+-+-+-+-+-+-+-+-+-+-+-+-+-+-+-+-+-+-+-+-+-+-+-+-+-+
     IP  |          Identification          |Flags|     Fragment Offset        |
          +-+-+-+-+-+-+-+-+-+-+-+-+-+-+-+-+-+-+-+-+-+-+-+-+-+-+-+-+-+-+-+-+
     IP  |  Time to Live  |0 0 0 0 0 1 1 0|       Header Checksum             | Prot. 6 = UDP
          +-+-+-+-+-+-+-+-+-+-+-+-+-+-+-+-+-+-+-+-+-+-+-+-+-+-+-+-+-+-+-+-+
     IP  |0 0 0 0 0 0 0 0 0 0 0 0 0 0 0 0|0 0 0 0 0 0 0 0 0 0 0 0 0 0 0 0| SA
          +-+-+-+-+-+-+-+-+-+-+-+-+-+-+-+-+-+-+-+-+-+-+-+-+-+-+-+-+-+-+-+-+
     IP  |1 1 1 1 1 1 1 1 1 1 1 1 1 1 1 1 1 1 1 1 1 1 1 1 1 1 1 1 1 1 1 1| DA
          +-+-+-+-+-+-+-+-+-+-+-+-+-+-+-+-+-+-+-+-+-+-+-+-+-+-+-+-+-+-+-+-+
     IP  :                  Options                    /  Padding           :
          +=+=+=+=+=+=+=+=+=+=+=+=+=+=+=+=+=+=+=+=+=+=+=+=+=+=+=+=+=+=+=+=+
     UDP |          Source Port              |      Destination Port      | DP = 67 (C->S)
          +-+-+-+-+-+-+-+-+-+-+-+-+-+-+-+-+-+-+-+-+-+-+-+-+-+-+-+-+-+-+-+-+    = 68 (S->C)
     UDP |      Length (UDP hdr + DHCP)      |         Checksum          |
          +=+=+=+=+=+=+=+=+=+=+=+=+=+=+=+=+=+=+=+=+=+=+=+=+=+=+=+=+=+=+=+=+
    DHCP |      op (1)      |    ht ype (1)   |    hlen (1)    |   hops (1)  |
          +-+-+-+-+-+-+-+-+-+-+-+-+-+-+-+-+-+-+-+-+-+-+-+-+-+-+-+-+-+-+-+-+
    DHCP |                          xi d (4 Bytes)                         |
          +-+-+-+-+-+-+-+-+-+-+-+-+-+-+-+-+-+-+-+-+-+-+-+-+-+-+-+-+-+-+-+-+
    DHCP |        Secs (2 Bytes)             |      Flags (2 Bytes)        |
          +-+-+-+-+-+-+-+-+-+-+-+-+-+-+-+-+-+-+-+-+-+-+-+-+-+-+-+-+-+-+-+-+
    DHCP |                          ci addr (4 Bytes)                      |
          +-+-+-+-+-+-+-+-+-+-+-+-+-+-+-+-+-+-+-+-+-+-+-+-+-+-+-+-+-+-+-+-+
    DHCP |                          yi addr (4 Bytes)                      |
          +-+-+-+-+-+-+-+-+-+-+-+-+-+-+-+-+-+-+-+-+-+-+-+-+-+-+-+-+-+-+-+-+
    DHCP |                          si addr (4 Bytes)                      |
          +-+-+-+-+-+-+-+-+-+-+-+-+-+-+-+-+-+-+-+-+-+-+-+-+-+-+-+-+-+-+-+-+
    DHCP |                          gi addr (4 Bytes)                      |
          +-+-+-+-+-+-+-+-+-+-+-+-+-+-+-+-+-+-+-+-+-+-+-+-+-+-+-+-+-+-+-+-+
     D   |                                                                 |
     H   |                                                                 |
     C   |                          Chaddr (16 Bytes)                      |
     P   |                                                                 |
          +-+-+-+-+-+-+-+-+-+-+-+-+-+-+-+-+-+-+-+-+-+-+-+-+-+-+-+-+-+-+-+-+
    DHCP |                                                                 |
    DHCP |                          Sname (64 Bytes)                       |
          +-+-+-+-+-+-+-+-+-+-+-+-+-+-+-+-+-+-+-+-+-+-+-+-+-+-+-+-+-+-+-+-+
    DHCP |                                                                 |
    DHCP |                          File (128 Bytes)                       |
          +-+-+-+-+-+-+-+-+-+-+-+-+-+-+-+-+-+-+-+-+-+-+-+-+-+-+-+-+-+-+-+-+
    DHCP |                                                                 |
    DHCP :                          Options (Variable)                     :
          +-+-+-+-+-+-+-+-+-+-+-+-+-+-+-+-+-+-+-+-+-+-+-+-+-+-+-+-+-+-+-+-+
```

FIGURE C.2 IP/UDP/DHCP packet format.

TABLE C.1   DHCP Field Descriptions from RFC-2131

op	1	Message op code / message type.
		1 = BOOTREQUEST, 2 = BOOTREPLY
htype	1	Hardware address type, see ARP section in "Assigned Numbers" RFC; e.g., '1' = 10mb ethernet.
hlen	1	Hardware address length (e.g. '6' for 10mb ethernet).
hops	1	Client sets to zero, optionally used by relay agents when booting via a relay agent.
xid	4	Transaction ID, a random number chosen by the client, used by the client and server to associate messages and responses between a client and a server.
secs	2	Filled in by client, seconds elapsed since client began address acquisition or renewal process.
flags	2	Flags.
ciaddr	4	Client IP address; only filled in if client is in BOUND, RENEW or RE-BINDING state and can respond to ARP requests.
yiaddr	4	'your' (client) IP address.
siaddr	4	IP address of next server to use in bootstrap;returned in DHCPOFFER, DHCPACK by server.
giaddr	4	Relay agent IP address, used in booting via a relay agent.
chaddr	16	Client hardware address.
sname	64	Optional server host name, null terminated string.
file	128	Boot file name, null terminated string; "generic" name or null in DHCP-DISCOVER, fully qualified directory-path name in DHCPOFFER.
options	var	Optional parameters field. See the options documents for a list of defined options.

In the future, values of the DHCP fields are maintained by the IANA, and are available from one of the following URLs:

```
<ftp://ftp.isi.edu/in-notes/iana/assignments/bootp-dhcp-parameters>
```

or

```
<http://www.iana.org/>
```

The fields that are important in the initial client DHCPDISCOVER packet are the flags, the chaddr (client hardware address), and the htype/hlen that determine the type and length of the hardware address. In the absence of other data, such as the transaction ID (xid, which is optional), the hardware address is the unique token that allows the DHCP server to track which IP addresses have been assigned to which machines.

The other key field that is used when there is a DHCP Relay present is the giaddr (gateway IP address) field. If one thinks about it, this field must be filled in so that the DHCP server will know from which subnetwork's assigned prefix the client's address should be drawn. The DHCP Relay will forward the packet to the DHCP server(s), but knowing the source IP address of the router doesn't tell a DHCP server which of the router's interfaces received the packet. Using the giaddr, the DHCP server(s) can know which IP prefix to use when assigning an address to this client.

Once a DHCP server has allocated an address to the client, should it try to inform the client directly? It can't, unless it is on the same subnetwork—and even then the capabilities of the client's IP stack determine the form of the DHCPOFFER packet. Either the DHCP Relay agent or the DHCP Server itself must properly format the DHCPOFFER to the client, or the client will not be able to receive the packet. Clearly, the router cannot rely on its ARP cache to help deliver the packet, since the IP address has not been used by the client yet. The DHCPOFFER includes all the necessary information to build the ultimate packet that will be sent to the client.

The DHCPOFFER indicates what address to use as the MAC DA (the chaddr field contains the client's hardware address), but not all IP stacks can receive a unicast MAC-layer frame that has their own MAC address as the MAC DA, but also has an unknown IP address as the IP DA. In such cases, the IP stack can often receive the packet if it is broadcast (at both the IP and MAC layers), which is what one of the bits (the Broadcast bit) from the flags field is for. In fact, so far, the Broadcast bit is the only bit of the 16-bit flags field that has been used. If a client sets the Broadcast bit in a DHCPDISCOVER packet, then it needs to receive the DHCPOFFER as a broadcast packet. Otherwise, the client can receive the DHCPOFFER directly via unicast from the DHCP Relay (or from the DHCP Server itself if they happen to share the same subnetwork).

REFERENCES

Kercheval, Berry, *DHCP: A Guide to Dynamic TCP/IP Configuration,* Prentice Hall, Upper Saddle River, NJ. 1999.

Request for Comment (RFC)

RARP

0903 Reverse Address Resolution Protocol. R. Finlayson, T. Mann, J.C. Mogul, M. Theimer. Jun-01-1984. (Format: TXT=9345 bytes) (Status: STANDARD)

1931 Dynamic RARP Extensions for Automatic Network Address Acquisition. D. Brownell. April 1996. (Format: TXT=27544 bytes) (Status: INFORMATIONAL)

BOOTP and DHCP

0951 Bootstrap Protocol. W.J. Croft, J. Gilmore. Sep-01-1985. (Format: TXT=28354 bytes) (Updated by RFC1395, RFC1497, RFC1532, RFC1542) (Status: UNKNOWN)

1048 BOOTP vendor information extensions. P.A. Prindeville. Feb-01-1988. (Format: TXT=15423 bytes) (Obsoleted by RFC1084, RFC1395, RFC1497, RFC1533) (Status: UNKNOWN)

1084 BOOTP vendor information extensions. J.K. Reynolds. Dec-01-1988. (Format: TXT=16327 bytes) (Obsoletes RFC1048) (Obsoleted by RFC1395, RFC1497, RFC1533) (Status: UNKNOWN)

1395 BOOTP Vendor Information Extensions. J. Reynolds. January 1993. (Format: TXT=16314 bytes) (Obsoletes RFC1084, RFC1048) (Obsoleted by RFC1497, RFC1533) (Updates RFC951, RFC0951) (Status: DRAFT STANDARD)

1497 BOOTP Vendor Information Extensions. J. Reynolds. August 1993. (Format: TXT=16805 bytes) (Obsoletes RFC1395, RFC1084, RFC1048) (Obsoleted by RFC1533) (Updates RFC951, RFC0951) (Status: DRAFT STANDARD)

1531 Dynamic Host Configuration Protocol. R. Droms. October 1993. (Format: TXT=96192 bytes) (Status: PROPOSED STANDARD)

1532 Clarifications and Extensions for the Bootstrap Protocol. W. Wimer. October 1993. (Format: TXT=51545 bytes) (Obsoleted by RFC1542) (Updates RFC0951) (Status: PROPOSED STANDARD)

1533 DHCP Options and BOOTP Vendor Extensions. S. Alexander & R. Droms. October 1993. (Format: TXT=50919 bytes) (Obsoletes RFC1497, RFC1395, RFC1084, RFC1048) (Obsoleted by RFC2132) (Status: PROPOSED STANDARD)

1534 Interoperation Between DHCP and BOOTP. R. Droms. October 1993. (Format: TXT=6966 bytes) (Status: DRAFT STANDARD)

1541 Dynamic Host Configuration Protocol. R. Droms. October 1993. (Format: TXT=96950 bytes) (Obsoletes RFC1531) (Obsoleted by RFC2131) (Status: PROPOSED STANDARD)

1542 Clarifications and Extensions for the Bootstrap Protocol. W. Wimer. October 1993. (Format: TXT=52948 bytes) (Obsoletes RFC1532) (Updates RFC0951) (Status: DRAFT STANDARD)

2131 Dynamic Host Configuration Protocol. R. Droms. March 1997. (Format:TXT=113738 bytes) (Obsoletes RFC1541) (Status: DRAFT STANDARD)

2132 DHCP Options and BOOTP Vendor Extensions. S. Alexander, R. Droms. March 1997. (Format: TXT=63670 bytes) (Obsoletes RFC1533) (Status: DRAFT STANDARD)

ENDNOTES

1. A DHCP client will only get information beyond an IP address if it asks for it.

2. Easing "moves, adds, and changes" is one of the most hyped reasons to want VLANs. Given the existence of DHCP, it would appear that VLANs are not a pre-requisite for solving this problem. VLANs are a tool, and DHCP is a tool.

3. Even though DHCP is "Dynamic" it is not fickle. A design goal of DHCP is to have the address assignment be as stable as possible, once an assignment is made.

4. Also, RFC-2137 requires that the DNS Security infrastructure be in place, which is a barrier to entry for RFC-2137-augmented DHCP software.

5. By looking up the source IP address in the DNS, one would hopefully find a useful machine name that would allow the owner of the machine, or the machine's location, to be found.

6. Each "resource record" in the DNS has an associated Time-to-Live (TTL). Before the move, the servers' domain names should have had their TTLs reduced to small values so that the old name-to-address mappings would age out of any domain name resolver caches. Once the new addresses are stable, the TTLs can be increased again, since it will be safe to cache them.

Index